INSIGHT GUIDES

Created and Directed by Hans Höfer

GERMANY

Edited by Bettina Schümann

Managing Editor: Tony Halliday

Editorial Director: Brian Bell

APA PUBLICATIONS

Part of the Langenscheidt Publishing Group

L

Höfer

Schümann

Ulbrich

Given Germany's high profile during the 20th century, encompassing both the depths of human conflict and the heights of economic success, it has generated more preconceptions than just about any other European country. For that reason, the Insight approach, which sets out to explain a destination as well as describe it, is particularly appropriate. What's more, the series' creator, Apa Publications, maintains an editorial office in Munich and so is ideally placed to provide a true insider's view. Working closely with the team in Apa's main editorial office in London, the Munich editors assembled a group of expert writers and photographers whose brief was to provide real insight into the country for an international readership.

This latest edition of *Insight Guide: Germany* has a solid history behind it. So rapid have developments been in Germany in recent years that the book has undergone continual change. The original edition, covering the old Federal Republic, was one of the key titles in the Insight Guides series. For Apa Publications' founder, **Hans Höfer**, it had represented a triumphal return home. A Bauhaus-trained designer and photographer, he had left his native Germany in the late 1960s as one of the generation who set out to discover Asia and in 1970 he launched the series with the ground-breaking *Insight Guide: Bali*, the first of a number of southeast Asia titles. Later, he set up an editorial office in Munich and brought out *Insight Guide: Germany* to mark the series' arrival in Europe. Today the company publishes nearly 200 Insight Guide titles, and with two further series, Insight Pocket Guides and Insight Compact Guides, Apa Publications has more guide book titles than any other publisher in the world.

Following unification in 1990, *Insight Guide: Germany* was radically altered and expanded to take account of all the new cities and lands that had opened up in the east. After unification, events moved swiftly, tourism patterns altered and the book needed to be updated constantly to reflect the enormous changes. But, as postunification period of transition moved into a more settled climate, it was clearly time to tear up all the past ideas and begin looking at the country from a fresh perspective.

The task of developing a whole new concept for the book fell to **Bettina Schümann** who, together with Apa's senior editor in Munich, **Dieter Vogel**, set about commissioning new material and adapting the old.

The 1990 edition began with Heidelberg, a trip down the romantic Rhine to the old capital of Bonn. But where else could a description of Germany now begin but Berlin, the new capital? In the 1990 edition, some areas of the eastern part of the country were dealt with in perhaps too much detail, while others, such as the coastal areas along the Baltic, received too little attention. The new "Coasts" chapter was written by Bettina Schümann herself, who was born and raised in the wild north.

The history section of the book, including articles by **Roger Jopp**, **Martin Clemens** and **Herbert Ammon**, had to be brought up to date. The new article analysing the most recent developments in the country and titled "United and Uncertain" was written by

Hanuschek

Reinhard Ulbrich, an experienced author and commentator who studied English in Dublin.

Dieter Vogel investigated the clichés about the Germans and also wrote the new chapter on the environment – something which has long been a subject of major issue in Germany but which has now become an integral part of the economy.

Sven Hanuschek, whose hobby is playing the tuba, wrote about Germany's famous composers, as well as its poets and philosophers, the writer Stefan Heym, and German film-making. Modern painting and sculpture is described by **Kerstin Dötsch**, while **Eva-Elisabeth Fischer**, who has long worked on the features section of the *Süddeutsche Zeitung*, examines the development of German theatre and dance.

Giebel

A taste of Germany's culinary delights was provided by **Petra Casparek**, a freelance journalist who was weaned on the subject through the various cookery book projects of her well-known parents. **Andreas Wirthensohn** dealt another vitally important aspect of German culture, namely beer. As a Bavarian born and bred, he regarded this as very familiar territory.

Most of the articles describing the new federal states in the east were written by **Wieland Giebel**, who edited the book's 1990 edition. The articles were revised and updated with the help of **Dr Karin Timme**, who lives in Leipzig and has intimate knowledge of Saxony, Sachsen-Anhalt and Thuringia.

The article about the lakes and coast of Mecklenburg was completely rewritten by **Thomas Gebhardt**, who

Pansegrau

spent his youth in the region. After reunification he began working for various western-based publications, including *Merian* and *Die Woche*, as well as continuing his career as a freelance journalist. He has written travel books on Mecklenburg-Vorpommern as well as Malta.

The original articles on Berlin and Potsdam were written by **Petra Dubilski**. The texts were revised for this edition by **Christianne Theiselmann**, who has lived in Berlin since the collapse of the Wall and has followed the dramatic changes in that city both as a private citizen and as a journalist and author for a variety of publishers.

For the updating and restructuring of the articles covering the old Federal Republic, Bettina Schümann drew on the expertise of the editors working in Apa's Munich editorial office. **Sigrid Merkl**, born near Regensburg, dealt with the southern part of the country, while **Monika Römer** from Düsseldorf provided new material on Cologne, Düsseldorf and the Ruhrgebiet.

Monika Römer also compiled the extensive and detailed Travel Tips section of the book.

Gebhardt

The final choice of photography for the new edition was made in the London editorial office by **Brian Bell**, Apa's editorial director. Apart from the pictures from Apa's own library, there were substantial contributions from **Erhard Pansegrau**, **Wolfgang Fritz** and **Rainer Kiedrowski**.

Translation of the original German text, overseen by Apa's resident Anglo-German specialist **Tony Halliday**, was by **Paul Fletcher, Susanne Pleines** and **Bob Tilley**. Proof-reading and indexing was completed by **Pam Barrett**.

Theiselmann

CONTENTS

Maps

TRAVEL TIPS

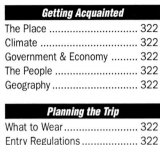

Germany, politically on Europe's centre stage, is one of the classic tourist destinations. A turbulent history, ever-changing landscapes, unspoilt nature reserves and a wealth of impressive cultural attractions provide a varied menu, and the ease with which English is spoken makes it a more accessible destination than many other European countries.

Its cosmopolitan cities throb with life, their boulevards lined with cafés, pubs, bars and discos inviting you to drop in and stay a while. Hamburg and Berlin are especially famous for their nightlife, and "closing time" is an unknown phrase.

Some of the world's greatest art can be found in Germany's magnificent museums, which also organise regular exhibitions of historical and contemporary significance. In World War II the cities were badly bombed, but most of the architecturally important buildings have been reconstructed or – miraculously – survived undamaged. Those which largely escaped the bombing include Cologne Cathedral, which ended the war in 1945 towering practically unscathed among the surrounding ruins (mirroring the survival of St Paul's Cathedral in London). Dresden's Church of Our Lady in the centre of the lovely baroque city of Augustus the Strong, on the other hand, is being restored to its pre-war splendour. And Berlin has become one large building site in the 1990s as the city rediscovers its role as German capital.

In the country's many castles and palaces – built in the choicest sites – the visitor can wander in the landscaped parks in which they're set and escape into the dreamlike world of knights and princes. Medieval towns beckon visitors into the past, and the open-air museums which are such a feature of the German countryside also offer a fascinating look into the life of bygone ages.

Leisure-time is cherished by Germans, many of whom particularly relish outdoor sports. The mountain terrain of the Alps is ideal for climbing, mountain biking, hang-gliding and skiing, while yachting enthusiasts, windsurfers and beach fans make for the seashores of the north and the banks of the country's lakes.

Not so well known are the tranquil but no less attractive landscapes of the Mecklenburg Seeplatte (Lake District), for instance – or the Sächsische Schweiz (Saxony's "Little Switzerland"), the heavily wooded tracts of the Spessart, Rhön and Odenwald and the picturesque valleys of the Black Forest. They can be explored by canoe or on foot, in excursions which end within the welcoming walls of a typical German country inn.

Preceding pages: Berlin's Reichstag wrapped by the artist Christo in 1995; Augustus the Strong as Golden Horseman in Dresden; facing the world head on; entertainment in Munich's Marienplatz; low tide on the mud flats; autumn pleasures in the Wetterau, near Frankfurt; the Kirmes fair on Düsseldorf's Rheinwiesen. **Left,** the television tower on Berlin's Alexanderplatz marks the historic centre of the city.

HAVE THE GERMANS CHANGED?

They played, sang and danced to the backdrop of the Reichstag, which was itself flamboyantly wrapped as a work of art in June 1995 by Christo and Jeanne-Claude – and the wider world was amazed that the Germans could be so free and easy.

"Nothing will remain the same, neither in the East nor in the West," prophesied Hans-Dietrich Genscher in 1990. Much has changed with the Germans. At that time, the world looked with some anxiety at this country of 80 million people in the heart of Europe. Would the spectre of the past arise again and Germany rediscover its old aggression? But, in the debate about allowing its army to participate in crisis missions around the world, the Germans at large showed scant enthusiasm for their military strength. In neighbouring France, the Germans' scruples were widely interpreted as malingering.

After reunification, the skinhead menace hit the international headlines, but the silent majority of young Germans don't hold much truck with violence, particularly in its military guise. Indeed, the number of conscientious objectors is rising. Figures show that thousands of young men refuse conscription yearly. They prefer to work in hospitals and social institutions. Are the new Germans, then, a bunch of softies? The Federal Army, already wound-down, has recruiting problems. In 1993, when a reduction in the period of conscription was considered, strong objections came from the charity organisations and social services: they warned that, if young men opting for civilian service had to work for a shorter period, the cost of nursing care would become prohibitive.

Multicultural society: In the 1950s, because of a labour shortage, millions of Italians and later on Yugoslavs, Turks and other nationalities were recruited for work in Germany. Many remained and established families. In Munich, the children of foreigners are in the majority in many of the city's primary schools. The integration of all these people doesn't always proceed placidly. Xenophobia

is often the way young people without job prospects take out their aggressive frustration on those weaker than themselves.

Remarkably, in many districts of Germany's big cities, every fourth person is a foreigner – a figure which includes the hundreds of thousands of asylum-seekers, resettlers from the East and the 400,000 refugees from former Yugoslavia. The country that rejected heterogeneity in the 1930s seems unwittingly to have embraced it, and for most Germans it isn't a big problem.

The hard fact that not all Germans share in the country's prosperity is borne out by statistics as well as by the many homeless people. The gap between rich and poor is increasing even in this country of the "economic miracle". The United Nations Children's Fund (UNICEF) published a study showing that every fifth child in the eastern part of the country lives on the poverty line. The disposable income of 63 percent of single parents was reported as than DM1,800 (£800/US$1,200) a month. "Poverty not in the Third World but in a part of one of the wealthiest countries on earth..." wrote the *Süddeutsche Zeitung* in moral indignation.

The unsatisfied yearning for faraway places:
If a fondness of travelling is anything to go by, then half of all Germans can by no means be considered poor. Thanks in part to favourable currency exchange rates, many have become globetrotters and can be found in the most out-of-the-way parts of the world. Young Germans are constantly on the move abroad as pupils and students; they've jetted to Asia and America and – though it's a mystery where they get the money from – have already ticked Australia and New Zealand off their travel destination list. And 80-year-olds are undertaking perhaps their final educational journey – to view the penguins of the Antarctic.

Location problems: The industriousness of the Germans has become proverbial since the much-vaunted economic miracle began in the 1950s. However, international tables of statistics have been doggedly declaring for some time that, in purely quantitative terms, less real work is done in Germany than elsewhere. If one takes vacation time and public holidays and adds them to the average number of days lost through illness (a recent sickness tally was 28 days in the case of civil servants and 26 for salaried workers), you find that many Germans have three months off a year, on full pay. While the machines run 73 hours a week in the car

factories of other European countries, they operate barely 60 hours a week in Germany.

Is the country, therefore, in danger of losing its treasured status as a location for industry? Wage costs average DM57 an hour in Germany and just half that in France and Italy – a good enough argument for Siemens to build a highly-subsidised microchip factory in northern England and for BASF and Hoechst to create 2,000 jobs in gene and biological research on the east coast of the United States. Rationalisation is under way. Nearly one German in 10 is unemployed, and that's been the case for several years.

Proof that the country is hard at work, however, is provided by the rapid reconstruction of the infrastructure in eastern Germany; many individuals and companies from all over the world, but particularly from the East, are helping there, too. Selfless "neighbourly help" (known as moonlighting) provided by friends and family in building houses, for example, also escapes the statisticians. The chairman of the Trades Guild made tireless attacks on this shadowy side of the economy – until somebody found in the workers' hostel of his own company Bulgarians who couldn't produce work permits.

Medieval romance: Since Madame de Staël explained the German Romantic Movement to the rest of Europe in 1830 (and unwittingly gave a modern hotel chain, Romantik Hotels, its name), many visitors to Germany have been drawn to medieval towns such as Rothenburg and Dinkelsbühl. If they had the choice, many Germans would also like to live in medieval times. The great historical pageants such as the Landshut Wedding regularly hold thousands of visitors and participants in thrall. Many small towns and villages celebrate medieval festivals or market jubilees, lovingly prepared by various organisations, where people don traditional costumes for days on end and revive long-extinct crafts once carried on by coopers, tanners, indigo-printers and candlemakers.

And, on the subject of organisations, in what other country could a town with 3,475 inhabitants boast 72 officially-registered local associations? Although it leads the European Union economically, Germany has clearly not been homogenised by it.

Above, youth in search of identity. Right, an artist and his work, observed in Hamburg.

In AD 60 the Roman historian Tacitus characterised the Germans thus: "They have blue eyes and red hair, and although they have an impressive build and are strong fighters, they are not given to hard graft." He was referring to the multitude of tribes living on the vague northern borders of the Roman Empire and partly within Roman conquered territory. These tribes must indeed have appeared unruly and uncultured to the sophisticated Romans. There were no cities and agriculture was not developed much beyond subsistence level.

The Romans under Caesar Augustus attempted to expand their empire towards the north. Their legions crossed the Rhine and the Danube in an attempt to annex Germania as part of the Roman Empire. However, they came up against stiff opposition and, indeed, the warriors of the Cheruscan tribe under their commander Arminius so soundly defeated three of their best legions at the Battle of Teutoburger Wald in AD 9 that the Romans opted to withdraw and accept the Rhine and the Danube as the frontier of the empire. They secured their territory by building a series of fortifications, the *limes,* along a length of 550 km (350 miles).

Along this distant frontier of the empire, cities such as Mainz, Trier and Augsburg, were built on the Roman pattern. The "Barbarians" thus came face to face with unimaginable luxury: theatres, public baths, roads, bridges and villas.

Clovis, king of the Franks: However, by AD 40, when Germanic Vandals poured across the Rhine, the death knell of the Roman Empire was sounded. This fate did not befall the Franks, however, who, having settled in present-day Belgium, had emerged as a second major power. Their success was down to their leader, Clovis, from the house of Merovingia. In the 30 years of his rule, he transformed his Frankish warriors into a mighty army and extended his realm eastwards as far as the Weser, westwards and southwards as far as the Atlantic and Spain.

Left, the minstrel Walther von der Vogelweide. **Above,** Maria Laach monastery, climax of the German Romanesque.

Wherever the Franks advanced, they found the country firmly in the control of bishops, because Christianity had been the state religion of the Roman Empire ever since AD 380. Doing business with the bishops was of mutual advantage. After Clovis was baptised in AD 496, he knew he could rely on the support of the bishops, and they, in return, could reinforce their position through the power and authority of the king. Christianisation of the Franks followed and Christianity spread as the realm expanded.

Charlemagne's empire: From AD 768 onwards, it was Charlemagne who guided the fortunes of the largest empire in the western world. Like his predecessors, he maintained no fixed residence, preferring to travel through the country with his entourage and to live on his various estates. Through a long series of bloody and cruel campaigns, it took Charlemagne more than 30 years to bring the Germans to heel, to Christianise them and to annex their territory.

Charlemagne regarded himself as the legitimate heir of the Roman emperor, and sealed this position by having himself crowned emperor on Christmas Day AD 800.

THE TEUTONIC KNIGHT

During the reign of the Hohenstaufen emperors, the status of the Teutonic knight rose. Tales of their exploits, often expressed in song, have survived through the centuries. The knights' historical importance does not just include their heroic participation in the Crusades and their bloody battles against the Infidel, but also their impressive cultural achievements and their sporting prowess in tournaments.

Around 1100, as the alliance between pope and emperor began to weaken, the royal dukes began to act more in their own interests, rather than that of the state. The emperor therefore turned for

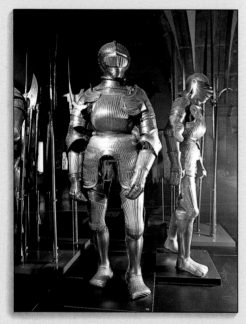

support to his appointed counts and lords, giving them hereditary rights in return for their backing in time of war. As a result, a new landed nobility emerged, who were vassals of the emperor and who also had a degree of security.

Merchants and the new administrative officials could rise up the social ladder by marrying aristocratic women and gaining access to the nobility's salons. At the core of this new social order, the knights became the bearer of an important new courtly culture that spread through the Imperial palaces, castles and large country estates.

An independent German literature hardly existed around the turn of the millennium. Literature was almost totally oriented towards Italy and Rome

Above, medieval armour for a virtuous knight.

where the language most commonly used was Latin. Slowly there emerged a secular literature which was based on traditional myths and legends, on reports of travelling minstrels and on oriental legends which had been picked up during the Crusades. In the heyday of Middle Age literature, the narratives were primarily based on descriptions and glorifications of German orders of knighthood. The medieval courts became the focal point of literary pursuits: "courtly" became synonymous with "well-bred", "brave" and "pure". Courage, strength and dexterity were required of the medieval knight, but he was also characterised by his inner harmony, self-discipline and pursuit of honour, loyalty and compassion. Only after achieving these virtues through a long, inner struggle with himself could the medieval knight match the ideals demanded by his social standing.

The literature of chivalry outlined the ideals for which the knight should strive. These same ideals applied to the whole of Christian Europe, largely because of the contribution made by the Crusades which, from the 11th to the 13th centuries, provided a common goal for all Europe's knights.

Influenced by the French troubadours, the Minnesang or court lyric emerged in Germany, enjoying great popularity during the late 12th century. In 1184, for example, Frederick Barbarossa invited 70,000 guests to join him in Mainz for a famous courtly festival. The German Minnesang is based on a social convention, the literary expression of what German poets call Frauendienst, a code expressing a lover's relation to his mistress. Written in passionate language but showing the utmost respect and dignity, the Minnesänger paid homage to his lady, someone of higher social status than the poet and unattainable.

And yet the life of a knight was anything but romantic. The training was extremely tough. At the age of seven, boys born into the nobility would be brought to serve as page boys in another castle. Here they would not only wait on their elders but they would also learn social poise and good table manners.

At the age of 14, the pages became squires and served the knights both in tournament and in battle. They practised jousting, riding and javelin throwing and when they were 20, they were considered fully-fledged knights. Reading and writing were not part of the curriculum – these were the domain of the higher ranking clergy and some daughters of the nobility. Becoming a knight did not necessarily mean acquiring a castle. Many simply joined forces with a wealthy knight of the same order or just travelled the country as "poor knights" without estate.

The invention of firearms rendered knights' armour useless. The once proud and distinguished orders, with all their ideals and virtues, became impoverished and disintegrated. ∎

His crowning achievements were the organisation of the empire's administrative structures and the establishment of its cultural base. He standardised the laws of all the tribes within his realm and divided it into states to which he assigned loyal leaders. He also summoned intellectuals to his favourite palace in Aachen and established schools in the monasteries throughout his empire in order to raise the standard of education.

With the help of the clergy and the monastery-trained laymen, Charlemagne succeeded in introducing Latin as the official language of the realm. The monastery and palace schools taught the art of book illustrating, drew up contracts, translated the classics and established libraries. We have these institutions to thank for translations of the writings of Caesar, Tacitus and Juvenal.

The beginnings of German history: Now only England, southern Spain and southern Italy lay outside Charlemagne's influence. Under his rule, the division of the empire into east and west would have been unthinkable. Yet, within 30 years of his death, it became reality: in 843 his grandsons divided the empire between them at the Treaty of Verdun and it is this year that marks the actual beginning of German history. The first king of the Eastern Empire, Ludwig the German (843–76), ruled over a land which for the first time could be called "German".

It was Otto, the son of Henry I (the Fowler), whom fate called upon to make one of the most important decisions for the west, namely to defend the realm against the advancing Hungarians. In AD 955 Otto and his army, which was composed of all-Germanic tribes, defeated the invaders at Lechfeld in southwest Germany.

The other major danger was presented by over-ambitious princes who threatened the empire with disintegration. However, he mastered this problem through clever personnel policy and the inclusion of the Catholic Church in the governing process. The bishops could often advance to important political posts, not only because they were educated and good administrators, but also because they had no heirs to threaten the power of the king.

Thus fortified, Otto, just like Charlemagne, succeeded in capturing the iron crown of the Langobard dynasty and intervened in the political chaos in Rome. He also managed to have the Western Slavic tribes incorporated in the Roman Church, and by doing so, was able to secure the realm's eastern borders.

Church and emperor: From AD 906 right up until the fall of the empire in 1806, the title of emperor was inseparably linked to that of the German king. Nobody who had not already been the German king could be crowned emperor. The realm came to be called "The Holy Roman Empire of German Nation" with the status of the German emperor defined as the ruler over "eternal" Rome with a

responsibility to fulfil the functions of both the German king and the Roman emperor.

The Carolingians and the church co-operated on the basis of mutual advantage. Charlemagne made his conquests in the name of the church and the church expanded its influence. However effective this partnership was, it carried with it a danger which came to the surface in the 11th and 12th centuries and rocked western Christendom. The church had taken on an increasing amount of secular responsibility. The emperor would intervene in the election of the bishop and make sure that only those who were interested in secular power got anywhere in the church. The bishops became prince-bishops, and naturally this secularisation of the church did not find favour with the pope in Rome.

The open struggle between the pope and the emperor began in 1076 when, according to the traditions of the time, Emperor Henry IV appointed the new Archbishop of Milan. Pope Gregory VII, who demanded that the emperor immediately revoke his decision, was dismissed. The pope hit back by excommunicating the emperor and forbidding him to rule over the German and Italian kingdoms. The emperor, whose position had been weakened by the immediate flare-up of opposition from the nobility, was forced in 1077 to beg the pope personally for forgive-

ness in order to release himself from excommunication. He was thus able to win back his position, but his authority within the church was severely shaken.

The powerful princes of the empire no longer recognise the power of the emperor to the extent that they had previously. The title of the king was no longer to be linked to birth but was to be decided by the nobility. Even the outstanding kings of the Hohenstaufen period, Frederick Barbarossa (1152–90), Heinrich VI and Frederick II (1212–50), ruling in an era regarded by many as the high point of medieval imperial rule, could not achieve a lasting return to the old order.

Medieval towns and cities: Until the turn of the millenium, the only cities were those that had been established in Roman times. After that time, cities emerged from monastic centres (Munich), castles (Nuremberg), river crossings (Frankfurt) or at the intersections of the few major European trade routes. The princes soon came to recognise the advantages of these settlements. Here they could exact customs and taxes and obtain rare goods and excellent craftsmen. The towns were also safe havens from which the princes could control their territory more effectively. Between 1100 and 1250 the number of towns in Germany increased tenfold.

While every citizen had a right to certain freedoms, this did not guarantee that people lived as equals in the crowded medieval towns. Inevitably, some were more equal than others. The most important class was that which the town had to thank most for its prosperity, namely the merchants. These organised themselves into associations which virtually controlled the town: only the associations were represented on the council and they thus had full responsibility for the town's administration.

Between the 13th and 15th centuries, the craftsmen succeeded in gaining their share of power in many towns. They were organised into guilds, which would set the price, quality and quantity of manufactured goods. Funds were established to look after the needs of those no longer able to work, as well as widows. In several cities the guilds managed to secure their place on the councils.

Between one- and two-thirds of the urban dwellers, including menial workers, maidservants, domestic servants, the illegitimate, beggars and outcasts, as well as those with despised professions such as hangmen and grave diggers, had no civil rights at all. These groups were often dependent on the goodwill of the church or charities established by wealthy citizens. Fortunately, the rich had been convinced that only those who gave something to the needy could expect God's mercy. As a result, they often financed hospitals, as well as old people's homes and sometimes special housing for the poor.

The Jews: The Jews lived as a separate entity. In every medieval city, there was a Jewish community which was generally detached from the Christian quarters. The Jews, repeatedly the target of pogroms and expulsions, were subject to strict laws laid down by their Christian fellow citizens. In many places the Jews were forced to earn their living as moneylenders and pawnbrokers. In difficult times many citizens were highly indebted to Jewish creditors, who were often driven out of town or murdered. During the 15th century persecution led to the disintegration of many Jewish communities (Mainz 1438, Augsburg 1439).

Originally the Germans were genuinely a free people. However, this all changed in centuries of upheaval punctuated by countless wars. Many small farmers, who found it hard to make a living when they were continually being called up to fight, were forced to hand over their property to the landowners as a means of buying their way out of military service. They got their land back for cultivation but only in return for dues and fixed services such as building and maintaining tracks and helping with the harvest. They sank into servitude, semi-free peasants who were forbidden to own land. Apart from the odd period of economic upswing, the economic and legal position of most peasants drastically deteriorated in the Middle Ages.

Religious devotion and Luther: Many people found comfort in the Christian religion, which promised compensation in the next world for earthly suffering. Their piety was manifest in the many chapels and pilgrimage churches, the worship of relics and the popular religious tracts of the time. This Christian zeal had its dark side, however, in the persecution of witches that spread throughout Europe towards the end of the Middle ages. It was as late as 1749 that the last alleged witch was burned on a hill outside Würzburg.

Against this background of religious devoutness, the deplorable state of affairs within the church was keenly felt. The moral decline of the papacy, the insatiable greed of the church and the theological ignorance of the clergy were the main objects of criticism. The church exploited believers' fear of purgatory and damnation to obtain the money required for ambitious building projects and the maintenance of a luxurious lifestyle. For a specified sum, anyone could buy a pardon and shorten the time spent in purgatory.

During the 15th and 16th centuries, critical theologians constantly attacked these practices. From 1517 the German Augustinian monk Martin Luther set about reforming the church through a series of damning theses. Luther denounced the authority of the pope, renounced the special status of the clergy as mediators between God and man and instead formulated the idea of having a general priesthood involving all believers.

The peasants' revolt: Luther found support among all levels of society; among the lower nobility, the townsfolk and the impoverished peasant. His campaign for an end to discrimination against peasants and his battle against the authority of the church in the

countryside led to an uprising against all authority. In the spring of 1525, the first monasteries and castles went up in flames in southwest Germany and the rebellion spread like wildfire throughout central Europe. But the peasants were poorly equipped and, in 1526, the revolt was brutally crushed by the superior forces of the nobility. More than 100,000 peasants either died in battle or were subsequently executed.

The unity of the church was now broken and western Christianity was split between the Catholics and the so-called Protestants. The teachings of Luther were a powerful weapon in the hands of those princes seeking

Left, the German imperial sceptre. Above, bust of Charlemagne, founder of the Holy Roman Empire of German Nation.

independence from the emperor and the Pope, particularly in northern and central Germany. Religion became a territorial matter and the schism was an important factor in the fragmentation of Germany into sovereign states.

A new era begins: Luther's successes would not have been possible without a changed world view and the accompanying developments in science, technology and economics. The medieval view that life on earth served merely as a hard test for the eternal life to come changed in the 14th and 15th centuries. People now tried to interpret the world by applying logic. The earth was deemed to be round and not flat. Christopher Columbus discovered America in 1492 and,

in 1445, Johannes Gutenberg invented the printing press, so enabling the population at large to have access to new ideas. Education expanded and in the 15th century a number of universities were founded in Germany (e.g. Leipzig 1409, Freiburg 1455), and their curriculum became increasingly devoted to secular subjects. In the cities, reading and writing rooms were established.

The Thirty Years' War: Despite all attempts on the part of the Catholic church to stem the spread of Lutheran Protestantism and to win back lost territory, by 1600 the new sect had become the most powerful religious-political force in Europe. The religious conflict was further exacerbated by the rivalry between the newly established sovereign states and the struggle between the emperor and his princes.

In 1618 the military confrontations began in Bohemia and soon enveloped the whole of Europe. France and Sweden joined in with the Protestants, England and Spain with the Catholics. The mercenaries, who were not averse to swapping allegiances, were fed and paid from the spoils of war. There was torture and rape and towns were besieged and put to the torch.

After 30 years of war, central Europe was so desolated and exhausted that peace negotiations finally led to an agreement. The Treaty of Westphalia brought about recognition for both sides and the dissolution of the German Empire into some 1,800 separate states. Only the emperor and the common language provided a last vestige of unity. The German population had been reduced by one-third. Epidemics were rife, hunger reigned and the Holy Roman Empire of German Nations had completely lost its influence.

The rise to a new great power: Germany gradually recovered from the wounds of war, and living conditions soon began to improve, promoted by monarchist absolutism which, following the example set by the French king Louis XIV, found favour among many princes. They saw themselves as the centre of the state, appointed by and answerable only to God. Through resulting improvements in law and order, agriculture could be reorganised and citizens resettled.

By far the largest states within the empire were the Austrian Habsburg realm and the Prussian house of Brandenburg, which in the 17th and 18th centuries emerged as the two new great powers in central Europe. Austria expanded to the south-east at the expense of the Turks and Prussia amalgamated a number of fragmented states with the help of its mighty army. In the 18th century rulers emerged in both states who regarded themselves more as "servants of the state" than as absolute rulers. In particular, Frederick II – the Great – of Prussia and Emperor Joseph II of Austria were strongly influenced by a new attitude which promised to change the world: Enlightenment.

<u>Above</u>, officer cadet in the Thirty Years' War. <u>Right</u>, Martin Luther.

The great masters of the German classical period, particularly Ludwig van Beethoven, Johann Sebastian Bach and, of course, Austrian-born Wolfgang Amadeus Mozart, have bequeathed their immortal musical masterpieces to the world.

In the baroque period the work of **Georg Friedrich Handel** (1685–1759) was of European significance. Born in Halle, he found his first engagements in Hamburg and Hanover and during his tours of Italy, where he played the organ as well as working on

compositions, he was acclaimed as *il divino sassone*, the divine Saxon. He finally settled in London, where the Elector of Hanover, who had made him his director of music, later became King George I. Artistically, he employed rigorous methods: he is said to have hung the tyrannical prima donna Francesca Cuzzoni out of a window, threatening to drop her until she agreed to follow his musical directions. In London he introduced the Italian style of baroque opera, but after his work was subjected to a musical caricature in *The Beggar's Opera* by John Gay and Johann Christian Pepusch, his response was to concentrate on oratorios. He

wrote *Belshazzar, Jephta, Judas Maccabaeus* and, greatest of them all, the *Messiah*. His orchestral works – the organ concertos, *concerti grossi* and his famous water music – were frequently performed.

There could not have been a greater difference in character than between Handel and **Johann Sebastian Bach** (1685–1750), the master of the pure form. Born in Eisenach, Bach was organist, choirmaster and royal orchestra conductor in Köthen, Weimar and Leipzig. He was an indefatigable worker, but he still found time to father, and care for, 20 children.

Bach is often regarded as primarily a composer of religious works, and the best known of these today are the *St John* and *St Matthew Passions,* the *Mass in B Minor*, and the *Christmas Oratorio*. But he wrote a wealth of secular music too, of which the *Brandenburg Concertos* are perhaps the greatest. His compositions for piano, including the *Goldberg Variations* and the *Wohltemperierte Klavier* also have an enduring popularity. Bach's works are pure and spiritual in form and often – as in the *Art of the Fugue* – not even related to particular instruments. Neither a tuba quartet nor a jazz combo can destroy his music; scarcely any other composer's work has inspired so many different interpretations.

Joseph Haydn (1732–1809), Mozart's friend and Beethoven's teacher, was the oldest in the Vienna triumvirate of classical composers. Through their influence, European music between 1781 and 1827 concentrated itself in the royal city of the Habsburgs. Haydn bequeathed to the world an enormous repertoire, ranging from pre-classical works to early romanticism and embracing all the musical styles of his time. He is sometimes known as "the father of the symphony" and is also regarded as the founder of modern chamber music His 80 string quartets and more than 100 symphonies offer a broad spectrum ranging from the entertaining music he wrote to please high society, whose darling he was, to individual self-searching compositions.

In the 20 years he spent as choirmaster on the estate of Prince Esterhazy on the

Neusiedler lake in Hungary he played all kinds of jokes on his noble audiences: in the finale of the *Farewell Symphony, No. 45,* one musician after another leaves the stage – a challenge, perhaps, to his royal patrons to grant them a longed-for holiday. In his *Symphony No. 94* the unexplained drum beat is said to have been intended to wake up sleeping members of the audience.

Wolfgang Amadeus Mozart (1756–91) was born in Salzburg, the son of a violinist, composer and theorist, Leopold Mozart. He displayed his musical gifts very early, and had mastered the keyboard by the time he was four, and the violin at five. After undertaking numerous tours throughout Europe with his family, by the time he was 16 he had written no less than 25 symphonies. Having been dismissed from the household of the Archbishop Colloredo of Salzburg, Mozart left his birthplace in 1777 and became the first freelance composer. He made his home in Vienna, where he received the support of the Emperor, but he was constantly in financial straits and not always sufficiently recognised. His greatest success was the premiere of *Don Giovanni* in Prague.

He is the most important operatic composer of the period, committed to the ideas of the Age of Enlightenment. The political dynamite to be found in the *The Abduction from the Seraglio, The Marriage of Figaro, Cosi fan Tutte* or *The Magic Flute* may not be as relevant today, but the psychological and dramatic power remains intact. There is hardly any other composer whose work remains so totally alive; one just has to think of the 25 piano concertos, some 40 symphonies, his *Requiem,* and his chamber music.

Ludwig van Beethoven (1770–1827) was born in Bonn, but at the age of 17 was sent by the Elector to Vienna, which he made his home. Beethoven created a musical language of an unmatched power of expression. Anyone with a musical ear can whistle one of his themes. His revolt against musical norms makes itself clear in his love of dissonance. Best known of his works are the five piano concertos, the opera *Fidelio,* the piano sona-

tas, the string quartets and above all the nine symphonies. The music of the romantic movement further developed his subjectivity, replacing rigidity of form with emotion and expression.

Franz Schubert (1797–1828) "set the art of poetry to music and let music speak". He created a new category of music, the artistic song, represented by the song cycles *Die schöne Müllerin* and *Die Winterreise.* In the *"Unfinished"* symphony and the great *C-Major* he spins out musical themes to "heavenly lengths", with a perfection of melody also to be found in the *Trout* quintet and the final string quartets (*Der Tod und das Mädchen,* among others).

Felix Mendelssohn-Bartholdy (1809–47) composed romantic music: his symphonies, chamber music and the overture to *A Midsummer Night's Dream* are worldly and elegant. *Fingal's Cave* is perhaps the most frequently performed of his works today.

Composers who rounded off the romantic movement were Carl Maria von Weber (1786–1826), with his operas *Freischütz, Euryanthe* and *Oberon,* Robert Schumann (1810–56) with his instrumental music and Johannes Brahms (1833–97). The "tonal pioneers" Richard Wagner and Anton Bruckner were already investigating new musical forms in the second half of the 19th century.

Preceding page: flute concert in Sans Souci, by Adolf Menzel. **Left,** Wolfgang Amadeus Mozart was already famous at an early age. **Right,** Ludwig van Beethoven shattered the musical rules of his time.

When Germany is described as the country of poets and philosophers, it is usually the era of Weimar classicism that is being referred to. In German literary terms, this roughly covers the time between von Goethe's Italian tour (1776) until the appearance of his autobiography *Dichtung und Wahrheit* (the final part published in 1830). Weimar classicism followed the artistic rules of the ancient classical period and the Renaissance, while also referring to the most important achievements of other epochs. It adopted from the

Many important writers of this period lived in Weimar, others such as Jean Paul, Johann Peter Hebel and Heinrich von Kleist stayed there for varying periods of time. The liberal Countess Anna Amalia is to be thanked for that. In 1772 she engaged Christoph Martin Wieland (1733–1813) as a teacher. He was followed by Goethe, Herder and Schiller, all of whom were brought to Weimar by the Countess's son, Carl August.

Wieland, particularly creative in his use of language, wrote the first educational novel

philosopher Immanuel Kant (1724–1804) the idea that all human beings should take responsibility for themselves, and make the most of their own intellect and potential. From Gotthold Ephraim Lessing (1729–81) the movements absorbed the principle of tolerance towards other religions.

The *Sturm und Drang* (Storm and Stress) movement was also influential at this time. Johann Wolfgang Goethe (1749–1832), Friedrich von Schiller (1759–1805) and Gottfried Herder (1744–1803) were its most important figures. Inspired by Rousseau, it was a revolt against literary conventions and a plea for a return to nature.

(*Geschichte des Agathon*, 1766), the first German-language opera libretto (*Alceste*, 1773), utopian-satirical novels, the first Shakespeare translation, and for 20 years published the magazine *Teutscher Merkur*. This publication aired the artistic and political debates of the day, in a light, journalistic style. Although Wieland counted Kant, Schiller, Schlegel, and other prominent personalities among his friends, they rarely wrote for the *Sau Merkur* (the Swinish Merkur), as Johann Wolfgang von Goethe deprecatingly described it.

When considering the high ideals of the period one should not forget that, compared to today, Weimar was a small town, in which the great thinkers of the time lived practically on top of each other, intrigued against each other and were not too sophisticated for the ways of provincial society.

In reading Wieland's satirical novel *Geschichte der Abderiten* (1774–81), one gets an idea of what life was like in Weimar. Each thinker had his own little problems: Herder, for example, tried unsuccessfully in his role as Superintendent General to reform the schools. Privy Councillor Goethe, a powerful figure in the city and close to the young Duke of Weimar, experienced difficulties because he hadn't married the much younger woman with whom he was living, the artificial flower-maker Christiane Vulpius (they eventually married in 1806).

For us today, Goethe and Schiller are the outstanding personalities of the period, but in those days they had a great deal of competition. They took a lively part in the literary gatherings at the homes of Countess Anna Amalia and Johanna Schopenhauer, but at the time popular taste tended towards lighter works and people were avidly reading the ironical fantasies of novelist Jean Paul and picaresque tales such as *Rinaldo Rinaldini* (1798), written by the Weimar librarian Christian August Vulpius, the brother of Goethe's Christiane.

Schiller's greatest and most enduring successes were the blank-verse drama, *Don Carlos*, the historical tragedies *Wallenstein* and *Maria Stuart* and his final work, *William Tell,* all of which grappled with problems of personal or political responsibility.

In 1799 Goethe and Schiller founded the Gesellschaft der Weimarer Kunstfreunde (Society of Weimar Friends of the Arts). They proclaimed their new concept of classicism, rooted in the ancients, in the pages of the publications *Horen* and *Propyläen,* in which they also campaigned against literary philistinism. The art historian Hans Heinrich Meyer, the language philosopher Wilhelm Humboldt and the philologist Friedrich August Wolf were all members of this illustrious literary circle.

Goethe may have suffered from literary competition for a while, but posterity has recognised him as a genius. His best-known work is *Faust*, written in two parts over a period of 60 years, and finished only just before his death. Among his other great works were *Iphigenie auf Tauris* and *Tasso*, both influenced far more by Italian classicism than by the ideals of the *Sturm und Drang* movement.

What makes Goethe so fascinating today is the universality of his intellect – he was interested in every aspect of the world around him and constantly strove for a straightforward, analytical approach. He immersed himself in philosophical, art-historical and scientific studies, and published a *Farbenlehre* (Treatise on Colours) in 1810, which chal-

lenged the theories of Isaac Newton, and was itself attacked by Arthur Schopenhauer. He carried out a geological survey for the duke, and conducted both botanical and medical research, becoming interested in comparative anatomy and discovering the intermaxillary bone in the human skull.

The first works on Goethe's genius appeared shortly after his death: *Goethes Briefwechsel mit einem Kind* (Exchange of Letters with a Child) by Bettina von Arnim, and Johann Peter Eckermann's *Gespräche mit Goethe in den letzten Jahren seines Lebens* (Conversations with Goethe in the Final Years of his Life).

Johann Wolfgang von Goethe, Friedrich Schiller (left) and Frederick the Great of Prussia (above) were major figures of German Enlightenment.

Germany at the end of the 18th century was neither an empire nor a united country. Instead, it looked rather like a patchwork quilt of 350 principalities and over 1,000 small states where kings, electors, dukes, counts and knights, monasteries and cities, sat on their limited rights of sovereignty and where bishops came to govern as secular rulers. There were only two powers of any distinction that stood out in the veritable Augean stable that Germany had become: Prussia and Austria. The loose union of states with

the grandiose title "Holy Roman Empire of German Nations" had no common system of taxation and no common army. After 200 years of constant strife, Germany had landed right back in the Middle Ages.

Four-fifths of this curious empire's 23 million inhabitants lived tied to the land. In the west the peasants paid their lords in money and in kind, providing services for little or no remuneration. The church demanded its tithe from the yearly harvest. Only a few peasants actually owned the land they worked. For better or for worse, most of them were simple tenants at the mercy of the landowners.

In the extensive Prussian lowlands east of the Elbe, the peasants and their families still lived as inherited subjects of the lords of the manor. Living as serfs, they had to do compulsory labour on a knight's or bishop's estate. They were not allowed to marry freely and could not leave the estate without the permission of the landowner. Their situation was made even worse by the constant wars which were waged by the nobility. Every Prussian peasant was a soldier of the king. They were simply carried off to fight, leaving the farms to decay and the harvest to rot. And the Prussian army wasn't exactly a bed of roses. Conditions were degrading in the extreme and many conscripts died before they even saw the battlefield.

The need for a free market: This structure of hundreds of small states was not conducive to the development of business and industry. Each state and town had its own trading conditions, its own coinage, weights and measures. No wonder, then, that the money from German states was not accepted abroad, and was even ridiculed. Restrictions imposed on the guilds and customs barriers made free competition impossible. Strict local legislation prevented the free movement of people.

In 1803, under the auspices of France, there began a radical clean-up in fragmented Germany. Many of the small states lost their independence. Napoleon declared Bavaria and Baden Württemberg to be kingdoms. Sixteen south and west German princes committed open treason and founded the Rhine Confederation under Napoleon's protection. From then on the peasants were required by their princes to serve in the French army.

To all intents and purposes the 900-year-old Holy Roman Empire of German Nations now ceased to exist. It simply fell apart. After Prussia had declared war against revolutionary France, its army's heavy defeat near Jena and Auerstedt in 1806 exposed the extent of its internal weakness. The army dispersed without further ado, the king fled and when Napoleon marched into Berlin there was no resistance. Europe's mightiest military state, with its 200,000 soldiers and senile officers, collapsed like a house of cards. With the Treaty of Tilsit, Prussia was forced to cede half of its territory.

Reforms and war of liberation: Defeated armies learn quickly and the Prussians learned too. Reformers came into the fold: men like Baron von Stein and Graf Hardenberg, officers of the calibre of Scharnhorst, Gneisenau and Clausewitz. The peasants were granted their liberty, the guild order was lifted for some trades and the civic administration was restructured. The army was completely reorganised. Mercenaries and the nobles' monopoly of officer posts were abolished and general military conscription introduced.

A national liberation movement grew in Germany. Gneisenau demanded mobilisation and a national uprising against the French, and after Napoleon's crushing defeat in Russia in 1812, the time was ripe. The hesitant Prussian king was faced with a *fait accompli* by the patriots when, in the spring of 1813, anti-French revolts broke out all over Germany. With the support of Russia, Great Britain and Austria, Prussia finally declared war on France.

The Battle of Nations near Leipzig on 17 October 1813 was a turning point in world history. Napoleon's army was surrounded and defeated, France was forced to withdraw to the west of the Rhine and, after his defeat at Waterloo, Napoleon was sent into exile. Germany's fate was now to be decided at a congress of the victors in 1815 in Vienna.

Triumph of the restoration: At the Congress of Vienna it was the powerful Prince von Metternich who tied together the threads of the new European order. Germany and Italy were once again divided into small states, Poland was made part of Russia and Hungary remained firmly under Austria's thumb. The European reaction was triumphant. The kingdom of God's mercy, the old feudal order and the Catholic Church were reinstalled in their ancestral positions.

Outside the German sphere, Austria's centre of gravity shifted towards the east, while within, Prussia now expanded westwards and became the most important power. At its feet lay 34 principalities and four free imperial cities, combined into a loose confederation without a leader. The result, and indeed

the intention, of the Vienna Congress was clear: Germany was to remain divided and powerless. The final agreement was fashioned by the monarchs of Russia, Prussia and Austria. They founded a "Holy Alliance" of the eastern powers, bound together by the ideals of monarchical absolutism.

In universities students organised a protest movement against the princes' confederation. Their symbol was a black, red and gold flag. When in 1819 the pro-Russian writer Kotzebue was murdered by a student, Metternich reacted with the Carlsbad Decrees. All opposition was suppressed, the students' societies forbidden and the universities placed under police control.

Reaction: The overthrow of the French king in Paris in July 1830 was the signal for a general outbreak of unrest throughout Europe. There was an uprising in Leipzig and uproar and the burning of a palace in Brunswick, destruction of the police headquarters in Dresden, followed by open revolt in Brussels and, at the end of the year, revolution in Poland. Although the protests were crushed by the troops of the Holy Alliance, the bourgeois-democratic opposition movement could not be extinguished. In May 1832, 30,000 people came together at Hambach Castle to demand a free united Germany. The Hambach so-called Festival was attended

<u>Left</u>, Berlin 1848 – Germany to the barricades. <u>Above</u>, the first German Parliament assembled in Frankfurt's St Paul's Church.

by townsfolk, peasants, craftsmen, academics and students whose leaders gave passionate speeches expressing bitterness at their wretched living conditions. Metternich's police arrested the ringleaders and the colours black, red and gold were banned.

In the south German states, the monarchs preserved their constitutions, but allowed the citizens a certain amount of participation in government by introducing so-called "second chambers". In Prussia, Austria and many other states, however, absolutism – the single-handed rule of the monarchs – continued to dominate the body and the soul of the people. "When I think of Germany at night, then I am robbed of sleep," wrote the poet Heinrich Heine.

Railways and poverty: The Industrial Revolution was knocking ever louder on Germany's doors. The age of the train had arrived and in 1835 the first German steam locomotive chugged its way along the 6-km (4-mile) stretch between Nuremberg and Fürth. The nation was entranced. It was with railways, canals and new wide roads, with money and steam, that the up-and-coming citizenry started to undermine the old feudal order. A German customs union including 18 states and 23 million inhabitants was introduced in 1834. The other side of the economic boom manifested itself in the increasing poverty of the lower classes.

Poor peasants were driven to working for a pittance for the rich landowners. There was no more room for all the craftsmen and many ended up in the factories. They were forced to work 12 or 16 hours a day for next to nothing, a situation that drove many families to despair and bitterness. In 1844 in Silesia the weavers revolted and smashed all the machinery. The appalling social conditions forced many to emigrate, primarily to America. Karl Marx and Friedrich Engels worked on their theories of revolutionary socialism in Paris, Brussels, London and Manchester. The air was thick with the smell of radical change.

Germany at the barricades: The year 1847 saw a general economic crisis in Europe: failed harvests, rising inflation, mass starvation, bank collapses, falls in production, and serious unemployment. To make things worse, the winter of 1847–48 was unusually hard. The first unrest was seen in the cities, and once again the struggle began in Paris.

The revolution quickly spread to Germany. The peasants set palaces on fire and withheld their taxes and other dues. Public meetings demanded reforms and a parliament. The rulers were put on the defensive and in order to avoid the worst they were forced to make certain concessions. Common citizens were granted ministerial posts, the bourgeoisie was allowed to share in government and to form armed militias.

On 18 March the revolt reached Berlin and barricades were erected in the streets. After being forced to order the retreat of his forces, the Prussian king appointed a liberal government. Parliaments were voted in the member states of the German Confederation and on 18 May 1848 an elected German National Assembly finally came together in the church of St Paul in Frankfurt.

The failure of the revolution: Would the French Revolution now be repeated in Germany? Would the National Assembly become a permanent body and would it proclaim the nation's sovereignty and abolish the nobility? Nothing of the sort happened. The German citizens talked and talked, but did not touch the established power centres. The National Assembly allowed the individual states to keep their armies. No powerful people's army was created under its auspices, and nobody could take a governing body without weapons very seriously. The liberal majority was afraid of the radical demands of the democratic left, which wanted a republic, and refused to sanction the lifting of feudal dues that the peasantry was still required to pay.

The German revolution ground to a halt. And when the liberals, shocked by the bloody fights in Paris that June, joined the nobility, the train of revolution began to roll backwards. The absolutist overlords knew how to use their power. In Vienna the rebels were shot down by Field Marshal Windischgrätz and in Berlin the revolution had to contend with General Wrangel. Rebellious Hungary was brought to its knees by the heavy boys acting for the European nobility – the Russian army. In Frankfurt, the St Paul's Assembly, which had resisted resorting to arms, was dispersed at sword-point.

Right, *Walker above the Mist* **by Caspar David Friedrich, a painter renowned for his romantic paintings of the countryside.**

1871.

Law and order returned to the land. But although the revolution had been crushed, the problems that had caused it remained. The national state had to be created: if not revolutionary or liberal-democratic, then reactionary; if not as a pan-German state (with Austria), then as a single state (without Austria and under the leadership of Prussia). Something had to be done, one way or another. What actually happened will forever be linked with the name Otto von Bismarck.

A loyal conservative: Bismarck was born in 1815, the year of the Vienna Congress, the son of a Brandenburg landowner, a captain in the cavalry. He had a humanistic education, studied law and was given to student pranks and free-thinking. It was only after he married that he began to take seriously his Christian faith. During the 1848 revolution he was on the staff of the pro-Russian and arch-conservative *Kreuzzeitung* newspaper, supporting a counter-revolutionary nation. He spent some time at the court of the Prussian king.

He learned the art of diplomatic intrigue during the eight years he spent as a Prussian delegate at the Bundestag in Frankfurt. He recognised that Prussia could prosper only if Austria became weak. From 1859 to 1862 he was ambassador to the Russian Czar at St Petersburg, a post which reinforced the pro-Russian sentiments he was to keep all his life. After a few months of diplomatic service in Paris, his career really took off.

In October 1862 King Wilhelm I summoned Bismarck to head the Prussian government. His first task was to bring the liberals in parliament into line – which he did, thoroughly. Then, without much regard for parliament or the constitution, he pushed through the modernisation of the Prussian army. His first master stroke, however, came a year later when he obtained the support of Austria in winning back from Denmark the states of Schleswig and Holstein.

The years between 1866 and 1870 were the best of Bismarck's life. He cleverly managed to keep all other European powers out of the German civil war. In 1848 he had screamed blue murder against general voting rights. Now, however, as a move against

Austria, he introduced those very same liberal rights into the Bundestag. He became a Prussian right-royal revolutionary. Against the will of the small German states he started a deliberately calculated war against the Habsburg monarchy. The decisive battle was near Königgrätz in 1866, where the Prussian army fought with muzzle-loading guns and won. Bismarck became Prussia's hero.

His revolution from the top changed the map of Germany. Prussia annexed large areas, including Schleswig-Holstein, and

France and Austria were forced to agree to this territorial expansion. The German Confederation disintegrated. Prussia forced Austria out of Germany and in the newly-established North German Federation it achieved unchallenged hegemony. Bismarck had granted the liberals their national wishes at the expense of their democratic ones.

Franco–Prussian War: After the defeat of Austria, for the Prussians there was now only one major competitor in central Europe: France. Bismarck used the deserted Spanish throne as a means of provoking Napoleon III. He decreed that a Hohenzollern prince should reside in Madrid, knowing that the

French emperor could not accept having to the south a government loyal to Prussia. But the prince was forced to give up his candidature, which should have ended Bismarck's provocation. Napoleon III, however, demanded that Prussia renounce its claims. Wilhelm I rejected the demand and, with encouragement from Bismarck, the desired war broke out. Led by the old campaigner General von Moltke, the superior German forces triumphed at Sedan on 1 September, 1870. Napoleon III was taken prisoner.

In France he was unanimously deposed by the people, who again proclaimed a republic. German troops marched into Paris, where in March 1871 the working population had

the Palace of Versailles. It was not born out of any national democratic movement, but out of diplomatic agreements between German kings and princes. It was not the result of a victory of the citizens over the nobility, but of the monarchy and nobles over the citizens. It wasn't a republic, but an empire that was proclaimed on 18 January 1871.

This imperial national state was to last for 47 years until its disintegration at the hands of the November Revolution of 1918. And it was home not only to Germans – against their will, oppressed Poles, Danes and Alsatians also belonged to the German Empire.

An industrial state: At the beginning of the 19th century, four-fifths of the population

hoisted the red flag of social revolution. France was forced to accept a harsh peace settlement, handing Germany the province of Alsace–Lorraine and 5,000 million francs in war reparations.

An imperial national state: The new German empire emerged under rather unusual circumstances. It came into being not in Germany, but in France, in the hall of mirrors in

Preceding page: proclamation of the 2nd German Empire in Versailles. Left, Otto von Bismarck, the "Iron Chancellor". Above, the dawn of the railways: the stretch from Berlin to Potsdam around 1850.

had been tied economically to the land, but by the end of the century this figure had been whittled down to barely one-fifth. Germany was transformed from a country of farmers to a nation of industry.

The 5,000 million francs of war reparation helped the German economy to achieve an unparalleled boom. In the so-called "years of promoterism" (1871–74), joint stock companies sprang up like mushrooms. The Ruhrgebiet developed into the most important industrial centre in Europe, with the Essen-based armaments manufacturer Krupp alone employing 50,000 people. In the 1870s, the gross national product soared past that of

A SUPERPOWER OF SCIENCE

For many people, Germany is the land of poets and philosophers, of Goethe, Schiller, Kant or Marx. Fewer people are aware that, for a time at least, Germany was the home and proving ground of the sciences.

Virtually everyone has undergone an X-ray examination at some time in his or her life. The discoverer of the process was a German, Wilhelm Conrad Röntgen, who was awarded the first Nobel Prize for Physics in 1901. Immunisations against tetanus and diphtheria developed by Emil von Behring (who won the Nobel Prize for Medicine in 1901) have dispelled the fears caused by these

two once dreaded scourges. Hundreds of thousands of sufferers succumbed to incurable tuberculosis until Robert Koch, a bacteriologist, demonstrated the most effective way to control the disease.

Today people complain of almost drowning in the flood of information with which they are constantly bombarded by the mass media. Whether such knowledge is a benefit or not, our modern communications-based society could not exist in its present form without radio or television, much of the technological basis for which was laid by German researchers such as Heinrich Hertz, Karl Ferdinand Braun and Adolf Slaby. Our knowledge of physical processes has made remarkable progress during the past 100 years, in particular as a result of the trail-blazing work of Max Planck (quantum theory), Albert Einstein (theory of relativity), Werner Heisenberg (quantum mechanics), Otto Hahn (atomic fission), and others.

The contribution of technicians and inventors of genius has been almost as significant as that of the theorists. Names that spring to mind include Nikolaus Otto, Carl Benz and Gottlieb Daimler.

Between 1901, the year in which the Nobel Prizes were awarded for the first time, and 1933, when the National Socialists came to power, Germany was the undisputed "superpower" of the scientific world. During this period, no fewer than 31 Nobel Laureates were German nationals (only six were American). Furthermore, German firms such as Siemens and AEG reigned supreme when it was necessary to adapt new discoveries in the fields of chemistry or electrotechnology to commercial use.

The standards for the high levels of technical and scientific expertise achieved were laid in 1871, at the beginning of the German Reich, when committed scientists such as the mathematician Felix Klein and far-sighted officials such as Friedrich Theodor Althoff founded scientific associations (for applied mathematics and physics, for example), thus forging closer links between university and industry, between theory and practice. The newly-created technical universities soon became an integral part of the German "Scientific Miracle". In order to further its national, military and mercantile interests the state financed promising research projects.

A large number of the scientists responsible for this remarkable series of brilliant discoveries were Jewish. The racist persecution unleashed by the National Socialists drove many outstanding thinkers such as Albert Einstein into exile; most fled to the United States. Today, modern German science has still not really recovered from this exodus. Between 1933 and 1990, the US was awarded 136 Nobel Prizes; Germany received 22.

Some post-war German Nobel Prizes, such as the Physics Prize awarded in 1986, harked back to scientific achievements during the period before 1933. The physicist Ernst Ruska, who was 79 in 1986, received his award for "one of the most important inventions of the 20th century", according to the accolade at the ceremony. He had invented the electron microscope in 1930–33.

One invention which failed to win its innovator the Nobel Prize was a development with which Hitler had hoped to win World War II: the V2 rocket, the work of Wernher von Braun and his team. These were the missiles used to bombard London. From 1959 von Braun worked for NASA, developing the *Saturn* launching rocket for the American space programme and making a significant contribution to the first landing on the moon. ∎

Above, **Albert Einstein, genius of relativity.**

France. By 1900 production had drawn level with England's, and it would actually nudge ahead during World War I.

The rise of social democracy: Encouraging and leading a process of industrialisation was a role that suited Bismarck. Both he and his Bonapartist ideology were overtaken by the new age, and he became superfluous to the requirements of the state. The affluent class he represented belonged to the land – and the past. Right until the end Bismarck opposed parliamentary democracy, especially of the social democratic workers. His law banning the socialists was in force from 1878 to 1890, but it actually had the opposite of its desired effect. The popularity of the SPD (Social Democratic Party of Germany) increased regardless and by 1912 it had become the strongest political force in the Reichstag. The workers accepted improved sickness and retirement benefits but, far from being placated, they demanded an eight-hour day, a republic and political power. In these changed circumstances the new emperor, young Wilhelm II, had little use for Bismarck, who was forced to retire.

Gunboat politics: On the international front, German tradesmen and troops acquired colonies abroad. In South-West Africa, East Africa, Togo, Cameroon, and in the Tsingtau enclave in China, the black, white and red flag of the German emperor was raised.

England, the main competitor, was to be paid back on its own territory – at sea. German imperialism plunged the country into a massive programme of warship building. The Deutsche Bank developed good relations with Turkey and, in 1902, the Turkish Sultan granted it the concession for a railway to Baghdad. To wrest Morocco (rich in iron ore) from France, the German government ordered the gunboat *Panther* to Agadir, but to no avail: Morocco remained French.

All the great European powers were arming themselves in preparation for the big show-down, which was to be fought over the re-distribution of colonies and markets. After two Moroccan crises and two Balkan wars, the imperial powers had grouped themselves for a war that had been on the cards for a long time. Germany and Austro-Hungary

Left, Albert Einstein, Germany's greatest scientist. **Above,** mass rally of the Communists Party in Berlin, 1942

against the alliance of France, Russia and England. When Serbian nationalists murdered the Austrian Crown Prince Franz Ferdinand in Sarajevo, the Berlin government exploited its historical chance to rise to a world power by waging a preventive war. The time seemed ripe: the German artillery and infantry were superior and Russia and France didn't appear to be ready for war.

The German Empire forced its ally in Vienna into a war against Serbia, throwing down the gauntlet to Russia and France. The hostilities wouldn't last for long – only a few weeks or, at the outside, a few months. At least that's what von Moltke and his general staff thought, as indeed did a great many

Germans, blinded as they were by patriotic warmongering.

German war aims: "I am no longer aware of any parties, I only recognise Germans," announced Kaiser Wilhelm at the outset of hostilities. Applause came from all factions, including the Social Democrats, who agreed to a pact and approved the massive credit required for war. Only Karl Liebknecht, at that time still in the SPD, refused to agree and protested against the capitalist war. Later he and Rosa Luxemburg would together found the Communist Party of Germany.

The Reich's Chancellor, von Bethmann Hollweg, had outlined the war aims in a secret memorandum: conquering the mining region of Briey, wearing down France, subjugating Belgium and Luxembourg and the non-Russian peoples ruled over by Russia, as well as establishing a European economic and customs union under German leadership. In the end, none of these plans came to fruition. As the war raged on, the military and economic inferiority of the Austro-German camp became clear. France could not be defeated in a blitzkrieg. In 1916, more than a million people died at Verdun and on the Somme. The switch to an underwater war waged by U-boats marked the beginning of the end, since it forced a hitherto reluctant America to enter the war against Germany.

Defeat and revolution: Germany had transformed itself into a military dictatorship. A state of siege, censorship and forced labour became part of everyday life, as did a diet of cabbage stalks. People were starving while gold was swapped for steel. The increasingly detested war was financed by loans. After the February and October revolutions in 1917, Russia's part in the hostilities was over, a fact confirmed by the Treaty of Brest-Litovsk in March 1918. But Germany knew the war could no longer be won militarily.

At the end of September 1918 its ally Bulgaria capitulated, cutting off Germany from oil supplies from the Balkans. General Ludendorff, a monarchist and conservative through and through, made the only sensible suggestion. He convinced Hindenburg and the emperor that an immediate ceasefire was needed and that a parliamentary government be formed to "pick up the pieces". The German people thus heard of the entry of the SPD into the new government of Prince Max von Baden at the beginning of October 1918, and of the petition for a ceasefire. The war was lost and the parliamentary monarchy couldn't be saved. The revolution continued apace.

Councils or national assembly: In the week of 3–10 November 1918 Germany was transformed from a military dictatorship into a republic of committees. Princes and military authorities fell. Armed workers and soldiers formed worker and soldier committees which took over local control. Kaiser Wilhelm fled into exile in Holland. The hour of social democracy and that of its chairman, Friedrich Ebert, had arrived.

The "council of the people's representatives" – as the six-member social democratic government called itself – was supposedly to steer the country towards a socialist republic governed by committees, which is what the workers' representatives throughout the country were demanding. But Friedrich Ebert had no intention of allowing this to happen and secretly secured the support of the German army.

The first Congress of German Councils met in the capital, Berlin, in 1918, with the vast majority of the 489 representatives coming from the ranks of the SPD. It was decided to hold elections for a national assembly and all political power was entrusted to Ebert's council of people's representatives.

Berlin was quickly consumed by a bitter civil war, and Rosa Luxemburg and Karl Liebknecht, the leaders of the Communist Party, were assassinated by a group of soldiers from the imperial army. While this internal conflict was being played out, the representatives of the national assembly gathered in peaceful Weimar to elect Friedrich Ebert as president of the first German democratic republic, the Weimar Republic.

Germany after the November Revolution: Germany was now a republic with a constitution based on adult suffrage, an eight-hour working day and recognised trade unions. But into the ranks of the conservatives came incorrigible monarchists, old generals, discarded soldiers, East Elbian nobles, anti-Semites, bankers and influential press barons. These forces created the legend that the war had been lost from within, by a stab in the back.

And then there was Versailles where, in July 1919, Germany, as loser of the war, had to sign a humiliating treaty. It lost all its colonies, with Alsace being returned to France, Gdansk to the League of Nations, West Prussia, parts of Pomerania and East Prussia to Poland. German territory on the west bank of the Rhine was occupied by the troops of the victorious powers. The Saar was administered by the League of Nations and its coal fields went to France. There were astronomical sums to be paid for reparations;

was a product of society at the time: a failed artist with a bourgeois background, stranded in Vienna without skill or trade. It was there that he joined the bandwagon of east European anti-Semitism and pan-German nationalism. He was a corporal in World War I and an informer in the service of the imperial army. Then he became the speech-maker for a small reactionary post-war party in Munich beer taverns, and by 1923 had failed in an attempted *putsch*.

Without Versailles, without the economic crisis in Germany with 6 million unemployed, without powerful backers in industry and without the army, this unscrupulous demagogue would never have made it to the

Paragraph 231 burdened Germany with the exclusive guilt for World War I. A union of Germany and Austria was forbidden.

These measures, interpreted as revenge, provided the ingredients for a new wave of German chauvinism and revanchism.

Hitler's rise to power: Some Christians believed Adolf Hitler to be Satan in human guise. Others saw him as a psychopath, a confidence trickster, someone with delusions of grandeur, or a criminal. Whatever else, he

Left, Joseph Goebbels, the Nazis' brilliant chief of propaganda and social enlightenment. **Above**, the masses salute the Führer.

head of the Weimar state. He organised a chauvinistic mass movement and controlled a powerful army in the SA stormtroopers.

Hitler propagated the destruction of Marxism and the Jews, and promised to restore Germany to the status of a world power. The man and his party, the National Socialist Workers' Party of Germany (NSDAP) became a useful tool in the hands of big business. Steel baron Fritz Thyssen later admitted in a book: "I paid Hitler." At the height of the economic crisis, when political differences came to a head and parliamentary government no longer functioned, reactionary circles favoured a transfer of power to the

NSDAP. After the cabinets of Brüning, Papen and Schleicher had been worn to shreds, President von Hindenburg appointed Hitler as Chancellor on 30 January 1933.

The Nazis in power: The curtain went up on the barbarous stage of the Third Reich – a terror that was to last for 12 years. First of all the Communist Party was banned and its leaders forced into exile or thrown into concentration camps. After the next elections, at which the NSDAP acquired 44 percent of the vote, all the parties in the Reichstag accepted the Enabling Act, with the exception of the SPD. The NSDAP thus came to power quite legally, without a *putsch*. Then the unions were broken up, and finally all other political

processions and party conferences fanned the patriotic flames.

The fascists made noises about the chosen northern race and began the grisly business of excising all "inferior" life. The Jews were declared second-class citizens, were targeted in the ruthless Kristallnacht attacks of 9 November 1938, and from 1941 were led to the "final solution". Millions of European Jews died a gruesome death in the extermination camps of Auschwitz, Treblinka, Madjanek and Buchenwald. The word holocaust was added to the vocabulary of war.

World war and capitulation: After coming to power, Hitler had explained the essence of Germany's foreign policy to army and navy

parties were abolished. The National Socialists called their one-party dictatorship the "leadership principle". Factories, offices, schools, universities, radio and the press – almost the entire spectrum of society – were forced into step and regimented.

There were the Sturmabteilungen (SA), the Schutzstaffeln (SS), the storm and defence brigades, the German Work Front, the National Socialist Women's Movement, the German Girls' Association, Hitler Youth, Strength Through Joy, and Beauty Through Work. The NSDAP aimed to exercise complete control over the body and minds of an entire people. Mass gatherings, torchlight

commanders: "acquisition by force of new export markets", "acquisition and Germanisation of new land in the east." The Nazis embarked on a four-year plan of war preparations and soon tanks were rolling on the new motorways which had been built specially for them. Within five years Hitler had recouped just about everything that Germany had lost at Versailles. In 1935 the Saar was returned to its "German mother", and one year later the Wehrmacht marched into the Rhineland. In March 1938 came the annexation of Austria and after the Munich Conference the Sudetenland in Czechoslovakia became part of the German Empire.

The British and French policy of appeasement at the Munich Conference had failed miserably. After the Soviet–German non-aggression pact of 23 August 1939, Hitler and Stalin decided how they would carve up Europe between them. In September, German and Russian troops invaded Poland, triggering the start of a massive conflict.

With a death toll of more than 50 million, it was to be the most terrible war ever known. For the first two years, as German forces, supported by their allies, marched unstoppably from one victory to another, it seemed entirely possible that Hitler would win. By 1941 the Nazis controlled Europe and now, in league with Italy, sought to bring Africa

war in December 1941 after the Japanese attack on Pearl Harbor, the final outcome of the war was no longer in doubt. Britain, the United States and the Soviet Union presented a militarily superior alliance, and fighting on so many fronts sapped the Nazis' strength. The defeat of the 6th Army at Stalingrad in 1943 and the allied landings in Normandy in 1944 signalled the end of Germany's aspirations.

Among the most devastating aspects of the war were the Allied bombing raids of German cities. During January and February 1945 American bombers reduced the centre of Berlin to rubble. On the night of 13–14 February, Dresden, filled with refugees, was

under their yoke. Vast numbers of dissenters were marched into forced labour. Any effective resistance within Germany to National Socialism was quashed and all attempts by military and civil groups to topple the Nazi regime ended in failure.

Fortunes began to change when Hitler, looking for "living space" to the east, sent 3 million troops to invade the Soviet Union in June 1941. No more successful than Napoleon had been, his advance came to a halt before Moscow. When America entered the

Left, Adolf Hitler marches into Prague. Above, prisoners at Dachau released in 1945.

so heavily bombed it created an unquenchable firestorm and 15 sq. km (6 sq. miles) of the city melted away. On 22 March, 816 RAF bombers wiped out Frankfurt's old town.

On the morning of 29 April the Russians launched a massive attack on Berlin's inner defence. The next day Hitler and his mistress, Eva Braun, committed suicide in their bunker. It was the end of the Third Reich. The Nazis surrendered unconditionally.

The dream had been to conquer new territory for Germany and to make the nation an invincible world power. But now the country lay in ruins, occupied and divided. The dream had turned to nightmare.

The end of the Third Reich came with the battle for Berlin. On 30 April 1945 Hitler committed suicide in the bunker of his chancellery and on 1 May the Red Army hoisted the Soviet flag on the ruins of the Reichstag that had been destroyed by fire in 1933.

On 5 June 1945 the Berlin Four Power Conference agreed on a combined administration of the country which had been divided into four zones of occupation. The Soviets obtained the east zone, the Americans the south, the British the north-west and the French the south-west. The erstwhile capital Berlin, as already envisaged by the London protocol of 1944, received a special status and was divided into four sectors.

At the Potsdam Conference, from July to August 1945, the "Big Three" – Joseph Stalin, US President Harry Truman, and Winston Churchill (succeeded after the British election by Clement Attlee) – agreed on the aims of the combined occupying regime: demilitarisation, denazification, democratisation and decentralisation of the economy and the state. Economically, Germany should be treated as a complete unit. A peace treaty was promised after an unspecified period.

"The idea of ruling Germany together with the Russians is madness", wrote the American diplomat Kennan in 1945 in Moscow. There were fundamentally varying interpretations of notions like "peace" and "democracy". However, world peace seemed to have been secured, particularly when, on 26 June 1945, 50 nations signed the United Nations Charter. By early 1947 that the agenda was set for the division of Germany.

Germany starts again: The Third Reich had reduced Germany to a heap of ruins. Cities like Hamburg, Cologne, Magdeburg, Nuremberg, Würzburg and Dresden had been devastated by bombs. Berlin and many other cities that had seen heavy ground fighting were little more than piles of rubble. In the regions west of the Oder-Neisse, more than a quarter of all residential buildings had been either obliterated or seriously damaged.

Most major German cities were reduced to rubble by the end of the war: picking up the pieces in Berlin (left) and Hamburg (right).

The war had destroyed one-fifth of Germany's manufacturing capacity and production sank to one-third of its 1936 level. The collapse of transport systems, the destruction of railways, bridges and tunnels all contributed to this gloomy state of affairs. Not a single major bridge across the Rhine remained intact. Between 1945 and 1948 a total of 12 million extra Germans flooded into this destroyed country, whose size had been reduced by a quarter. Over 2 million people lost their lives during this period of

exodus and forced expulsions from the German-settled areas in the East. A large proportion of the population suffered from starvation and illness, particularly during the "hunger winter" of 1946–47. In order to survive, they bartered, hoarded, dealt on the black market and stole. City dwellers headed for the country to swap pianos, carpets and jewellery for eggs, ham and potatoes. With the continuing decline in the value of gold, the unit of currency on the black market became the American cigarette.

In this climate of destruction, misery and general demoralisation, the populace set about the organisation of its survival. In the cities, the *Trümmerfrauen* ("rubble women") extracted the bricks from the ruins for the rebuilding of houses. Railways, bridges and machinery were repaired so that the wheels of industry could begin to turn once more. For most Germans, the daily routine was devoted to finding a place to live, and procuring food and heating material.

Despite all that they had suffered, the anti-Nazis, including many who had survived the concentration camps and prisons, who argued most fervently for the right of Germans to seek a democratic self-rejuvenation. In many cities the so-called "anti-fascist" committees spontaneously sprang up to organise economic and political development, only to

accused (including the absent Martin Bormann) were sentenced to death; three were sentenced to life imprisonment and two to between 10 and 20 years. The remaining three were acquitted.

The trials were continued in 1950, and now the Germans were confronted with the reality of the Nazi atrocities which until then many had either not wanted or not been able to recognise. While some of the guilty escaped, the denazification process affected the entire population, divided as it was into five categories ranging from "principals" to "exonerated". In the American zone every citizen over 18 years of age had to complete a questionnaire containing 131 questions.

be dispersed by the occupation authorities. The fate of Germany lay firmly in the hands of the victorious powers.

The Nuremberg trials: On 24 November 1945 the surviving leaders of the Nazi regime were put on trial at Nuremberg. Twenty-four politicians, ideologists, military men and industrialists, including Hermann Goering, Alfred Rosenberg, Wilhelm Keitel and Gustav Krupp were charged with crimes against the peace and crimes against mankind. The unprecedented arraignment and trial were to set new norms for international law. On 1 October 1946 the International Military Court passed sentence: 12 of the

Based on the answers given, the "judgement chambers" passed sentences ranging from 10 years in prison to denial of voting rights.

In the Soviet zone, the anti-fascist cleansing process bore the mark of Stalinist terror from the moment it began. Between 1945 and 1950 in camps like Buchenwald and Sachsenhausen it was not only the functionaries and supporters of the Nazi regime who were killed, but also tens of thousands of randomly arrested people who had been denounced to the authorities.

The policies of occupation: Regardless of the Allied Control Council, the occupation authorities under their respective military governors very much did as they pleased. In the Soviet zone, under the catchphrase "anti-fascistic-democratic reform", a revolution took place from the top aimed at eradicating the "roots of fascism, militarism and war". This included a comprehensive land reform, the nationalisation of the banks, the expropriation of all "those interested in war", extensive dismantling of industrial plant and the establishment of the "Soviet joint-stock company", which took over more than 30 percent of industrial capacity. After 1 million people had fled the east zone, not least because of a desperate lack of food, the Soviet Military Administration closed the zone boundary in the summer of 1946.

Americans in particular. The private relief campaigns and the "care parcels" sent by the American people contributed to this pro-American stance, which was then further reinforced by the events that were being witnessed in the east.

Somewhat later than the Russians, the western military governments allowed parties to indulge in political activities and trade unions to be established in their zones. In the late summer and autumn of 1945 they appointed governments for the newly structured German states.

In summer 1946 the American military governor proposed that the Allied Control Council establish a central economic admin-

In the western zones, too, the dismantling of industry continued right up until 1949, resulting in soaring unemployment. France took a particularly hard line. It refused to allow the emergence of any German central authority, demanded the internationalisation of the Ruhrgebiet and for Saarland to become part of the French economic sphere. Nevertheless, many Germans continued to pin their hopes on the West, and on the

Left, Nazi war criminals stand accused at the Nuremberg Trials, which opened in November 1945. **Above**, Young Pioneers march to Stalin's tune in East Berlin.

istration in the four zones. France and the Soviet Union rejected the idea. By the beginning of September the differences of opinion among the Allies became even more pronounced. The Americans and the British agreed on the establishment of the "bizone", a combined economic region for the two zones under their occupation. The Soviets and the French protested and on 6 September 1946, the plan was also turned down by the US Secretary of State James Byrnes. He proposed the establishment of a combined German government (on a state basis) and proposed a revision of the eastern border (Oder–Neisse line) in the peace treaty.

The Cold War: The different policies in the occupied zones reflected the differences in the political systems as well as the increasing conflicts of interest between the two super-powers. In 1947–48, the east–west conflict erupted in different parts of Europe and quickly spread to some of Asia as well. In Eastern Europe – the huge area that had been handed to Stalin at Yalta in February 1945 – the communists installed dictatorships in their "peoples' democracies". When in Greece the left wing threatened to emerge victorious in the civil war and when similar tensions began to erupt in Turkey, the Americans announced that they would stamp out the spreading flames of communism. The many only with the financial assistance of the Americans. The military governor, Lucius Clay, made it clear that the Germans would have to pay for their own imports, something that was possible only through an increase in industrial production and exports. As agreement with the Soviets on this issue did not seem to be possible, the establishment of the West German state was organised.

In the West the CDU chairman, Konrad Adenauer, supported the integration of the west zones into the western family of nations. And the SPD chairman, Kurt Schumacher, who had suffered for 10 years in Nazi concentration camps, also turned down any deal with the communists.

Marshall Plan, the American-funded reconstruction of Germany, was also intended to halt Soviet expansion. Under pressure from Stalin, Poland was forced to forgo this aid. In February 1948 the communists took over power in Prague. The only communist country that broke with Stalin was Yugoslavia. As the Iron Curtain descended in Europe, it was clear to all where the political-strategic centre of the Cold War conflict would lie: in defeated and occupied Germany.

The division of Germany: The decision to divide Germany was made by the western powers. The British and the French could pay for the delivery of foodstuffs to Ger-

The final decisions were made in London at a six-power conference on 7 June 1948. It was agreed that western Germany should be involved in the rebuilding of Europe (OEEC), that the Ruhrgebiet be subject to international control, and that a new West German Federal Republic be created. The Russian representative left the Allied Control Council in Berlin in protest.

On 20 June 1948, the currency reform, that had also been decided upon in London, was carried out. The Soviet Military Administration responded with its own currency reform in the east zone. The conflict came to a dramatic head when the Soviets imposed a complete blockade of the western sector of Berlin. The Allies organised a massive airlift which supplied the West Berlin population with food and coal until the blockade was lifted on 12 May 1949.

Berlin was divided in September 1948. A parliamentary council made up of elected representatives of the West German state assemblies was set up by the western powers and from 1 September, in King Ludwig's castle of Herrenchiemsee in Bavaria, set about formulating a provisional constitution, the Grundgesetz – the "basic law". After its ratification by the state assemblies, this constitution of the Federal Republic of Germany was announced. In September 1949

The other German state: The SED (Socialist Unity Party of Germany) attacked the West Germans' "politics of division" but then set about founding an East German state. On 29 May 1949 the elected People's Congress approved a constitution for the German Democratic Republic, which occupied 30 percent of the area of pre-war Germany (the states now known as Berlin, Brandenburg, Mecklenburg–Western Pomerania, Saxony, Saxony–Anhalt and Thuringia). Wilhelm Pieck became the president of the GDR and Otto Grotewohl, formerly a social democrat, acted as the president of an SED government. By 1952 the SED boss Walter Ulbricht, a longtime member of the German Commu-

the newly-elected Federal Parliament came together for the first time. Theodor Heuss (FDP) was elected the first president and Konrad Adenauer (CDU) the first chancellor at the head of a civil coalition government.

The new state was a parliamentary democracy made up of a number of federal states. But the Western powers made quite sure that they retained control of Berlin, with all the symbolism which that city held for a "united Germany".

Left, "raisin bombers" relieve blockaded Berlin in 1948. Above, riots on the steets of Berlin in June 1953.

nist Party, had swung the policy firmly behind the "development of socialism" and better relations with other Communist states.

Uprising: During this critical period, rebellion broke out on 17 June 1953. Construction workers in East Berlin reacted to an increase in work quotas by strike action and mass demonstrations, and these quickly developed into an insurgent movement throughout the GDR. The strike slogans developed into outright demands for free elections and the reunification of Germany. The SED reacted sternly, claiming the strike was stirred up by supporters of the West, and used Russian tanks against the protestors. This uprising in the east not only succeeded in securing the political survival of Walter Ulbricht, but it also helped the West German Chancellor Konrad Adenauer to election victory in 1953 and reinforced his policy of integration with the West.

The "economic miracle": In Western Germany it took some time for the currency reform to have its desired effect on economic stability. After its reform in 1948, consumer goods appeared once again in shop windows and industrial production increased correspondingly. A further important thrust was provided by the Marshall Plan, America's blueprint for rebuilding Europe, of which the Federal Republic became a beneficiary in

December 1949. Thereafter, over DM3 billion worth of cash and credits was poured into West German production.

In the 1950s the world began to talk of the German "economic miracle" – the *Wirtschaftswunder* – high growth rates of around 8 percent, a marked reduction in unemployment and a steady increase in the standard of living. The economic recovery went hand in hand with the development of a socially-oriented market economy.

The system could only be as successful as it was through the restrained wage policy practised by the West German trades unions. Under their parent organisation, the DGB (German Trades Union Council), the strong unions limited their class struggle to rhetoric and acted as upholders of the economic system – as "social partners". The West German Social Democrats also differentiated between Marxist theory and practice and made Keynesian redistribution concepts the theme of their Godesberg Manifesto in 1959.

By the end of the 1950s the West German economy was producing half of all industrial commodities in the European Economic Community, which was founded in 1957 as the basis for further economic and political integration within Europe.

As the economic gap between the two Germanys became a chasm, the GDR leadership erected the infamous Berlin Wall in August 1961 to help prevent any further exodus of refugees from East Germany. Now the Federal Republic became a magnet for unskilled workers from Italy and Southern Europe, whose recruitment had already begun back in 1955. After the 1966–67 recession came a flood of hundreds of thousands of further "guest workers" from Turkey.

Military integration: After the Korean War (1950–53), the Western powers insisted on the rearmament of the West German state. Chancellor Adenauer exploited this military interest in exchange for the acquisition of a higher degree of sovereignty for the Federal Republic. A conservative Catholic, Adenauer was less concerned with the question of eventual reunification than with gaining an equal say for the Federal Republic in the chambers of the new European Economic Community.

As far as the Soviets were concerned, a rearmed Western Germany as part of a western alliance represented a provocation of incalculable proportions. In 1952, in order to prevent Germany's integration with the West, Stalin offered a peace treaty for a united, neutral Germany. The Soviet Union was prepared to sacrifice the East German state for a political price, and its offers were repeated several times before the Federal Republic's entry into NATO in 1955. The chance for a reunification of Germany had been presented but it was a chance that Adenauer, who rejected neutrality, chose to ignore.

Realising that American forces would not be withdrawn from Germany, the Soviet Union now proceeded with the consolidation and expansion of the area under its control. In 1955 the GDR was equipped with an army and entered the Eastern Bloc's new military alliance, the Warsaw Pact.

The new *Ostpolitik* and the status quo: After the Cuba crisis in 1962, when America challenged the USSR's right to base missiles on the Caribbean island, it seemed as though the superpowers had arrived at détente. In West Germany, Willy Brandt, heading a social democrat-liberal coalition, geared his new *Ostpolitik* towards the preservation of the unity of the German nation under the prevailing conditions of division. Communication was the basic requirement for the survival of the nation. On the international level, this policy was aimed at forcing a "recognition of

astic reception when he arrived in Erfurt for the first negotiations with the GDR Minister President Willi Stoph.

Student protest and the 1968 generation: The late 1960s marked a turning point in the development of the Federal Republic. In 1966–67 the West German state experienced its first serious recession, the result of the structural crisis in the coal and steel industries. The country was rocked by student revolts at the universities. The protests were directed primarily at the Vietnam War, but at the same time they discovered the revolutionary theme of global emancipation. As their idols, the students chose Ho Chi Minh, Mao Tse-Tung and Che Guevara.

reality" – the reality of the post-war borders.

With Brandt's election as Federal Chancellor in 1969 there emerged a leader who was, largely for tactical reasons, reviled by various political opponents both for his anti-fascist stance during the war, when he had fled to Norway, and for now acknowledging the reality of the "other Germany". As for the ordinary East Germans, many pinned their hopes on Brandt. They gave him an enthusi-

Left, Konrad Adenauer, first Chancellor of the Federal Republic of Germany. **Above**, In Warsaw in 1970, Willy Brandt acknowledged German guilt for the death of Polish Jews.

More important in the long run than the expounding of these ideologies was the revolution that took place within German society itself through the "1968 generation". In a roundabout way, the "68" philosophy of life led to the emergence of the powerful German ecological movement that was later known as "the Greens".

Conflict and agreement: The long-term perspective of the liberal *Ostpolitik* towards a reunification of the country became rather lost in the 1970s and 1980s. The preservation of two German states came to be defended, especially in German intellectual circles. The two states had gone their separate ways for so long that many felt that reunification had no longer any place on the political agenda. Only occasionally – as, for example, in 1976 when the SED expelled the poet and singer Wolf Biermann whose songs had attacked the East German leader Erich Honecker – were doubts cast on this ideology of division.

The beginning of the end: German unity came about very suddenly, when nobody really expected it would happen at all. In September 1987, when Honecker officially visited Bonn and was received by Chancellor Helmut Kohl with all the honours accorded an equal head of an almost sovereign state, he probably felt that he had reached the zenith of his career: after all, did not this visit

The average East German was less dogmatic: although the GDR's economy might be the most productive among the socialist countries, living conditions had fallen far behind those in the West. For months, thousands of resigned citizens had been leaving the country daily across the Hungarian border, which had been opened in June 1989. Before the eyes of the world, these refugees presented the inflexible regime in East Berlin with the spectacular bill for its anti-reform line. Western television beamed into East German living rooms each evening pictures of the apparently inexhaustible stream of refugees, but the SED leadership would not be deflected from its propaganda.

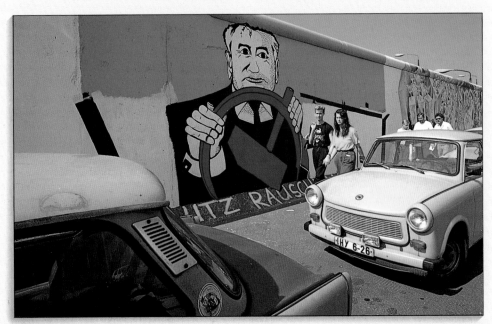

demonstrate the existence of two equal-ranking German states?

It was one of the ironies of history: on 7 October 1989, East Germany celebrated its 40th birthday with the leaden slogan "The development of the German Democratic Republic will continue to be the work of all the people." This motto would prove to be true – but in a very different way than the regime of old men in the GDR had hoped.

When Mikhail Gorbachev came to power in the USSR in 1985, the Socialist Unity Party of Germany (SED) made it clear that it would continue on its dogmatic course, if necessary against the will of the reformer in the Kremlin.

Under the pressure of the emigration crisis, the face of the East German opposition also changed. A group of 100 people, impressed by the wave of emigration, published an "Appeal 1989" for the founding of a "New Forum". The appeal was perfectly tailored to the popular mood. It called for a broad dialogue on acute problems and a common search for solutions. In only a few weeks, some hundred thousand citizens had joined the New Forum.

The wall collapses: Before that fateful Monday demonstration in Leipzig on 9 October 1989 – these demonstrations had been occurring each week for months – the situation became critical. Task forces were placed on the alert and local hospitals prepared blood supplies. The press announced that "counter-revolutionary activities" would be stopped for good, if necessary "with weapons in hand." But on that evening, 70,000 people gathered and Leipzig experienced the largest demonstration since the uprising on 17 June 1953. The state held back.

On 18 October, Erich Honecker, the head of the party and state, resigned. His closest confidantes went with him – the absolute ruler of the East German economy, Günter Mittag, and the country's top censor, Joachim Herrmann. Honecker's successor was Egon Krenz, who until then had been responsible

German television. The tenor of the meeting was clear: uncompromising demands for a pluralist democracy that guaranteed GDR citizens all the freedoms available in Western societies.

On 9 November, almost the entire Honecker Politburo resigned and, at the end of a press conference, it was announced that the travel laws were no longer in place. A few hours later, astonishing scenes of joy were beamed by the TV cameras from the intracity border crossings in Berlin. East German border guards, armed to the teeth, had protected socialism here for 29 years, but on this evening hundreds of thousands crossed without hindrance to the city's western side.

for security matters within the Politburo.

But the party leadership in Berlin had not begun to recognise the changing times. Instead of entering into negotiations with opposition groups, it attempted to save itself with non-committal announcements of reform once things had quietened down. But this wasn't good enough. On 4 November, Berlin experienced its largest demonstration by far since the November revolution of 1918, with over 1 million participants. The demonstration was broadcast live on East

In the elections of 18 March 1990, the parties that had consistently supported unification received well over 70 percent of the vote. In the summer of that year, Mikhail Gorbachev agreed to a unified, but demilitarised Germany becoming a member of NATO – the American pre-condition for German unification – and on 3 October 1990 the two countries were formally merged. The postwar period had ended. In the first parliamentary elections in a united Germany on 2 December 1990, Chancellor Helmut Kohl and his governing coalition of the Christian Democratic Union and the Free Democrats were returned to power.

Left and **above**, Mikhail Gorbachev's reforms led to the ultimate collapse of the Berlin Wall.

They were fine, stirring pictures which travelled around the world on 3 October 1990, the day of German reunification: fireworks bursting over Berlin's Reichstag, thousands of waving flags and banners, proudly posturing politicians, and crowds of people moved to tears of joy and disbelief. At long last, everything seemed to be turning out right. The Cold War had ended, the threat of a hot one had vanished, the Germans were once again a united people, and the few remaining difficulties would rapidly be tackled and

resolved. At least, that's what most people thought – back in the autumn of 1990.

Before long, however, some harsh economic realities began to dilute that original enthusiasm. As one commentator put it, half Germany now sits on the couch and sulks. No-one had expected the road leading to unity to be so wearisome, so demanding of sacrifice and, above all, so costly. Foreigners observed this unexpectedly listless German mood with a mixture of bewilderment and suspicion. After all, Germany is a state with 80 million inhabitants, the third largest economic power in the world, an important member of the United Nations, and one of the largest contributors to the budget of that organisation. It could naturally expect to take a seat within the UN Security Council as a permanent member. At the same time, the Germans are anything but clear about their future foreign policy role. Whether or not the Federal Army should now be engaged in international crisis management, how the integration of the East European states within the European Union and NATO should be accomplished – these central issues are as controversial as the question of further financial commitment to the reconstruction of eastern Germany. Uncertainty is the dominant political mood in the country, which still has to find an agreed role and to clarify its relationship with its neighbours.

The threat of bankruptcy: The great transformation actually began with the fall of the Berlin Wall in November 1989. A glance at the balance sheets of the GDR didn't bode very well even then. The economy of the smaller German state was on the verge of bankruptcy; for years, insolvency had been avoided only by the availability of repeated Western credits. One final shove towards inevitable bankruptcy was given by the collapse of its major export market, the Soviet Union. In the face of the looming economic melt-down, the only sensible solution seemed to be to accept being absorbed as rapidly as possible by its big brother.

The big brother stepped in first with money, in the form of a currency union declared on 1 July 1990. This measure was wholeheartedly welcomed in the East, despite the less than fraternal exchange rate of one D-Mark for two East German Marks. But what to buy with the new currency? Soon it was realised with dismay that East German manufacturers had lost their old market outlets at one blow. Who wanted to wait another 12 years for an uninspiring Trabant motor car when shining limousines fresh from Western factories were now available?

It was the same with other goods. "Comet" powdered foods, Club Cola or Rotplombe pudding – whatever the East German product, it sat like lead on shop shelves, while sales in the east of Western goods shot up. It was this enormous domestic demand that masked for several years the looming economic crisis in Western Germany and which fed the slightly unrealistic hope that the market would somehow regulate everything by itself. The market just didn't oblige.

A state authority, the famous (or infamous) Treuhand, therefore had to take on the daunting task of privatising the ailing East German enterprises. That meant deciding the future of around 12,000 former state-run concerns, virtually all of which been now been sold off.

The Treuhand winds up: Help came too late, though, for 1,700 firms which became victims of the form of bankruptcy known in the East as *Gesamtvollstreckung*. A change in

less of what their region is called, the people of the former GDR still lack one important prerequisite of a market economy: capital. That's by no means their own fault, of course; under the rule of Erich Honecker and his associates, few people managed to accumulate great wealth. The result was that, after reunification, only about 1,500 Treuhand-managed enterprises passed into the hands of East Germans – mostly small businesses such as pharmacies and greengrocers.

Most people in the East had little reason to welcome the process of privatisation. One in two former GDR citizens lost their old jobs; in industry, two-thirds of all jobs just disappeared, permanently. Despite these unprece-

vocabulary accompanied the spread of capitalism: eastern Germany was no longer known simply as "the East" but as the "new Federal states", jokingly also as Neufünfland (because five, or *fünf*, is the number of the eastern states which joined the Federal Republic) or East-Elbe (because the new states lie mostly east of the Elbe river). But, regard-

Preceding pages: popular celebrations outside Berlin's Reichstag on 3 October 1990, the "Day of German Unity". Left, not everyone can get to grips with the enormous changes in the new Federal states. Above, an old Trabant is given a new lease of life in an ecology-conscious age.

dentedly drastic economic and sociological changes, the readjustment to the new circumstances did proceed extraordinarily peacefully.

That's even more remarkable in view of the fact that, at the same time as their jobs were disappearing, practically everything in the everyday lives of the East Germans was changing. New laws took effect, new account numbers, new passports, new health insurance coverage, new pensions, new street names – there were even demands for a while in the press that driving tests should be retaken by East German motorists. The troublesome fraternal strife over land and property gave rise to further insecurity. West Germans turned up demanding the return of property which had long passed into East German ownership – this prickly area was governed by the adamantly held but scarcely workable principle of returning property to its former owners instead of granting them compensation.

Unclear ownership: Unsuspecting pensioners in the East suddenly found themselves confronted with the absurd accusation that they had obtained their property only by being close to the GDR state. Places like Kleinmachnow, south of Berlin, where restitution claims have been made on 80 per cent of all properties, show that this problem not

such as Hof, had to put up with veritable invasions by hordes of shoppers from the East, and there were new postal codes to get used to, but the future was called into question only when people were affected personally by the changes or when they felt the effects in their pockets.

Tougher times in the West: The economic recession which many thought they had escaped caught up with the West, too. Subsidies for the former border zones came to an end, the Berlin bonus was scrapped and unemployment reached unprecedented new levels in the whole of Germany. For the first time since the economic boom years, the average individual German's prosperity

only represents a major hindrance to investment but will also tie up lawyers and courts for years to come. At least, East Germans weren't evicted from their homes and country houses *en masse*, as had been feared. Instead, a so-called social restitution is to come into being. Behind this rather elaborate term lies the simple fact that people living above their means because of escalating rents and property taxes will have to move out in the end anyway.

In the "old" federal states it was felt at first that life would continue along its accustomed course despite reunification. True, many former West German border towns,

failed to increase. That was a shock – one which was hard to cope with after decades of steady increase.

Vacillating policies caused further difficulties. A solidarity tax surcharge was introduced to help the East, then abolished, then reintroduced together with a social security insurance charge for nursing care. The result was that the German worker's tax burden took on painful proportions. When for the first time the state budget deficit shot through the psychological barrier of 1 billion D-Marks, there was no suppressing the fear that the East could become a bottomless pit into which not only the man on the Western street but the entire Federal Republic could disappear, economically ruined.

Admittedly, the economic statistics tell another story. The D-Mark is still one of the world's most stable currencies, and the annual transfer payments of 150,000 million Marks from West to East have proved to be economically acceptable. Also, contrary to a widely-held view, the solidarity tax levy is paid by East as well as West Germans, so the burden is distributed more equally than is popularly believed.

While on the subject of popular beliefs: in view of the many and various difficulties encountered in the process of reunification it was hardly to be avoided that clichés and prejudices arose in relations between East and West Germans. Thus, you'll find the *Besserwessi* (the West German who knows better) standing alongside the *Jammer-Ossi* (the East German who just moans and complains), two figures who are meant to symbolise personal characteristics which have come about during 28 years of separate development. But, because there's a grain of truth in every stereotype, these two types can readily be identified in real life. The *Wessi* is used to marketing himself, which is why he has an opinion on everything and is always interfering – sometimes in matters which seriously overtax his knowledge and personality. The *Ossi*, on the other hand, has learnt to take his place in the community and to assign it a large share of the responsibility for his life. He avoids open contradiction and prefers to let off steam by moaning or, even better, by persistent nagging.

Everyone tells himself or herself that there's no such person as a *Wessi* or an *Ossi*, but ill feelings have the curious property of reinforcing themselves despite evidence to the contrary. For many Rhinelanders the entire, far-off east of the country is as full of Stasi agents as it was at the time of reunification and clings ever closer to the PDS, political heirs of the GDR Communists. There are many Mecklenbergers, on the other hand, who – after years of siege by insurance company representatives and fraudulent

salesmen – dismiss the entire western half of their country as society of crafty *Abzocker*.

The ecological imperative: Yet such resentments can distort the overall picture and obscure the undeniable advances that have been made as a result of reunification. Life has taken on more colour in the new federal states. Thousands of buildings which were on the point of collapse have been restored. Irreplaceable historic structures, such as the Cranach courts in Wittenberg or half the old town centre of Stralsund, escaped demolition at the very last minute. Bitterfeld, only a few years ago the filthiest corner of Europe, is on the way to becoming a model example of ecological restoration. The entire infra-

structure from the island of Rügen to the Thuringian Forest, where people once had to wait half a lifetime for a telephone, is being modernised so rapidly now that the West could soon become the more backward part of Germany.

In the area of nursing care for the disabled and elderly, humane conditions are at last coming into being after the catastrophic situation which ruled in GDR times. And many East German pensioners who once had to survive on 300 Marks a month have experienced the first real increase in their incomes. Nevertheless, it must be admitted that in the area of pensions there are still some very

Left, the Opel company, whose new Eisenach works are seen here, is only one of many investors in eastern Germany. **Above**, the construction industry is booming – cranes dominate the skylines of many cities.

serious inequalities to be found. And wages in the East have lagged just as far behind. Only in Berlin have public service workers achieved equivalent living standards measured in real income terms.

Otherwise, the equalisation of living standards developed with greater complexity than had been expected in 1990. That wasn't just because the matter had been excluded from the economic equation. Rather, psychological obstacles are largely to blame. According to a public opinion poll, nearly 60 per cent of all East Germans say they have become better off since reunification, although at the same time just about the same percentage claim that they don't feel their experience

and personal profile are sufficiently accepted in the new, larger Federal Republic.

Apart from a general right to a kindergarten place for their children and the retention of the green arrow which allows motorists to turn right when a traffic light is red, not many of the laws and regulations have been kept from the old GDR.

As a result of this feeling of rejection, there's a dominant mood in the East not only of disappointment – as the West would have people believe – but frequently also of considerable frustration. In the new federal states different books are being read, for instance; even separate best-seller lists are sometimes

to be found. A whole range of daily newspapers which have big sales in the East have hardly been heard of in the West. Conversely, there are prominent weekly magazines and newspapers in the West which do not sell well in the East.

Big supermarket chains are increasingly forced to offer different ranges of goods, depending on where their branches are located. Those in Saxony or Brandenburg, which sell no goods produced in the East, increasingly have to face the anger of customers who scorned the same products not so long ago. Even advertising campaigns suddenly adopt different approaches: Western lifestyle is disapproved of in the East, where keen prices, availability of spares and guarantee terms are valued above fashion and frippery.

Difficult relationships: The relationships among Germans from East and West are certainly difficult ones. Like relatives brought together after a period of estrangement, they recognise each other's personalities but still don't really get along together very well. That happens in the best of families, of course, and it may be no cause for great concern. But everyone realises that the future will demand considerable goodwill on all sides.

On the international front, Germany remains the prime mover behind European integration. Such integration, insists Chancellor Kohl, is vital if the disasters of the first half of the 20th century are not to recur. Not all Germany's partners are so enthusiastic, but they agree that Germany is bound to play a central role in the expansion of the European Union. The geopolitical centre of gravity in Europe has certainly moved eastwards and a shifting of political weight has begun. The fact that the country will change greatly in the process is accepted by some as inevitable, yet for others it's unimaginable, even after a few years of unity. At least one great concern has not materialised: despite much doom-mongering, the policies of right-wing radicalism have been rejected by nine Germans out of ten.

One of the democratic virtues is not to lose nerve in times of change. The Germans are now being put to that test.

Left, an epoch comes to an end – dismantling the monumental Lenin memorial in Berlin.

STEFAN HEYM

There is scarcely any other German writer whose life reflects so well the vicissitudes of eight decades of German history as Stefan Heym. In his 850-page autobiography *Nachruf* (1988) he describes, somewhat controversially and with no undue modesty, his extraordinary and adventurous life.

Born plain Helmut Flieg, in Chemnitz in 1913, he began to write at a young age and was expelled from high school at 18 because of his opposition to rising nationalism. His expulsion came after an anti-militaristic poem of his was published in the local newspaper.

Two years later, like so many others, he fled from the Nazis. He went first to Prague and then to the United States where he studied German literature and worked as a journalist and editor for a German-language émigré publication in New York. In 1943 he enlisted in the American army and took part as a sergeant trained in "psychological warfare" in the Normandy invasion.

After the war, Heym remained in the United States, where his first major novels were published. He tackled critical contemporary issues in a journalistic style, entertaining and yet analytical, with the result that several of his books became best-sellers. In *Hostages* – to take one of his works – he wrote about the assassination of the Nazi leader Reinhard "the hangman" Heydrich in May 1942 by members of the Czech resistance in Prague. The book was also made into a film. In his novel *The Crusaders* he questioned the point of war, particularly relating to his own recent experiences. In *The Eyes of Reason* (1951), he returns to a Czechoslovakian background to examine the development of a bourgeois family after the struggle against fascism. He wrote most of his works in both English and German.

As a result of the McCarthy witchhunts in the United States and the outbreak of the Korean War, Heym left the country in protest in 1952 and settled in the GDR, where he soon ran into trouble because of his work as a contentious newspaper columnist. From 1976 until shortly before German reunification his books could be published and sold only in the West.

He experienced the greatest difficulties with his book *5 Tage im Juni (Five Days in June)*, which dealt with the riots in the GDR on 17 June 1953. Heym had to abandon plans to publish the book in 1959 because of censorship. He revised it many times and finally had it published in 1974 – but even then only in the West. For 21 years it was unavailable to his fellow countrymen in East Germany. Based on documentary material, the novel was attacked in

Right, Stefan Heym: appealing for solidarity.

East and West as a falsification, although admittedly for varying reasons; Heym shunned an evaluation of the events either as a counter-revolution plotted by the West (the East German version) or as a workers' uprising against the Communist regime (which is how West Germany saw it).

Heym involved himself in the civil rights movement and enjoyed enormous popularity in the GDR right up until reunification. In no way did he want to renounce the socialist state in 1989 but argued in favour of making it "truly socialistic". In doing so he manoeuvred himself into a minority position.

From then on he wrote laconic stories and pamphlets directed against the profiteers of reunification, in East and West alike. But that wasn't all: the author whose books had been banned in the GDR now stood as an independent candidate for the PDS, the party which hankered

after the "achievements" of the GDR. What was the reason for this apparent change of heart? It was quite simply that he felt that those who had been deceived for 40 years were once again being betrayed. He believed that the Western authorities imposing new rules on the East, particularly over property ownership, exerted more power than the GDR Politburo ever possessed. His words fell on eager ears among the disappointed people of eastern Germany. In the 1994 general election 82-year-old Heym was elected to the Bundestag.

The opening speech of the 13th legislative session fell to him as "doyen President". In this time of great change he directed a conciliatory appeal for solidarity to all Germans: "Chauvinism, racism, anti-Semitism and Stalinist ways should be banned for ever from our country". ∎

"I'm convinced that Babelsberg will soon belong again to the world's best studios", said Billy Wilder in February 1993 as Berlinale guest of honour at the Babelsberg gala film evening. A few months earlier DEFA, the former GDR film factory, had been sold by the Treuhand to CIP Deutschland, daughter company of the Compagnie Immobiliere Phenix SA and Britain's Chelsea group. And since then great efforts had really been made to integrate again the studios of the Babelsberg GmbH into the inter-

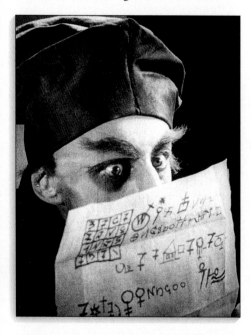

national media world. With the gigantic infrastructure of a modern media centre, including Europe's largest sound mixing facilities, the studios pick up once more their legendary UFA past, when – with the discovery of the "talkies" – they were the biggest film studios in all Europe.

UFA film pioneers: In those days the German film industry experienced its heyday in the UFA studios. It was here that both German and Austrian directors invented a variety of new stylistic methods in a motion picture industry that was still very much in its infancy. Robert Wiene directed the first expressionistic silent film, *The Cabinet of Dr*

Caligari. Fritz Lang made a series of crime pictures around the figure of Dr Mabuse, and his *Metropolis* is regarded as the first science fiction film, one which set new standards of animation technique. Friedrich Wilhelm Murnau established with his *Nosferatu* – a Symphony of Horror – the genre of the vampire film. For *The Last Man* he invented the "freed" camera. Previously the camera had stood firmly fixed in one place but now it was movable, lifted by crane, looking at people and buildings from new perspectives and sometimes almost to the point of distortion – an enormous gain in film vitality.

Emigration to Hollywood: All these film pioneers have something in common with many of their colleagues – the comedy directors Max Ophuls and Ernst Lubitsch, the early psycho-thriller experts Otto Preminger and Robert Siodmak, the scriptwriter-turned-director Billy Wilder, with Josef von Sternberg and Marlene Dietrich, who had become famous with *The Blue Angel*, Peter Lorre and Fred Zinnemann: they all emigrated around 1933 to Paris or Hollywood because they were Jewish or because they saw their work endangered by the rise of the Third Reich.

A few, especially younger artists such as Billy Wilder (*The Lost Weekend, Sunset Boulevard, The Apartment, Some Like it Hot*) and Fred Zinnemann (*High Noon, From Here to Eternity*), first achieved fame in Hollywood, and some, such as Lang and Lubitsch, managed to continue their success in their new home; the majority, however, went under, both artistically and financially. Marlene Dietrich was one of the exceptions among the actors and actresses: she was forgiven her first, bad Hollywood films. Her acting and singing ability were enough reason for producers to place their faith in her.

A trend to triviality: With the emigration of its greatest talent, the German film industry sank into obscurity. The Nazi propaganda films were followed in the 1950s by the so-called Heimat (Homeland) films, ingenuous comedies and superficial period pieces. Films were able to put the events of the immediate German past out of mind successfully enough for a few years. Their plots were schematic but often exciting and their casts were not without their star quality (Romy Schneider, Heinz Rühmann). And some directors – Helmut Käutner, Bernhard Wicki, for example – knew their trade thoroughly. But to learn anything about that time or the political context in which they were made we must turn to the films of Wolfgang Staudte – for example, *Roses for the Prosecutor* or *The Subject*, based on Heinrich Mann's novel.

Youthful resurgence: German film-making only regained its international esteem at the end of the 1960s, through the work of young authors involved in the so-called Junger Autorenfilm. Artistically, it was influenced by France's *nouvelle vague*, in which Jean-Luc Godard and François Truffaut were

soon after great successes like Schlöndorff's version of *The Tin Drum* (which won the Golden Palm at Cannes), the German film industry drifted to a fringe position in its own country. At the same time, an internationalisation process, even an Americanisation, could be seen.

International themes: The chief reason for this is most likely to be found in the production conditions in Germany. The only large studios, Munich and Berlin, could not be compared to Hollywood or Rome, and money was short. German directors faced the choice of either making uncompromising films for the avant garde cinema and a small public – the road followed by Achternbusch – or

among the most prominent names. Politically, it rejected the continued suppression of the German past and found support from the student movement of 1968. Alexander Kluge, Rainer Werner Fassbinder, Volker Schlöndorff, Werner Herzog, Reinhard Hauff and Wim Wenders directed their first films in those years; they were followed by Margaretha von Trotta, Helma Sanders, Herbert Achternbusch and Hark Bohm. Yet

Left, *Nosferatu – a Symphony of Horror;* with this film Friedrich Wilhelm Murnau founded the genre of the vampire film. **Above**, Marlene Dietrich soared to fame in *The Blue Angel*.

changing countries. Trotta went to Italy, Schlöndorff and Wenders filmed in the US, the successful director Wolfgang Petersen (*The Boat*) and his producer Bernd Eichinger went to work in Hollywood. But this situation was not without its positive side: a growth in the universality of German films, which no longer clung exclusively to domestic issues.

New possibilities: Only the future can tell how the development of German film will continue. Volker Schlöndorff, who went to live in New York in 1984, is now back in Germany and, as one of the business directors in Babelsberg, is responsible there for all development, production and artistic areas of activity. That's a project that offers hope. Perhaps the title of Margarethe von Trotta's last film, *The Promise*, can be taken as an omen. This story, set on both sides of the former east–west German border, was filmed in the Babelsberg studios.

Trends of modern art: Strongly influenced as it was in its early days by expressionist theatre and art, the German film industry turned, with the arrival of the "talkie", increasingly to purely naturalistic forms of representation. Its experiments in pictorial expression ran dry. But that wasn't the case with fine art. Here the development of photography and film had long since contributed

group, Der Blaue Reiter ("The Blue Rider"), formed itself in Munich around Vassily Kandinsky, Franz Marc, August Macke, Gabriele Münter, Alexeij Jawlensky and Marianne Werefkin. Their trademark was abstraction, with which they aimed at a spiritual deepening of reality. The leading personality of the group was Kandinsky, whose influence was to become decisive for post-1945 west German art.

Two outsiders: A few great German artists were close to the expressionists, but were too uninteresed in the fashions of modern art to actually join them. With her strongly expressive drawings and sculptures, Käthe Kollwitz (1867–1945) drew attention to the misery of

to the general reluctance to depict nature in its objective state of realism.

Expressionist artistic groups: In 1905 the artistic society known as Die Brücke ("The Bridge) was established in Dresden, with its founder members including Ernst Ludwig Kirchner, Emil Nolde, Max Pechstein, Erich Heckel, Karl Schmidt-Rottluff and Otto Mueller. Much influenced by primitive German woodcuts, their common programme was the direct expression of the emotions. In their concentration on the subjective they broke objective forms and freed colours from their purely illustrative function.

Six years later a second expressionistic

disadvantaged sections of the population. Her cycle *A Weavers' Revolt* (1893–98), *Peasants' War* (1903–8) and *The War* (1924) are particularly famous. After being expelled by the Nazis from the Prussian Academy, she made a moving series of eight prints on the theme of Death (1934–35).

The sculptor, artist and poet Ernst Barlach (1870–1938) also went his own way. At the centre of his sphere of interest stood man himself, whom he represented in highly original sculptures of great severity and yet of inspiring, almost fragile radiance. His antiwar memorials made him the subject of a Nazi persecution campaign. Not until 1978 was a memorial erected to him, in Güstrow.

Dada and Surrealism: World War I brought about a radical change of direction. In 1916 the Dada movement arose in Zürich. Because of the European-wide slaughter during the war it declared art to be a game of nonsense. German citadels of Dadaism arose: in 1920 Kurt Schwitters built the first of his three *Merz* constructions in Hanover – bizarre collages made out of plaster and wood, whose form was constantly changed by the artist. Max Ernst created collages in Cologne. Hannah Höch, George Grosz and Raoul Hausmann produced Dadaist posters, magazines and various happenings in Berlin, where the first international Dada exhibition was staged in 1920. Chance or coincidence became an artistic principle, and everyday objects were declared to be works of art.

But this anarchistic art soon destroyed itself. From the mid 1920s the principles of Dadaism found deep and permanent expression in the surrealistic, dream landscapes of Max Ernst (1891–1976) and Paul Klee (1879–1940). With his rich repertoire of work and his innovative painting methods and draughtsmanship, Klee can't really be tied to any particular style.

New realism: In the 1920s the artistic style of penetratingly sharp New Realism established itself. In its exaggerated representation of reality, it sometimes took on surrealistic characteristics. Otto Dix and George Grosz are among its most important representatives. Grosz was fined on many occasions in the Weimar Republic times because of the mordant social criticism of his drawings and paintings.

Existential questioning lies at the roots of the great *oeuvre* of Max Beckmann (1884–1950). With its sensual colours and violent forms, his Welttheater (World Theatre) represents a society living in violent times. Human fears and brutality appear as mythical phenomena, which neither the artist nor the viewer can escape (*Die Nacht*, 1918–19; *Versuchung* 1936–37).

The Bauhaus as a programme: The architect Walter Gropius opened the Bauhaus in 1919 in Weimar (in 1925 it moved to Dessau). The Bauhaus was a school of art and architecture.

It included the teaching of various crafts, which Gropius saw as allied to architecture, and by training students equally in art and in technically expert craftsmanship, it sought to end the schism between the two. At the same time, the Bauhaus preached that function and aesthetics were inseparable, and the school's philosophy was directed towards producing pleasing objects for the masses rather than individual items for a wealthy elite.

Leading contemporary artists such as Klee, Kandinsky, Lyonel Feininger, Oskar Schlemmer and Laszlo Moholy-Nagy taught at the Bauhaus, introducing new ideas and didactic methods. In 1933 the Bauhaus was closed down by the Nazis, but the school's teaching

methods and ideals continue to have a huge influence today.

After World War II: After 1945 there were very few points of contact with the interrupted artistic tradition which existed before the Third Reich. A synonym for contemporary art came into being in 1955 with the Dokumenta in Kassel, which brought new impulses with it. Its first three exhibitions stressed the European moderns and the abstract expressionism of Ernst Wilhelm Nay, Fritz Winter and Willi Baumeister, and revealed the the preference of the 1950s for lyrical-abstract art or non-objectivism.

In the 1960s art was confronted with the

Left, The *Blaue Reiter*, by Wassily Kandinsky. **Right**, *Tisch mit Aggregat 1958–87* by Joseph Beuys.

world of commodities. Following on Dada, the artists Gerhard Richter, Sigmar Polke and Palermo founded the German variant of pop-art, "capitalist realism". Consumer goods ranging from department store materials to bath tubs and ordinary sausages served as motifs and creative material.

Joseph Beuys: Post-war Germany's most famous artistic personality, Joseph Beuys (1921–86), is represented in museums throughout the world, often with entire galleries devoted to his work. Having studied art at the Düsseldorf Academy, he broke the confines of traditional artistic vehicles, such as draughtsmanship, painting and sculpture, and confronted his public with spectacular

ening, actions and performances blazed a trail along which the separation of the theatrical and the real was suspended for a few moments at a time. Theatre was combined with pictures, spectacle with movement and time-honoured classics with comics – constantly on the search for new forms of expression for new ingredients.

The theatrical panorama: Actors and directors from other European countries often look enviously at Germany's theatrical panorama. Certainly no other country possesses such a wealth of theatres, large and small. There are historical reasons for Germany's good fortune. In the 18th century, kings and princes maintained, as patrons of the arts,

"happenings", the physical remains of which were later taken over and displayed by the museums. In his sculptures or "assemblages" he commonly used materials and objects such as felt, fat, lead moulds, concert grand pianos and school blackboards. Influenced by traumatic wartime experiences (as a Luftwaffe pilot, he was shot down), later fed with anthroposophical and utopian socialist ideas, Beuys wanted to convey a unified and universal experience, embracing all senses and developing creativity.

Fluid borders of art: A blending of the arts sprang at the same time from the representational sphere. In a time of experimental awak-

their own theatres and acting ensembles. Friedrich Schiller celebrated his successes in Mannheim, Johann Wolfgang von Goethe shone in Weimar. These theatres, built through the grace of Germany's various rulers, form the basic foundations of today's state and municipal theatre system.

Subsidised theatres: The multiplicity is striking. There are 185 subsidised theatres in Germany, most of them staging opera, drama and ballet, possessing their own ensembles and workshops and offering a varied repertoire. In contrast to the commercial theatres, they have an educational function to fulfil.

But subsidised theatre doesn't only bring

advantages; the system is also plagued by huge inefficiencies. Management, technical support and salaries consume some 85 per cent of a typical annual budget, leaving just 15 per cent for new productions – in other words, for art.

This practice of cost-intensive subsidy gives the politicians a lot of headaches, however. The closing in 1993 of Berlin's Schiller Theatre – a house rich in tradition – rang alarm bells and brought prophesies of the death of good theatre in Germany. A countrywide outcry led to the postponement of plans to shut Reinhild Hoffmann's Tanztheater Bochum.

But beyond plain policies of economy, these decisions signalled the temporary end of a unique development. At the end of the 1960s and in the early 1970s a renewal of the German theatre got under way, inspired by the student movement. With provocative personalities like Peter Zadek, politically tendentious "director's theatre" conquered the theatrical venues; the Berliner Schaubühne at the Hallesches Ufer, under Peter Stein, achieved international recognition.

Dance as "choreographic theatre": Apart from these impulses and successes in drama, though, the really radical change in artistic repertoire occurred in the dance form. The Austrian Johann Kresnik staged dazzling political revues in Cologne, Bremen and Heidelberg and called them "choreographic theatre". In Wuppertal a young woman by the name of Pina Bausch presented psychologically-based dance theatre rooted in the everyday. Her uncompromising productions divided the ballet world, whose conservative representatives, stuck in their rigid mind-set, saw in them not enough dance and too much theatre. Her choreography and particularly her unusual stagings mark a turning point in contemporary dance and remain a powerful influence. In *Bluebeard* (1977) the stage is strewn with dead leaves and in *Carnations* (1982) with 15,000 pink and white carnations. After Pina Bausch, Reinhild Hoffmann and Susanne Linke achieved international fame. All three studied at Essen's Folkwang School. Meanwhile in Cologne's Tanzforum, a collective ensemble leadership was developed and American-style modern dance was cultivated.

German expressionist dance: Between the wars, Germany was the home of the internationally-acclaimed expressionistic dance movement with its prominent exponents Rudolf Laban, Mary Wigman, Kurt Jooss and Harald Kreutzberg. But the Nazis perverted the genre, attempting to use it for their own mass rallies. Those choreographers who did not conform or who refused to distance themselves from their Jewish colleagues (Kurt Jooss, the founder of the Folkwang School, was a prominent example) decided to emigrate. After the war, the German public had had enough of expressionistic dance,

even in its original form, and turned to untainted neo-classical ballet.

New theatre forms: So dance theatre picked up late from a rudely interrupted tradition and created a completely new genre, in which the front-stage was taken by neither the narrative line nor pure dance. Instead, associative thought and feelings dictated form and content. This also had its influence on theatre directors, changing their concept of space and bringing to the stage a new corporeality in which the attention was focused on the choreographic movement of the actors.

At the same time, independent theatre and

Left, scene from the dance-drama *The Seven Deadly Sins* by Pina Bausch. **Right**, *Frida Kahlo* by Johann Kresnik.

dance groups sprang up all over the country, mostly presenting political material in experimental form on tiny studio stages, in former factory halls or marquee tents. In Munich a whole range of similarly politically motivated theatres opened their doors to an enthusiastic public.

Dance theatre today: And what has remained of this post-war artistic rejuvenation? The Wuppertal Tanztheatre is now known worldwide as a result of its extensive tours – every one of Pina Bausch's pieces carries the guarantee of an extraordinary theatrical experience. In Bremen, Susanne Link and Urs Dietrich attempted a promising new beginning. Their predecessor Johann Kresnik continues to provoke with his choreographic theatre – but these days in Frank Castrof's theatre, the Volksbühne on Rosa Luxembourg Platz in east Berlin. Kresnik, the angry agitator, and the East German director Frank Castorf, who made a name for himself as "destroyer of the classics", find their public mostly among the young. Castorf opened his theatre to vagabonds and skinheads and the discussions that his hospitality inevitably invited, making it a noteworthy place.

In Weimar, the young choreographer Joachim Schlömer attracts the national press and a wide public with ambitious and demanding dance theatre productions. Others to watch out for in the "independent scene" include the artist V. A. Wölfl and his Düsseldorf group Neuer Tanz, the choreographer Wanda Golonka or the anarchic Lower Bavarian Alexeij Sager, whose remarkable theatrical experiments can be seen at his "ProT" venue in Munich.

Avant garde: Although experimental theatre is rarely found these days, there are still a handful of theatres in Germany which concentrate on nurturing the international avant garde. They campaign for theatrical forms which fit no previously known patterns – from music and dance theatre to Cyberspace and Techno performances.

The most exciting is undoubtedly Frankfurt's Theater am Turm under the direction of Tom Stromberg, who has made his home in the enormous, reconstructed Bockenheimer Depot. New York's Wooster Group plays here regularly, presenting shrill, intelligent "multi-media-theatre". Antwerp's Jan Fabre is developing his pictorial theatre techniques at the Depot, where enthusiastic audiences are also teased and puzzled by the Frankfurt composer Heiner Goebbels and the Japanese choreographer Saburo Teshigawara. A similar programme is offered by Berlin's Hebbel Theatre, while in Hamburg the Kampnagel-Fabrik tries to keep pace with its own programme. In Munich's Marstall, the city's former royal stables, Elisabeth Schweeger follows her own highly individual course. Apart from her own productions and guest performances, she has cultivated the so-called "media salon", where the latest technical media are presented and their effects discussed.

And the established theatres? In the past two decades, the former revolutionaries have returned from director's theatre to the actor's stage. A selection of the most exciting German productions is offered annually at the Berlin Theatertreffen. The finest dramatic theatre is guaranteed by Thomas Langhoff at the Deutsches Theater in Berlin and by Dieter Dorn at the Kammerspiele in Munich. Frank Baumbauer, manager of the Hamburg Schauspielhaus, provides a forum for Switzerland's Christoph Marthaler with his wildly eccentric theatrical deconstructions.

A "must" for anyone interested in the dance form is the Ballet Frankfurt, whose director, William Forsythe, is justifiably regarded as the most innovative figure on the international ballet scene. Visits are also recommended to the Stuttgart Staatstheater, for the ice-cold, sublimely violent scenic theatre of the Carinthian Martin Kusej, and to anywhere where the work of stage designer Michael Simon is to be seen.

Is this a pretty lean balance in view of the 185 theatre communities? Certainly not, for only the outstanding names are mentioned here. There is something for every taste in Germany's rich theatrical landscape – from *My Fair Lady* in small provincial theatres to musicals in highly technological, luxurious productions, from classical stagings faithful to the original to the muscular linguistic acrobatics of Elfriede Jelenik or Werner Schwab. And, finally, let's not forget the innumerable summer festivals up and down the country in picturesque castle ruins or forest clearings. You just have to study the programme details.

<u>Right</u>, "Ruski go home" became reality earlier than Berlin's "Theater des Westens" dreamt.

The diversity of Germany's regions, between the coastal stretches of the north and the Alps in the south, is also manifest in the variety of the country's centuries-old cuisine – from rural, peasant-style to urban-bourgeois.

High calories to lean cuisine: To make up for the lean times following World War II, when shortages and ration-cards created a culinary slump, the 1950s were marked by a veritable *Fresswelle* (wave of gluttony): at last, people could eat their fill – and this they did with Teutonic abandon.

Regional specialities: In Bavaria the beer gardens are the places for home-style cooking. Roast pork with its crusty crackling, dumplings and cabbage, white sausage (the famous *Weisswürste*) with sweet mustard and pretzels are only some of the highlights on the menu. Guests at Alfons Schubeck's culinary temple in Waging am See in southeastern Bavaria are treated in noble fashion to plump farm duck and dumplings made from pretzel-dough or to light dumplings coaxed to fluffy opulence with sweet yeast.

Changes in German culinary tastes came about with the travel bug which bit the Germans in the 1970s and with the arrival of migrant workers from Mediterranean countries. They brought with them pizzas, pasta, moussaka, paella, kebab and wines pressed from sundrenched grapes. At the same time, the Germans began to take another look at their own traditional specialities, and today regional cooking is to be found in many local inns and restaurants. The progressive cuisine of top-bracket restaurants produces creative variations of traditional recipes, with popular preference for lighter dishes, using only the freshest produce.

In Swabia and Baden-Württemberg they delight in their pancake soup, cabbage dishes and pasta-like traditional specialities such as *Spätzle*, *Maultaschen* and *Schupfnudeln*. Black Forest smoked hams are world famous, while the onion tart from Baden is scarcely less prized. Both are complemented by the excellent wines and schnapps from this sunny region of southern Germany.

Franconia is the region for the greatest selection of sausages, such as the delicious, finger-sized *Nürnberger Bratwürste*. Nuremberg, though, is even better known for its spicy *Lebkuchen*, aromatic cakes which are particularly popular at Christmas time.

Franconian wine is justifiably famous, and not only because of the familiar *Bocksbeutel* bottles in which it comes.

Further north, in Hessen, they still enjoy the "green sauce" much celebrated by Goethe. Made from no less than nine kinds of fresh herbs, it tastes particularly good with beef and asparagus.

Marinated beef (*Sauerbraten*), potato salad, black bread, potato pancakes and apple sauce count among the delicacies of the Rhineland. At Christmas time the streets of Cologne are heavy with the smell of the thin almond biscuits known as *Spekulatius*, while the Yuletide speciality of nearby Aachen is the equally aromatic *Printen*.

coasts fish recipes dominate, with Hamburg offering eel soup, fried sole, herrings, shrimps and many kinds of smoked fish. In Lower Saxony, mutton comes to the table as *Heidschnuckenbraten*, with *Rote Grütze* a delicious, chilled melange of berries and custard, to follow. And Lübeck's marzipan is simply not to be missed.

In Berlin, the *Königsberger Klopse* (small meat dumplings) at the Café Kranzler on the Ku'Damm are much to be recommended, followed by a selection from the café's patisserie. Or you can prepare yourself for a tour of the city's nightspots with helpings of pickled pork knuckle (*Eisbein*), sauerkraut, creamed potato and mashed peas.

Westphalian kitchens beckon with hearty meat dishes, delicate hams and Pumpernickel, a dark, sweet wholemeal bread.

Green cabbage and *Pinkel* make up a hearty stew served in Bremen, a particularly welcome dish when a cold wind blows from the North sea. It goes well with another Bremen heart-warmer, *Köm*, a schnapps made from caraway seeds. On the North Sea and Baltic

In Saxony, specialities include *Leipziger Allerlei*, a light terrine of young vegetables and freshwater shrimps. The Christmas cakes of Dresden – the sugary *Christstollen* and *Baumkuchen* – are world-famous.

Thuringia rings the changes with all kinds of dumplings, and they are to be recommended with the region's goose dishes. In Erfurt's Linderhof, master chef Erhard Theumer will serve you up a delicious *Rostbrätel* (roast meat) in a beer sauce (Schwarzbiersauce), garnished with onions and potato pancakes, a typical example of new German cuisine. His Thuringian-style roast lamb is a tempting alternative.

Preceding page: a waitress's job at the Oktoberfest is no easy task. **Left**, a good selection of sliced Wurst makes an excellent snack. **Right**, more than 300 different varieties of bread are baked in Germany.

"A juice from barley or wheat, which acquires through fermentation a certain similarity to wine, serves as a drink... if one wanted to yield to their intemperance and provide them [the Teutons] with as much of it as they could drink, they could be conquered more easily through their vice than by force of arms." It's a good 1,900 years since the Roman historian Tacitus wrote these words, characterising what he viewed as the somewhat unfamiliar drinking habits of the Germanic people.

Superlatives: The Germans have remained a nation of sociable beer drinkers to this day. According to recent figures, 140 litres (31 gallons) of the golden liquid disappear down each German throat every year. Bavarians are top of the drinking league, with North Germans trailing in final position. Only the Danes and the Irish can offer the Germans competition. Commensurate with consumption are the number of breweries, and Germany has the most breweries in Europe (1,280, of which 730 are in Bavaria). Among them is the world's oldest commercially functioning brewery, in Weihenstephan near Munich (it's been going since 1040).

Between the lot of them they market 5,000 different brands. Dortmund is Europe's number one brewery centre, even edging out Munich, site of the largest beerhall (the Mathäser-Bierstadt), the best known (the Hofbräuhaus, built in 1589) and the annual Oktoberfest (the climax of the Bavarian beer drinking season).

At the centre of all these unique statistics is the purity law (*Reinheitsgebot*) enacted by the Bavarian nobility in 1516. The ancient ruling, the oldest foodstuffs law in the world, decrees that only barley, hops and water can be used to brew beer. In 1906 the law was extended to the entire German Empire, and retained its unrestricted validity until 1987. After that date, the importation was allowed of beers which did not match the purity laws, as long as their ingredients were declared.

Barrels of beer: The variety of the beer landscape is also unique. Anyone who simply orders a "beer" in Germany reveals himself as a novice. It's true that the bitter *Pils* has advanced since the 1960s to become the market leader and has also established itself south of the so-called *Weisswurst Äquator* (meaning Bavaria, region of the white sausage), while the mild *Hefeweissbier* of the south (the region's yeast-fermented wheat beer) conversely has gained territory and acceptance in the north. Nevertheless, regionally differentiated taste still rules, and this enables even the smallest breweries to compete with the giants of the brewing business. Beers which had almost disappeared from memory, such as the naturally cloudy *Zwicklbier*, are being rediscovered, and more and more breweries are concentrating on so-called eco-beers. Even the nostalgic snap-capped bottles are coming back.

A beer paradise is to be found in Franconia. Nowhere else in Germany are there so many small breweries as in the region lying between Kulmbach (which boasts the world's strongest beer, the EKU 28), Bamberg (with its famous *Rauchbier*, or smoked beer) and *Hof*. But Cologne, home of the legendary *Kölsch*, can't be accused of monotony; the city has more than 20 breweries. *Kölsch*, by the way, can only be brewed in Cologne and the surrounding area.

A few kilometres further on down the Rhine lies Düsseldorf, citadel of the copper-brown *Altbier*, while in the nearby Ruhr *Dortmunder Export* rivals Pils as the favourite brew. Other unusual beers include the *Berliner Weisse* and the *Leipziger Gose*, which connoisseurs enjoy with a dash of raspberry syrup, *waldmeister* or liqueur.

Far up in the north a few breweries still offer unfiltered *Kräusenbier* or *Broyhan*. In Lower Saxony, Bremen and Hamburg are to be found the largest beer exporters – a worldwide reputation that stretches back to the Middle Ages. For beer established itself as a national drink far earlier up here than in Bavaria. One place was responsible: Einbeck.

Bavarian beer experienced its boom during the course of the 19th century, when the dark, malty *Münchner* was regarded to all intents and purposes as the south German beer. It was fixed so deeply in the Bavarian soul that a beer price war raged for 66 years (1844–1910). With the coming of the lighter *Helles* around the turn of the century the "good old days" were over for many beer-drinkers. The annual fuss over the ever-increasing price of Oktoberfest beer has in the meantime attained a ritual character.

Where beer fans meet to drink: North and south also have their differences when it comes to where beer is drunk. Bavarians love their beer gardens, where they are al-

With its extraordinary collection of 700 breweries the Hanoverian town was the unrivalled German brewery centre in the 14th century, keeping even the Bavarian court supplied. Only with the enticement of an *aimpöckisch* (crafty) master brewer away from Einbeck in 1612 did the Bavarians free themselves of the need to import beer. Einbeck's memory is kept alive today in the name the Bavarians give to one of their most traditional beers, the *Bock*.

Left, the friendly local is second home to more than a few. **Above**, Munich's Oktoberfest – high point for many beer-drinkers.

lowed to bring their own food. In North Rhine–Westphalia, pubs, or "Pinten" and "Weetschaften", are where the beer is drunk, and the best place to enjoy it is at the bar. And in Berlin they say that every road intersection has four corners and five pubs.

Whether bar or beer garden, litre mug or fancy "Molle", *Kölsch* or *Altbier*, *Pils* or *Bock* – the special relationship Germans enjoy with their beer can really be understood only when the tongue gets under the noble hop juice. And don't be shy of the first taste, for Goethe himself said: "The first time, one shudders, but after drinking it for a week there's no leaving off."

Where nuclear energy, environmental protection and health foods are concerned, the Germans get more het up than any other nation. The *Los Angeles Times*, no less, reported that law and order and punctuality were no longer the national obsession of the Germans in the 1990s. Environmental protection and ecologically-aware behaviour were more important concerns.

The protest movements formed in the 1970s by popular initiatives and rainbow political coalitions have developed into a political force which compelled the state to enact new laws for the protection of natural resources, water and the atmosphere.

A bottomless pit: In April 1995, a so-called Castor container with spent nuclear fuel rods was sent to Gorleben in Lower Saxony, accompanied by the largest police operation in the history of the Federal Republic. Anti-nuclear activists wanted to stop the transport at any price. More than 15,000 police were called into action to escort the train and its load on its journey from Baden-Württemberg and to get it through the blockades set up by sitdown-striking demonstrators.

The police operation cost more than 60 million Marks, and fears were raised that the transport of the many other containers of nuclear waste, waiting in temporary dumps, would become an undertaking whose cost would run into billions.

And on the subject of billions – there really were billions available, in parliamentary budgets and company funds, for what was believed to be the cheapest form of energy. Eight billion Marks were spent on the fast-breeder nuclear plant in Kalkar on the Lower Rhine, close to two billion were invested in the nuclear reconversion plant at Wackersdorf in the Upper Palatinate before construction was halted on the grounds that the grand project was "politically unpracticable". The development of nuclear energy in Germany has virtually come to a halt.

Preceding page: ecologically-friendly energy production by wind power. **Left**, protests against the storage of nuclear waste in Gorleben, 1994. **Above**, waste has gained a place in the German public consciousness.

Shell also loses out: The Shell group's disposal of the redundant North Sea oil-drilling platform Brent Spar in July 1995 also became unpracticable. Shell wanted to sink the useless wreck in the Atlantic, but the plan was scuppered by a very effective, if slightly misleading, Europe-wide Greenpeace campaign and the powerful voice of the German government. A piquant note was added to the story by an advertising campaign which Shell had shortly before launched in Germany, underlining the company's engagement in

the cause of environmental protection. In Germany the protests weren't only verbal. Shell petrol stations experienced a 15 percent fall-off in sales, and the oil multinational was faced with losses running into millions. The company decided it was best to change its plans and to arrange for the Brent Spar to be dismantled on shore.

Ecologically-orientated organisations like the Society for the Environment and Nature Protection (BUND, with several thousand members), Robin Wood and Greenpeace, as well as alternative political parties, headed by the Greens, have succeeded in informing the public so well about threats to climate, atmosphere and water that individuals can decide for themselves whether to go to work by car or bike, whether to save or squander electricity, whether to sort out household waste or tolerate the pollution emitted by power stations. What's at stake is a liveable future, particularly for children. Environment and ecology are prominently on the political agenda, claiming the largest share of the political vocabulary. One of the leading economic organisations encouraged industrial firms to improve their image, arguing that they could expect long-term market benefits if they did so.

A fresh wind in Parliament: The Greens grew into a political party from their origins as a people's initiative, becoming in the late 1970s a kind of reservoir pooling energies for the fight for better environmental protection and alternative living. Apart from representatives of environmental organisations, the antinuclear lobby and peace movement, feminists and homosexuals began to get organised. Varied and various as these groups were, all of them felt their interests were not represented in the political landscape of the Federal Republic and sought to take their protests into Parliament itself.

The new party experienced a boost in support in the autumn of 1981 when tens of thousands demonstrated against the stationing of new American medium-range missiles in Germany and fought against the construction of Frankfurt International Airport's planned Runway West. In the federal elections on 6 March 1983, the Greens cleared the five percent hurdle with a 6.5 percent result which won them seats in the Bonn Parliament. Since then the Greens have taken their place behind the CDU and SPD as Germany's third strongest party both in the federation as a whole and in the states. In many public opinion polls they come out with more than 10 percent support. Following German reunification the Greens entered into alliance with the reformists of the former GDR, who had organised themselves as "Bündnis 90".

German fears: There are, of course, alternative parties throughout Europe. So why did ecological concepts meet with such remarkable support in Germany, of all countries? The relationship the Germans enjoy with nature always had a romantic quality. You have only to read the descriptions of nature

in Goethe's work: he writes of secluded meadows and rushing streams, and when people have problems in love they find solace in mother nature's lap.

But this nature is under threat. Such an understanding of nature might appear strange or even comical for, say, a South American whose ancestors had to wage a stubborn fight to clear a path for civilisation through jungle and wilderness. But in Germany the situation has become even more critical: a network of highways with four and often six lanes cuts through the land from west to east and north to south. Undeveloped countryside can be found only in a few areas, such as the Lüneberger Heide, the Eifel uplands or

the Bavarian alpine foothills, and the concentration of population in Germany is among the highest in Europe. While in Finland there are 15 people per square kilometre, in Germany the figure is 228. The density of population and infrastructure is clear to anyone who flies over Germany. While mountain chains form the relief map of Spain or Greece and the sheer endless stretches of steppes and forests dominate the ground plan of some other continents, Germany appears as a well laid-out panoramic work of art, fresh from an architect's drawing board. From this vantage point, the fears of the Germans become a little easier to understand.

No general speed limit: The commitment of many Germans to environmental protection has its contradictions, however. Many people become involved in citizens' initiatives for a pedestrian zone in their home towns, for instance, they perhaps buy chemically untreated foodstuffs but then remain infatuated motorists and bowl down the autobahn with no thought about the consequences. Millions take advantage of the services of the German motoring organisation ADAC, which is vehemently opposed to speed limits and ensures the failure of attempts to reduce traffic emission levels.

Many critics are already detecting a typical German tendency towards double stand-

ards. You can't have everything: clean air and at the same time the convenience which a car brings, less rubbish but also elaborately packed groceries, unspoilt landscapes but perfectly organised holidays in the form of package tours to all four corners of the world. And here it should also be pointed out that Germany sends large amounts of its harmful waste abroad to be disposed of and relieves itself in this way of an unsolvable problem.

<u>Left</u>, so-called "alternatives" weren't the only ones involved in the battle against nuclear power programmes. <u>Above</u>, protests in Dannenberg in March 1995.

Environmental technology: As a result of political protest, environmental protection is becoming a decisive economic factor. Social Democrats and Greens want a departure from nuclear energy and have been demanding for years past that state and business and industry must invest more in the development of alternative, regenerative sources of energy, particularly solar power. And it must be said that much has occurred in this area. A series of new laws requiring firms to introduce greater emission controls and energy-saving measures have had a significant impact. A network of state regulations and grants demands, and at the same time, promotes active environmental protection. A home-builder who installs a solar-cell panel on the roof can claim a grant of DM1,500.

German companies have also become pioneers in other areas of environmental technology, especially in heat retention and other heating techniques, for which the Federal Parliament has enacted strict environmental laws. Munich's Kraus-Maffei company, known for its production of the Leopard tank, now earns most of its income from projects employing environmental technology. Other firms such as Buderus and Siemens could also be sure that their products using environmental technology could become export hits if the strict standards in force in Germany also applied in other countries of the European Union and elsewhere. Siemens already has the largest construction plant for solar panels to be found anywhere in the United States.

Economic factors: Innovative environmental technology has become one of the few economic areas showing powerful rates of growth. The 1,000 firms producing environmental-technological plant in 1990 grew to a total of more than 8,000 in 1995. Many observers already speak of the emergence of a new industrial revolution.

When the Federal Parliament decreed that power stations were to be converted in order to lower by around 90 percent the pollution levels blamed for acid rain many companies groaned under the sheer burden of the millions of required investment. Meanwhile, not only have the power stations been converted but many German companies are now in the position to export their related know-how and new technology and to open up new markets in this area of industrial endeavour.

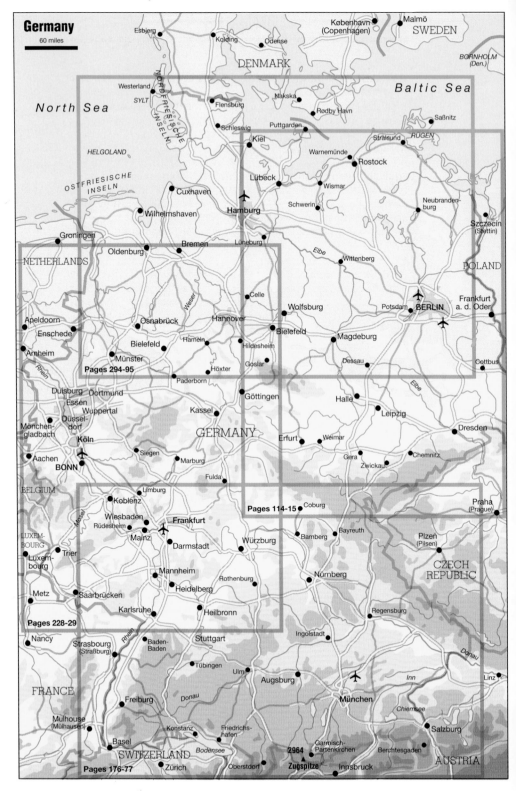

Germany

60 miles

North Sea

SWEDEN

København (Copenhagen)

Malmö

BORNHOLM (Den.)

Esbjerg

Kolding

Odense

DENMARK

Baltic Sea

Westerland

SYLT

NORDFRIESISCHE INSELN

Flensburg

Nakská

Rødby Havn

Saßnitz

Schleswig

Puttgarden

Stralsund

RÜGEN

Kiel

Warnemünde

HELGOLAND

OSTFRIESISCHE INSELN

Cuxhaven

Wilhelmshaven

Hamburg

Lübeck

Wismar

Schwerin

Rostock

Neubrandenburg

Szczecin (Stettin)

Groningen

NETHERLANDS

Oldenburg

Bremen

Lüneburg

Elbe

Wittenberg

POLAND

Apeldoorn

Enschede

Arnheim

Rhein

Osnabrück

Weser

Celle

Hannover

Wolfsburg

Bielefeld

Potsdam

BERLIN

Frankfurt a. d. Oder

Bielefeld

Hameln

Hildesheim

Magdeburg

Cottbus

Münster

Höxter

Goslar

Dessau

Pages 294-95

Paderborn

Göttingen

Halle

Elbe

Duisburg

Dortmund

Essen

Wuppertal

Mönchengladbach

Düsseldorf

Köln

Kassel

GERMANY

Leipzig

Dresden

Aachen

BONN

Siegen

Marburg

Erfurt

Weimar

Gera

Chemnitz

Zwickau

BELGIUM

Fulda

Limburg

Koblenz

Wiesbaden

Rüdesheim

Mosel

Frankfurt

Pages 114-15

Coburg

Praha (Prague)

LUXEMBOURG

Mainz

Darmstadt

Würzburg

Bamberg

Bayreuth

Plzeň (Pilsen)

Luxembourg

Trier

Metz

Mannheim

Rothenburg

Nürnberg

CZECH REPUBLIC

Saarbrücken

Heidelberg

Karlsruhe

Heilbronn

Regensburg

Pages 228-29

Nancy

Strasbourg (Straßburg)

Rhein

Baden-Baden

Stuttgart

Ingolstadt

Donau

Linz

FRANCE

Tübingen

Ulm

Augsburg

Inn

Freiburg

Donau

München

Chiemsee

Mulhouse (Mülhausen)

Konstanz

Friedrichshafen

2964

Garmisch-Partenkirchen

Salzburg

Berchtesgaden

Basel

SWITZERLAND

Bodensee

Zugspitze

Pages 176-77

Zürich

Oberstdorf

Innsbruck

AUSTRIA

It is hard to find a single image that fairly conjures up Germany, in the way that a beret-wearing wine drinker would suggest France or a cuckoo clock would identify Switzerland. One reason is that Germany is less homogeneous than most European countries and any familiar image – such as that of the *lederhosen*-clad beer imbiber – represents only one distinct part of the staunchly federal nation, not all of it. In that respect, perhaps Germany is Europe's equivalent to the United States. It offers a variety of landscapes, all packed into a country that stretches around 1,000 km (600 miles) between the north coast and the Alps, and about 700 km (400 miles) at its widest point from west to east. There is much to discover, from the regional character and customs of rural Bavaria to the Berlin snout, from the unchanging delights of the countryside to the vibrant culture of the cities.

Because of its federal structure, Germany does not have just one dominant political and cultural centre, such as you find in France or the United Kingdom, but several. For this reason, we chose four cities as the starting points on our voyages of discovery: the three largest state metropolises – Berlin, Hamburg and Munich – as well as the communications centre, Frankfurt.

Lots of lines run through the colourful mosaic on the map. The north and east are mainly Protestant, but in the south and west Catholics are in the majority. Nowadays Bavaria and Baden-Württemberg are the prosperous states of the republic, whereas in its time the Hanse and later the structurally weak north were richer. Rich and poor does not equate to east and west.

The Bavarians jokingly describe the veal sausage equator (*Weisswurst Äquator*) which runs along the River Main as the border between them and the Prussians, who seem to include everyone who isn't Bavarian. In reality, the border of the Roman empire ran along the Main and the Rhine and left its mark on both culture and lifestyle. That the Romans didn't succeed in moving this border further north had its compensations, as they didn't have to go without their customary wine – it is only grown in Germany on the other side of the Rhine–Main line at Dresden on the Elbe. Baden is excellent wine country but in the north they prefer beer and *klaren* (clear schnapps). The enjoyment of beer is something the Prussians and the Bavarians do have in common.

Dreamy, richly forested mountainous landscape beginning south of the rugged northern German plains... Anticipatory excitement filling the east, while the industrial centre of the Rhine struggles to come to terms with reunification... These descriptions could go on forever, but we will leave them here and begin the journey.

Preceding pages: magnificent decorative detail at the Charlottenburg Palace in Berlin; the bold shapes of the Wallraf-Richartz Museum in front Cologne Cathedral.

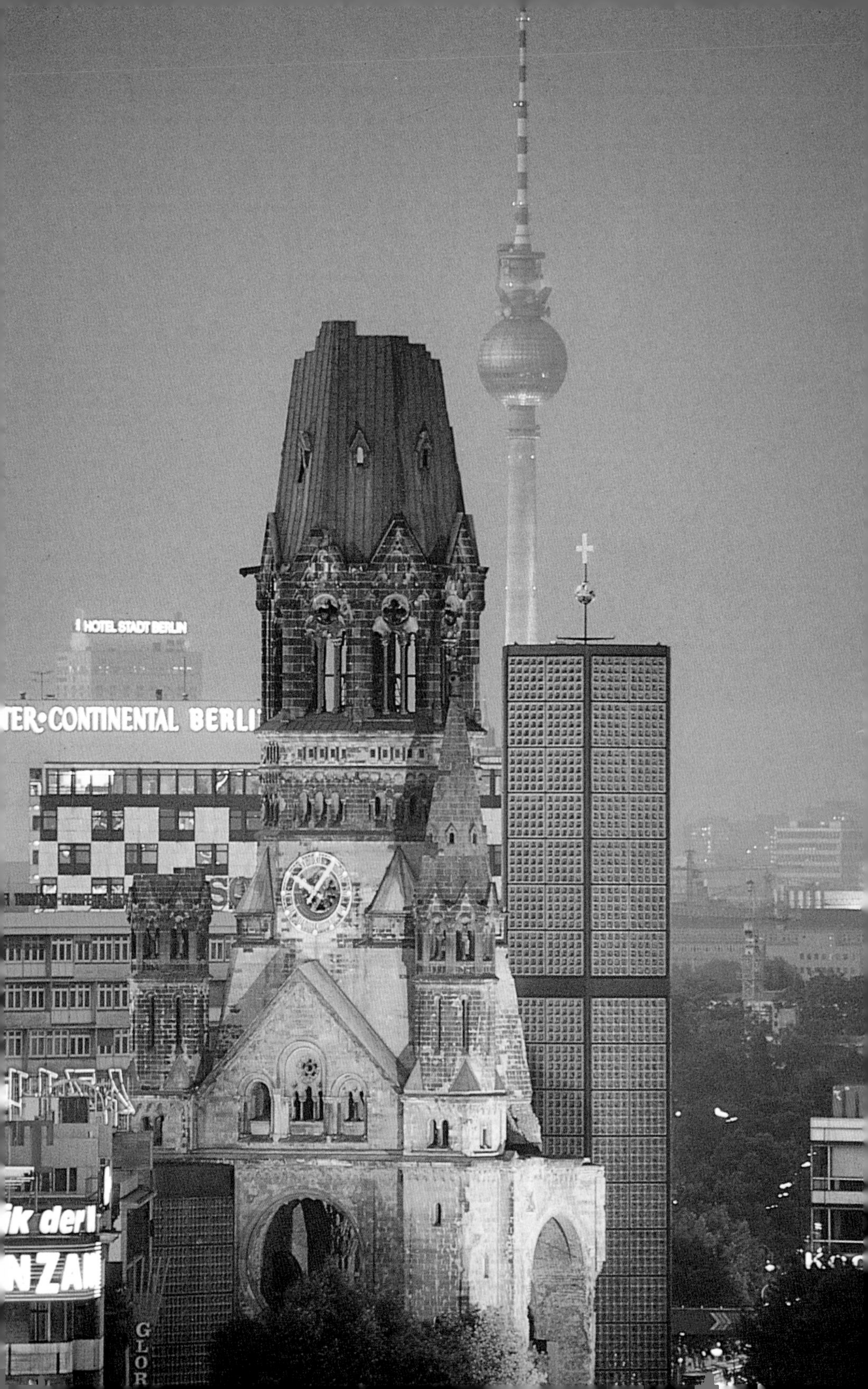
HOTEL STADT BERLIN
TER·CONTINENTAL BERLI
ik derl
NZAM

BERLIN AND THE NEW STATES

When visiting the eastern part of the country, many West Germans still think of their destination as unknown territory. This is quite understandable, even if they can no longer quite tell where the old border used to run.

In Berlin, at least, there is hardly a trace of the old border crossings. Nowhere else do east and west lie so close together; nowhere else are the consequences of reunification felt so strongly. Berlin is frenetically preparing itself for its old/new role as the capital of Germany. Will it be the same as it was in the legendary 1920s? In the summer of 1995, the artists Christo and Jeanne-Claude dealt in their own inimitable way with the past and the future by wrapping up the Reichstag: for two weeks the city centre watched with awe the transformation of the building. Pictures also shape history even if it is only fleetingly. The festival atmosphere is spreading and there is a new feeling of belonging together.

Visitors will relive the classic Berlin, the Kurfürstendamm and the historic centre in the throes of change. They can also look forward to the reliable old mainstays: the Berlin museum landscape is richer than ever, the theatre, even after budget cuts, is still lively, the green oases are as attractive as ever – in terms of the amount and variety of species of birds and plants, the surrounding parks and forests are some of the richest areas in Germany.

Berlin is no longer an island, it stretches its feelers out towards the surrounding countryside. Lying in the middle of eastern Germany, it is counted as one of the five new federal states. Mecklenburg-Vorpommern, Brandenburg, Sachsen (Saxony) and Sachsen-Anhalt make up the other four. While these areas possess countless attractions, many Germans from the south and west are much less familiar with them than they are with neighbouring European countries. The infrastructure has changed dramatically in the past few years to keep up with the needs of the spoilt travelling public.

Here are some of the high points of the journey through this new Germany: around the Mecklenburg Lakes are large areas of beautiful, unspoilt nature. The largest fleet of paddle steamers in Germany operates on the Elbe river between the wild, romantic sandstone mountains on the Czech border and the vine covered terraces near Dresden.

Hardly anyone would want to leave out Weimar, which is not far from the Thüringian Forest, and is the birthplace of the German classical era, so it is hard to avoid the large crowds of visitors to the Goethe House in Frauenplan. In Harz, Otto the Great left untouched the countless Romanesque buildings among the numerous small, half timbered houses.

As a famous old saying has it, "Chemnitz works, Leipzig trades, Dresden lives." So let's go and enjoy it.

Berlin and Surroundings

4 km/ 2,5 miles

Hohen - Neuendorf

Mühlenbeck

Mathiasberg
▲
56

Bötzow

Henningsdorf

Schil

E46

Glienicke / Nordb.

Schönwalde

FROHNAU

BERLINER
FORST
TEGEL

HERMSDF.

LÜBARS

HEILIGENSEE

WAIDMANNS-
LUST

Humboldt-Palace

NOR

Falkensee

BERLINER FORST
SPANDAU

KONRADS-
HÖHE

BORSIG-
WALDE

WITTENAU

WILHEL
RUI

TEGEL

TEGELORT

HAKENFELDE

REINICKENDORF

P.-FALKENHÖH

SPANDAU-
NEUSTADT

Airport
Berlin-Tegel

K.-Schumacher-
Damm

WEDDING

HASELHORST

SPANDAU

Citadel

SIEMENS
STADT

KLOSTER-
FELDE

STRESOW

Charlottenburg
Palace

TIERGARTEN

STAAKEN

WILHELM-
STADT

WESTEND

Bellevue Palace

Brandenbu
Gate

Seeburg

PICHELSDORF

CHARLOTTENBG

Victory Column

Radio Tower

AB.- Dr.
Funkturm

WILMERS-
DF.

SCHÖNE

Finkenberg
▲
75

GATOW

BERLINER

Karlsbg.
▲
78

GRUNEWALD

AB.- Kr.
Schöneb

Fahrland

Groß-
Glienicke

Gatow Airfield

FORST

Grunewald
Hunting Lodge

SCHMARGEN-
DF.

FRIEDENAU

2

KLADOW

Havel

GRUNEWALD

DAHLEM

STEGLITZ

ZEHLENDF.

P.-NEDLITZ

NIKOLASSEE

LICHTER-
FELDE

LANKWITZ

P.-BORNIM

P.-SACROW

WANNSEE

Berlin-
Zehlendorf

Cecilienhof
Palace

273

Kl. Glienicke
Palace

MARIENFEL

SCHÖNOW

Sanssouci
Palace

Babelsberg
Palace

P.-KLEIN-
GLIENICKE

Kleinmachnow

Potsdam

R.-
BABELSBERG

STEIN-
STÜCKEN

Teltow

Stahnsdorf

101

2

Kl.
Ravensberg
▲
114

P.-DREWITZ

Güterfelde

Großbeeren

Mah

Bergholz

Rehbrücke

100

BE.-NIBELUNGEN

BE.-EICHWERDER

Börnicke

BE.-BIRKENHÖHE

Zepernick

BUCH

Weesow

Abzweig.
Berlin - Pankow

Birkholz

Löhme

Werneuchen

ANKEN-
LDE

109

E 74

158

CHHOLZ

KAROW

Lindenberg

Blumberg

Krummensee

EDER-
HÖNHSN.

BLANKENBG.

Ahrensfelde

ANKOW

MALCHOW

WARTENBG.

Mehrow

Altlandsberg

HEINERSDORF

FALKENBG.

Eiche

WEISSENSEE

HOHEN-
SCHÖNHSN.

Bruchmühle

RENZLAUER
BERG

BERLIN

Neuenhagen

LICHTENBG.

Fredersdorf

TV Tower

Socialist Memorial

FRIEDRICHS-
HAIN

TTE

FRIEDRICHS-
FELDE

BIESDF.

KAULS-
DORF

MAHLS-
DORF

1/5

EUZBG.

STRALAU

Spree

Münchehofe

Vogelsdorf

TREPTOW

Soviet
Memorial

MAHLSDF.-
SÜD

Schöneiche

E 74

KARLSHORST

ort
empelhof

NEU-
KÖLLN

OBER-
SCHÖNEWEIDE

UHLEN-
HORST

MPEL-
OF

NIEDER-
SCHÖNEWEIDE

Spree

FRIEDRICH-
HAGEN

WILHELMS-
HAGEN

Wolters-
dorf

RIEN-
RF

BRITZ

JOHANNISTHAL

ADLERSHOF

Gr. Müggelsee

KÖPENICK

RAHNSDORF

Erkner

KOW I

BUCKOW II

ALT-
GLIENICKE

GRÜNAU

Müggelberge

HESSEN-
WINKEL

MÜGGELHEIM

BUCKOW

▲
115

RUDOW

Abzweig.
Berlin - Zentrum

BOHNSDORF

Langer
See

Große
Krampe

HTEN-
ADE

KAROLINEN-
HOF

Seddinsee

Schönefeld Airport

Eichwalde

Neu-Zittau

96

E15

179

SCHMÖCK-
WITZ

Wernsdorf

Zeuthener
See

Schulzendorf

Zeuthen

BERLIN

Following the fall of the Wall, Berlin is exploiting the unique chance to redesign its city centre and make the metropolis the seat of government of the entire republic and once again a place for all Germans. It has to be done quickly in order to take advantage of the remaining post-reunification euphoria before it is dissipated by economic angst.

The old but new capital city is now experiencing its second *Gründerzeit* (its time of foundation). Breakfast is accompanied by radio reports alerting Berliners to the latest roadworks and other traffic hold-ups – either it's the opening of the Brandenburg Gate, Christo's Reichstag "wrap-up", the tunnelling work under the Tiergarten or a visit by some foreign dignitary to the Museum Island. Great historical events have passed with fetching matter-of-factness into the Berliners' everyday life: on Sunday they pedal their bicycles through the former "death strip" of the Wall or play football on the grass in front of the Reichstag.

Berlin, this bizarre city, is an exciting place to live, work and visit. Existentialist artists and innovative young entrepreneurs alike feel themselves drawn by the same Berlin atmosphere. But it is also possible to escape the chaotic bustle very quickly, for example by visiting the Nikolskoe beer garden high above the Wannsee lake when the evening sun spreads its warm light, or by leisurely dipping the oars into the stream on a boat outing among the maze-like backwaters of the River Havel.

Great historical importance: Berlin's history goes back further than one might imagine. Two Slav settlements on opposite sides of the Spree river developed into the trading towns Cölln and Berlin, which united for defensive reasons in 1307 and joined the Hanseatic League in 1359. The event which sealed the city's fate came in 1415, when King Sigismund named the Hohenzollern Friedrich von Nürnberg as Prince of Brandenburg.

From that point, the Hohenzollern dynasty dictated the course of the city's history. In 1486 Berlin became the royal seat of residence, and from 1642 on it was magnificently developed by one Hohenzollern prince after another. Under their rule, Prussia grew to become the greatest state of the German Empire, alongside Habsburg Austria. The coronation of Friedrich III as King of Prussia in 1701 was a further step in this process. The rivalry between the young kingdom and Austria reached its climax in the Seven Years' War (1756–63), from which Prussia emerged strengthened by the official recognition accorded to its place as a European power. The first losses suffered by Prussia didn't come until 1806, when Napoleon's forces occupied Berlin for two years.

This challenge to Prussian power created room for reformist activity, encouraged by the French Revolution and the ideas inherent in the British economic system. With the foundation of the first Berlin University by Wilhelm von Humboldt in 1810 the centre of

Left, a pavement café on the Kurfürstendamm with a view of the Memorial Church. Right, underground at Wittenbergplatz.

reformist ideas moved from Königsberg to the royal seat of residence. Freiherr vom Stein and Prince von Hardenburg were among the most important figures who worked for Prussia's political and economic revival, which ended in 1819 with the resignations of the reformist ministers Boyen and Humboldt.

In 1848 Berlin was the centre of Germany's March Revolution, in which conservative forces again retained the upper hand. After the foundation of the German Empire in 1871 the Prussian King also ruled as German Emperor, and Berlin became the imperial capital.

With the coming of the industrial revolution the populations of Germany's big cities grew at an explosive rate, and workers' settlements sprang up around the large factories. At the close of World War I the last German Emperor had to abdicate and Karl Liebknecht proclaimed the Free Socialist Republic from the walls of Berlin's Stadtschloss.

After the short-lived Weimer Republic Adolf Hitler chose Berlin as his political powerbase from 1933. World War II led to the unconditional surrender of Germany, and of course of Berlin, which was almost completely destroyed. The city had four-power status (USA, Great Britain, France, the Soviet Union) until 1990. The Soviet-ruled sector was cut off from the rest of the city in 1961 in the dramatic overnight construction of the Berlin Wall.

The Berlin Wall: It now belongs to history, the Wall which was the symbol of the city for 28 years. Visitors who want to see what remains of it today must seek out the former Prussian provincial parliament building in **Berlin-Mitte** or the East-Side-Gallery in Friedrichshain, where artists work away for their own posterity on bits of the demolished Wall. Its old line can hardly be recognized in present-day Berlin. City planners have long since been falling over themselves to develop the wasteland of the former "death strip" – it had, after all, cut right through some of the best land in the city.

The scenes of 13 August 1961, the day Berlin was so abruptly cut in two, are still vivid in many people's minds.

Literally overnight, not only were capitalism and communism divided but perplexed families, too – children from parents, friends from one another, Berliners from their places of work. The Soviet-inspired Wall was 161 km (100 miles) long, 4 metres (13 feet) high, studded with watchtowers. To Erich Honecker's East German regime, it was an "antifascist protective wall". To the rest of the world, it was a symbol of repression and the place where more than 70 people died.

Although Honecker declared as late as the spring of 1989 that the Wall would stand for another 100 years, the opening of the Hungarian border for fleeing East Germans on 9 November of that year led inevitably to its fall: masses of people flooded out of East Berlin, welcomed by jubilant West Berliners. The whole city was overjoyed.

Today there are deliberations on how the era of the Wall can most appropriately be remembered. An extensive memorial complex is being prepared on Bernauerstrasse, and one woman artist **The Wall was sold off as art.**

put forward the suggestion in a competition entry for the former course of the Wall to be marked in the ground by a copper band.

Now that the Wall has gone, perhaps the most striking thing about Berlin is that it has two city centres. On the one side, on Alexanderplatz, the TV tower, built as the unmistakable emblem of the "capital of the GDR", marks the historical centre of Berlin, Berlin-Mitte. On the other, the blue Mercedes Star affixed to the Europa Center marks the location of the Kurfürstendamm, the bustling centre of the western part of the city. It is *still* the bustling centre, but since the collapse of the Wall the elegant boulevard Unter den Linden has begun to usurp the position held by the "Ku'damm" as *the* street for taking a stroll. And as far as the "No. 1 business address" is concerned, Friedrichstrasse is busily making up for the lost years.

The Kurfürstendamm: Nevertheless, the Ku'damm has not yet lost its powers of attraction. "I so long for my Kurfürstendamm," once sang Berlin's very own inimitable singer and actress Hildegard Knef. There's not much left, though, of the proud and beautiful late 19th-century mansions which once lined the noble boulevard and which suffered severe bombing in World War II. For centuries the Ku'damm had played an important role in Berlin after Prince Elector Joachim II had it laid out in the 16th century as a bridle path leading out to the hunting grounds. Kurfürstendamm means "The Electors' Road".

Only with Germany's rapid industrial expansion from 1871 onwards did the street begin to take shape. Inspired by the Champs Elysées in Paris, Bismarck decided that he wanted just such a boulevard for the new capital of the *Reich*. Building work proceeded in "Wilhelmenian" style: generous, ornate and even florid; truly representative of the age.

The Kurfürstendamm became the place where Berlin was youthful, where the wildest entertainment could be had and where everything considered bohemian was on offer. That was particularly the case during the "raving '20s".

The most famous meeting-place in those days was the Romanische Café, situated where the austere Europa Center now stands.

After the ravages of World War II and the division of the city into east and west, the Kurfürstendamm recast itself as the cultural centre of West Berlin. But the old splendour of the Ku'damm could never be recreated. Ugly new buildings replaced the fine old ones lost in the war. The finer businesses, such as chic boutiques and expensive antique shops, moved to better addresses between Adenauerplatz and Fasanenstrasse, while Wittenbergplatz became the home of fast-food chains, porno shops and department stores.

But Wittenbergplatz (at its corner with Tauentzienstrasse) is also the address of the stylish store Kaufhaus des Westen (the Department Store of the West), known as KaDeWe, a huge department store with a floor to please every taste. The building was the only one of Berlin's great department stores to withstand the war-time bombing.

The first place on the Ku'damm most people head for is **Breitscheidplatz** with the ruins of the **Kaiser Wilhelm Memorial Church**, together with its blue-glazed rebuilt version. The towering church was built in 1895 in memory of the well-loved Emperor Wilhelm I. It was left in its ruined state after the war, and a slender bell-tower with a low church assembly hall was built beside it, a structure the Berliners refer to as their "lipstick and powder compact". Since 1983, particularly in the summer, all sorts of people have tended to gather around the **Wasserklops**, a huge fountain created by the sculptor Schmettau which stands next to the **Europa Center**. The building is one of the tallest in Berlin, crowned by that highly symbolic Mercedes Star and housing a huge range of shops, restaurants, bars and even a casino.

A few steps away is the famous **Café Kranzler**, renowned for its fine pastries. It's no longer the Kranzler of the pre-war days – that was in Berlin-Mitte – but it's still a pleasant place to take a pavement table and watch Berlin life go by. Entertainment of a cultural nature can be enjoyed in the evening by booking seats for the **Schaubühne** on Lehiner Platz. Originally in Kreuzberg, this theatre made a name for itself through the brilliant productions of its director, Peter Stein. It remains one of the city's best theatres – although, since it moved into its new domicile, performances have tended to lack something of their experimental vivacity.

Historical centre: Things are a lot more leisurely over in **Berlin-Mitte**, where Berlin was really born. That isn't to say that it's a boring part of the city – quite the contrary. Here one is endlessly confronted by Berlin and Prussian history, reminders of the city's beginnings as two small settlements, Berlin and Cölln, which united in 1359. Of course, most of the historical buildings to be seen here are not the originals and much – the City Palace of the Hohenzollern Emperors, for example – has been lost forever. Although severely damaged during the war, it was the Stalinist authorities of the former GDR who actu-

Pavement cafés on every corner.

ally finished the building off, back in the 1950s. The copper-coloured Palace of the Republic, seat of parliament and popular amusement during SED rule, now stands in its stead.

The gateway to Berlin-Mitte is the **Brandenburg Gate**. Since its inauguration in 1791, this structure has always been a symbol of the fate first of Prussia and then of Germany. Napoleon marched triumphantly through it on his way to Russia, and sent back to Paris as war booty the gate's crowning ensemble, the Quadriga, the goddess of victory on her chariot drawn by four horses. Eight years later, in 1814, it was brought back in triumph by Marshal Blücher.

Barricades were erected at the gate during the revolution of 1848. Kings and emperors paraded here. The revolutionaries of 1918 streamed through it on their way to the palace to proclaim the republic. The Nazis also staged their victory parades through the Brandenburg Gate, and after their downfall in 1945, Soviet soldiers hoisted the Red Flag on the Quadriga.

Following the construction of the Berlin Wall, the entire area around the monument was cordoned off, both from the east and the west. During and after the collapse of the Wall, the gate became a central symbol of the hopes and expectations of a united Germany. It also became the meeting place for all those who counted themselves, in the words of the former West Berlin mayor Walter Momper, among "the happiest people in the world". So much for the rhetoric. The Brandenburg Gate has now been turned into a traffic island: while bicycles and taxis can go right through the middle, cars have to go round.

At the other side of the gate is Pariser Platz. World War II obliterated the houses that used to surround the square, once the abode of important personalities such as the Prussian Prime Minister Friedrich Karl von Savigny, the composer Giacomo Meyerbeer, the dramatist August von Kotzebue and the painter Max Liebermann. The Prussian Academy of Arts was also based here. The periphery of the square is now begin-

The Brandenburg Gate.

BERLIN MUSEUMS

L ike so many things in Berlin, museums often come in pairs. Each half of the divided city, after all, made the claim to be the administrator of the Prussian cultural heritage. The reorganisation of the "Staatliche Museen zu Berlin – Preussischer Kulturbesitz" ("State Museums of Berlin – Prussian cultural possessions") is under consideration; temporary closures are unfortunately unavoidable.

Museum Island (Museumsinsel): The Pergamon Museum contains Berlin's most highly-regarded artistic treasure, the Pergamon Altar (180–159 BC) from Western Turkey, one of the seven wonders of the world. Under the same roof can be found the Near Eastern Museum (Vorderasiatische Museum) and the Ethnological Museum. The Bode Museum contains examples of late antique, Byzantine and Egyptian art, as well as German, Italian and Dutch paintings and sculptures from the 15th to the 18th centuries. The Old National Gallery (Alte Nationalgalerie) is being renovated and its paintings and sculptures from the 18th to the 20th centuries are being shown until the year 2000 in the Hamburger-bahnhof, Invalidenstrasse, which also houses

the Erich Marx Collection of Andy Warhol and other modern painters.

Nearby, in the Unter den Linden boulevard, is the German Historical Museum (Deutsche Historische Museum). Apart from exhibitions with Prussian-German themes, exhibits illustrating the more recent history of the GDR are to be seen.

Cultural Forum (Kulturforum, Kemperplatz): The Museum of Musical Instruments (Musikinstrumentenmuseum) on Tiergartenstrasse contains an impressive collection of more than 2,500 instruments. In the airy Museum of Arts and Crafts (Kunstgwerbemuseum), which was built in 1985 by Rolf Gutbrod, there are textiles, furniture, glassware, fashion and goldsmiths' work from the Middle Ages until the present day.

The New National Gallery (Neue Nationalgalerie) was conceived as a modern building by Ludwig Mies van der Rohe but is basically a classical temple. Apart from well-known GDR artists, Oskar Kokoschka, Otto Dix and many others of the 20th century are exhibited. The Copperplate Engraving Cabinet (Kupferstichkabinett), which moved here from Dahlem in 1994, has 80,000 drawings, watercolours, gouache works and 520,000 graphic pages by artists from all over the world. The Painting Gallery (Gemäldegalerie) on the corner of Sigismundstrasse has paintings from the Middle Ages to the late 18th century.

Charlottenburg: The Nofretete in the Egyptian Museum (Ägyptisches Museum), the chalk bust of the wife of the Egyptian Pharaoh Echnaton (1358 BC), is of course world-famous. Across the way, the Antikenmuseum (Museum of Antiquities) presents Greek and Roman works of art, including the Hildesheimer Treasure Trove (Hildesheimer Silberfund) from the time of the Emperor Augustus. Charlottenburg Palace itself contains several collections: the historical rooms (middle section, right wing, upper storey of the new wing) were the living rooms of Frederick I and of Frederick the Great. On the ground-floor is the popular Galerie der Romantik (Gallery of the Romantics), with paintings by Caspar David Friedrich, Ludwig Richter and Carl Blechen. The Berggruen Collection in the Stüler building has 69 Picasso's and a number of African exhibits.

Dahlem: This museum complex, between Arnimallee and Lensstrasse, combines the Sculpture Collection (Skulpturensammlung), the Museum for Later Antiquities (Museum für Spätantike), Indian, East Asian and Islamic art, as well as an eye-opening and colourful collection of ethnic art. It is certainly worth the extra effort at reaching this part of the city. ∎

Sculpture on the Pergamon Altar.

ning to take shape once again, with a variety of new buildings.

The square marks the beginning of **Under den Linden**, undoubtedly the most Prussian of Berlin's streets, planned by the Great Elector in 1647. Here, too, much was annihilated during the war and ruined by socialist misplanning in the post-war years. However, strolling down this elegant boulevard today the ambience of the old metropolis can almost be touched. The classical structures conceived by the 19th-century architect Karl Friedrich Schinkel, which transformed the city into "Athens on the Spree", testify to the fact that Berlin once ranked among the most beautiful European cities.

It is open to debate which of Schinkel's buildings is the most beautiful. Some maintain that it is the **Schauspielhaus** (theatre) on **Gendarmenmarkt**. Framed by the German Cathedral and the French Cathedral the entire square is an aesthetically perfect ensemble. The old Opern Platz, now renamed **Bebel Platz**, is where the Nazis burnt more than 20,000 books in 1933. At its centre, the Equestrian Statue of Frederick the Great is one of the most important works of Berlin sculptor Christian Daniel Rauch. The square was planned by Frederick the Great as the Forum Fridericianum. The opera house, the Old Library and St Hedwig's Cathedral combine to create a masterpiece of urban architecture.

On the opposite side of Unter den Linden are two more bastions of German culture, the **Staatsbibliothek zu Berlin** (Library for Prussian Cultural Heritage) and the adjacent **Humboldt University**, whose alumni include Albert Einstein and the brothers Grimm.

The **Neue Wache** on Unter den Linden is Schinkel's most complete work. It was his first building in Berlin, and it certainly possesses the harmony of Classical simplicity. In GDR days, People's Army soldiers goose-stepped in front of the Neue Wache which served as a memorial to the victims of Fascism and militarism. After much discussion, the temple-like building was re-inaugurated as the **Central Memorial** of the Federal Republic of Germany in 1993. The bronze pietà *Mother and Son* by Käthe Kollwitz is dedicated to "all victims of war and violence".

Further towards the river, the **Zeughaus** (former Arsenal) is Berlin's largest baroque building and one of Germany's finest. Schlüter's 22 warriors' death masks in the courtyard are well worth closer inspection. The building is now a museum.

The **Old Museum** on the **Museum Island** is regarded as Schinkel's most impressive building. Inside and out it was entirely designed to serve its purpose, namely to display works of art. But then the whole museum island is, in both form and content, an extraordinary artistic ensemble. It requires more than an afternoon to visit all the museums, the **Old** and **New Museum**, the **National Gallery**, the **Pergamon Museum** and the **Bode Museum** (*see* page 108).

Berlin Cathedral is a monument to the Wilhelminian expression of splendour. The Cathedral was built in 1894, as the "chief church of Protestantism". It served as the family church of the

Hohenzollerns, where the imperial children were baptised, confirmed, later married and where family members were buried. Ninety-seven Hohenzollern tombs can be viewed in the crypt.

From here it's not far to legendary **Alexanderplatz**. At the moment there's not much to be found there of the bustling scene of the 1920s described by Alfred Döblin in his book "Berlin Alexanderplatz". In the coming years, however, a high-rise ensemble of offices, shops and flats is to thrust its way skywards. Whether the architects succeed in bringing to it the flair demanded by the Berliners remains to be seen.

Culture al fresco: The name of the **Tierpark** district may justifiably be associated with the well-loved park of the same name, but the Tierpark is much more than that. Its Kulturforum, planned as a post-war equivalent of the Museum Island, is dominated by architect Hans Scharoun's **Philharmonie** concert hall. This is where the Berlin Philharmonic shone under the direction of Herbert von Karajan; now it's conducted in different but still masterly style by Claudio Abbado. In the old diplomatic quarter, the **Diplomatenviertel**, imposing villas which once housed embassies and consulates still stand in the Tiergartenstrasse, although many ruins still scar the overgrown park-like gardens. The imperial-era **Reichstag** has reawoken to new life after decades of slumber. The English architect Sir Norman Foster is redesigning it as the future home of the German Parliament, the Bundestag.

Lordly residences: Before its incorporation by Berlin, **Charlottenberg** was the richest town of the Brandenburg Marches. Imposing villas around central **Savignyplatz** still give an idea of its past wealth. Its central attraction now is the **Charlottenburg Palace**, named after Queen Sophie Charlotte, grandmother of Frederick the Great. Apart from its many famous collections (*see page 108*) its magnificent park is well worth a visit (S-Bahn Westend).

A less elegant contrast is provided by the aluminium-clad **International Congress Centre,** beside which the **Funk-**

A game of football in front of the Reichstag.

turm television tower (with viewing platform) and the **fair grounds** of the 1920s and 1930s seem positively old-fashioned (S-Bahn Witleben).

The Nazi reign of terror is commemorated at the **Gedenkstätte Plötzensee.** Hundreds of political prisoners and freedom fighters of many nations were murdered in the infamous execution centre (S-Bahn Beusselstrasse). The **Berlin Olympic Stadium** at the Reichssportfeld was built by the March brothers for the 1938 summer Olympics. The Olympic grounds also contain the **swimming stadium,** the **German Sport Forum,** the **Maifeld** festival site and the **Waldbühne,** one of Europe's finest open-air stages and a mecca for rock fans (U-Bahn Olympia Stadium).

Multicultural life: After the militant street battles and house squatter scandals of the early 1980s, unruly **Kreuzberg** has in the meantime quietened down somewhat. It lives on its reputation, which has become a legend since the fall of the Wall. The area has developed into a show piece of "multicultural

Charlottenburg is home to many famous collections.

life". Much has changed since German unification. Kreuzberg is no longer on the edge of west Berlin but back in the centre and the Wall isn't its neighbour any more but the suburbs of Berlin-Mitte and Treptow. Kreuzberg still has a high proportion of foreigners: Turks, Greeks and citizens of former Yugoslavia make up 30 percent of its residents.

Kreuzberg took its name from the eponymous hill, which at 66 metres (216 feet) is one of the highest points in Berlin. The **Kreuzberg Memorial** at its summit was designed by Karl Friedrich Schinkel in 1821 in memory of the victories of the wars of liberation. Around the Kreuzberg is the **Viktoria Park,** an oasis of relaxation for local residents. The street battles which used to be a feature of Kreuzberg life every 1 May have moved to **Friedrichshain** and Prenzlauer Berg. Friedrichshain's Mainzer Strasse in November 1990 was the scene of the fiercest battles between squatters and police ever seen in Berlin.

A new trendy district: Life sometimes gets unruly, too, in the **Prenzlauer Berg**

district. During the industrialisation and land speculation of the 19th century this district just outside the Berlin city limits arose as a housing area for low-paid workers and the poor. War-time bombing and the demolition and clearing which followed left airy backyards where children today play and their parents hold barbecue and beer parties.

The heart of Prenzlauer Berg is the area around **Kollwitzplatz.** When the evening sun glows mellowly on the faded street facades and the restaurants and cafés have opened their doors and the gates to their beer gardens the area throbs with life and you could almost think you were in Italy.

This is the home territory of the "alternative" society, students and many elderly people. Friendly bars and pubs, art galleries and studios have established themselves here. One street, **Husemannstrasse**, was spruced up in the GDR days as a showpiece of "Old Berlin" urban style, and today it has the atmosphere of an open-air museum, although it's undeniably beautiful.

An old village on the Weisser See: One peripheral area with typically Berlin suburban ambiance is **Weissensee**, named after the Weissen See lake, around which the village with the same name was founded in about 1230. Today the lake, with its **park** and **open-air theatre**, is one of the chief attractions of this area. The **Jewish Cemetery** on Herbert-Baum-Strasse is one of the most important of its kind in all Germany. Here lie such leading Berlin cultural figures as the architect Walter Gropius, the sculptor Hugo Lederer, the hotelier Berthold Kempinski and the publisher Rudolf Mosse.

Peripheral sights: Fame attached itself to **Reinickendorf**, a surprisingly green district of northern Berlin, because of its **Märkische Viertel**, a collection of gleaming white high-rise residential blocks for 50,000 residents, built from 1963–74. The area was once the centre of a raging controversy, but most of its residents are not proud to live here. Another local attraction is the Humboldt-Schlösschen, a small palace which Wil-

Escaping the bustle.

helm von Humboldt redesigned to his own plans in 1824, and the old farm village of **Lübars**, with its parish church of 1793, ancient farmsteads and welcoming "Alte Dorfkrug Lübars".

Berlin's green corner: The charm exuded by **Zehlendorf** is defined by its successful combination of moneyed mansions, forests and stretches of water and its cultural offering. The Grosse Wannsee, a lake with a famous beach, the **Strandbad**, comes to life as early as Easter, when the water-sport clubs ceremonially sail into the new season. **Dahlem** is the site of the main buildings of the **Freie Universität**, with their nearby **Museum Complex** (*see page 108*). The pearl of the Havel river and lakes is romantic **Peacock Island** – the Pfaueninsel – reachable only by ferry. Its gardens take hours to explore.

Older than Berlin: When Berlin and Cölln established themselves in the 13th century in the Spree basin they lay between two fortified settlements which looked back on a longer history: **Spandau** and **Köpenick**. Both fought hard but unsuccessfully in 1920 against their incorporation within Berlin, and since then they have tried to retain their original character. Located astride important trade routes, the **Spandau citadel** won strategic importance in medieval times. Under the rule of Prussia's "Soldier King" the city became, along with Potsdam, the kingdom's arms factory. In more recent times, Spandau became known for the prison for war criminals in which Rudolf Hess, Adolf Hitler's deputy, was detained for many years. When he committed suicide there in 1987 the prison was torn down and a shopping centre built in its place.

Köpenick won headlines in 1906 when the cobbler Voigt took over the city treasury, disguised in a captain's uniform. The Kaiser is said to have been so amused by the ruse that Voigt was pardoned. Carl Zuckmayer based his 1932 play *Der Hauptmann von Köpenick* (*The Captain of Koepenick*) on the incident. Köpenick has the loveliest area of water in Berlin, together with the city's largest lake, the **Müggelsee**.

The Wannsee.

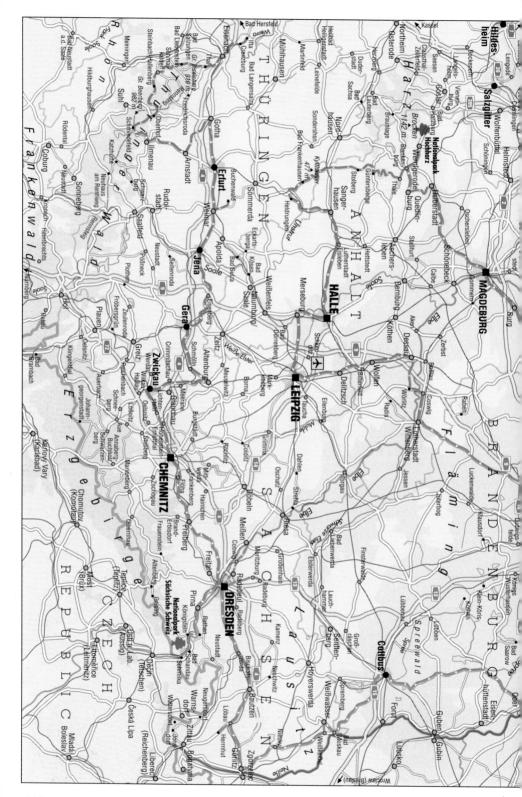

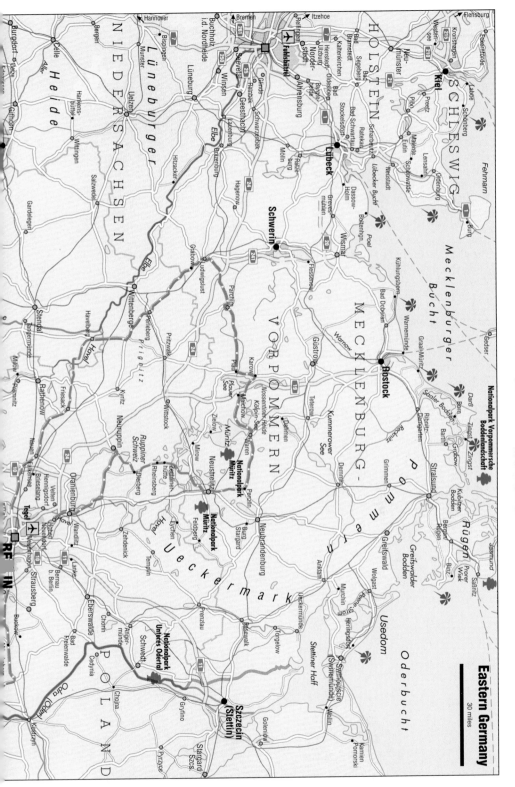

Eastern Germany

30 miles

Nationalpark Vorpommersche
Boddenlandschaft

SCHLESWIG-
HOLSTEIN

NIEDERSACHSEN

Lüneburger
Heide

MECKLENBURG-
VORPOMMERN

Mecklenburger
Bucht

Pommern

Rügen

Usedom

Oderbucht

Ueckermark

POLAND

Flensburg
Eckernförde
Westen-see
Kronshagen
Laboe
Schönberg
Schönberg
Kiel
Preetz
Probstei
Mielente
Schwentine
Oldenburg
Eutin
Fehmarn
Burg
Neustadt

Hannover
Bremen
Itzehoe
Pellingen
Neumünster
Bad Bramstedt
Kaltenkirchen
Henstedt-Ulzburg
Norder-stedt
Bargteheide
Stockelsdorf
Bad Schwartau
Lübeck
Scharbeutz
Lübecker Bucht
Kühlungsborn
Warnemünde
Rostock
Graal-Müritz
Darß
Zingst
Zingst
Born
Grabow
Bartli
Ribnitz-Damgarten

Westerland
Buchholz i.d. Nordheide
Bispingen
Seevetal
Reinbek
Geesthacht
Schwarzenbek
Lauenburg
Mölln
Ratzeburg
Dassow-Holm
Grevesmühlen
Poel
Wismar
Boitzenburg
Flessenow
Schwerin
Bad Doberan
Kubitzer Bodden
Bergen
Binz
Prorer Wiek
Saßnitz
Jasmund

Burgdorf
Uelzen
Celle
Bergen
Munster
Lüneburg
Hitzacker
Bleckede
Boizenburg
Ludwigslust
Parchim
Gustrow
Teterow
Dahmen
Stralsund
Grimmen
Greifswalder Bodden
Greifswald
Wolgast

Gifhorn
Hankens-büttel
Wittingen
Salzwedel
Grabow
Plau
Karow
Nossentiner-Heide
Plauer See
Matchow
Malchin
Kölpin-See
Varen
Müritz
Kummerower See
Demmin
Murchin
Heringsdorf
Swinoujscie (Swinemünde)
Zinnowitz

Gardelegen
Wittenberge
Perleberg
Pritzwalk
Zielow
Mirow
Neustrelitz
Perdin
Burg Stargard
Neubrandenburg
Anklam
Ueckermünde
Torgelow
Stettiner Haff
Ahlbeck
Uecker

Stendal
Tangermünde
Miesow
Havelberg
Wittstock
Neuruppin
Zechliner-hütte
Rheinsberg
Nationalpark Müritz
Feldberg
Lychen
Templin
Prenzlau
Pasewalk

Milow
Rhinow
Rathenow
Friesack
Kyritz
Oranienburg
Velten
Hennigsdorf
Zehdenick
Wandlitz
Bernau b. Berlin
Chorin
Angermünde
Schwedt
Oder

Nauen
Falkensee
Tegel
Neuenhagen
Michael-Neuenhorst
Lanke
Bernau b. Berlin
Strausberg
Buckow
Eberswalde
Bad Freienwalde
Cedynia
Chojna
Schwedt
Nationalpark Unteres Odertal
Szczecin (Stettin)
Gryfino
Golenow
Kamien Pomorski
Stargard Szcz.

Küstrin
Oranienburg
Briesetang
Havel
Küstrin
Odra (Oder)
Gryfino
Chojna
Pyrzyce

POTSDAM

For hundreds of years this small Slavic fishing town on the Havel was of absolutely no importance. It was originally the Great Elector who lost his heart to this sleepy town. Potsdam was first mentioned in the record books in AD 993, and was known as Potztupimi (which literally translated means "under the oak tree"). The Great Elector Friedrich Wilhelm made this town his second home after Berlin and had the city's castle built in 1662. Potsdam became an important part of the history of Prussia due to the Tolerance Edict of 1685 through which the Elector introduced asylum for people who were expelled from France, the principal benefactors being the Huguenots.

The Great Elector's son, Friedrich I, held an extravagant court at Potsdam, in imitation of Versailles, but his son Friedrich Wilhelm I, who was later known as the Soldier King, had no time for such frivolity. He was the first European monarch to wear uniform, and his motto was "the soul is for God the rest is for oneself". He drummed into his subjects the virtues of prayer, duty hard work and thriftiness. These are all traits which have become identified with the Prussian character. Wilhelm I expanded Potsdam into a garrison city to house his elite troops.

The city's present wealth and glory is mainly thanks to Friedrich II, also known as Frederick the Great. The **Sanssouci Palace** was the result of one of his own designs. Having come here to escape the business of the government in the capital, he went on to bequeath numerous beautiful rococo buildings to Potsdam, which became known as the "pearl on the Havel".

His great nephew Wilhelm IV continued in this great tradition. The Prussian chief architect, Karl Friedrich Schinkel, made a classical impression on the face of Potsdam. The sprawling gardens were laid out by the landscape designer Peter Joseph Lenné. A unique and harmoni-

Sanssouci Palace was the favourite home of Frederick the Great.

ous symbiosis between buildings and nature emerged, a heritage which still characterises Potsdam.

The popularity of Potsdam flourished and, just before World War I, Crown Prince Wilhelm (who never came to the throne) had the **Cecilienhof Palace** built in the English manorial style. As soldiers were dying in the trenches, the prince allowed himself the luxury of this summer retreat. In the summer of 1945, the Cecilienhof was chosen as the conference venue for the three victorious powers who decided on the future of the defeated Germany. The inside of the palace was swiftly reconstructed to enable it to be used as a working environment for the delegates. The conference room with the famous round table and the studies of Churchill, Stalin and Truman have been preserved in their original state and are open to the public.

The Cecilienhof is also the home of a first-class hotel and a fine restaurant.

Sanssouci: Whenever anyone speaks about a visit to Potsdam they are usually referring to Sanssouci. Frederick the Great had this small palace designed in 1744 according to his own plans and had it built in an old vineyard despite objections from his architect, Knobelsdorff. It is here that Frederick patronised the fine arts and gave his renowned flute concerts. He also welcomed and entertained his famous guest, the French philosopher Voltaire, in order to debate literature and philosophy with him. Today, tourists flock to Sanssouci, where seeing the 12 tastefully and expensively decorated rooms can become a real test of one's patience, especially on hot summer days. Outside, the 97-metre (300-ft) garden front (parterre) with its 35 huge caryatids and dome with the name Sanssouci inscribed in gold letters, is very impressive.

The Prussian Palace and Berlin-Brandenburg Parks Foundation not only sponsors the palace but also the expansive, 290-hectare (717-acre) park which contains numerous architecturally interesting objects that are well worth seeing. Left of the main alley, behind the precisely planned and planted groups

Powerful delegates at the Potsdam Conference.

of trees, the gold of the **Chinese Tea House**, with the figure of a rotund mandarin on the roof, dazzlingly reflects the sunlight. The clover leaf-shaped house represents the preference for exotic Chinese styles prevalent in the 18th century. At the end of the long main path there is the **New Palace** (Neue Palais), a typical example of palace architecture, which was the home of Friedrich's household and guests towards the end of his reign. Nearby, there is the impressive **Charlottenhof Palace**, which was designed and built in a classical style by Schinkel for Wilhelm IV, as were the atmospheric **Roman Baths**. On the other side of the park you will find the **Orangery**, which was erected in the Italian Renaissance style. The orange trees were not the only visitors spending their winters in these long halls. The crowned heads of friendly nations also stayed here.

The city centre: Potsdam was once one of Germany's most beautiful cities, next to Dresden and Würzburg, but today one would have to look very closely in order to find evidence as to how this reputation came about. Before the reunification, the ignorance of the founding fathers of East Germany destroyed the beauty of the town centre by building high-rise blocks side by side with historically important buildings. Afterwards, renovations on the crumbling facades and caved-in roofs were never started early enough because of local political problems.

The Broadway of Potsdam is Brandenburgerstrasse, a pedestrian zone which stretches between the bright yellow Brandenburg Gate on the one side to Saint Peter and Paul's Catholic church on the other. A very active commercial area is finally developing, with antique shops, leather goods shops and small bars in the surrounding side streets, such as Lindenstrasse and Dortustrasse.

The **Dutch Quarter** (Holländische Viertel) is a big attraction. Friedrich Wilhelm I was inspired by the red brick gables of Dutch houses when building these four blocks. The Soldier King even tried to lure Dutch craftsmen and artists to settle in this area, but few

actually came. He therefore moved Prussian craftsmen and his infantry into some of the buildings. The world-famous Alexander Schuke organ building company was based here during the years that the city was part of East Germany. Because there are still many unsolved problems concerning the ownership of property, many of the buildings seem sadly run down, while others have been beautifully restored.

If you wander down Mittelstrasse or Benkertstrasse you can see that a few craftsmen have chosen to settle in this area again. For example, you will find a violin maker, a goldsmith, a manufacturer of scales and a brass instrument maker running businesses here

There is a rather surprising building in the old market place (Alten Markt) in front of the **Church of St Nicholas**, which is yet another example of Schinkel's work. Known locally as the tin can, it is in fact a modern theatre which the city fathers decided to construct soon after reunification on what had been, up until 1960, the site of the im-

Frederick the Great.

118

posing Potsdam Palace. This metal monstrosity was built in response to the lack of suitable space for the Hans-Otto theatre. The hasty decision was made solely in order to save time until an agreement could be made about whether to rebuild the city palace or to erect a modern building on this historic site.

The powers that ruled in East Germany also decided to tear down the **Garrison Church** (Garnisonskirche), once a symbol of Prussian militarism and God-fearing morality, which used to stand on the land at the corner of Dortustrasse and Breite Strasse. In 1945, shortly before the end of World War II, this church was burnt out, when Potsdam was subjected to intensive bombing, but the walls were left standing. It was the demolition experts who finally brought these walls down in 1968. The Data Centre now stands on the site.

The internationally known **Babelsberg Film Studios**, under the aegis of the UFA and DEFA organisations, have not lost their magic. The silent film *The Death Dance (Der Totentanz)* starring Asta Nielsen and, later, Paul Wegener's *Golem* are still remembered today. One famous film after another was shot here with stars such as Lida Baarova and Gustav Fröhlich. During the war, the propaganda minister, Joseph Goebbels, ordered the production of the so-called rallying films which were designed to animate the demoralised nation. Films such as *The Great Freedom Number Seven (Die grosse Freiheit Nr. 7)* emerged from these studios.

Anyone interested in the history of film and cinema should visit the **Film Museum** in Potsdam's Breitestrasse. The building that was once the Royal Stables is now home to an exhibition of well-diplayed cinema posters and other relics of the past. For a glimpse into the modern film industry there is the Studio Tour that explores film-making techniques, the make-up and wardrobe studios and the props stores. Whole streets have been constructed for background scenery. The stunt shows, called "film experience shows", promise racing hearts and sweating palms.

Polish restorers at Sanssouci.

THE MECKLENBURG LAKES

There is a choice of routes from Berlin to the Mecklenburg Lakes. You can either join the stream of city dwellers queued up along the Berlin–Rostock motorway, or you can follow the Brandenburg side roads and enter a landscape that seems, like Sleeping Beauty, to have just been woken up. The best piece of advice is to take this leisurely route along the centuries-old avenues and the bumpy cobbled roads.

The countryside is pleasantly varied. On the one hand you have the sandy earth with its dusty fields and dark pine woods. On the other, you can enjoy the soft meadows, which virtually drip with water and always end up in a lake. The towns and villages were named after old noble families such as Bredows and Ribbecks. The writer Theodor Fontane (1819–98) described the villages and the area in his book *Strolls through the Brandenburg Marches* and thus brought the area to the attention of outsiders.

On the trail of writers: Fontane was born in **Neuruppin** (population 27,000), which was rebuilt in an early classical style following a fire which destroyed the original town in 1787. In the town **museum** there are numerous Fontane memorabilia as well as exhibits on the life of Karl Friedrich Schinkel (1781–1841), the town's second son. Schinkel made his career in Berlin as a master builder, but here in his hometown, too, the **Dominican Cloisters** (13th century) were rebuilt according to his plans.

The surrounding areas, with forests and water in abundance, are known as the Rhin, Luch and the Ruppin Switzerland respectively. Fontane's descriptions of this area can be used as a guide. A visit to **Rheinsberg** (population 5,500) is another literary must. Rheinsberg is the setting of *Rheinsberg: a Book for Lovers* by Kurt Tucholsky. With a gentle romantic touch, he managed to change this small town into a place of pilgrimage for people in love who wished to enjoy a "series of dazzling days" as Tucholsky's characters Claire and Wölf-

chen did. Above all, there is a palace, a small Sanssouci surrounded by a fairy tale park and an old town laid out like a chess board. There are round towers, a colonnade of pillars which stretch down to the Rheinsberg lake and plenty of northern German rococo, which all go back to the time of Wenzeslaus von Knobelsdorff (1699–1753), a companion and favourite architect of Frederick the Great.

Unique landscapes: It would take a lifetime to get to know the meandering rivers and lakes which belong to the Mecklenburg Lake District north of Rheinsberg. If the mathematical facts are correct, there are about 1,800 lakes in the Mecklenburg-Vorpommern area, which is one and a half times the size of Greater Hamburg. Wildlife has flourished in this region following the creation of three nature reserves in 1990: the Feldberg-Lychener Lake District (1,120 sq. km/432 sq. miles), the Müritz National Park (313 sq. km/121 sq. miles) and the Nossentiner-Schwinzer Heath (320 sq. km/124 sq. miles). Müritz and

the other lakes have become home to wildlife such as kites, falcons, sea eagles, ospreys, black storks and numerous species of duck.

Densely forested hills, sandy plains with moors and pine woods, inland dunes and broad reed belts form the landscape of the countryside that was created by the last Ice Age. It is best to experience the idyll by canoe or inflatable dinghy with the right maps and a tent in your luggage. Even if you are conducting a spur-of-the-moment tour of the area you can still arrange a canoe for one or more day trips on short term hire from local clubs. Here too, advice can be obtained about such things as tour maps.

Parkland scenery: Past large and small stretches of water, the country road takes us to **Neustrelitz** (population 26,000), a baroque town planned and built in 1733 as a residence for one of the dukes of Mecklenburg-Strelitz. Unfortunately, not many of the baroque buildings are left, but there are still some beautiful neoclassical monuments, such as the Town Hall, dating from 1841. You will search in vain for the baroque palace, which was destroyed by fire in 1945 and whose ruins were subsequently dismantled. The **palace park**, laid out in the style of an English country garden remains, however, and holds numerous small gems, such as the raised temple, the neogothic palace church and an avenue lined with sandstone statues of ancient divinities and the four seasons.

The Müritz: The Müritz, which is Germany's second biggest lake after Lake Constance, is only one and a half hours' drive away from the 8-million strong conurbation of Berlin. It's the beginning of the Mecklenburg Lake District. Those who visit the lake cannot miss **Waren** (population 24,000), which has been a health resort since 1845. Fontane knew that "in the whole of God's world there is no better place in which to take a cure". Nowadays there are also facilities for sailing, diving and windsurfing, but the town itself, more than 700 years old, is also worth exploring. There are some beautiful half-timbered buildings such as the Löwenapotheke (apothecary) **Warehouses in Plau.**

dating from 1623. The **Müritz Museum** near the lake will tell you all about the history and nature of the countryside and it also has the biggest **freshwater aquarium** in Germany. A beautiful view of the town, which is built up in terraces, can be enjoyed from the water, aboard one of the many pleasure steamers that go to Röbel on the southwest shore or steam across Kölpin, Fleesen, Malchower and Plauer Lakes to reach the half-timbered town of Plau.

"Make the most of your time" is written on the façade of the Town Hall in **Plau** (population 6,500). Those who follow that advice will find many treasures here. Apart from the abundance of water, there is the **Town Church** (13th century) with a late Gothic, richly decorated altarpiece, an old **Castle Tower** with an 11-metre (36-ft) deep dungeon and an ingenious lift bridge over the Elde, which was built in the year 1916. An **exhibition** near the church displays the work of Wilhelm Wandschneider (1866–1944) whose sculptures are scattered all around Mecklenburg.

Little Versailles: Some names are full of music, at times elegiac and heavy, at others dainty and light, but they all played their part in history. In **Ludwigslust** (population 12,600) there once stood a hunting lodge where Duke Christian Ludwig II resided, one presumes in not altogether unhappy circumstances.

From 1756 to 1837 the area rose to become a Residenz (or royal seat) and was planned and developed as the "Little Versailles" of Mecklenburg, with lots of baroque, even more classicism, a **palace** well worth seeing and an enormous **park** in which you can quite easily lose yourself. For a truly magnificent display of splendour the duke's purse was too small – at least as far as the palace interior is concerned, where everything is made out of *papier-mâché*. As the beautiful province lost its usefulness the sovereign moved once again to Schwerin in the north, which was the original royal seat.

Back to Berlin: Before returning to the city, you pass through more unspoilt landscape. Between Ludwigslust and Berlin, around the little towns of Perleberg, Pritzwalk and Kyritz lies the **Prignitz** – a flat, forested region dotted with sleepy villages. There is the occasional lake to bathe in and the roads are mostly narrow. There is little dramatic landscape, just forest and fields in this remote, almost forgotten part of the country. It's an idyllic place for cyclists.

During the first weekend of September (Thursday to Sunday) especially it's worth taking a detour through the little town of **Havelberg** (population 7,500) which rises up out of the agricultural plain on the B107. Every year a **horse market** is held here on Havel meadow – along with the flea market traders and carousel owners in tow. Transactions require little formality. A simple handshake, exchange of notes, and the horse has a new owner.

Nearby is the confluence of the Havel and the Elbe, the river which once formed the border between the Germans and the Slavs, which explains why the **Cathedral** (1170) has some of the characteristics of a castle. Trade was important, as the big market square illustrates.

THROUGH THE HARZ TO LEIPZIG

The journey from Berlin through Sachsen-Anhalt to Leipzig and back past Dessau and Wittenberg is a series of contrasts. In the Harz, visitors will be struck by the picture-book landscape of half-timbered houses and fine Romanesque buildings. They may also intrude into the fantastical world of the witches of Brocken. The industrial present takes over in Halle, while Leipzig is clearly a busy city currently being rebuilt after decades of neglect. Dessau and the Lutheran town of Wittenberg are both associated with some important names in German history and culture.

On the way to the Harz: Just beyond Potsdam to the west of the Grosser Zernsee lies the island town of **Werder**. Busy Berliners often come here at the end of April for the Blossom Festival. Later on in the year they return for the berry and fruit harvests, but relaxing in one of the cafés overlooking the Havel and treating themselves to freshly-made fruit cake or fruit wine is something that they do all the year round.

Follow the road beneath a canopy of oak, linden, chestnut and maple trees to the town of **Brandenburg**, passing the flat, watery and wooded Havelland.

The town, originally called Brennabor, was once the main fortress of the Slavic Hevellers. In AD 928 Emperor Heinrich I tried to capture this strategically important bastion on the Havel, but it was not until 1157 that the fortifications were finally taken by Albrecht the Bear. The town only really established itself when it became a bishopric. In the 14th and 15th centuries the area flourished as a centre for trade and the manufacture of cloth, but Brandenburg's importance declined following the rise of Berlin as the residence of the Elector. Prosperity returned in 1690 when Huguenots who had been expelled from France arrived in the region, bringing with them new tanning techniques.

Today, the townscape of Brandenburg (pop. 94,000) is dominated by the steel industry and rolling mills. And yet there are still some gems to be uncovered. For example, the **Saints Peter and Paul Cathedral**, which dates back to the Middle Ages, is the oldest surviving building in the Brandenburg Marches. First built in Romanesque style, the church was transformed at the end of the 14th century into a Gothic basilica. Among the many art treasures are various altars, 13th-century stained-glass windows and the bishops' tombstones.

The **Cathedral Museum** contains exhibits of calligraphy and textiles from the Middle Ages. In the old town it is worth taking a look at the **Old Town Hall** (1470) and, in what used to be called the new town, the parish church of **St Catherine** which was completed in 1401, is also of interest.

Romanesque roots: Magdeburg, the capital of Sachsen-Anhalt, lies at an important intersection of road, rail, river and canal routes and is easily the biggest inland port in eastern Germany. First impressions of this city tend to be rather disappointing due to the extent of the damage suffered during World War II.

Left, in need of renovation: half-timbered houses in the Harz. **Right**, a friendly local.

At an earlier time, Magdeburg did attain considerable historical significance. Under Otto I the city developed into a centre for Slavic missionary work. He elevated the status of the city by building a castle and installing an archbishop.

Many of the Romanesque buildings that were constructed during this period have survived. The **Unser Lieben Frauen Monastery** (1064–1160) is one of the most important Romanesque buildings in Germany. The church, which now serves as a concert hall, is dedicated to the composer Georg Friedrich Telemann who was born in Magdeburg in 1681 and a festival is held in his honour in June. The **museum** is home to numerous modern sculptures. The "Magdeburger Reiter", said to be the oldest free-standing **equestrian statue** in Germany, stands in the **Alter Markt** in front of the baroque **Town Hall**.

The city's **Cathedral** towers above the other buildings and is visible from afar. Dating from 955, the cathedral was rebuilt in Gothic style in 1209 after it had been destroyed by fire. The opulent furnishings within include 14th-century choir stalls, 15th-century alabaster statues, a late 16th-century pulpit and numerous tombstones. A monument by **Barlach** pays tribute to those Germans who fell during World War I.

The name of **Otto von Guericke** (1602–86) will be familiar to students of physics. He was not only born in Magdeburg but was also the city's mayor for a short time. In 1656 he pumped the air out of two hemispheres to create a vacuum. As the two halves remained firmly together, his experiment proved the existence of atmospheric pressure. The fertile soil of the surrounding countryside lies close to the city boundaries and the vast fields are of North American prairie proportions.

Halberstadt (population 47,000), formerly an episcopal residence, was almost completely destroyed during World War II. Grants worth millions of marks from a fund set up to preserve the neglected cities of the former GDR will safeguard most of the city's medieval treasures. The Cathedral and the Lieb-

Left, Halberstadt Cathedral. Below, facades in Quedlinburg.

fraukirche, a Romanesque basilica from the 12th century, have already been restored. After 250 years of building work, the **Cathedral** was finally consecrated in 1491. The cloisters contain the most impressive of the **cathedral's treasures**: Romanesque tapestries, crystal crosses and liturgical vestments. Near the cathedral the **Heineanum** displays some 16,000 stuffed birds and 10,000 eggs.

The half-timbered wonder: At the foot of the Harz mountains lies **Quedlinburg** (pop. 26,500), famous for its old town. With no fewer than 1,200 half-timbered houses, most of which date from the 15th and 16th centuries, the inner quarter resembles an old-fashioned picture postcard and UNESCO has listed the town as a World Cultural Heritage Site. The highly recommended **Fachwerkhausmuseum** at Wordgasse 3 in the oldest half-timbered house in Germany – thought to date from around 1300 – documents the development of this building style.

On the castle hill stands the late Romanesque **St Servatius Collegiate Church** (1070–1129). In the crypt lies the tombstone of King Heinrich I. Although lots of pieces from the church's treasury disappeared after 1945, some precious sacred relics remain. Exhibits in the museum at the **castle**, which was built between the 13th and 17th centuries, include paintings from the 16th and 17th centuries and Renaissance and baroque furniture. Nearby lies the **Klopstockhaus** where an exhibition documents the life and work of the well-known writer who was born in Quedlinburg in 1724.

The Hochharz National Park: At the heart of the Hochharz National Park is the **Brocken** mountain which reaches a height of 1,142 metres (3,747 feet) above sea level. In good weather, the panoramic view from the summit is quite stunning. Many people make the journey to the top on the **Harzquerbahn** steam railway from Wernigerode, a trip which takes about an hour and a half. As an alternative you can take a wonderful drive through dark, dense spruce forests

Rape and bees in the Harz foothills.

along the winding, picturesque country roads to Nordhausen, but that is a good three-hour trip. From the Brocken the waters of the river Ilse roar along an attractive valley and down a series of rapids, the **Ilse Waterfalls**. From **Thale**, set between the wild and rugged **Teufelsmauer** – the Devil's Wall, which makes a marvellous ridge walk – and the impressive **Bode** valley, a cable car crosses to the **Hexentanzplatz** or "Witches' Dance Square", the place where the *Walpurgisnacht* scene in Goethe's *Faust* is said to have taken place. The mountains, lakes and rivers of the Harz can boast a unique range of flora and fauna and the area ranks as one of the most remarkable nature reserves between Scandinavia and the Alps.

Reformers of the Middle Ages: Stolberg in the Harz is the birthplace of the reformer and revolutionary **Thomas Münzer** and a museum documents his contribution to German history. Although he was influenced in the beginning by Martin Luther, he soon realised that Luther's views were not radical

enough. Münzer strove to create God's kingdom on earth. His goal was the creation of a system in which all men are equal and land is shared for the common good. He soon established a liaison with the rebellious farmers and, in contrast to Luther, preached a militarist philosophy. In 1525 around a third of Germany opposed feudal law and the church was in tumult. However, the feudal lords joined together and 5,000 farmers were slaughtered in **Frankenhausen** at the foot of the Kyffhäuser hills. Münzer himself was beheaded. To commemorate this event, during the 1980s the East German government commissioned the construction of a **circular memorial** in **Bad Frankenhausen**. Close by lies the largest karst cave in the southern Harz foothills, the Barbarossa Cave. It may be viewed as part of a guided tour.

Martin Luther (1483–1546) was born in **Eisleben** and a statue in the market reminds the townsfolk of their most famous son. The house where he died has been converted into the **Luther Museum**. For over 4,000 years, copper mining has been of great importance in the region. The weapons and tools in the town's **local history museum** – some over 2,000 years old – testify to this long-standing tradition.

Industrial centres and more: Eisleben is the last of the romantic Harz towns. From here, the scenery becomes less attractive. Although **Halle** and **Merseburg** occupy nice locations on the banks of the river Saale, they lie at the heart of eastern Germany's industrial centre.

After a short stroll through the town centre, which was spared during the war, it will become apparent that **Halle** (pop. 300,000) is not a just a dull, industrial town. In 968 Halle came under the jursidiction of the bishops of Magdeburg and from the 11th century onwards the saltwater springs provided the foundation for the prosperity and power of the people. Around 400 years later a bitter struggle between the people and their episcopal masters ended with defeat for the rebellious middle classes.

In the 17th and 18th centuries, the university, founded in 1694, developed into a stronghold of enlightenment and

Beware of witches!

pietism. At the end of the 19th century the ban on the existence of socialist parties was lifted and Halle was the venue in 1890 for the first conference of the SPD (German Socialist Party). The local workers' movement strongly resisted the emergence of the right-wing nationalist parties during the 1920s. During the period of industrial development in the 1960s **Halle-Neustadt** developed into a giant dormitory town for over 100,000 chemical workers and their families. The factories were responsible for considerable damage to the environment, but after reunification many of the chemical plants were forced to close and the air has become much cleaner.

The spacious **Market Square** in the centre of Halle has retained its unique combination of churches and historic buildings. The **Council Chambers**, **Town Hall** and **Market Hall** are overlooked by the four towers of the market's **Church of Our Lady** (1529–55). Martin Luther preached here, and Georg Friedrich Händel, the town's best-known inhabitant, was at one time the organist. More about his life can be discovered in the **Händel Museum**, his birthplace, which can be found on the Grosse Nikolaistrasse 5. There is also a statue of him opposite the church on the market place and the city holds a Händel festival. Immediately adjacent, the free-standing **Red Tower** with 76 bells soars to a height of 84 metres (275 feet). Near the **Cathedral**, which contains some fine examples of late-Gothic sculpture, stands the former **residence** of Cardinal Albrecht II (16th century). This houses the **Geiseltal Museum** with a display of notable fossils. One of the most important art collections in eastern Germany is in the **Moritzburg** (1484–1503) on the Schlossberg, or Castle Hill. This contains exhibits of German painting and sculpture from the 19th and 20th centuries, including works by Caspar David Friedrich, Franz von Stuck, Wilhelm Lehmbruck and Ernst Barlach.

Merseburg is the home of some of the earliest German history. On the Stadthügel, originally the raised site of

Luther was born in Eisleben.

a fortified palace built by Heinrich I in the 10th century, the **Cathedral** and **Schloss** (15th–17th centuries) are close neighbours. In the days of the German Empire, more than 20 Imperial Diets convened here between 933 and 1212.

The complex of buildings has its focus in the beautifully-tended **Castle Gardens**, a haven of delightful treasures which provides the setting for the Assembly House, the Palace, the Orangery and a Café. Of greater cultural significance, however, is the **Cathedral**. Originally consecrated in 931 as the palace chapel for Heinrich I, it was elevated to the status of cathedral when the bishopric was established in 968.

The building we see today was started in 1015 and took on its present form, characterised by its four towers, in the 16th century. Showpieces of the luxurious interior include the bronze memorial (1080), the font (around 1150) and the richly decorated choir stalls. The famous **Cathedral Collegiate Archive**, founded in 1004 by Bishop Wigbert, contains a collection of medieval manuscripts which are among the earliest extant examples of German literature, among them the priceless **Merseburger Zaubersprüche**, an ancient charm to protect fighting men and their horses from harm. They date back to the 9th–10th centuries, and lay undiscovered in the cathedral library until 1841.

Two centuries ago, Goethe named **Leipzig** "Little Paris", and with a population of just under 500,000 it was the second-largest city of the former GDR. In 1930 the population was around 700,000, but the division of Germany hit this established centre for publishing and exhibitions particularly hard. Many publishing houses relocated to the West after 1945, and Leipzig surrendered to Frankfurt am Main its status as *the* city for book fairs.

The earliest signs of habitation date back to the 6th and 7th centuries, when Sorbs settled here and named it "Lipzi" (under the lime trees). As foreign trade grew, two important routes crossed the lowlands around Leipzig, and where they met, merchants and craftsmen be-

The market place in Halle.

gan to make their home in the 10th–11th centuries. In 1268 the Margrave of Meissen pronounced it a free trade town, and it was granted a market in 1497 by Kaiser Maximilian I. Thus the town flourished as a trading centre.

With the founding of the **University** in 1409 Leipzig also became a cultural centre which attracted many influential students, among them the historian Leopold von Ranke, the philosopher Gottfried Wilhelm Freiherr von Leibniz, the poets Friedrich Gottlieb Klopstock, Gotthold Ephraim Lessing, Johann Wolfgang von Goethe and Jean Paul, and the philosopher Friedrich Nietzsche.

There has been a publishing industry in Leipzig since 1481, and this grew to monopolise the German book trade in the 19th century. In 1842, a central ordering and delivery centre was established, so that nearly all publishing houses in Germany had to distribute their books via Leipzig. This practice continued until 1945.

The **Leipziger Congress** took place in 1863, initiated by German workers' unions. The political programme was the brainchild of Ferdinand Lassalle, who was elected President of the General German Workers' Union at the congress. The influential socialists Clara Zetkin, Rosa Luxemburg and Franz Mehring were employed on the left-wing newspaper, the *Leipziger Volkszeitung*, founded in 1894.

Leipzig's contemporary history also shows a dynamic tendency towards change. The city became well-known for its Monday Demonstrations, which were a forerunner of the peaceful revolution in 1989.

Today's Leipzig is known as the "Boomtown of the East". The skyline is punctuated with cranes, symbolising its renewal, and a modern exhibition hall opened in 1996.

On first sight of the **Hauptbahnhof**, or Main Station, constructed in 1915 and the largest terminal station in Europe, the visitor may be somewhat surprised by the unusual symmetrical layout of the building. The reason for this does not lie with any aesthetic concept,

but in the fact that two completely independent railway companies used to share the building; the eastern side was owned by Saxony, the western by Prussia. Two open-air staircases lead from the main concourse which is around 300 metres (980 feet) long, 33 metres (108 feet) wide and 27 metres (89 feet) high. The town centre, with its market square, is 15 minutes' walk from here, passing through the wide Sachsenplatz.

The fine Renaissance **Old Town Hall** on the **Market Square** is a marked contrast to the station. Built in 1556 on the foundations of the previous Gothic Town Hall and the former Wool Weavers' Guild House, it only took the nine months between fairs to complete. The arcades were added in 1907, and today it houses the **Local History Museum**. Directly opposite, the **Handwerkerpassage** was reopened in 1989, recreating the lives of medieval craftsmen. At the end of the alley, over the entrance to the "Coffe Baum", the oldest coffee house in the town (closed in 1995), there is a carving showing a Turk offering a bowl of coffee to a small boy.

The Thomasgasse leads to the **Church of St Thomas**, home of the **Thomaner Choir**. The church was founded in around 1212 by Markgraf Dietrich dem Bedrängten as the Augustinian collegiate church, and assumed its current late-Gothic form in the 15th century at the hands of Claus Roder. When the opening of the university was celebrated in 1409, the Thomaner had already been in existence for nearly 200 years. At first it consisted of only 12 boys, pupils at the School for the Children of the Poor, who sang at the Mass. But they soon went on to sing at church and state ceremonies. Johann Sebastian Bach, who became choirmaster and organist in 1723, wrote the majority of his motets for this choir. The Thomaner, one of the best boys' choirs in the world, can often be heard in this, their home church. More can be learnt about Bach's life in the **Bach Museum**.

Returning to the Town Hall, to the rear can be found the idyllic **Naschmarkt** and the **Alte Handelsbörse**, the

The elegant Mädlerpassage.

baroque exchange building constructed along Italian and Dutch lines. Once it was a meeting place for merchants during the fairs; now it is a venue for cultural events and festivals. If you continue past the statue of the young Goethe which stands in front of this building, you will come directly to **Auerbachs Keller** in the **Mädlerpassage**. This old student pub was the setting for the famous scene in *Faust*. Pictures from the legend already adorned the walls in Goethe's day. The clear notes of a Meissen porcelain chime can be heard echoing through the elegant passageway.

At the exit, to the right, the **Städtische Kaufhaus** has stood since 1901. This store was formerly the site of the old Gewandhaus (Cloth Hall) which accommodated not only the cloth trade but also the city's orchestra. The new **Gewandhaus** is on the Augustplatz. The orchestra was founded in 1781, and among its most famous conductors are Felix Mendelssohn-Bartholdy, Bruno Walter and Wilhelm Furtwängler.

The **Church of St Nicholas** was be-

gun in the 12th century in the Romanesque style. The Gothic chancel dates from two centuries earlier, and the late Gothic triple nave was consecrated in 1523. Decorative plasterwork on pillars and vaults and the classical interior are evidence of the city's former wealth. In 1989 the weekly services in this church led to the famous Monday Demonstrations. The history and lifestyles of Leipzig are on exhibition in the **Museum of the Round Corner** (Runde Ecke).

Opposite the church is Leipzig's oldest school, the **Alte Nikolai-Schule**, founded in 1512. The building has been renovated and now houses, among other things, the **Ancient History Museum**.

South of the city, the **Völkerschlachtdenkmal** commemorates the victory over Napoleon in 1813. A 91-metre (300-ft) monument on a 30-metre (100-ft) high mound was dedicated by Kaiser Wilhelm II on the battle's centenary.

The route from Leipzig to Berlin passes **Dessau**, the Bauhaus town, and **Wittenberg**, Martin Luther's town, both of which are well worth a visit.

The Bauhaus Building in Dessau is now a museum.

Bauhaus in Dessau: In 1919 Walter Gropius founded the Bauhaus school in Weimar which was to become one of the most important art schools of this century. In 1925 it was moved to Dessau. The group of budding artists, architects, planners, designers and photographers, with Walter Gropius at its centre, lasted until 1932. There was an attempt to set up the Bauhaus in a disused factory in Berlin, but the school was closed by the Nazis in 1933.

The Bauhaus movement sought to unite craft and art. There was no insurmountable contradiction between technology and craft, either according to the artists Mies van der Rohe, Feininger, Moholy-Nagy, Klee, Kandinsky, Marcks and Albers. Their aim was to design and produce works and buildings whose styles were functional and dictated by their materials, yet maintaining a human perspective. Teaching and learning, theory and practice, should be closely linked.

It was not until 1977 that the town decided to reopen the **Bauhaus Building** as a **museum**. Nearby is the former house of the artist Lionel Feininger, now the **Kurt Weill Centre**, which houses the work of the composer. Further examples of Bauhaus architecture include the old labour exchange on August-Bebel-Platz designed by Gropius, the Bauhaus housing estate with the Co-operative Building in the Törten district, and the Meisterhäuser in Ebert-Allee.

A British bombing raid on Dessau on the 7 March 1945 destroyed over 80 percent of the town. All that remained of the royal residence was a ruined wing of the **Royal Palace** (1530), which has subsequently been restored. **St George's Church** (1712–17) has been rebuilt.

Around Dessau: Dessau's heyday was in the time of Prince Leopold Friedrich Franz von Anhalt-Dessau (1740–1817), who surrounded himself with artists, poets and architects. He established one of the finest English-style country parks (1764–1800) in Germany at **Schloss Wörlitz** (1769–73), which houses an art collection with works by Averkamp, Rubens and Canaletto. A boat trip through the canals and artificial lakes

Crisp morning in the grounds of Schloss Wörlitz.

takes about an hour, but this is no substitute for walking. Over 800 varieties of trees and innumerable exotic plant species are planted among hills, winding paths and antique sculptures. The grounds are dotted with various buildings, including an Italian farmstead, a Greek temple, a Gothic folly and a palm house. A rococo castle stands on the on the nearby estate of **Mosigkau**, and the museum there displays handicrafts, porcelain, faience and a collection of paintings by Rubens, van Dyck and Jordaens. Nearer the town centre, **Schloss Georgium**, surrounded by landscaped parks, houses an art collection with works from the 16th–20th centuries.

Wittenberg – Luther's town: Approaching **Wittenberg** (pop. 50,000) from the west the first impression is of the tower of the **Schlosskirche** whose dome looks like a well-fitting crown. It was to the door of this church, on the 31 October 1517, following peasant uprisings in Hungary, Transylvania, Slovakia, Switzerland and southern Germany, that **Martin Luther** posted his famous 95

Theses against, *inter alia*, the Catholic practice of indulgences. News of this quickly spread throughout Europe, and the Reformation began. Three years later, Luther, excommunicated by the Pope, finally broke away from the church authorities. By the **Luther Oak** to the east of the town he burned the Papal Bull and the Canon, the basis of medieval law. Close to the oak is the Lutherhaus, where the state-owned **Luther Hall** is the largest museum in the world dedicated to the history of the Reformation. Luther and his colleague Melanchthon are buried in the Schlosskirche.

In addition to the legacy of the Reformer, there are many other places of interest in Wittenberg. These include the Gothic **Parish Church of St Mary** (13th–14th centuries, the church where Luther preached), the **Melanchthonhaus**, dedicated to the memory of the scholar and theologian, the electoral **Royal Castle** (1489–1525) and the **Cranachhaus**, dedicated to the painter Lucas Cranach the Elder, who lived in Wittenberg from 1505 until 1547.

Wittenberg, where Luther lived.

FROM BERLIN TO DRESDEN

Following the roads southwards along the rivers Oder and Neisse, you arrive at the splendid city of Dresden, the "Florence on the Elbe" and beyond it, the natural beauty of the sandstone mountains which stretch right up to the Polish–German border. Since the reunification of Germany in 1990, this is now the easternmost border of the European Union which, if German and Polish politicians have their way, should also include Poland by the year 2000. For the moment, however, lorries heading to and from eastern Europe remain stuck in never-ending traffic jams.

Trade on the Oder and Neisse: The Germans and the Poles are endeavouring to foster a close relationship, something which is clearly evident in **Frankfurt-on-the-Oder** (pop. 86,500). It was here, in 1991, that the **University of Viadrina** was created in order to establish a spiritual bridge; of the 2,000 students, one-third come from Poland. The college is carrying on its tradition as the first university of the state of Brandenburg; it was founded here in 1506 but moved to Breslau in 1811.

In 1430, Frankfurt-on-the-Oder joined the Hanseatic League and developed into a rich and prosperous trading city. It was during this time that three important buildings were constructed in the North German, red-brick, Gothic style: the **Town Hall**, **St Mary's Church** and the **Franciscan Monastery**. The latter is now used as a concert hall bearing the name of Carl Philip Emanuel Bach, who worked as the choirmaster from 1734 to 1738. An exhibition dedicated to Bach is held here.

Another of the prominent sons of the city is the writer Heinrich von Kleist (1777–1811). A museum devoted to his life and works is situated in the former garrison school (founded in 1777).

Until reunification, the textile industry and brown coal mining provided **Cottbus** (pop. 123,000) with an economic basis. Over the years a number of radical changes have taken place. In 1991 the Technical University was inaugurated, leading to financial investment in the surrounding area. The success of the National Garden Exhibition in 1995 enhanced the image of the "little metropolis" and drew parallels with the city's historical masterpiece of landscape gardening, **Branitz Park**, designed in 1846–71 by Prince Hermann von Pückler-Muskau. The Stables, Palace and Park Smithy blend harmoniously with the surrounding gardens.

In the centre of the town lies the **Old Market**, bordered by fine Baroque townhouses and the Lion Pharmacy (Museum). By contrast, the Brandenburg Art Collection is devoted to 20th-century collages, photographs, posters and design. The **State Theatre** is a first-class example of Art Nouveau architecture; it was built by Bernhard Sehring in 1908. The **Wendish Museum** describes the history of the Sorbian minority which originated in Niederlausitz. The late Gothic Upper Church (begun in 1468), the **Baroque Palace Chapel** (1707–14) and the early Gothic Monastery Church (14th-century) are all interesting.

Prince Pückler-Muskau was born in **Bad Muskau** in 1785. Here, too, in the aristocratic-rural idyll of the Old Castle (16th-century), he created a 600-hectare (1,480-acre) park which is a masterpiece of garden design.

Görlitz (pop. 70,000), the most easterly town in Germany, experienced its economic heyday in the 15th century. In those days they mainly traded in cloth, but above all in woad, a plant used in the production of blue dye. It is here, at the most important crossing over the river Neisse, that two major trade routes met: between Stettin and Prague via Frankfurt-on-the-Oder, and between Leipzig and Breslau.

The most important Renaissance buildings around the **Town Hall** originate from this era. These include the **Schönhof**, which is the oldest Renaissance house in Germany, as well as numerous late-Gothic churches. Visible from afar are the towering spires of the 15th-century parish church of **Saints Peter and Paul**. With its main altar (1695), pulpit (1693) and the late-Gothic

Georgian chapel, it is well worth visiting. The double-winged altarpiece in the Trinity church in what was once a **Franciscan monastery** dates back to 1510 and looms over a Gothic pulpit (14th century). The grave of the mystic philosopher Jakob Böhme (1575–1624) is to be found in the cemetery of the **Church of St Nicholas** (15th century).

The **Kaisertrutz** and the neighbouring fortified tower are today home to the town's art collection; as well as alternating exhibitions, there are exhibits relating to local archaeology and history. The highlight is the **Holy Sepulchre**, a copy of the original in Jerusalem. An example of the town's later prosperity is the magnificent **Art Nouveau department store** on Marienplatz.

Minority interests: To the south of Löbau, between Bautzen and Görlitz, lies Herrnhut, the home of the religious minority of the Moravians (or Herrnhuter). The brotherhood was founded in 1722 by the pious Count Nikolaus von Zinzendorf and his Bohemian-Moravian fellow-believers. The **Museum of Anthropology** has a display of objects collected from their missionary work.

There are still around 100,000 Slavic Sorbs living around Bautzen and as far as Cottbus and Spree Forest. Their parent organisation, the "Domowina" is based in **Bautzen** (pop. 51,000), where the **Sorb Museum** provides an informative introduction to these people.

Bautzen was also a flourishing trading centre, a fact reflected today in the core of the old town, with the **Town Hall** (1729–32), **St Michael's Church** (1498), the ruins of the **St Nicholas Church** and some fine baroque houses. **St Peter's Cathedral** (1293–1303) has been used by both Catholics and Protestants since the reformation (1524), when it was agreed that the Protestants take the nave and the Catholics the choir. Standing proudly on a granite outcrop, **Ortenburg Castle** was built as a border outpost during the eastwards expansion of the Germans. It first belonged to Bohemia and after 1635 to Saxony.

The most notorious building in Bautzen is the prison (1903), where political

Religious motifs are the theme of this Sorbian woodcarver's creations.

prisoners of the GDR served out their sentences.

The Florence on the Elbe: It is only another 50 km (30 miles) until the high point of this tour, **Dresden** (pop. 470,000), which proudly calls itself the most beautiful city in Germany. Millions of visitors each year flock to the "Florence on the Elbe", which in 1990 took up its role once again as the capital of Saxony. Apart from the city itself, the surrounding countryside, dotted with old towns and palaces, is well worth exploring.

Dresden will forever be associated with the devastating bombing raid that took place on the night of 14 February 1945, when almost the entire city centre was completely destroyed by a series of firestorms. At least 35,000 people, including many refugees, lost their lives in the inferno. A great deal of restoration was done during the days of the GDR, a process that has continued apace since reunification. The **Frauenkirche** (Church of Our Lady), whose ruins long stood as a reminder of the senselessness of war, is now being rebuilt a precise copy of its former self.

It was on the site of the this church that the foundations of Dresden were laid, in the middle of the 11th century, when a Christian missionary centre was established by monks out to convert the heathen Slavic Sorbs. Merchants settled here on the crossing point over the Elbe. In 1485, the Albertine, the Saxon line of the the ruling Wettin family, elevated Dresden to a royal city.

Dresden's most resplendent era came after the Thirty Years' War with the arrival of the king of Poland and elector of Saxony, Augustus the Strong (1670–1733). Most of the the city's baroque masterpieces are due to this one man, a leader with a boyish soul who not only enjoyed life to the full but, as a man of great vision, was responsible for the planning of this, *his* city.

The view from the 100-metre (330-ft) high **Town Hall** tower provides a good initial impression of the layout of Dresden. Nearby stands the 13th-century **Kreuzkirche**, the oldest place of wor-

Augustus the Strong as the "Golden Horseman" in Dresden.

ship in the city which is said to contain a fragment of the Holy Cross. After it was destroyed in the Seven Years' War, it was rebuilt between 1764 and 1792 and remains a beautiful example of the baroque style. Vespers take place every Saturday in the company of the world-famous **Kreuzchor**.

Around Theaterplatz: No visitor to Dresden should miss the **Zwinger Palace**, a masterpiece of the baroque on the Elbe. Commissioned by Augustus the Strong and completed between 1710 and 1732 by the court architect Matthäus Daniel Pöppelmann and sculptor Balthasar Permoser, the original design was based on the orangery at Versailles. But with its mighty gateways, its pavilions, galleries, and gardens, the complex grew to take up an enormous area. By 1719 enough of the palace had been completed for it to host the marriage of Prince Friedrich August II (1696–1763) to the Archduchess Maria Josepha (1699–1757), a daughter of Austria's Habsburg empress Maria Teresa.

The Zwinger houses a number of galleries and collections, of which the **Gemäldegalerie Alte Meister** (Old Masters' Art Gallery) is the most important. It was designed by Gottfried Semper (1803–79) and completed in 1854. There are over 2,000 works of art to be admired here, including the *Sistine Madonna* by Raphael, Rembrandt's *Self portrait with Saskia*, as well as Dürer's *The seven pains of Maria*.

The **Historical Museum**, located in the east wing, contains a superb weapons collection (15th–18th centuries) and court costumes (16th–18th centuries). Scientific instruments (the earliest of which date from the 13th century) are exhibited in the **Mathematical-Physics Room**. Meissner porcelain, in addition to early Chinese ceramics, is displayed in the **Porcelain Collection** in the long gallery, the second-largest such collection in the world after the Serail collection in Istanbul.

Architecturally and musically, the **Semper Opera House** (1870–78) is of equal prominence. Standing next to the Zwinger in the grandly-proportioned

The Semper Opera House from the Brühlsche Terrace.

Theaterplatz, it was designed and built by Semper in the Italian high baroque style on the site of an earlier theatre which, prior to burning down, had staged the premieres of Richard Wagner's operas, *Rienzi* (1842), *The Flying Dutchman* (1845) and *Tannhäuser* (1845). In 1905 and 1908 respectively, the premieres of *Salome* and *Elektra* by Richard Strauss were performed in the new building. In front stand the equestrian statue of King Johann and the memorial to the composer Carl Maria von Weber, who was the musical director in Dresden from 1817 to 1826. The building, which was destroyed by bombs in 1945, reopened after eight years of restoration work in 1985 with a production of Weber's opera *Der Freischütz*.

The restoration of the **Taschenberg Palace** was completed in 1995 and today it serves as a hotel. Inside, it is possible to view the stairwell, built in 1707–11 according to the design of Pöppelmann. The neoclassical **Old Town Guard House** with its temple-like facade consisting of six ionic sandstone columns, was built between 1830 and 1832 according to the design of Karl Friedrich Schinkel, contemporaneous with the Neue Wache in Berlin. Theaterplatz is dominated by the baroque **Hofkirche** (Court Church, 1739–55). The exterior niches contain 78 statues, while highlights of the interior include Permoser's beautifully carved wooden pulpit (1712–22) as well as the Silbermann organ (1753).

The utterly destroyed **Castle** (1547), the restoration of which was begun in the 1960s, is scheduled to be completed by the year 2006 in time to celebrate the city's 800th anniversary. The four-winged renaissance building will then act as the cultural centrepiece of this great Saxon city. The Green Vault, which is at the moment in Albertinum, is planned to return to its original home, as are the prints and drawings and coin collections.

From here the **Lange Gang** (Long Passage) leads to the **Johanneum**, the erstwhile royal stables on the Neumarkt, which now houses the **Transport Museum**. Along the external wall of the passage 35 Wettin rulers are depicted in a royal parade. In 1876, the mural was rendered in scratchwork, but in 1906 this was overlaid by 24,000 ceramic tiles from Meissen.

Rising from the rubble: The **Frauenkirche** (1726–43), potent symbol of Dresden's destruction, stands almost in the middle of the square. In front of this church Martin Luther looks sagely at his Bible. The 95-metre (312-ft) high dome of the Frauenkirche caved in after a bombing attack in 1945. It was finally decided to go ahead with the rebuilding of Germany's most important Protestant church in 1994, and the project is scheduled for completion in 2006. Meanwhile, the church has reopened for services and recitals.

Passing by the Dresden Hilton Hotel, opened in 1989, you come to the **Sekundogenitur** – once the library of every second-born prince and now a café and wine bar – and on to the **Brühlsche Terrace**. The latter was originally part of the old city's 16th-century fortifications until Heinrich Graf

The Catholic Hofkirche.

von Brühl had it converted into a landscape garden in 1738.

Initially built as the Armoury, the **Albertinum**, behind the Frauenkirche, is now home to a variety of unique collections. The most famous in the **Green Vault** are the treasures of the Saxon princes, including jewellery, precious stones and some 14th- and 15th-century paintings. In the **Galerie Neuer Meister**, 19th-century masterpieces such as Caspar David Friedrich's *Cross in the Hills* and Paul Gauguin's *Two women from Tahiti* are displayed alongside more recent contemporary works. Further collections include the **Sculpture Gallery** (ancient and modern pieces) and the **Coin Collection**.

Dresden's environs: The most popular weekend excursion for the people of Dresden, elegant **Loschwitz** was once a haven of peace for the nobility and educated elite of the city. One can reach it via Germany's oldest suspension railway (from the *Blaues Wunder* on the road to Pillnitz) that leads directly up to Loschwitzer Heights. From here there is an impressive view over the Elbe and the city. There is a good restaurant in the Luisenhof Hotel.

Nearby is the wooded area of **Dresden Heath**. In devising an organised system of paths through the woods, Heinrich Cotta (1763–1844) was an early pioneer of nature walks. Summer concerts are held on the open-air stage at the **Bühlau Cultural Centre**, while open-air swimming pools guarantee refreshment on hot days.

The museum at **Graupa** is dedicated to the life and works of Richard Wagner who was director of music in Dresden from 1843–49. A visit to the Carl Maria von Weber museum in **Klein-Hosterwitz** is best carried out in conjunction with a trip to **Pillnitz Palace**, the riverside summer residence of Augustus the Strong, who would come here by Venetian gondola to visit his various mistresses. Conforming to the exotic tastes of the courtly late-baroque, this pleasure palace was designed by the architect responsible for the Zwinger, namely Matthäus Daniel Pöppelmann.

Pillnitz Palace, summer residence of Augustus the Strong.

With its sweeping pagoda-like roofs, it is an important example of the Chinese vogue so prevalent at the time. In the extensive grounds the large camellia imported from Japan in 1770 immediately draws your attention. It is a riot of blossom in the spring.

Downstream on the Elbe: Following the river downstream **Radebeul** (pop. 35,000) can be reached by tram. Passing the old wine growing estates, you arrive at the yellow **Spitzhaus** (built around 1650), today a popular restaurant. Beneath the flight of steps (designed by Pöppelmann) leading up to the building stands **Haus Hoflössnitz** which contains the Viticulture Museum. This was originally Augustus the Strong's "summer-house" and he would come here during the the grape harvest to join in the wine festivals and vintner parades.

With his gripping tales of lands he had never even visited, Karl May was Germany's answer to Sir Henry Rider Haggard. The **Karl-May Museum** is located in Villa Shatterhand, where the writer lived out his final years. Not only does it exhibit material relating to the author but also to the culture of North American Indians. Children will enjoy a visit to the **Puppet Theatre Collection** in the Hohenhaus.

Moritzburg Palace (15 km/9 miles from Dresden) is accessible by a narrow guage railway which spookily howls its way through the forest. The palace, originally a renaissance building (1542–46), was converted and expanded by Pöppelmann from 1723 to 1736 in baroque style. It served Augustus the Strong as a hunting lodge.

The **Baroque Museum** houses an excellent, extensive collection of crafts and other treasures (including porcelain, furniture and a collection of portraits). The beautiful countryside around Moritzburg attracted many artists. In 1995, on the 50th anniversary of the death of the artist Käthe Kollwitz, a **museum** was opened in the house where she died dedicated to the life and work of this important and highly revered expressionist artist.

The wine producing town of **Meissen** (pop. 35,000) became a diocesan town back in AD 968 and used to be the hub of Saxony. Most of the buildings surrounding the market place date from the Middle Ages and the medieval atmosphere has been preserved.

The **Albrechtsburg**, completed in 1525, was the first of the Wettin family's residential castles. In 1710 Augustus the Strong had moved the production of porcelain here in order to keep the formula a secret. Augustus had apprehended the runaway apprentice chemist Friedrich Böttger, so that he might employ his alchemy skills in the production of gold and thereby rescue the shattered finances of the state. However, Böttger's experiments only resulted in porcelain. Today, the castle houses an art collection with a variety of exhibits including a Saxon sacred statue collection from the 15th and 16th centuries and, of course, a collection of early Meissen porcelain. Porcelain is still produced in Meissen today, and a workshop has been set up in the **Porcelain Museum** in the town.

Meissen Cathedral (which was start-

Moritzburg Palace.

ed around 1260) possesses numerous treasures such as sacred paintings and a number of important sarcophagi. The **St Afra Church** (13th century), part of the former Augustinian seminary is also well worth a visit as is the **Church of St Nicholas**, which preserves large figures of Meissen porcelain. There is a fine view of the town from the tower of the Church of our Lady.

Sächsische Schweiz National Park: The delightful "Little Switzerland" of Saxony encompasses the Saxon part of the Elbsandstein Mountains, the sandstone uplands straddling the Czech border to the southeast of Dresden. The gateway to the region is the beautiful town of **Pirna** (pop. 47,000), a major trading centre in the Middle Ages, whose entire centre is under a protection order. As restoration work progresses, a stroll through the narrow streets provides an insight once more into the prosperity of the citizens of the time.

The area around the market place has been partly restored. In the centre, the **Town Hall** stands alone. The building

displays architectural influences spanning five centuries, starting with the ground floor which dates back to 1485. The portals and gables are of Gothic origin and the tower was added in 1718.

The **town houses** surrounding the market place excel with their fine arcades and oriel windows. Particularly worth inspection are **No 3** with its five canopied niches (1500) and **No 7**, the **Canalettohaus** (1520), with its steep and richly decorated gable. Remarkably, it is still possible to appreciate fully the "Canaletto view" which presented itself to the master as he painted scenes of this market place. The tower of the **Church of St Mary**, to the east of the town centre, is a good vantage point from which to view the town, the rolling foothills of the Erz Mountains and the Sächsische Schweiz. The single-naved church with its ribbed vaulting was built between 1504 and 1546.

Five km (3 miles) outside Pirna are the romatic **Grossedelitz Baroque Gardens**. The property was acquired by Augustus the Strong in 1723. He completely redesigned the place to provide a suitable setting for his extravagant parties, commissioning the addition of statues, flights of steps and an array of fountains from his specialist, Matthäus Daniel Pöppelmann.

The Sächsische Schweiz was declared a national park in 1991. A popular area for climbing and hiking, the name was actually coined by two Swiss artists who studied at the academy in Leipzig. The paintings of Adrian Zingg (1734–1816) and Anton Graff (1736–1813) can still be seen in the galleries of Dresden. But with the Grosse Winterberg topping out at only 552 metres (1,810 feet), the mountains here are just molehills when compared to the mighty Alps. The biggest lure of the region is the fascinating topography, with cliff faces carved in a multitude of forms, freestanding pillars of rock and deep ravines running between them. Over millions of years the Elbe and its tributaries sculpted this land from a single sandstone plateau.

Over the centuries, the region has drawn numerous artists, including the **The jetty at Pirna.**

painter Caspar David Friedrich and the composer Richard Wagner, whose *Lohengrin* is supposed to have been inspired here. The area was only developed for holidaymakers relatively late. Before the railway was completed in 1850 and steamships first started sailing in 1875, the wealthy were carried by litter through these rugged hills.

River trip: One of the best ways to appreciate the countryside is by taking the steamer from Dresden to the border town of Schmilka. The first really stunning feature is the rugged cliffs of the **Bastei**, from the top of which there are superb views. At the Rockfall, one of the most popular crags, a 76-metre (250-foot) long stone bridge crosses the impressive **Mardertelle Gorge**.

The ship soon draws in at the health spa of **Rathen**, a town closed to vehicles. In summer, the amphitheatre of cliffs provides a natural backdrop to the open-air theatre (seating capacity 2,000). **Königstein Fortress** stands sentinel 360 metres (1,180 feet) above the river. You can visit the living quarters and work rooms of the inventor of the "white gold", Friedrich Böttger, who was imprisoned here from 1706 to 1707. There is also a museum which has, among other exhibits, an antique weapons collection. While the views from here are impressive, from the **Lilienstein** (415 metres/1,360 feet), only reachable on foot, they are stunning.

Bad Schandau stretches along the river for some distance. Built in 1704, the local parish church is a great attraction. Both the pulpit and the altar are carved from local sandstone and the altar is also set with locally occurring precious stones. Hikers can take the **Karnitztal Railway**, incorporating the very best technology that the 1920s could provide, to the Lichtenheimer Waterfalls. This is the starting point for the climb to the **Kuhstall** (Cow Shed), a deep cave 11 metres high by 17 metres wide (36 ft by 56 ft) in which the robber knights would hide the cattle they had stolen. Finally, the Czech border is reached near **Schmilka**; the river itself marks the border for several miles.

The rugged crags of the Bastei.

FROM CHEMNITZ TO JENA

In the course of this short stretch from Saxony to Thuringia it will be possible to peer into deepest space with the aid of precision technology and then consider the philosophical truths propounded by some of Germany's most famous thinkers – including, of course, Karl Marx.

Chemnitz (pop. 300,000) was once the region's most important industrial centre, thanks mainly to its heavy engineering, locomotive factories and textile industry. In recent years, however, many of these major employers have had to close, although Volkswagen have invested in the area and created jobs. Other large-scale sources of industrial employment are desperately needed.

One of the city's attractions is the huge statue of Karl Marx's head, known as the **Marxkopf** (Lew Kerbel, 1971) which has since become an accepted symbol for Chemnitz. Until it was renamed in 1990, the city was known as Karl-Marx-Stadt.

Almost the whole of the inner city was destroyed during World War II. The **Rote Turm** or Red Tower, dating from the 12th century, is the last remaining section of the city's fortifications and now houses an exhibition documenting the city's growth. Over the centuries, this tower has served as the law courts, as a prison and as residence for the local governor. The complex of buildings in the **Theaterplatz** consisting of the **Opera House** (1906–09), a neo-Romanesque church and the **König Albert Museum** have also survived. The museum is perhaps the most interesting of the three, not least for its *Jugendstil* (Art Nouveau) interior. It also houses the state art collection which, *inter alia*, displays important examples of Impressionist and Expressionist paintings. The **Sterzeleanum** is worth seeking out as it is one of the few places in the world where it is possible to see a petrified forest. The **Schlossberg-museum**, originally a Benedictine monastery (1136) and later the Elector's Palace, is now used for exhibitions on

local history. Concerts and other functions are often held in the delightful Renaissance Hall and Kreuzhof. Some areas of the city, such as Kassberg, with its *Jugendstil* houses, Sonnenberg, and the area around the castle, illustrate the city's architectural developments.

It seems almost as if the citizens of **Zwickau** (pop. 120,000) had wanted to ensure that their town would always be the last entry in a gazetteer. In the first document relating to the town (1118), the place was recorded as "ZZwickaw". It initially grew up around a tollbooth on the Prague to Halle trading route, but the town flourished in the 15th and 16th centuries thanks to its clothmaking industry and silver mining in the surrounding ore-rich hills. Zwickau was the GDR's centre for bituminous coal mining until 1977. The Trabant car was manufactured at the old-fashioned Sachsenring works. The first cars to be produced in the area – at Mosel near Zwickau – rolled off the production line in 1904. After German unification, Volkswagen agreed to invest in the plant.

Left, the university tower in Jena. Right, the huge head of Karl Marx has become the most popular attraction in Chemnitz.

The history of the Trabant is displayed in the **Automobilmusuem** and a rally is held here in June.

All the most interesting sights are grouped around the **Hauptmarkt**, the main market place. These include the recently renovated neo-Gothic **Town Hall**, the **Cloth Market** or Gewandhaus (1525), converted into a theatre in 1823, as well as a number of grand patrician houses, one of which was the birthplace of Robert Schumann (1810–56). The museum, which is run by the Schumann Society and the Conservatory, is dedicated to his life and work.

The late-Gothic parish **Church of St Marien** (1206) has undergone numerous alterations and extensions – mostly during the 15th and 16th centuries – as a result of fires. Among its treasures are an early-Renaissance pulpit, a late-Gothic altar cross, many tombs, and a mobile Sacred Tomb which reaches a height of at least 5 metres (16 feet). Also of particular interest is the late-Gothic high altar made by the Nuremberg Wohlgemut workshop.

Altenburg (pop. 53,000) is the first Thuringian town along this route. Dedicated players of the card game skat might be familiar with this town. The modern game grew out of several older card games between 1810 and 1817 and the committee responsible for administering this popular game is based here. Surrounding the market place or the **Brühl** are the **Seckendorfsche Palais** (1725), former government buildings, a number of impressive town houses – and the **Skatbrunnen**, the only memorial dedicated to a card game.

The **Schloss**, dating originally from the 10th century, but rebuilt in the 18th, is the home of the **Spielkartenmuseum**, a museum which confirms Altenburg's claim as the home of skat and which boasts a large collection of playing cards and a playing card manufacturing studio dating from 1600. The **Lindenau-Museum**, built in the Italian Renaissance style between 1873 and 1875, houses several valuable art collections. On display here are Italian paintings from the pre- and early-Renaissance

Altenburg Palace is home to a substantial collection of playing cards.

periods as well as sculptures and paintings from the 19th and 20th centuries.

Gera, first mentioned in official records in 1237, lies picturesquely on the middle reaches of the White Elster. Its population of about 125,000 makes it the second-largest town in Thuringia. Gera's history stretches back over more than 750 years and traces its growth via its heyday as the principal city and residence of the princes of Reuss to become an important industrial centre. Since reunification, it has become the focal point of East Thuringia.

The Market Square is one of the prettiest in the country. It is dominated by the medieval Renaissance **Town Hall** (1573–75), noted for its richly-decorated six-storey staircase and tower (57 metres/187 feet). It is surrounded by a number of beautifully restored buildings, notably the Renaissance **Stadtapotheke** (chemist) with an elaborately carved oriel window and a baroque, three-storey **government building** (1722).

Of particular interest are the Gera Vaults, constructed at the beginning of the 18th century as underground cellars for the brewery. In Vault No. 188 there is an exhibition illustrating "Minerals and Mining in East Thuringia". The largest private housing complex in Gera can be seen in the Ferber House, which houses the **Museum of Applied Arts**. The Gera Art Collection which is in both the **Orangery** and the **Otto Dix** house has exhibitions of contemporary art. Dix was born in Gera in 1891 and his birthplace house is also a museum.

Three churches in the town are worth a visit: the **Pfarrkirche St Marien**, a late-Gothic, single-nave church (15th century), the triple-nave, baroque **St Salvatorkirche** (1720) with early 20th-century *Jugendstil* paintings and the **Trinitätskirche** (14th century).

Jena (pop. 100,000) is the last stop before Weimar. But unlike its more illustrious neighbour, Jena is known mainly for its technical achievements.

Carl Zeiss (1816–88) recognised early on that industrial progress depended on close co-operation between the world of science and business. He opened his first optics workshop in 1846, but it was 20 years later when he was joined by the physicist Ernst Abbe, that he achieved commercial success. Abbe built the first microscope using scientific methods, while the precision optical lenses needed were developed by the chemist Otto Schott. Schott was responsible for the invention of heatproof Jena glass.

The glass industry continues to be the town's lifeblood. The **Optical Museum** in Carl Zeiss Platz documents the achievements of the two main glass producers and has a display of 13,000 optical instruments. The **Zeiss Planetarium** (1926) in the **Botanical Gardens** offers presentations and laser shows.

However, Jena doesn't owe its academic reputation solely to the natural scientists. In 1789 Friedrich Schiller presented his inaugural lecture on the ideals of the French Revolution at the city's university (founded in 1558). A **memorial** to the celebrated dramatist can be seen in the summer house where he wrote *The Maid of Orleans* between 1797 and 1802.

The philosophy professor Johann Gottlieb Fichte encountered problems with the university authorities when in 1799 he was accused of being an atheist. He responded with a letter asking that "it be read before it is confiscated". But the irony was lost on his superiors and Fichte was suspended from his post. Two other famous philosophers, Schelling (from 1798) and Hegel (from 1805) also studied at the university.

Collegium Jenense, originally a 13th-century Dominican monastery, and the oldest university building, stands on the edge of the market place. Its founder, Prince Johann Friedrich, is remembered by a memorial in the market place. One of the few well preserved buildings in Jena is the late Gothic **Town Hall** (1377) with "Schnapphans". On the hour, a figure in a jester's cap opens his toothless mouth and snaps after a ball held out to him by a pilgrim, whereupon an agonising scream rings out. The **Romantikerhaus** not far from the Town Hall is dedicated to the legacy of Tieck, Novalis, Brentano and the Schlegel brothers, all heroes of the German Romantic literary movement.

FROM WEIMAR TO THE WARTBURG

Weimar is the natural starting point for any journey across the Thuringian Forest to the historic castle of the Wartburg. From the mid-18th century the duchy formed the centre of German cultural life. Traces of the German classical writers, above all Johann Wolfgang von Goethe, are to be found throughout the region. After a tour of the museums visitors can relax in the beautiful landscape of the Thuringian Forest, where the legends surrounding the Wartburg, which watches over Eisenach, will carry them away to another world.

Cultural recognition: When Weimar (population 62,000) assumes the title of European City of Culture in 1999 to coincide with the 250th anniversary of the birth of Goethe, it will strongly assert its traditional role as a crucible for the arts. The city's fame as a cultural centre is largely due to the influence of one lady, the cultured Duchess Anna Amalia, daughter of Duke Karl I and niece of Frederick the Great. The government of the duchy of Saxony-Weimar-Eisenach was left in her hands after her husband died in 1758. She made sure her sons, Karl August and Konstantin, had the best education and to this end summoned as tutors the poet and professor of philosophy, Christoph Martin Wieland and the Prussian officer Karl Ludwig von Knebel. The latter soon introduced Karl August to Goethe, who had already become famous through his work *The Sorrows of the Young Werther.*

Karl August took over the affairs of state after his mother in 1775, and it was not long before he summoned Goethe to an elevated office in the duchy. Goethe's position as privy councillor enabled him to initiate a series of reforms. In 1786, after around 10 years of state affairs, Goethe left for his sojourn in Italy. On his return to Weimar in 1788, he assumed new responsibility as education minister and director of the Weimar theatre. This period saw the growth of a special relationship, founded on their mutual passion for the theatre, between Goethe and Friedrich Schiller, who had come to live in Weimar from 1799. For example, Goethe was actively involved in the preparation and rehearsals for the first performance in 1799 of Schiller's drama *Wallensteins Lager.*

The early years of the following century saw the death of several leading literary figures. The theologian and philosopher Johann Gottfried Herder who came to Weimar in 1776, died in 1803, Schiller in 1805, Anna Amalia in 1807 and Wieland in 1813. Goethe outlived them all, dying on 22 March 1832.

The **Castle** houses the **State Art Collection**. This contains masterpieces by Cranach the Elder, Tintoretto, Rubens and Caspar David Friedrich. Nearby, the Green Castle is the repository of the **Herzogin Amalia Library**, containing 840,000 volumes. A further 600,000 volumes are to be found in the "Goethe and Schiller Archives" (1896) on the opposite bank of the River Ilm.

Goethe's **Summer House** is also located on the eastern side of the river. It

Left, Goethe and Schiller, Weimar's dynamic duo. Right, a welcoming smile.

still looks as if the great poet has just popped out and will be back any minute. It was here that he and his future wife Christiane Vulpius spent some of their happiest days.

Goethe's House is on the Frauenplan, not far from the market. Here, too, everything is just as he left it. Only his living and working quarters at the back of the house, to which only very close friends had access during his lifetime, are preserved from close public scrutiny. The library is protected by a screen, and the 8,000 volumes contained within are still arranged according to Goethe's system. The **Goethe Museum**, next to the house, is well worth a visit, and the **Schillerhaus** is also not far away. Schiller lived here until his death, and the rooms have been recreated with historical accuracy. The **Schiller Museum** next door is housed in a light and airy modern building.

Anna Amalia spent a good 30 years of her life in the baroque **Wittumspalais** (1767), at that time Weimar's intellectual and cultural centre. Today it is used to display furnishings from Goethe's era together with the **Wieland Museum**. The **Goethe and Schiller Memorial** stands in front of the **German National Theatre**, where the Weimar Constitution was passed in 1919. The baroque **Kirms-Krackow-Haus**, closed until 1999, contains rooms dedicated to the memory of the writers Johann Karl August Musäus, Johannes Daniel Falk and Johann Gottfried Herder. The latter's grave is to be found in the **Parish Church of St Peter and St Paul**, diagonally opposite. This church is well worth a visit, both for its architecture, originally late-Gothic and rebuilt in the baroque style, and for its winged altarpiece by Lucas Cranach the Younger.

Another of the many famous inhabitants of Weimar was Johann Sebastian Bach, who was court organist here from 1708 to 1717. Franz Liszt, Richard Strauss and Friedrich Nietzsche also lived here. It was in Weimar, too, that Walter Gropius founded the Bauhaus School, which later moved to Dessau. The **Bauhaus Museum** chronicles the founding of this school.

Weimar's magnificent library.

154

Apart from the historical sites, the traditional culinary venues of the city have also been preserved. These include the "White Swan", the "Black Bear", the "Elephant Hotel" which served as the location for Thomas Mann's novel *Lotte in Weimar*, and, not least, "Goethe's Café".

Buchenwald concentration camp: However splendid a past Weimar might have had, the image of the city remains tarnished by the fact that it was the site of the Buchenwald concentration camp, established in 1937. More than 60,000 people from some 35 countries were murdered in the camp, which was especially notorious for medical experiments on living human beings. The camp was liberated by the Americans on 11 April 1945. The memorial, whose 50-metre (164-foot) high clock tower is visible for miles around, is situated on the **Grossen Ettersberg**, approximately 1 km from the camp.

The capital of Thuringia: Following the political changes of the past few years, Erfurt, with a population of 213,000, has become not only the largest town in Thuringia but also its state capital. Once it has been renovated, it could become an architectural masterpiece, with such historic buildings as **Das goldene Rad**, the **Krone**, the **Fructbasar** and the **Andreasviertel**.

One site which has already been restored is the medieval **Krämerbrücke**, the only covered bridge to be found north of the Alps. This once formed part of the old east–west trade route, and today houses artists' studios and antique shops.

It was from Erfurt that the monk St Boniface set out to convert the heathen Germans to Christianity. He founded an independent bishopric in 742, although this was soon integrated with Mainz. In the Middle Ages Erfurt derived a great deal of wealth from the export of woad, the raw material for rich blue dyes. Market gardening developed into an important source of revenue from the 17th century onwards, giving rise to the permanent garden exhibition, which is today run by the EGA (*Erfurter Garten-*

Below, Erfurt's narrow streets. Right, history was made in Schmalkalden.

bau-Ausstellungsgesellschaft, or Erfurt Garden Exhibition Company).

In 1891, Erfurt saw the Party Conference of the SPD (Socialist Party), whose resolutions (the Erfurt Programme) replaced the Gotha Programme. A meeting between Willy Brandt and Willi Stoph in 1970 heralded the new *Ostpolitik* of the Federal Republic, relieving the tension between the Eastern bloc and the West.

Of particular interest in the **Cathedral**, founded in 742, are the Gloriosa, one of the largest church bells in the world, and the Wolfram, a candelabra dating from the 12th century. Other treasures to be found here include stained glass windows some 15 metres (50 feet) in height, the choir stalls and the baroque altar. The **Church of St Severin** (12th century) houses the tomb of St Severin, who died around 1365.

The city's skyline is punctuated by the towers of around 20 further **churches** and **monasteries** of the various holy orders who settled here, including Dominicans, Augustinians, Benedictines and many others. The visitor can get an idea of the former wealth of the city by taking a stroll through the square of the **Fish Market**, fronted by the neo-Gothic **Town Hall** (1869–71) which stands near the **Statue of Roland** (1591) and two fine Renaissance houses.

Former royal seat: The town of **Gotha** (population 54,000), can be recognised from afar by the distinctive Schloss Friedenstein standing out above the town's skyline. The town is one of the oldest in Thuringia and was once a royal seat. In the Middle Ages its economic prosperity reached its peak through trade in cereals, timber products and woad for blue dyes.

The **Castle** was built after the Thirty Years' War, between 1643 and 1657. The earliest example of a baroque castle in Germany, its rooms are magnificently furnished. The **Painting Collection** includes works by Lucas Cranach the Elder, Rubens and Frans Hals. Additional attractions include a small **Copperplate Exhibition** and an **Art Room**. In 1774, the **Ekhof Theatre** housed in

Sausages are a Thuringian speciality.

the castle was the first in Germany to offer its actors fixed engagements. The stage accoutrements are preserved largely in their original condition. In the same building the **Cartographic Museum** is dedicated to Justus Perthes, whose cartographic institution, founded in 1785, formed the basis for the Gotha publishing method.

If all this has still not satisfied your thirst for knowledge, you can visit the **Natural History Museum**. This can be followed by a relaxing stroll in the castle grounds or a refreshing drink in the Café der Orangerie.

All the medieval buildings are clustered together around the delightful **Market Place**, with the red **Renaissance Town Hall** (1567–77) forming the centrepiece. A little further on is the **Augustinian Monastery**, with its beautiful cloister and Gothic church (of particular note are the chancel, royal box, and the 16th- and 17th-century graves and memorial stones).

Gotha also supplies an important date in the struggle for workers' rights. In May 1875 the German Social Democratic Workers' Party united with the General German Workers' Union to become the forerunner of today's SPD.

Towns of the Thuringian Forest: To the south of the towns of Weimar, Erfurt, Gotha and Eisenach lie the undulating hills of the Thuringian Forest. A deceptive amount of history and culture is hidden in these beautiful surroundings.

From 1620 the Bach family made their contribution to the musical world in the attractive town of **Arnstadt** (population 30,000). The most famous among them, Johann Sebastian, was from 1703 until 1707 the organist in the church which today bears his name. His **memorial museum** is to be found in the **Haus zum Palmbaum**.

With its beautifully preserved Old Town, Arnstadt is one of the most ancient towns in Germany (first cited in 704). In the baroque **Castle** (1728–32), the unique **Mon Plaisir Dolls' Town**, containing over 400 dolls from the period 1690 to 1750 collected by Princess Auguste Dorothea, is on show for all to wonder at. There are further collections

of valuable exhibits – 16th-century Brussels tapestries, a display of porcelain, *Dorotheenthaler* faience pottery, paintings from the 16th to the 20th century, and rococo carvings. There is a steam locomotive collection at the **Museum im Lokschuppen**.

Goethe often spent time in **Ilmenau** (pop. 32,000), simply relaxing or else on official business, as he was inspector of the silver and copper mines here. The poet's apartment on the Market Place has been opened as a **Goethe Memorial Museum**. Ilmenau is the beginning of the **Goethe Way** which ends in Stützerbach (waymarked G, 18 km/11 miles).

A winding road leads from here to **Oberhof** at 830 metres (2,720 feet). Most of its 100,000 annual visitors come for the winter sports, attracted by the ski-jump complex, the biathlon stadium and the speed-skating rink.

The small town of **Schmalkalden** (pop. 17,000) made history with the *Schmalkaldischen Bund* (League of Schmalkalden), formed in 1531: the Protestant clergy united to confront the

Foxgloves in bloom.

power of the central Catholic Imperial regime. In the 1546–47 War of Schmalkalden, Charles V finally overpowered the league's army, but the Imperial force was waning.

The first historical mention of the town was about 700 years earlier, in 874. At that time it was in the hands of the House of Thuringia, later the counts of Henneberg, and finally the counts of Hessen (Kassel). Wilhelm IV von Hessen had **Schloss Wilhelmsburg** (1585–90) built as a hunting lodge and summer retreat. The ornamental walls of the rooms display fine examples of plaster work and frescoes. The **Castle Museum** has an interesting display on the rise of the iron and steel industries from the 15th century.

The **Neue Hütte Monument to Technology** represents the iron smelting industry of the 19th century. From 1745 Schmalkalden was a centre for gunmaking, and in World War II hand grenades and anti-tank guns were manufactured here. Two bombing raids destroyed houses and factories, but a small part of the medieval town was left undamaged, including fine, half-timbered houses, churches and the Town Hall.

The narrow winding road now leads across the narrow **Trusetal** with its waterfall to **Bad Liebenstein** where cottage industry goes hand in hand with the area's natural resource of healing waters. Since 1610 this spa town has prided itself on cures for heart disease.

Thal is a small village with a great history. As a result of the 1920 revolt in Berlin, led by the East Prussian Officer Kapp, workers throughout the whole country joined the general strike. In Thal the proletariat furthered their cause by seizing privately owned weapons. Fifteen workers who were volunteers in the Marburg Student Corps were arrested and shot, while the perpetrators were absolved. A memorial to the murder can be seen in the cemetery.

Nature in the Thuringian Forest: Undulating, thickly forested hills, narrow river valleys and rounded mountain tops all combine to form the unique quality of the Thuringian Forest, known as the

The town hall in Gotha, city of cartography.

"Pearl of Germany". Goethe himself enjoyed the natural surroundings of this region, and today's hiker will be in good company if he follows the **Rennsteig** – the famous, 168-km (105-mile) long-distance ridge path which crosses the whole area, from Höschel, past Eisenach, to Blankenstein (five days).

The route also passes by the **Grosse Inselsberg** (916 metres/3,000 feet). Although this is only the fourth highest mountain in the region, it offers the most beautiful view, and boasts the title "King of the Thuringian Forest".

Not far from Eisenach is the impressive **Drachenschlucht** (Dragon's Gorge), with its 10-metre (33-foot) high sheer cliff walls which lean towards each other to a 73-cm (30-inch) gap. A 3-km (2-mile) path leads from Sophienaue through the mossy gorge.

A visit to the glittering **Marienglashöhle** near Friedrichroda, one of the largest crystal caves in Europe, is a must. Its walls are covered in patterns formed by gypsum crystals up to 60 cm (24 inches) long. A natural geological window reveals the rock strata.

On the northern edge of the Thuringian Forest, near Sattelstadt (on the B7 in the Gotha direction), lie the **Hörselberge**, a 7-km (4-mile) long limestone feature steeped in legend. This is the home of Frau Holle, who is reputed to keep a stern watch over both the hard-working and the lazy. Here also is the cave of Venus, who is said to have ensnared the knight Tannhäuser for seven long years. Wagner used this story in the plot of his opera of the same name. The ridge of this escarpment, which provides a rich habitat for a variety of flora and fauna, gives a further panorama of the Thuringian Forest.

At the northern tip of the forest is **Eisenach** (pop. 45,000), whose biggest attraction is the mighty Wartburg. Before embarking on an ascent to the castle, however, it is well worth taking time out for a stroll around Eisenach's idyllic streets. One of its oldest town houses was the home of the reformer and Latin scholar Martin Luther, who lived there between 1498 and 1501. The **Lutherhaus** is mainly dedicated to Luther him-

self, but also contains an interesting collection of religious publications from the 16th century.

Another famous name associated with the town is that of Johann Sebastian Bach. The **Bachhaus**, which also houses a display of ancient musical instruments, was set up at Am Frauenplan 21, believed to be where the great composer and musician was born in 1685.

As in Erfurt and Gotha, the fight for workers' rights is also represented here. The Eisenach party conference in 1869 led to the foundation of the Social Democratic Workers' Party. Since 1896 the town has developed as an important centre of the motor industry, and under the GDR, the Wartburg was manufactured here. In 1989 Opel took over and invested a billion marks in the factory, which today provides jobs for just under 2,000 employees.

The mists of time: On a rocky plateau 400 metres (1,300 feet) above the town, the historic **Wartburg Castle** is steeped in history. It is so well hidden that in all its 900 years it has only been besieged

The market place in Eisenach.

once, but never captured or severely damaged. Legend has it that it was founded in 1067 by Ludwig dem Springer.

The Wartburg's reputation as the most quintessentially German of all German castles, and all the legends which surround it, are due in no small degree to the special interest devoted to it by the Romantic artists of the early 19th century. Their search for the origins of German culture led to a reverence for all things medieval.

Thus the theme of the legendary *Sängerkrieg* (*War of the Poets*) which took place at the Wartburg reappears in several works of the Romantic era: in E.T.A. Hoffman's *Die Serapionsbrüder* (1812), Ludwig Tieck's *Phantasus* (1816), and Richard Wagner's opera *Tannhäuser* (1845). The *Sängerkrieg*, a Middle High German literary piece, describes a meeting between the most famous *Minnesinger* – Walther von der Vogelweide, Wolfram von Eschenbach and Heinrich von Ofterdingen – at the Wartburg during the time of Prince Hermann I (1190–1217). By the 19th century the castle had fallen into decay, and a restoration programme was carried out at Goethe's instigation.

Another story connected with the Wartburg tells of the life of the pious **Elisabeth** (1207–31), canonised in 1235. At the age of 14 the Hungarian king's daughter married the 20-year-old Earl of Thuringia, Ludwig IV. Deeply influenced by the conviction of the Franciscan friars that poverty saves the eternal soul, Elisabeth founded churches, homes for the elderly and several hospitals. The legend of the Miracle of the Roses tells of how she hid bread and meat under her coat to take to the poor in the hospital. When she was stopped and searched by her husband's men, the food was suddenly turned to roses beneath her coat. The walls of Elisabeth's Bower are decorated with a splendid glass mosaic (1902–06) showing scenes from the legend.

The most famous connection with the Wartburg is that of **Martin Luther**. Because of his severe criticism of the Catholic Church, he was excommunicated by the Pope in 1521 and brought before the Reichstag in Worms to recant his thesis. Luther refused and was placed under the ban of the Empire. His overlord, the Elector Friedrich the Wise, brought him in secret to the Wartburg, where he translated the New Testament.

The theme of unity: The whole of the second storey of the castle is taken up by the magnificent banqueting hall supported by 12th-century columns. Here are hung the banners of the German Students' Societies who celebrated the renowned **Wartburgfest** in 1817. They proposed the unification of Germany into one empire, contrary to the interests of the conservative princes and monarchs of individual small states.

Just as it was then, the theme of unity is relevant today. While the evidence of a single German cultural inheritance is to be found throughout the region, it was only a few years ago that the area was divided by the border between West and East, which ran near **Creuzburg** (pop. 2,500) and **Ifta** (pop. 1,350).

Both places were designated in the "prohibited area" which was subject to certain zoned restrictions. Within 500 metres (550 yards) of the border there was a curfew after 10pm, and any movement in the direction of the border was strictly forbidden. Even those living within the 5-km (3-mile) zone were allowed visitors from outside only by official permit. Immediate relatives were granted a three-month permit, others were allowed only daily visits.

The border today: Not many visible traces of the border remain. The minefields have been cleared, and only in one or two places is a small stretch of the fence left standing. There is a positive aspect to the whole business – the only one. In the former no-man's-land, nature lay undisturbed and a unique self-contained eco-system developed.

The **National Park of Werratal-Eichsfeld**, stretching from here to Heiligenstadt, was created to preserve this system. It can only be hoped that journeys such as this one through the "other" German areas will play an important role in promoting a deeper mutual understanding.

The Wartburg, a castle steeped in history.

Some call it the "world metropolis with a heart", others refer to it as "the village of a million people". Munich, capital of the Free State of Bavaria is certainly a city of world status, not only because of its size but also because it is the headquarters of international companies like Siemens and BMW. In addition, with its Pinakothek art galleries, it possesses two of the world's greatest museums, as well as several top orchestras. Munich has remained a "village" because it exudes that atmosphere the world now describes as *Gemütlichkeit*, even though at times this has something to do with the influence of beer. Whenever opinion polls go looking for Germany's favourite city, Munich always takes first place. The Nymphenburg Palace, the River Isar, the Deutsches Museum, the Oktoberfest, the Olympic Stadium – Munich certainly has a lot to offer.

A Bavarian King became one of the most famous of Europe's rulers: Ludwig II. The palaces and castles of the "Mad King", whether Neuschwanstein, Herrenchiemsee or Linderhof, put all other tourist attractions, far and wide, entirely in the shade. Ludwig or no Ludwig, an excursion to his Herrenchiemsee Palace is an absolute must.

Mention Munich, too, and the Alps come to mind. In Bavaria they might be slightly lower than elsewhere, but no less impressive. The foothills, too, form a picture postcard landscape, in which baroque churches thrust their onion-domed towers heavenwards. Only some 56 km (36 miles) from Munich, the 2,000-year-old city of Augsburg offers magnificent art treasures and historic old buildings such as the Fuggerei. A visit to this hospitable trading city, one of the biggest in Germany back in 1500, should certainly be considered. A journey north along the Romantic Road takes the traveller back to the 16th and 17th centuries in places like Nördlingen, Dinkelsbühl and Rothenburg. These towns, which have survived the centuries virtually intact and present well-preserved little worlds of their own, appeal to the romantic in any visitor.

Further afield, southern Germany opens up great expanses of rich landscape and offers a wealth of sights to enjoy. The baroque Residenz of Würzburg has been described as one of the finest palaces in all Europe. Make up your own mind by visiting this town, the Franconian wine centre. On the shores of Lake Constance palm trees and banana trees are quite at home. The Black Forest is a paradise for those who enjoy the great outdoors. Ulm, on the Württemberg–Bavarian border, stands sentinel over the Danube with its lofty Münster tower, the highest in the world, while Stuttgart is dominated by the shining Mercedes star.

Preceding pages: about one-third of the territory of southern Germany is covered with forest. Marienplatz is the most important meeting place for locals and visitors alike. **Left**, the Oktoberfest gets underway with a grand procession of Bavarians in their traditional costumes.

MUNICH

With a population of nearly 1½ million, the Bavarian capital is Germany's third largest city after Berlin and Hamburg. Lying on the banks of the Isar River, with the majestic Alps and several scenic Bavarian lakes just a short drive away, Munich offers a wealth of recreational activities and a wide palette of cultural attractions.

The large number of museums and art collections and the variety of music and theatre events make Munich a cultural metropolis of international rank. Here, too, Germany's largest university, with almost 100,000 students, is located. More publishers have their headquarters in Munich than in any other German city. In recent decades, the city has developed into a high tech centre.

Despite copious amounts of international seasoning, Munich has managed to retain an almost provincial flavour. The true natives, having found a way to ignore all the hustle and bustle around them, retain a serenity and lust for life which is unmatched. They take pride in their Bavarian customs and traditions, thus ensuring their continuation in this otherwise cosmopolitan city.

Wealth based on salt: A monastery known as *Munichen* (meaning monks in High German) is known to have existed here from the 8th century. In 1158, Duke Henry the Lion had a vital bridge over the Isar moved south to Munich, diverting the salt trade route between Bad Reichenhall and Augsburg and enabling Munich to prosper from the taxes levied on this valuable commodity. Emperor Frederick I of Barbarossa legalised Henry's action and the rapidly growing settlement soon won the right to hold markets and to mint coins. In 1180 Barbarossa awarded Palatinate Duke Otto von Wittelsbach the imperial state of Bavaria, whose dynasty guided the fate of Bavaria for almost 750 years, until 1918.

Duke Wilhelm IV (1493–1550) chose Munich as his residence and the capital of Bavaria. He and his successor Duke Albrecht V enforced exclusive Catholicism throughout Bavaria. During the reign of Maximilian I (1597–1651), the city suffered the ravages of the Thirty Years' War (1618–48). The column outside the Town Hall, the Mariensäule, was erected at the end of the war and marked a period of recovery and reconstruction. Under the Elector Max II Emanuel (1679–1726) Munich attained the rank of a European city.

In the following century, the city once more became involved in the tumults of war and occupation. Famine and poverty struck. After the alliance with Napoleon in 1806, which made Bavaria a kingdom, the city entered a new period of prosperity as a royal capital and seat of residence. Napoleon dissolved the monasteries and had their estates nationalised. In 1819 the first Bavarian parliament assembled in Munich. King Ludwig I (1825–48) continued with monumental architectural works (including the National Theatre and the Prinz Carl Palais) which greatly influenced the present appearance of the city.

Revolution: After the death of the fairy-tale King Ludwig II, Munich developed into a large modern city under the regentship of Prince Luitpold (1886–1912) and by the turn of the century had a population of about half a million. But Munich again suffered heavily under war – this time World War I. Popular revolutionary pressure brought about the abdication of Ludwig III, the last king of Bavaria, in November 1918. A council of workers, soldiers and peasants was formed, with the leader of the revolution, Kurt Eisner, at its head. Eisner became Bavaria's first Prime Minister but shortly afterwards was assassinated. His death at the hands of Anton von Arco sparked bloody street battles which raged for six months and left some 600 dead.

Capital of the "movement": The end of the revolutionary Räterepublik ushered in a new and unhappy chapter of German history. It was in Munich that Adolf Hitler rapidly rose to the leadership of the NSDAP, the Nazis. On 8 November 1923 he staged an abortive coup against the national government. The *putsch* was put down and Hitler was imprisoned. With the 1938 Munich Agreement in which Hitler, Mussolini, Chamberlain and Deladier sealed the fate of Czechoslovakia, the "city of the [Nazi] movement" won further questionable significance. Hitler's expansionism was to bring Munich great wartime misery; 70 bombing raids reduced the city to little more than a pile of rubble. Eventually Munich was occupied by American troops with the people offering no resistance.

What Munich has to offer: Munich's true centre, its extensive pedestrian shopping area, begins near the **Hauptbahnhof** or main railway station at busy **Karlsplatz**, which is known by the locals as Stacchus. At the end of the 18th century, the square and its imposing gate, the 14th-century **Karlstor**, were part of the city walls. Passing through the gate you step into the pedestrian area, passing the **Richard Strauss Fountain**, the German Hunting Museum and the **Church of St Michael**,

Famous Munich landmarks: the town hall and the Frauenkirche.

one of the most famous Renaissance churches in Germany where Ludwig II, the doomed fairy tale king of Bavaria, is buried, together with other members of the Wittelsbach dynasty. Munich's landmark cathedral, the **Frauenkirche** or Church of Our Lady is a late-Gothic edifice of red brick, consecrated in 1494. The soaring building, with its two distinctive onion-domed towers (now Munich's popular symbol), represents the pride and the prosperity of the city's population in the late Middle Ages. The interior of the church, which is among the largest hall churches in southern Germany, consists of three naves of equal height. Of particular note are the three Gothic stained-glass windows in the choir gallery. The crypt contains the tombs of 46 Wittelsbach princes and several cardinals of the Munich-Freising diocese. From the south tower there's a fine view over the city and the Alps, which look deceptively near when the warm dry wind known as the *Föhn* is wafting in from the south.

Central **Marienplatz** throbs with life throughout the year – in spring and summer, when the street entertainers are doing their thing, and in deepest winter when the Christmas market takes over, the stalls clustering around the statue of Munich's patron, the Virgin Mary, who looks down on the scene from her place atop a marble column.

One entire side of the square is taken up by the neo-Gothic **Rathaus** or City Hall (built between 1867 and 1908), with a world-famous **Glockenspiel** in its 85-metre (278-feet) tower. The carillon and its mechanical figures depict two episodes from Munich's history: a tournament held in Marienplatz in 1568, and the *Schäfflertanz* (dance of the coopers) commemorating the end of the plague in Munich in 1517. There are performances twice a day in summer (11am and 5pm) and every day at 11am in winter. The **Old Town Hall** (1470–74) sits rather forlornly amid all this attention on the eastern side of Marienplatz. But its modest exterior contains one of Germany's finest Gothic halls.

Across the road from the old town hall

Chess al fresco.

is the **Church of the Holy Ghost**, originally built in the 14th century, but fully restored in florid rococo style between 1724 and 1730. Behind the church is the **Viktualienmarkt**, Munich's colourful open-air food market (*Viktualien* means victuals), with its enormous variety of produce, ranging from rosy Bavarian apples to exotic tropical fruits, simple sausages to expensive venison, hearty home-brewed beers to fine French wines. There are friendly bars and a couple of small beer gardens to recover from the rigours of shopping.

From the tower of the nearby **Alter Peter**, as the locals call the venerable **Church of St Peter**, Munich's oldest parish church, there's a fine view as far as the Alps.

The **Rindermarkt** (Munich's former cattle market) leads to Sendlinger Strasse, with its richly-stocked shops and the incredible **Asamkirche**. The famous Asam brothers built it between 1733 and 1746 giving the little church a magnificent rococo interior which bursts from the gloom on the visitor's eye with a theatrical and almost mystical force.

The **Munich City Museum**, a short walk from Sendlinger Strasse, was built as an arsenal and livery stable in the 15th century and now has regular showings of mostly contemporary art and design and a permanent exhibition devoted to the history of the city. The first floor has a **Puppet Museum** where regular performances are given.

Fun-loving Munich: Munich works hard and plays hard. Its carnival season, Fasching, is as well known as its beer "temple", the imposing **Hofbräuhaus**. No sooner is Fasching over than it's strong beer time at the **Nockherberg** Starkbier festival. Munich has more than 100 beer gardens, the largest of which – the Hirschgarten – accommodates more than 7,000 people under its spreading chestnut trees. At the end of September it's time for the 14-day Munich beer festival, the **Oktoberfest**, which draws 5 million visitors every year to the vast **Theresienwiese**. Affectionately termed *Wies'n* by the locals, it was originally an agricultural fair attended by the citizens

Bavarians take their costume seriously.

of Munich and the farmers from the outlying countryside. Then, during this century, the small booths selling food and beer were replaced by enormous temporary beer halls, each accommodating over 6,000 people. The "tents" belong to the city's major breweries.

Cultural metropolis: Opera and ballet festivals, a Film Festival and a Biennale pack Munich's cultural calendar, in which open-air concerts and ballet performances at the Schleissheim palace and in the courtyard of the Residenz are among the repertoire.

Beyond the **Isartor**, another of the old city gates (containing a museum devoted to the popular Munich comedian Karl Valentin), lies the world's largest science and technology museum, the **Deutsches Museum**, situated on an Isar island. Its astonishing 55 sq. km (21 sq. miles) of floor space contain more than 15,000 exhibits, from sailing boats to aeroplanes and from steam engines to microchips. Replicas of coal and salt mines record the development of the mining industry. Days, if not weeks, are required to see everything.

From the museum it's a short stroll along the right bank of the Isar to the **Maximilianeum** (1857–74), the seat of the Bavarian Parliament. It stands proudly at the end of **Maximilianstrasse**, laid out as an avenue of regal magnificence. The wide street has retained much of its opulent character, attracting some of Munich's most elegant shops, boutiques, bars, cafés and art galleries.

Here too is the **Museum of Anthropology** with its ethnological collection and the **Munich Kammerspiele**, one of Germany's best theatres.

Wittelsbach residence: Maximilianstrasse opens out into **Max Joseph Platz**, dominated by the columned facade of the **National Theatre**, contrasting strikingly with the modern Residence Theatre next door, named after the neighbouring royal palace, or **Residenz** (Royal Palace), home of the Wittelsbach rulers for 800 years.

Priceless Wittelsbach treasures, including coronation crowns and accoutrements, are on view in the **Königsaal** and the **Schatzkammer**, or Treasury.

The former royal theatre, the **Cuvilliés Theatre**, is a rococo jewel and still in use, as are the **Herkulessaal** concert hall and the grand **Antiquarium** reception hall.

Before the Residenz was built, the Bavarian dukes' power base had been the **Alter Hof** between Max Joseph Platz and Marienplatz.

A visit to Schwabing: From Max Joseph Platz, Residenzstrasse leads to Odeonsplatz, dominated by the **Feldherrnhalle** and the 17th-century **Theatinerkirche**, with twin towers and imposing 71-metre (236-foot) high dome. Its interior has a magnificent high altar and more Wittelsbach tombs. From Odeonsplatz, elegant **Ludwigstrasse** leads north towards Schwabing. Ludwig I commissioned architects F. von Gärtner and Leo von Klenze to design it as another regal Munich thoroughfare. They lined the street with impressive neoclassical buildings, including the **Bavarian State Library**, one of the largest German libraries, and the **Ludwig-Maximilians-University**. Situated shortly before it is

Boating in the English Gardens.

the Victory **Siegestor** (Victory Gate), which was erected in 1850 to commemorate the Bavarian soldiers who fell during the Napoleonic wars.

At this point, Ludwigstrasse gives way to **Leopoldstrasse**, once the bustling heart of the legendary artists' district of Schwabing and still a pulsating nightlife centre, with cafés, bars and discos. Munich's famous park, the **English Gardens**, east of Leopoldstrasse, was laid out in 1785. It acquired its name because of its informal, so-called English style and is one of Europe's biggest parks. A fine view of Munich's distinctive silhouette can be enjoyed from the park's **Monopteros** (a Greek temple), which shares a corner of the park with the famous beer garden by the **Chinese Tower**. Completed in 1791, it was modelled on the outlook tower in Kew Gardens. It did not survive World War II but was rebuilt in 1952 according to the original plans.

At the southern end of the park is one of Munich's few remaining Hitler-era buildings, the **Haus der Kunst** (Museum of Modern Art), from which the Nazis once banned "decadent" art. It is now a home for some 20th-century masterpieces with works by Picasso, Matisse, Dali, Klee and Warhol. The **Bavarian National Museum** further along Prinzregentenstrasse is one of the best-known museums in the city and provides a comprehensive insight into the history of Bavarian art and culture from the Middle Ages to the present.

An art eldorado: The densest concentration of the city's art treasures is to be found to the west of the city centre in the so-called Maxvorstadt. **Königsplatz**, probably the most impressive square in Munich, is lined on all sides by neoclassical buildings, the **Propyläen**, the **Glyptothek** and the **Antikensammlung**. Commissioned by Ludwig I, they earned Munich the sobriquet "Athens on the Isar". The Antikensammlung contains collections of world-famous Greek vases, Roman and Etruscan statues and artefacts made of glass and terracotta, while the Glyptothek is devoted to Greek and Roman sculpture. Around the cor-

The Alte Pinakothek exhibits the works of many European masters.

ner on Luisenstrasse is one of Munich's most attractive galleries, the **Lenbach Villa**, which boasts a lovely Italianate garden. It was built in 1890 in Tuscan style for the Munich painter Franz von Lenbach. Today it houses the **Municipal Art Gallery** and displays works by Munich artists from the 15th to the 20th centuries, with the Blauer Reiter group featuring prominently.

Nearby Karolinenplatz has an **obelisk** erected in 1812 as a memorial to Bavarians killed in Napoleon's Russian campaign. On the left Barerstrasse leads to the **Alte Pinakothek**, one of the most important art galleries in Europe, exhibiting works of European masters from the 14th–18th centuries (which has been undergoing extensive renovations). The adjacent **Neue Pinakothek** has about 400 paintings and sculptures covering all the important modern periods, from impressionism to art nouveau and symbolism.

A royal garden house: The summer residence of the Bavarian princes and kings, **Nymphenburg Palace**, was built at the start of the 18th century by the Italian master Agostino Barelli and is one of the most famous late-baroque palace estates in Germany, complete with gardens, pavilions, galleries and the building in which Nymphenburg porcelain has been produced since 1761. The main building has a marble hall; the Wittelsbachs' living and reception rooms are in the north and south wings. There is a fascinating **Gallery of Beauties**, commissioned by Ludwig I. One of the attractions is a painting of the Irish dancer Lola Montez, whose affair with Ludwig I was one of the reasons for his abdication in 1848. The **Marstallmuseum** or Stables Museum contains a fine collection of royal coaches, sleighs and ceremonial vehicles.

The park was laid out on the French pattern and contains a number of smaller buildings, including the **Badenburg**, a lodge with baroque baths built in 1721, the octagonal **Pagodenburg** from 1719, the **Magdalenenklause**, which Maximilian Emanuel had built as a hermitage for himself in 1725 and the **Amalienburg**, a hunting lodge completed in

1739 by Franz Cuvilliés the Elder and now regarded as a masterpiece of European rococo.

Munich's Mittlererring ring road (or the U3 underground) brings you to the **Olympiapark**, built for the Olympic Games in 1972. The **Olympic Stadium** has a tent roof which spans the whole site in a series of giant "spider's webs", covering a total surface area of nearly 75,000 sq. metres (90,000 sq. yards). The **Olympic Hall** is now a concert venue. The restaurant at the top of the 290-metre (960-foot) high **TV tower** affords some magnificent views of Munich and the Alps.

Bavarian lakes: On fine weekends in summer and winter all roads lead south and east to the lakes. The nearest of them, **Lake Starnberg** (on the S6 suburban railway) is crisscrossed by steamers. One popular stop is **Berg**, where a cross in the water shows the spot where the drowned body of King Ludwig II was recovered in 1886.

Ammersee, 35 km (22 miles) from Munich and also accessible on the S-Bahn railway, is not as crowded as Lake Starnberg, although its main town, Herrsching, is a good starting point for walks into the hills to a beer-lovers' mecca, **Andechs**. The reputation of this famous Bavarian monastery is largely based on the outstanding Andechs beer brewed there.

King Ludwig's own Versailles: Another popular outing is **Chiemsee**, a large lake to the south-east of Munich at the foot of the beautiful Alpine Chiemgau foothills. On the island of Herrenchiemsee stands Ludwig II's imitation of the palace of Versailles, completed in 1878. It was intended as the highest expression of princely splendour and regal might of the Bavarian throne. In summer, concerts are held in the stately hall of mirrors. The King Ludwig Museum offers a fascinating insight into the king's life and his love of music and theatre. A boat crosses to the island from Prien.

The Benedictine Abbey of St Mary (766) on the neighbouring **Fraueninsel** is a beautiful, harmonious combination of Romanesque, Gothic and baroque architectural styles.

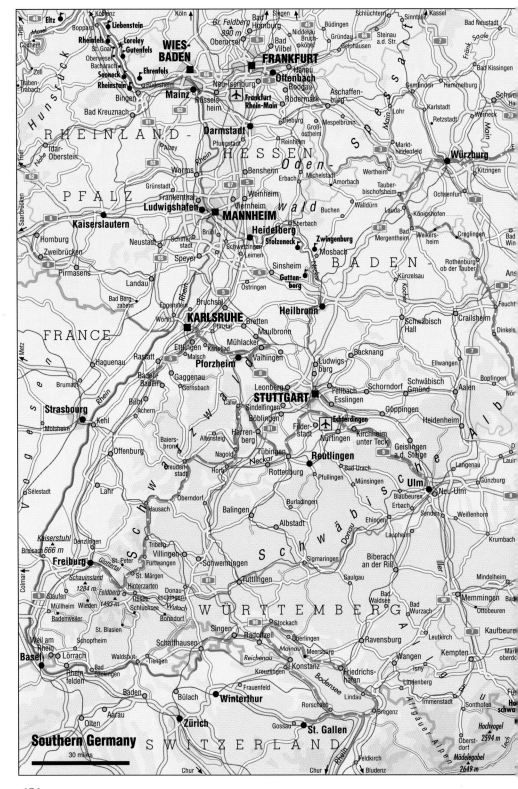

Southern Germany

30 miles

176

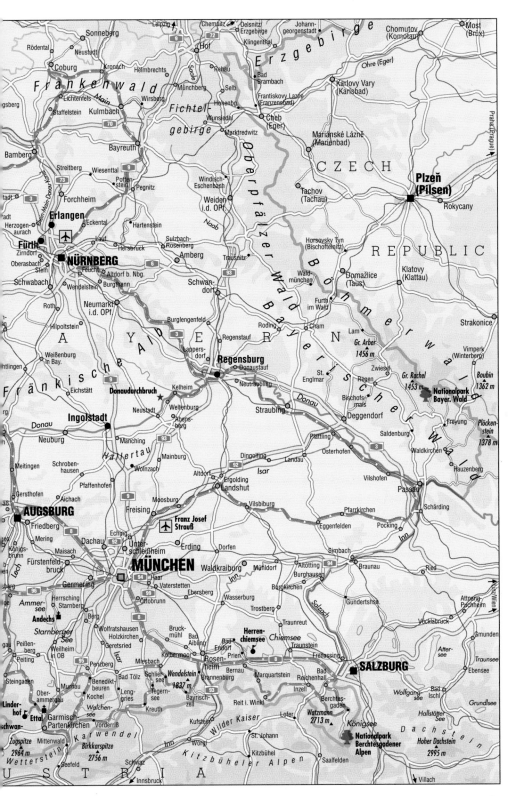

177

THE GERMAN ALPINE ROAD

Wending its way from Königsee near Berchtesgaden in the east to Lindau on Lake Constance in the west, the German Alpine Road is the oldest tourist route in Germany. In most road atlases, its serpentine, 465-km (290-mile) course is marked by additional colouring. Allow plenty of time for the scenic sections of the route which follow a number of byways and diversions. A toll is payable on some private roads.

From Munich, the A8 motorway to Salzburg leads to **Bad Reichenhall**. The old centre of the town with its spa resort is well worth a visit. Inhaling and drinking the saline spa waters offers visitors relief from respiratory disorders. In the salt refinery, 400,000 litres of this spa water drip over a brushwood grating. Some of the water evaporates, thereby increasing the salt content of the air and imparting a curative effect.

The section of the German Alpine Road between Bad Reichenhall and Berchtesgaden is without doubt one of the most attractive panoramic routes in the entire Alps. Astonishing views across the spectacular mountain scenery of the **Berchtesgadener Land** lurk behind every bend, with the **Watzmann** (2,713 metres/8,901 feet), Germany's second highest mountain, dominating the scene.

The basis for the wealth of the present mountain spa of **Berchtesgaden** was established by Emperor Frederick Barbarossa when he granted the local Augustinian monks prospecting rights for salt and ore. The salt mine is still in operation and a visit is highly recommended. Visitors descend about (500 metres/1,640 feet) into the depths.

On walking through the old town centre, the most striking sights are the typical Upper Bavarian buildings in the Weihnachtsschützenstrasse and its side streets, featuring pastel-coloured facades decorated with fine stucco. In the Metzgerstrasse, the outdoor wall paintings on the former hotel *Zum Hirschen* (now a bank) depict the sumptuous pleasures of Bavarian cuisine.

One of the scenic highlights is the trip along the Rossfeld-Höhenstrasse (toll road). Numerous vantage points offer breathtaking views of the Watzmann, the Hoher Göll (2,522 metres/8,275 feet), the Tannengebirge, the Steinernes Meer and the Dachstein (2,995 metres/9,830 feet).

In 1935 Hitler had the famous "Eagles' Nest" built on the **Obersalzberg**, where he would receive party luminaries and important visitors from abroad. A boat trip can be made across the approximately 8-km (5-mile) long, crystal-clear **Königsee,** deep in the Berchtesgadener Nature Reserve.

The German Alpine Road continues from Berchtesgaden through Schönau and Inzell, passing inviting country inns with beer gardens shaded by chestnut trees and on to **Reit im Winkel**. This famous winter sports resort with guaranteed snow on the Winklmoosalm (1,160 metres/3,800 feet) is also superb for walking in the warmer months. After a short section of motorway driving, along the A8 and the A93 (Brandenburg

exit), the German Alpine Road weaves its way between the steep gorge of the Tatzelwurm (toll road) towards the Sudelfeld ski resort (1,100–1,450 metres/3,610– 4,760 feet).

The route continues through hilly pastureland at the foot of the Wetterstein massif, past the winter sports resort of **Bayerischzell** and continues on towards **Schliersee**, a village oasis centred around the Parish Church of St Sixtus, whose stucco and frescoes are the early work of Johann Baptist Zimmermann (1680–1758).

In the midst of a picture postcard landscape of gently sloping meadows lies **Lake Tegernsee**. First to arrive here were the monks; then came the Wittelsbachs, the Bavarian royal family, followed by a host of famous artists. After the war, Tegernsee became a haven for politicians and super-rich businessmen, who secured expensive plots of land by the lake shore.

In the picturesque town of **Tegernsee**, the **Monastery Church of St Quirin**, whose baroque doorway opens on to a triple-naved basilica with a ceiling fresco by Johann Georg Asam, is well worth a visit. Those who enjoy more raucous entertainment should call in at the **Herzogliche Bräustüberl** to sample the beer. Beautiful examples of Upper Bavarian domestic architecture can be found in the Rosengasse.

At the southern end of the lake is the twin community of **Rottach-Eggern**. A sign at the far end of the town, pointing to the left, indicates the station for the cable car to the summit of the **Wallberg** (1,722 metres/5,650 feet). This mountain is a starting point for some moderately tough hikes; colourful hang-gliders hover around its summit. On bright winter days, lazy sunworshippers take it easy on their chalet terrace while keen alpine skiers make the most of the slopes.

The **Achen Pass** (944 metres/3100 feet) leads to **Kreuth**, another popular winter sports venue. Soon after this, the River Isar, which is dammed in the **Sylvensteinsee Lake**, comes into view. The road crosses the long lake over an

The craft of violin making has a long tradition in Mittenwald.

elegantly arched bridge. In 1959, this lake engulfed the old poaching village of Fall. A literary memorial to the village can be found in the novel *Der Jäger vom Fall* (*The Hunters of Fall*) by Ludwig Ganghofer (1855–1920).

In **Vorderriss**, the *Gasthof zur Post* restaurant marks the start of a 15-km (9-mile) long, narrow forest toll road through the **Karwendel Mountain Nature Park** leading via Wallgau and Klais bei Krün to GarmischPartenkirchen. From **Hinterriss**, you can walk through the **Ahornboden Woods** with their unique stock of deciduous trees.

A detour to Mittenwald: Mittenwald lies in the valley that separates the Wetterstein Range from the towering summits of the Karwendel Range to the east – the village character of this small town has been largely preserved. Mittenwald developed into a world-famous centre for violin-making after Matthias Klotz, who had learned this difficult art in Italy from Antonio Stradivari (1644–1737), returned to his home village. Six violin makers continue to produce the instruments today, and visitors can learn more about their rare skill at the **Violin Making Museum** (Ballenhausgasse 3). Mittenwald's outstanding landmark is the baroque tower of the **Church of St Peter and Paul**, one of the finest church towers in Upper Bavaria.

A fixed base: It is well worth spending a few days in **Garmisch-Partenkirchen** and using it as a base from which to make trips into the surrounding countryside. When the Olympic Games were held here in 1936, the two towns of Garmisch and Partenkirchen were merged to form a twin community. In the former Garmisch, the central Marienplatz is surrounded by a number of especially attractive buildings, including the Old Apothecary with its black and white scratchwork facade.

The summit of Germany's highest mountain, the **Zugspitze** (2,966 metres/9,730 feet) can be reached either by taking the rack and pinion railway from Partenkirchen or the even faster cable car from nearby Eibsee. On a clear day, visitors are greeted by a spellbinding panoramic view extending from the

Grossglockner to the ridge-line of the Bohemian Forest. The high corrie of the **Zugspitzplatt** to the south-west of the *Schneefernhaus* (Germany's highest hotel) is the highest altitude ski resort in the country, with snow guaranteed for most of the year. The Olympic ice-skating and skiing stadia are located in Partenkirchen.

Off the beaten track, a flight of steps on the western slopes of the **Wank** mountain leads to the late-baroque votive Chapel of **St Anton** (18th century). The dome fresco by the Tyrolean painter Johannes Holzer is a masterpiece.

The walk from Garmisch- Partenkirchen through the mountain gorge of **Partnachklamm** where the track leads you beneath overhangs with cascading waterfalls, presents some delightful scenery.

Another beautiful excursion leads via Walchensee and Kochelsee to Murnau and Benediktbeuern. The highest mountain lake in Germany, the Walchensee (802 metres/2,630 feet), is situated at the edge of the steep slopes of the

Walchensee offers ideal conditions for windsurfers.

Karwendel and **Wetterstein** mountain ranges. In clear weather, the Herzogstand (1,730 metres/5,680 feet; there is a cable-car), offers superb panoramic views of the High Tauern, the Grossglockner and the glacial scenery of the Ziller and Ötz Valleys. After Urfahr, the Kesselberg road leads down in a series of hairpin bends to the **Kochelsee Lake**. Shortly before the end of the mountain route, a sign indicates the cul-de-sac road to the Walchensee Power Station (tours available).

The painter Franz Marc, an important representative of German Expressionism, lived in **Kochel**, where a museum in Herzogstandweg now commemorates his work.

In **Murnau** on the **Staffelsee Lake**, the "Russian House", where the painters Gabriele Münter and Vasili Kandinsky lived from 1909 to 1914, will also be of interest to art lovers (Wednesday, Saturday and Sunday 4–6 pm). The Castle Museum also has absorbing exhibits relating to the Blaue Reiter group of artists, the Austrian writer Ödön von Horváth (1901–38), and life in the Murnau Moors.

Benediktbeuren, a formerly powerful, 17th-century Benedictine monastery has recently been restored to its former glory by the Salesian Don Bosco order. The **Anastasia Chapel** (1751–53) by Johann Michael Fischer is a rococo masterpiece.

Just outside Garmisch, at the foot of the steeply rising slopes of the Ettaler Mandl (1,633 metres/5,358 feet), lies the **Ettal Monastery**, a baroque Benedictine abbey. The fresco under the dome depicts no less than 431 figures on a total painted area of (1,300 sq.metres/13,993 sq.feet.

The Passion Plays of **Oberammergau** have brought fame to this little town. After an epidemic of the plague in 1633, to which one in every 10 inhabitants succumbed, the survivors vowed to perform Christ's Passion every 10 years thereafter as thanksgiving for their deliverance. The first performance was staged in 1634 and the next is due in the year 2000. A commercial enterprise

The Passion Plays in Oberammergau are staged once every 10 years.

operated according to stringent rules under the supervision of the parish council has also been set up. The auditorium of the Passion Play theatre has a seating capacity of 4,800 and overlooks the world's largest open-air stage, (at 45 metres/148 feet across and 30 metres/98 feet deep).

Oberammergau is also famous for the fine frescoes on the facades of its typical Upper Bavarian houses, which is not surprising when one considers that Franz Zwinck, the "inventor" of the Italian-influenced fresco technique known as *Lüftlmalerei* lived and worked in the town during the 18th century. Only a mile or two away is one of Ludwig II's three famous castles.

Regal dream worlds: This king of Bavaria, who even looked like a fairy-tale prince charming, was only 18 years old when he ascended to the throne in 1864. Ludwig was a musical person who loved the theatre and music more than anything else. In the first year after his coronation, however, he devoted himself with great passion to ruling the land. It was a task for which he was ill-prepared and ill-suited. Consequently, he withdrew further and further into the solitude of the Bavarian forests and mountains. His favourite residences were **Berg Castle** on the Starnberg Lake and **Hohenschwangau**, both of which he had inherited from his father. From these retreats, he organised the building of the Linderhof and Neuschwanstein castles.

Linderhof is a monument to Ludwig, designed according to plans by Georg Dollmann and set in the secluded Graswangtal Valley. The castle embodies stylistic elements from the baroque and rococo but was built between 1870 and 1879. Its 10 rooms are adorned with almost stifling pomp. The two most interesting rooms are probably the bedroom and the dining hall. In the latter, the table was designed as a "Magic Table" straight from *Grimms' Fairy Tales*, which would appear from a trap door in the floor. There are also artificial caves in the park, a Moorish Pavilion and the *Hundinghaus*, a type of hunting

lodge which Ludwig modelled on the stage set of Wagner's opera, the *Valkyrie*. The gardens surrounding Linderhof are uniquely beautiful. French formality near the castle gives way to an Italian-style, terraced garden, and this in turn merges with an English landscaped garden.

Hohenschwangau Castle near Füssen was originally a medieval castle which Crown Prince Maximilian of Bavaria had had restored in neo-Gothic style in 1833. King Ludwig II spent much of his youth here and was no doubt inspired with many romantic ideas which he later tried to incorporate in Neuschwanstein Castle.

For his dream world, rooted in medieval ideals, he chose a secluded eyrie far above the **Pöllat Gorge**. **Neuschwanstein Castle** is more akin to a theatrical stage-set than a place for living, ruling a kingdom and accommodating court society. The interior of the castle reflects the operatic fantasy world of Richard Wagner. In the **Sängersaal**, the centre piece of the fairy-tale castle, Ludwig II staged performances of scenes from the opera *Tannhäuser*, and other rooms are reminiscent of oriental palaces.

At a time in which the monarchy had long been in decline in Germany, Ludwig erected a last, great monument to the mythical kings of fairy-tale and legend. In June 1886, the government had the king declared insane by four psychiatrists who had never previously met him. Ludwig was deposed and forcibly moved from Neuschwanstein to Berg Castle on the Starnberg Lake where, on 13 June 1886, he was found drowned, together with his doctor. Since the circumstances of his death has never been clearly established, the interpretation that Ludwig had committed suicide in despair, taking the doctor with him, has frequently been suggested. The work on Neuschwanstein Castle was completed after 17 years.

From Hohenschwangau and Neuschwanstein, a wide view opens out over the Forggensee Lake, the Allgäu Alps and **Füssen**, above which rises the 16th-century **Hohes Schloss**, a former sum-

Left, was King Ludwig really so mad? **Below**, rococo detail on the Town Hall facade in Landsberg.

mer residence of the Bishops of Augsburg. Füssen is now considered one of the foremost spa and winter sports resorts in the Allgäu region.

Art and culture in the Allgäu: In the heart of the hilly Allgäu region lies the essentially Romanesque **Steingaden Monastery**, where the famous architect and stucco worker of the School of Wessobrunn, Dominikus Zimmermann (1685–1766) is buried. In the church at nearby **Wies**, he was able to realise his plans for a synthesis of rococo artistic forms, embodying perfect harmony between architecture and decoration. In 1745, he was commissioned by the Steingaden Monastery to plan a pilgrimage church to accommodate a statue of the *Flagellation of Christ*, on whose face a farmer's wife had discovered tears in 1739. From this date onwards, the rural chapel was the destination for countless pilgrims. The magnificent ceiling painting, which creates the illusion of vaulting on a flat surface, is by Johann Baptist Zimmermann. Another perfect example of rococo architecture is to be found in the **Rottenbuch Monastery.** The masters of the School of Wessobrunn devoted their considerable talents to transforming the Gothic basilica into a contemporary style.

On a clear day, the entire Allgäu Region can be viewed from the **Hohenpeissenberg** near Schöngau.

Rococo treasures: In recent years, the small town of **Landsberg** has carried out fine restoration work on its historical centre. As a settlement under royal protection, Landsberg grew rich on revenue from bridge tolls and the salt trade, subsequently investing its wealth in the obsessive decoration characteristic of the rococo. Dominikus Zimmermann was mayor of the town from 1749 to 1754, he planned the Rathaus (Town Hall) in the main square and worked on the Dominican Church and St John's Church, encouraging other rococo architects to visit. A further point of historical interest is that, after his failed *putsch* in Munich in 1923, Adolf Hitler was imprisoned in the jail in Landsberg, where he also wrote *Mein Kampf*.

The market place in Landsberg. The town hall is on the right.

THE ROMANTIC ROAD

Wars, destruction and bitter poverty dictated life for many centuries in Swabia and Franconia. The lack of municipal means for the reconstruction and modernisation of its hapless towns and villages was deeply regretted for a long time. But, in view of the growing awareness of the value of historical sites the disadvantages soon became vital assets in the rising tourist industry.

Attractive cities which were once royal and episcopal residences or trading centres, idyllic little medieval towns, sturdy old inns offering hearty meals and comfortable beds, wide open stretches of countryside for hiking and biking – that sums up what the regional tourist authority's Romantische Strasse has to offer along its 340-km (211-mile) itinerary, which stretches from Füssen and Augsburg to the episcopal residence city of Würzburg.

Augsburg and the Fuggers: First-time visitors to Augsburg are usually surprised at the wealth of artistic treasures in a city of only 250,00 inhabitants. But Augsburg looks back on more than 2,000 years of history rich in tradition: in 15BC the Roman *Augusta Vindelicum* was founded close to a military camp. The medieval trading city of the 11th century soon grew to a commercial centre and episcopal seat situated at the cross-roads of the important routes linking Italy and the centre of Franconian–Carolingian power. By about the year 1500 Augsburg was among the largest cities in the German speaking world. Emperor Maximilian I and Charles V raised money from the Fuggers, one of the wealthiest families in Europe, in exchange for trading and mining rights.

Augsburg has this wealthy banking and merchant family to thank for an extraordinary social housing settlement, located in the old Jakobervorstadt artisan quarter, the **Fuggerei** (1516). In accordance with the testament of its founder, Jakob Fugger, poor citizens of the Catholic faith can rent a small home here for a peppercorn rent. The Fuggerei

Museum is located at Mittlere Gasse 13.

Ten minutes' walk east of the Fuggerei brings the visitor to the glorious centre of the old city axis: Maximilianstrasse-Karolinenstrasse-Hoher Weg, to the imposing **Rathaus** (City Hall) and neighbouring Perlachturm (Perlach Tower). The Renaissance City Hall, the work of Elias Holl (1615–20) with its onion-domed towers and a magnificent Goldener Saal (Golden Hall), was intended to symbolise bourgeois wealth. The same purpose was assigned to the fountains which mark the route of the broad Maximilianstrasse.

Passing the Moritzkirche (Church of St Maurice), the visitor arrives at the former financial centre of the world, the 16th-century Fuggerhaus (Maximilianstrasse 36/38). Further up the street at number 46 is the fine **Schaezlerpalais**, an ideal home for the Deutsche Barockgalerie (German Baroque Gallery), which includes work by German masters of the 16th–18th centuries.

At the head of the street stands St Ulrich's Minster, a late Gothic basilica

with an interior decorated by Renaissance masters. From here, it's worth the walk to the old defence walls at the Rotes Tor (Red Gate), where outdoor theatre productions are staged in summer, and then along the streams back to the city centre, past the ancient homes of tanners and smiths. On the way, you can call in at the Handwerkermuseum (Crafts Museum) in the former Heilig-Geist-Spital, or visit the Roman Museum.

The earliest signs of settlement in Augsburg are to be found in the area of the **Dom** (Cathedral). The Romanesque-Gothic Cathedral is the home of precious works of art, including valuable altar pictures and the oldest known glass window in Germany (from the 11th century). The beautiful window, with representations of the prophets, is in the southern section of the central aisle. The Cathedral's south portal has magnificent 11th-century bronze doors, replete with biblical motifs.

On the section of Roman wall south of the Cathedral is a plaque commemorating the 1555 Augsburger Religionsfrieden, which brought the residents of the Free Imperial City of Augsburg religious freedom.

Augsburg's churches give an overall impression of the rich creative energy of the town's artists. The Annakapelle, for instance, with its Fugger tombs; the birthplace of dramatist Berthold Brecht at Auf dem Rain 7 (re-opening 1998); and the home of Mozart's father Leopold (Frauentorstrasse 30) are among Augsburg's museums. On the premises of the MAN vehicle factory, there is also a museum dedicated to Rudolf Diesel, inventor of the eponymous motor.

Hot air: The little town of **Gersthofen** just outside Augsburg is a centre for hot-air ballooning. It was from here in 1786 that the first German balloon journey was undertaken – a feat celebrated in Gersthofen's **Balloon Museum** in the Wasserturm, the old water-tower.

The Wörnitz is a tributary of the Danube, the river that follows much of this itinerary. Shortly before it opens into the Danube it embraces a small island, known as Werth. In the shadow of the **Augsburg's Town Hall Square.**

Schwäbische Alb uplands, the trading and free imperial city of **Donauwörth** emerged during the Middle Ages from the island's fishing community.

The city's main sights lie along its main trading route, today's Reichstrasse: the **Fuggerhaus** (1536) on the west side, the 13th–18th century **Rathaus** (City Hall) on the east, and between them the parish church with the heaviest bell in all of Swabia, the 6.5-tonne Pummerin, the Tanzhaus, the Stadtkommandantenhaus and Baudrexlhaus. **Käthe-Kruse Puppet Theatre** museum has over 200 puppets and figurines, carousels, puppet houses and miniature theatre stages.

Outside **Harburg** is one of Germany's largest castles (12th–18th centuries), which looms above the Wörnitz Valley. The indomitable fortress watched for centuries over the important trade route between Augsburg and Nuremberg.

Free cities, free citizens: The townscapes of Nördlingen, Dinkelsbühl and Rothenburg are a reflection of 16th- and 17th-century history and old German

imperial glory. From the 90-metre (295-ft) tower of the late-Gothic St Georgs-Kirchein **Nördlingen**, fondly known as the **Daniel**, there's a panoramic view of the 99 villages of the Nördlingen Ries.

The city's 3.5 km (2-mile) long fortification wall took shape between the 14th and 17th centuries, and a walk along the wall gives the visitor a view of ancient tanners' homes with their drying lofts, and dwellings ranging from almshouses to patrician Renaissance mansions. The Rathaus (Town Hall) and Tanzhaus were also designed in noble, imposing style. The Reichsstadtmuseum in the former Spital (infirmary) documents local and regional history.

A crater for the astronauts: The Ries crater around Nördlingen was formed by a huge natural catastrophe. Fifteen million years ago a meteorite some 1,200 metres (1,310 yards) in diameter hit the surface at a speed of around 100,000 km (62,137 miles) an hour. The impact discharged enormous amounts of rock and earth, which came down in a wall-like formation about 13 km (8 miles) in

Rothenburg is a honeypot for tourists.

diameter. In 1970 NASA sent its Apollo 14 astronauts to train in the Ries because the geology of the Ries crater is exactly the same as the moon's.

A fine view of **Dinkelsbühl** is to be enjoyed from the banks of the Wörnitz. The four medieval gates are still the only entrances to the town. To reach the town centre, follow the tower of St George's. The church below has a 20-metre (70-foot) high aisle and a late-Gothic altar. The market square was for centuries the traditional trading centre, while horse-drawn carts were parked on the nearby Weinmarkt (wine market). The half-timbered Deutsches Haus (German House) and the Schranne, the town's former granary, are two particularly fine buildings. On the third Monday of every July there are performances of the **"Kinderzeche"**, a tradition which goes back to the Thirty Years' War (1618–48), when Dinkelsbühl was under siege by Swedish forces. In 1632, when the situation seemed hopeless, the watchman's daughter Lore and other children of Dinkelsbühl appealed to the Swedish

commander to spare the town. The incident is commemorated every year by Dinkelsbühl children who parade in historical dress through the town to the Altrathausplatz, where they encounter the "Swedes". A high point of the "Kinderzeche" is the appearance of the young commander wearing the red and white rococo uniform of the Dinkelsbühl Knabenkapelle (Youth Band).

A statue of the Dinkelbauer (Dinkel farmer) in the park recalls the cultivation of dinkel, a very basic type of cereal, which was planted widely in earlier times in the Tauber valley and Franconian uplands – the Frankenhöhe.

Back on the Romantic Road (the B25), **Feuchtwangen** is recommended as the next stop. In summer the Romanesque cloisters of the Stiftskirche, the collegiate church, serve as a stage for high-class open-air theatre. The church's altar is the work of Michael Wolgemut, Dürer's teacher. The Romanesque Church of St John, the 16th-century tithe barn (the Zehentstadel or Kasten) and the Heimat Museum (local history museum), all grouped around the market square are also worth visiting.

Rothenburg ob der Tauber has become the embodiment of Germany's romantic past. The number of visitors who descend on Rothenburg every year (1 million) speaks for itself. Yet an overnight stay in Rothenburg can be thoroughly recommended, coupled with an evening stroll through the quiet lanes, a meal of Franconian specialities in one of the atmospheric restaurants, such as the famous Baumeisterhaus (1596), and perhaps a visit to Trexler's Figurentheater (a puppet show at the Burgtor).

The streets of Rothenburg radiate like the spokes of a wheel from the city gates and defensive walls and all lead to the central market place, with its **Rathaus** (Town Hall), a combination of Renaissance front and Gothic rear. From the 55-metre (180-foot) high town hall tower the historic town centre and the course of the original defence wall can be made out. To the south it's marked by St John's Church and to the east by St Mark's tower with its archway and a second tower called the Weisser Turm.

A detail of the Riemenschneider altar in Creglingen.

190

The special status of early Rothenburg (a free imperial city as early as 1274) provided the town with the basis for its prosperity. Its citizens traded in wine, livestock and wool, and very soon a new city wall had to be built. That second wall is very well preserved and the half-hour stroll along its walkway is well worth the effort.

The walk could begin at the Klingen-bastei bastion in the northern part of the wall, following a visit to the 14th–15th century **Church of St James** (St-Jakobs-Kirche), with its Heilig-Blut-Altar containing a masterful representation of Christ's Passion, executed in 1501–05 by Tilman Riemenschneider. Follow the wall eastwards and then south and you come to the Spitalbastion (the Infirmary Bastion). Returning towards the centre of town along Spitalgasse you'll find yourself in Plönlein, the prettiest part of Rothenburg and one much favoured by amateur photgraphers. The **Kriminal-museum** (Museum of Crime) next to the Johanniskirche has some grisly exhibits recalling the horrors of the Thirty Years' War, which did not spare Rothenburg. One of the central events of the war, a wager which saved the town from destruction in 1631, is marked by a scene on the astronomical clock which adorns the former Ratstrinkstube (town hall tavern), next to the present town hall, and by regular theatrical performances. The fabled wager pitted an elder of the town, former Mayor Nusch, against an enormous *Humpen*, or tankard of wine. Tilly, commander of the besieging troops, offered to spare the town if anyone could down the 3.25 litres (5.7 pints) of wine in one go. Nusch accepted the challenge, accomplished the feat and saved the town – at least, that's how the story goes.

Nusch's feat is not the only thing celebrated on stage; a summer festival every September includes a programme of Hans Sachs plays featuring the wit, slyness and simplicity of the local peasants, and performances of the traditional Schäfertänze (Shepherd's Dances).

The woodcarver's art at its height: With enchanting little **Detwang** (and its

The castle square in Tauber-bischofsheim.

Riemenschneider altar) behind us, we arrive at **Creglingen**, whose Herrgottkirche (Church of Our Lord) has been a pilgrimage church ever since the 14th century, when a local peasant is said to have ploughed up some eucharistic bread. Around 1500 the Princes of Hohenlohe had a church built on the site and Tilman Riemenschneider was commissioned to carve an altar dedicated to the Virgin Mary.

The **Fingerhutmuseum** (Thimble Museum), only a stone's throw away, contains some 2,000 examples of the seamstress' vital tool.

Courtly elegance in miniature: Weikersheim and Bad Mergentheim, both only a few miles from Würzburg , are towns with royal connections. In Weikersheim, the seat of the princes of Hohenlohe, the former servants' quarters by the village square mark the entrance to the **Schloss**, an archetypal courtly residence in miniature. The belfry dates from the 12th century, but its baroque cap was added between the 16th and 18th centuries. The coffered ceiling in the palace's south wing is a masterpiece of the period, while the garden with its orangery and statues of scenes from ancient mythology is pure baroque. The gnomes represent caricatures of figures from court life.

It is worth making a detour to **Stuppach** to see Mathias Grünewald's Madonna (1519). A priest named Blumhofer acquired the painting from the estate of the Order of Teutonic Knights in 1812 and until 1908 it was thought to be a Rubens. The complex symbolism and the brilliance of the paintwork are the main points of interest.

In 1826 a shepherd rediscovered the lost salt springs of **Bad Mergentheim**. A hotel was opened up a few years later when the water was found to be helpful in the treatment of kidney, gall bladder and bladder complaints and the town has never looked back since. The settlement was founded by the Franks but the Order of Teutonic Knights put Mergentheim on the map when they moved their headquarters here in 1525. With the help of generous donations from grand masters, kings and dukes, around 1600 the 13th-century moated castle was lavishly converted into a palace for the knights. A baroque church was completed in 1736. The palace now houses the Deutschenordenmuseum (Knights' Museum) and the modern sanatorium is to be found in the palace's extensive grounds.

Mergentheim's market place is surrounded by ornate half-timbered and plasterwork buildings. Near the 16th-century Town Hall, a statue of Wilhelm Schutzbar, also called Milchling, adorns the Milchlingbrunnen (fountain). Schutzbar was responsible for bringing the Knights' order to the town.

The enchanting Tauber Valley: For centuries, **Lauda** has been a wine-producing region. A 16th-century house at Rathausstrasse 25 used to belong to a grower and now houses an interesting wine and local history museum. The half-timbering and baroque ornamentation demonstrate clearly that Lauda's citizens have profited handsomely from the noble grape.

Gerlachsheim and **Distelhausen** both have impressive baroque churches. Motorists will notice the occasional roadside shrine; these explain why the locality is sometimes described as the "Land of God" or "Madonna country".

Tauberbischofsheim is the highlight of the Tauber Valley. Take a stroll from the bridge through to the pedestrianised zone. Haus Mackert (1744), a baroque mansion built for a wine merchant, and a pharmacy, form the gateway to the market square with its neo-Gothic Town Hall (1866). The small baroque church on the south side of the square is dedicated to St Lioba. St Boniface, the Devon-born monk, who later became the Archbishop of Mainz, founded a convent here around 725, hence the name of the town, which means "home of the bishop". Lioba, probably related to St Boniface, was the convent's first abbess. Both the wheel in the town's coat-of-arms and the **Schloss** (14th–16th centuries) serve as reminders that the Mainz prince-bishops held sway here from the 13th to the 19th centuries. There is a fine view over the town and the Tauber Valley from the watchtower.

Right, keeping in step in Dinkelsbühl.

FROM WÜRZBURG TO MUNICH

The city of **Würzburg** (pop. 127,000) has been a bishopric since the 8th century and this long history of successive rule by prince-bishops has dictated the majestic appearance it presents today.

High above the city, surrounded by vineyards, the mighty **Marienberg** served from 1253 to 1719 as the residence of the prince-bishops who used it as a stronghold to keep the ever-more powerful townsfolk at bay. It received a baroque facade in 1600 under the prince-bishop Echter von Mespelbrunn, who went on to enlarge the complex in Renaissance style and added the Echter bastion and the Fürstengarten (princes' garden).

From 1631 to 1634, during the Thirty Years' War, the city was occupied by Gustav Adolf of Sweden. The fortress was extended and began to take the form of the building seen today, with its baroque facades.

The high point of baroque architecture:

The city experienced its heyday in the 18th century under the rule of the House of Schönborn. In 1719 Johann Philipp Franz of Schönborn became prince-bishop and moved his residence from the Marienberg to the city. The famous master builder of the baroque, Balthasar Neumann (1687–1753), was given the commission to plan a new princely residence. Neumann built the "palace of all palaces", the **Würzburg Residence** (1720–44), designing it in south German baroque style. It is ranked today as one of the finest baroque palaces in Europe.

Neumann created his own memorial within the palace by designing what is undoubtedly one of the most beautiful staircases of the baroque-rococo era. The stair well extends right up the two-storey building and is crowned by a single concave vault 30 metres (100 feet) long by 18 metres (59 feet) wide. More renowned than the vault itself is the **ceiling fresco** painted by the Italian artist Giovanni Battista Tiepolo who was summoned to Würzburg in 1750 to

On every weekend in October, somewhere in the Würzburg area there's a wine festival.

194

create the largest painting in the world. Tiepolo depicted the Gods of Olympus and allegories of the four continents known at the time. The painting also alludes to the marriage between Emperor Frederick I of Barbarossa and Beatrix of Burgundy in the year 1156. Miraculously, the fresco survived the allied bombing. Neumann continued with the design of the *Käppele* pilgrimage church in 1748, but died in 1753 before he could complete it. He is buried in the St Mary's Chapel.

Tragedy of an artist: The woodcarver and sculptor Tilman Riemenschneider came to Würzburg from his home in the Harz Mountains in 1483 and rapidly rose to fame in Franconia. In his workshop he carved altars from limestone, made tombstones from sandstone and supplied the whole of Main-Franconia with splendid sculptures. He became a member of the city council in 1509 and even served as mayor from 1520 to 1521. During the Peasants' Revolt, Riemenschneider supported the oppressed peasants against the prince-bishop Konrad von Thingen. When the peasants were ultimately defeated at the Marienberg fortress, he was imprisoned and tortured. He died a broken man in 1531 and his name passed into oblivion. Interest in his work was only reawakened centuries later when his grave was discovered during road excavations. The world-famous works of Tilman Riemenschneider are now displayed in the **Mainfränkische Museum** in the Marienberg, along with a splendid collection of other Franconian works of art.

A city walk: More Riemenschneider creations can be seen on a walk through Würzburg, starting at the **Hofgarten** (court gardens) behind the Residence, with its impressive wrought-iron gates and beautiful baroque group of figures. The **University**, only a short walk away, has in its southern wing a remarkable Renaissance church known as the Neubaukirche. The nearby early Gothic **Franciscan Church** (1221) contains a *pietà* by Riemenschneider.

Domschulstrasse leads to the Romanesque **Cathedral**, dedicated to St Kilian,

Tiepolo's ceiling fresco in the Würzburg Residenz.

the apostle of the Franks and the patron saint of the city who was murdered in AD 689. The **Schönborn Chapel**, one of Balthasar Neumann's most important works, is built on to the cathedral transept and contains the shrine of the prince-bishops of Schönborn. St Kilian lies buried in the crypt of the adjacent **Neumünsterkirche** (New Cathedral).

The **Old Town Hall** has Roman origins, was acquired by the city in 1316 and given many extensions. One of them is the imposing late Renaissance town hall tower, the **Grafenackhart**, erected in 1659. The nearby **Carmelite Monastery** (1712) has been part of the town hall since the 19th century.

Home of Franconian wine: One of the statues on the old Main bridge is that of St Kilian, patron saint of Würzburg and of vintners. October, the month of the wine harvest, is the best time to explore the vineyards and wine-producing Franconian villages. Every weekend in October a wine festival is held in one the nearby villages, such as Volkach, Frikkenhausen or Eisenheim.

The puzzling statue: The journey through Franconia continues towards the delightful medieval jewel of **Bamberg**, an old imperial and episcopal city first mentioned in AD 902. The **Cathedral** contains the tomb of its founder Emperor Heinrich II who elevated Bamberg to a bishopric in 1007, and of Pope Clement II, the only Papal tomb north of the Alps.

The Cathedral was consecrated in 1012, but it burned down twice and was finally rebuilt in 1237. Particularly impressive is the **Fürstenportal** (Prince's Door). The Cathedral is the home of an unsolved riddle, namely the **Bamberg Horseman**, a medieval equestrian statue of unknown origin. It's not even known who the horseman is. On the left of the Cathedral, in the former chapter house erected by Balthasar Neumann in 1730, is the Diocesan Museum with its cathedral treasury of unique exhibits including Heinrich II's cloak.

A narrow street separates the **Alte Hofhaltung** (old residence) from the cathedral. This magnificent Renaissance

Bamberg's old Town Hall on the river Regnitz.

building completed in 1569 was once the imperial and episcopal palace. It is now the **Museum of Local History**.

Aufsessstrasse leads to the 290-metre (951-feet) heights of the Michaelsberg, with its **Church of St Michael**, part of a former Benedictine Abbey founded at the request of Heinrich II in 1015. The famous facade above the broad staircase leading up to the entrance (1677) is the work of the Dientzenhofer brothers. Suttestrasse, or Maternstrasse, leads up to the 12th-century **Carmelite Monastery**. Its late Romanesque cloisters are the largest in Germany.

The **Old Town Hall** stands on an island in the River Regnitz, linked to the banks by a bridge. It also houses the **Sammlung Ludwig** collection of baroque porcelain and glazed earthenware. There is also an excellent view of Bamberg's **Little Venice**, with fishermen's old houses on the right bank of the river.

From here wend your way back to the cathedral square through a maze of narrow alleys, passing the former **Domini-** can Church with its attractive 14th-century cloisters. Today it houses the famous **Bamberg Symphony Orchestra**. At the top of the picturesque steps of the Katzenberg is the **Schlenkerle**, one of the best *Rauchbier* inns. *Rauchbier* (smoked malt beer) is a Bamberg speciality.

Idyllic Main Valley: Between Staffelstein and Lichtenfels are two rare jewels of baroque architecture. On a 421-metre (1,380 ft) hill stands the fortress-like **Banz Abbey**. Founded in 1069, it served as a Benedictine abbey until 1803 and later as a palace belonging to the ruling Wittelsbach family. It is one of the greatest achievements of the German baroque. On the opposite side of the valley (3 km/2 miles from Lichtenfels off the B173 road) is the absolute zenith of the era – the **Vierzehnheiligen** (the Pilgrimage Church of the Fourteen Saints) by Balthasar Neumann. It was built between 1734 and 1751 and named after 14 saints whom a pious shepherd in the 15th century claimed to have seen several times.

Gala evening at the Bayreuth Festival Theatre.

Grilled sausages and other delicacies:
The market place in **Coburg** is watched over by the statue of Coburg's patron saint, St Maurice, dubbed *Bratwurst-männle* (Sausage Man) from his place on the town hall. The opulent facade of this rococo building (1580), with its richly-decorated high gables, is typical of Coburg. Dominating the town is the large, well-preserved **Fortress** where Martin Luther stayed in 1530. **Ehrenburg Castle** displays a fine collection of furniture. From 1547 until 1918 it was the city residence of the Dukes of Coburg. The **Dolls' Museum** next door houses some 600 antique dolls.

From Coburg the route continues to the medieval town of **Kronach**, the birthplace of the artist Lucas Cranach (1472–1553). The **Franconian Gallery** is the former commander's building of the dominant Rosenburg Fortress and contains masterpieces of Franconian art from the 13th–16th centuries.

The Wagnerians' Mecca: The town of **Bayreuth** (population 70,000) is first and foremost associated with the com-

poser Richard Wagner, who built an opera house here in 1876. Every year it is the setting for the Wagner Festival, which runs from 25 July to 28 August. The city's operatic tradition, however, was begun by the cultured Margravine Wilhelmina, Frederick the Great's favourite sister, who commissioned the architect Saint Pierre to design the first Bayreuth **Opera House**. It is now regarded as one of Germany's best-preserved baroque theatres.

Saint Pierre was also responsible for the **New Palace**, now the home of a beautiful faience collection, with some attractive fountains outside. Richard Wagner and his wife Cosima, Liszt's daughter, lie buried in the park close to Franz Liszt himself.

The **Hermitage Palace** is another famous building in the east of Bayreuth, as is the baroque **Old Palace**, with an interior grotto and fountains to rival the splendour of its historic rooms.

Further on towards Nuremburg is the region known as the Franconian **Little Switzerland**, so-called because at that time the German Romantics believed this was exactly how Switzerland looked. There are indeed some impressive looking crags such as those that tower above the romantic hill village of **Tüchersfeld**. The high point of a tour through this beautiful national park is the one-kilometre long limestone cave, the **Devil's Cave** near **Pottenstein**, a fascinating underground world of caverns and grottoes.

Free imperial city on the Pegnitz: To the south is the old, free, imperial city of **Nuremberg** (pop. 500,000), the second largest city in Bavaria and an important industrial and commercial centre. Devastated by bombs in World War II, it has been faithfully restored and much of its old charm remains.

Nuremberg was founded in the 11th century by Emperor Heinrich III as a base for his campaigns in Bohemia and the settlement rapidly developed into an important trading centre. Elevated to a free imperial city by Emperor Friedrich II in 1219, it retained this status until 1806 when it was annexed by the Kingdom of Bavaria. From the 12th to the

Outward bound in Franconia's "Little Switzerland".

16th centuries nearly all the emperors maintained their residence in the Kaiserburg (castle), and held their imperial diets (meetings) here. At that time, Nuremberg was regarded as the unofficial capital of the Holy Roman Empire of German Nations.

Between the 15th and 17th centuries, the rich city attracted artists and scientists. Names such as Albrecht Dürer, Adam Krafft and Veit Stoss are testimony to this age of artistic achievement. From 1600 onwards the political and economic importance of the city declined and real prosperity only returned when the first German railway between Nuremberg and Fürth was inaugurated in 1835. Splendid specimens of the first German steam engines can be viewed in the **Transport Museum**.

One hundred years later another less celebrated chapter in Germany's history was written in Nuremberg. The Nazis wanted to revive the city's tradition as the old capital of the Reich and so they built a massive stadium in which between 1933 and 1938 the now notorious rallies were held. The weed-overgrown hulk of the stadium is still standing. From 1945 to 1949 Nuremberg again became the focus of world attention when Nazi war criminals were put on trial by the victorious allied powers.

Back to the Middle Ages: The river Pegnitz divided Nuremberg's **Old City** into the Sebalderstadt in the north and the Lorenzerstadt in the south, both surrounded by a sturdy 13th-century defensive wall with 46 fortified towers – the landmarks of the city – and five main gates: the Spittlertor, the Königstor, the Frauentor, the Laufertor and the Neutor. The **Emperor's Castle**, built on sandstone crags high above the old city, consists of three architectural components, each from a different historical period. The western crags provide the foundations for the Kaiserburg which was erected in the 12th century during the reign of the Hohenstaufen Emperor Frederick Barbarossa. Then there is the **Burggrafenburg**, the first royal castle built by the Salians in the 11th century. The **Kaiserstallung** (imperial stables),

Nuremberg is dominated by the Emperor's Castle.

originally built by the city fathers as a granary in 1485, is now a youth hostel.

Near the castle, the Tiergärtnertor leads to the **Albrecht Dürer House**. This 15th-century building where the famous artist lived from 1509 until his death in 1528 is now a museum.

Right and left of the Pegnitz: On the Town Hall Square stands the protestant **Church of St Sebald**, a late Romanesque columned basilica from 1256. St Sebald's tomb inside the church is a masterpiece of the German iron foundryman's art and was cast by Vischer at the beginning of the 16th century. The moving Crucifixion group by Veit Stoss dates from the same period.

Opposite the church, in a splendid late Renaissance patrician house dating from around 1600, is the **Fembo Municipal Museum**.

Crossing the narrow Pegnitz river we come to the **Main Market**, (the tourist office can be found here) the site of Nuremberg's famous annual **Christmas Market**. The richly carved **Schöne Brunnen**, a beautiful 19-metre (62-feet)

high fountain, stands before the **Church of Our Lady** (1349). The church has an interesting facade with the famous **Männleinlaufen**, a clock which at noon every day re-enacts the homage of the Seven Electors to Emperor Charles IV. The interior contains the **Tucher Altar** (1440). The **Town Hall**, whose oldest part is the hall with stepped gables, dates from 1340. In the basement are medieval dungeons with gruesome torture chambers. Nearby is the well-known **Gänsemännchen** (1555), a figure of a peasant with two geese spouting water.

Situated on an island of the river Pegnitz, the **Heilig Geist Spital** (Holy Ghost Hospice) was founded in the 14th century for old and needy citizens. The German emperor's imperial insignia were kept here until 1796. Within the inner courtyard lies an impressive Crucifixion group by Adam Krafft and the 14th-century Hansel Fountain.

Beyond this is the **Church of St Laurence**, built between the 13th and 15th centuries. Particularly impressive is the chancel with its wonderful star vaulting, suspended from which is the beautifully carved Annunciation created by Veit Stoss in 1517. Another work by the same artist is the Crucifix which can be seen at the high altar together with Adam Krafft's worldfamous Tabernacle.

Königstrasse, the shopping street, extends from St Laurence's past the **Mauthalle**, which was built as a granary around 1500 and is now an inn with a beautiful old vaulted cellar. The **German National Museum** at the Kornmarkt, founded in 1852 "to save the German cultural heritage" displays folklore items, artefacts from pre- and early history and copper engravings.

Past the early-Gothic **Church of St Clare** stands the **Old Nuremberg Handwerkerhof**, formerly a craftsmen's yard, now a living museum displaying medieval handicrafts and pieces in gold and other precious metals. It also covers the manufacture of the famous Nuremberg gingerbread.

A cross-section through time: The A3 autobahn leads to **Regensburg**, founded as Castra Regina by the Emperor Marcus

Young and old in Bavarian traditional costume.

Aurelius in AD 179. The Irish missionary St Boniface made the city a bishopric in 739. Five hundred years later, in 1245, it became a free imperial city and developed into an important medieval centre and a hub of European commerce. It was the regular seat of the Reichstag from 1663 until the disintegration of the old empire in 1806.

Regensburg lies at the northernmost point of the river Danube, which is navigable to the Black Sea. World War II left the city and its Roman and medieval heritage largely undamaged.

A fine view of the city can be enjoyed from the 12th-century **Stone Bridge**, a masterpiece of medieval engineering, 310 metres (1,017 feet) in length. The river is lined by stately mansions, over whose roofs tower the 105-metre (345-feet) spires of the Bavarian Gothic cathedral (1250–1525).

Near the Cathedral is the *porta praetorius,* the northern gate of the former Roman citadel. Pass the bishop's palace and then turn right at the Niedermünster church where there are some interesting

Roman excavations. Beyond it lies the picturesque Alter Kornmarkt (old corn market) and the **Herzogshof** (ducal palace), the residence of the Bavarian dukes from AD 988. Its Ducal Hall has a magnificent ceiling.

The Gothic hall in the Old Town Hall (1350) was once the meeting place for the Reichstag. Down in the cellars of the Reichstagmuseum is a grisly medieval torture chamber. German law in those days specified that if an accused criminal survived three days of torture without confessing he could go free, even if had been convicted by a court. Bachgasse leads to the 7th-century **Benedictine Monastery of St Emmeran** and adjacent palace of the Thurn and Taxis princes.

One culinary note: Regensburg is noted for *wels*, a fleshy Danube fish, and sausages. Try them at the riverside Würstküche near the Stone Bridge.

Where the Danube is at its deepest: Near the town of **Kehlheim**, King Ludwig I commissioned his architects Friedrich von Gärtner and Leo von Klenze to

Typical scene in a Bavarian beer tent.

build a **Liberation Hall** on the Michaelsberg in memory of those who fell in the Wars of Liberation (1813–15). Kehlheim also has an interesting archaeological museum.

Take a detour to the **Altmühltal**, still a popular destination despite the construction of the Rhine-Main-Danube Canal in 1992. Further on stands the rococo **Weltenburg Monastery** with its baroque abbey church of St George (Asamkirche). One way to view it is from a boat that passes through the deepest and narrowest section of the river, the Donaudurchbruch.

Hop fields: From this point on the Danube, the direct road route to Munich follows the **Deutsche Hopfenstrasse** (B301). It leads through villages lined with linden trees and into the Holledau, where hops are cultivated on the hilly slopes. Every year in mid-September a Hop Queen is elected in Wolnzach.

The Bavarian Parthenon: On the northern bank of the Danube, the upland, heavily-wooded **Bavarian Forest** extends as far as the Czech border. On the river bank, 11 km (7 miles) east of Regensburg, just outside Oberstauf, stands the Bavarian **Valhalla**, a copy of the Parthenon temple on the Acropolis in Athens. It was designed by royal architect Leo von Klenze and built between 1830 and 1842 for King Ludwig I as a hall of fame for illustrious figures from the German-speaking world.

The Bavarian Forest joins with the Czech Republic's Bohemian Forest in the northeast to form the largest uninterrupted stretch of forest in central Europe. Adalbert Stifter described the beauty of this landscape in many of his stories and novels.

The people of the Bavarian Forest live from forestry, glassmaking and tourism, notably on the ski slopes of the Lusen (1,371 metres/4,496 feet), Dreisessel (1,378 metres/4,519 feet), Rachel (1,452 metres/4,762 feet) and the Grosser Arber (1,457 metres/4,778 feet), four mountains criss-crossed with trails and paths for hikers.

The **Bavarian Forest National Park**, near Grafenau, has enclosures where wolves, lynx, otters and bison roam in relative freedom. Numerous resorts nearby offer comfortable accommodation, sporting and recreational facilities and the Czech Republic is only a short drive away.

South of the Danube, the landscape flattens out into the Gäuboden plain, Bavaria's grain belt. There's an annual Gäuboden Festival in Straubing which attracts around 900,000 visitors, making it Bavaria's biggest folk festival after Munich's Oktoberfest.

City on three rivers: The geographer and writer Alexander von Humboldt included **Passau** (pop. 51,000) on his list of "the world's seven most beautifully-situated cities". Passau's location at the confluence of three rivers, the Danube, the Inn and the Ilz, is indeed spectacular, with the old town huddling on one narrow stretch of land between Danube and Inn.

The old streets and the riverside atmosphere give the town an almost Venetian feel. Residenzplatz has a huge bishop's residence and facades in baroque style. At noon every day, the world's largest organ in **St Stephen's Cathedral** resounds with special recitals.

Excursions into the 15th century: In the old ducal city of **Landshut**, a very special wedding is celebrated every four years: the Landshuter Fürstenhochzeit, Germany's largest historical pageant. The tradition goes back to 1475, when the Archbishop of Salzburg officiated at the marriage of the Polish Princess Hedwig and the duke's son, Georg, in Landshut's Gothic minster.

Towering over the medieval old town is the sturdy **Trausnitz castle**. Dating from 1204, it was converted, in the 16th century, into a Renaissance palace which served as the Lower Bavarian seat of the Wittelsbach dukes.

The last town on the road back to Munich, **Freising** (at the end of Munich's suburban railway line 1) was once a powerful episcopal centre. Its **Cathedral** and the Diocesan Museum testify to its long traditions. During 1146 the world's first brewery was founded in the Benedictine abbey of **Weihenstephan** and it is still producing one of Bavaria's finest beers.

Full of myth and legend: the Bavarian Forest.

LAKE CONSTANCE

The lucky people who live along or near **Lake Constance** (Der Bodensee) don't need to go on holiday. The climate here is so mild that orchards of apples, pears and plums flourish. Long hours of sunshine ensure that the grapes in the vineyards ripen at the same time as those in Mediterranean countries. The lake, backed by the mighty panorama of the Alps, is more the size of an inland sea. Over half of its 538 sq. km (208 sq. miles) belongs to Germany; the rest is shared by Switzerland and Austria.

The silent lion: A tour of the lake commences in **Lindau,** an island town on German soil connected to the mainland by a road and rail causeway. In 15 BC the Romans established a military base on the island. At the end of the 13th century, Lindau became a free imperial city, whose economic prosperity was closely linked to the Lindau Messengers. This courier service – at that time a complete novelty – operated all the way between Italy and northern Europe. The climax of the town's importance came in 1496 when the Imperial Diet assembled here. In 1803, Lindau lost its free imperial city status and in 1806 became integrated with Bavaria.

With its broad promenade, the **Seehafen** (harbour) is flanked by a number of hotels and inviting cafés. The harbour entrance is guarded on one side by a 33-metre (108-foot) high lighthouse and on the other by the symbol of Bavaria, a stone lion. The lion has never been able to roar because the sculptor forgot its tongue.

The **Mangturm** tower, which is all that remains of the old fortifications, stands in the middle of the promenade. From here it isn't far to the **Reichsplatz,** the main square, with its **Lindavia Fountain** and the Gothic **Old Town Hall.** Both the back and the front of the building are richly decorated with frescoes depicting events from the Imperial Diet.

The **Brigand's Tower** (Diebesturm) stands to the northwest of Maximilianstrasse, adjacent to the Romanesque **Church of St Peter**, in which frescoes depicting the Passion are attributed to Hans Holbein the Elder. Another interesting sight on the **Market Place** is the baroque painting on the facade of the **Haus zum Cavazzan** (No 6). It houses a museum with the largest art exhibition in the Lake Constance region.

The Austrian side: From Lindau it is only 10 km (6 miles) to **Bregenz,** The town comes to life during July and August when the Bregenz Opera Festival is performed on the largest floating stage in the world. The lakeside promenade draws thousands at weekends, although better views of the lake itself can be enjoyed from the summit of the **Pfander** mountain (1,064 metres/3,491 feet) which can be reached by cable car.

The Swiss side: Switzerland is just a few minutes away from Bregenz. The former prosperity of **Rorschach** (corn market and weaving mill) is reflected in the fine facades of the patrician houses on the Marienberg and the high street. A local crafts museum has been established in the baroque corn exchange.

Some 15 km (9 miles) to the west, **Romanshorn** is the terminus for ferries to **Friedrichshafen** on the German side of the lake. On the way it is well worth making a detour south to **St Gallen**. Founded in 612, the Benedictine abbey was one of the first education centres in Christian Europe and contains a magnificent library.

Lakeside university town: Konstanz (pop. 80,000) is the largest town on the lake. The Romans erected a camp here and named it after the emperor Constantinus Chlorus. Konstanz became a bishopric in 540. The most important event in the town's history was the Reform Council of 1414–18, during which the only election of a pope (Martin V) on German soil took place. The princebishops also sentenced the reformer John Hus to death here. He was burned at the stake in 1415. The council met in the **Council Building** (old town), built in 1388 as a corn and wine warehouse. Other buildings worth inspection are the Romanesque-Gothic **Minster** (11th–16th centuries) and the town hall.

An early-Gothic replica of the Holy Sepulchre is to be found in the **Mauritius Rotund**, which has a viewing platform offering a panorama of the town and the lake. Historians come to the Kunkel Haus to view the fine **Weber Frescos** (late 13th century) which depict the individual stages in the manufacture of silk and linen.

Fruits and flowers: To the southeast of Radolfzell, the island of **Reichenau** is connected to the mainland by a man-made causeway. It is the most important centre of market gardening in Germany, with 15 percent of the island being taken up by huge glasshouses. The **Benedictine Abbey** on Reichenau was a major spiritual centre of western European culture for 300 years (724–1000).

On the other side of the Bodenrücken peninsula in Überlinger See lies the famous flower island of **Mainau**. This sub-tropical paradise is in full bloom between March and October and can be reached by ferry from the mainland.

The Rhine Falls: Strongly recommended is the journey along the Rhine **Medieval Meersburg.**

to the west of Lake Constance to the **Rhine Falls** near Schaffhausen in Switzerland. The impressive spectacle of the Rhine plunging 21 metres (69 feet) along a length of 150 metres (450 feet) is best enjoyed from one of the boats which goes right up underneath the falls

Back to the Stone Age: Once a free imperial city, **Überlingen** is a pretty little town with much of its medieval fortifications still intact. From its long harbour promenade steep streets lead up to the old town centre. The town hall contains the splendid **Council Chamber** created by Jacob Russ in 1490, with its wonderful wood-carved frieze of statuettes representing the 41 medieval trades.

Surrounded by vineyards, the pilgrimage church of **Birnau** has a magnificent rococo decor. Its main attraction is a life-size, roguish putto, *The Honey Sucker*. Nearby at **Uhldingen-Mühlhofen** is a reconstruction of a Stone Age village, built on stilts in the lake.

Magic of the Middle Ages: Meersburg is considered to be one of the best preserved medieval towns in Germany. The magic of the place is best appreciated in the evening. Time then to admire the half-timbered houses in peace, accompanied by the melody of bubbling fountains and church bells. The historical centre is marked by the **Old Castle**, one of the oldest in Germany dating from Merovingian times. In the **New Castle**, the erstwhile summer residence of the prince-bishops of Konstanz, classical concerts are now performed.

The **Fürstenhäusle** formerly belonged to Annette von Droste-Hülshoff (1797–1848), one of Germany's leading poets, whose crime novel *Judenbuche* is on the reading lists of many German schools. Her statue stands before the bridge to the Old Castle.

Friedrichshafen (pop. 52,000), the second largest town on Lake Constance, rose to fame at the end of the 19th century when airships were built here. Their inventor, Graf Ferdinand von Zeppelin (1838–1917) came from Konstanz. The museum, located in a wing of the railway station, has an entire department devoted to his achievement.

Graf Zeppelin built his famous airship in Friedrichshafen.

THE BLACK FOREST TO STUTTGART

The **Black Forest** is no longer as dark and forbidding as it once was. The region has been made accessible by road, rail and an extended network of walking trails, and there is little left of the dense pine forest which the Romans knew.

From the 16th century onwards, the woodland was cleared from the navigable river valleys and agriculture established. Small industries arose, notably glass and watch making, and together with forestry and tourism these remain the backbone of the Black Forest economy.

Tourists have been drawn to the Black Forest ever since the 18th century, attracted by the beauty of the Rhine Plain with its backdrop of mountains and many opportunities for walking. Grouse and pheasant, buzzards and hawks, deer, foxes and badgers populate the more remote areas, where the mountain folk still wear their beautifully embroidered costumes on public holidays. In summer, the evenings are warm, perfect for sitting outside to enjoy a meal and a glass of good local wine.

Catholic love of life: The development of **Freiburg** has always been closely linked to the Catholic Church. Only 80 years after the grant of the city charter in 1120 the people began construction of a parish church which soon grew into one of the most magnificent minsters of medieval Germany. Many consider its 116-metre (380-foot) high tower to be the finest in Christendom. The **University**, founded in 1457, was famous throughout Europe as a centre of liberal humanism, until the middle of the 16th century, when it became a Jesuit bastion of the Counter-Reformation. It remained true to this strict Catholic tradition right up until the 1920s. Nowadays its students are responsible for the *joie de vivre* of the city, whose unique character is also due to its wonderful location between the Black Forest and the vineyards of the Rhine.

The city centre is characterised by narrow cobbled streets and the fast-flowing rivulets called *Bächle* which are perfectly clean now but in medieval times acted as sluices for carrying away sewage. This area centres on the bustling Münsterplatz which provides the setting for the Gothic **Freiburg Minster** (1200–1520). Marvellous classical concerts are often staged here. An ascent of the tower can prove a memorable experience when the mighty bells ring and shake the tower. The southern side of the square is bordered by three beautiful buildings, including the **Kaufhaus**, dating back to 1520.

Begin exploring the old city by walking eastwards from Münsterplatz to the Swabian Gate, the gate tower to the old city walls. To the south the **Gewerbebach Canal** was once the main artery of the city's medieval economy and to the west is the Rathausplatz featuring Freiburg's early Renaissance **Town Hall**. An example of late-Gothic architecture is the Haus zum Walfisch on the corner of Franziskanerstrasse. Behind the town hall in Turmstrasse the old **Jesters' Guild Hall** displays collections of carnival masks and *Häs* (jesters' costumes) which lend the *Fasnet* (Alemannic for carnival) a pagan air. Only five minutes from Münsterplatz, the **Schlossberg** is an area of parkland providing the ideal setting for a stroll.

Five excursions from Freiburg: A trip to the top of the nearby mountain, the 1,284-metre (4,200-feet) high **Schauinsland** promises a fine panorama over the surrounding landscape. This can be reached by taking the No 2 tram and then the No 21 bus to Horben. On clear days there is a magnificent view from the top, from the Black Forest across the Rhine Plain to the Vosges beyond.

Just a 10-minute drive to the north of Freiburg on the B 3/B 294 is one of the most beautiful valleys in the Black Forest, the idyllic **Glottertal**, where a popular TV serial, *Black Forest Hospital,* was filmed. There is an abundance of restaurants, hotels and shops here. The road continues to climb until the towers of the Benedictine **Abbey of St Peter**, founded in 1093, come into view. The journey onwards towards **St Märgen**, is accompanied at every turn by wonderful views of the hills and valleys. Here the Black Forest still retains its original character, with dense woodland, wild streams and peaceful valleys, where the roofs of the typical Black Forest farmhouses almost touch the ground. St Märgen offers a perfect compromise between remoteness and the comforts of modern-day tourism. The focus of this idyllic holiday centre is the 12th-century Augustinian monastery.

When venturing east of Freiburg to **Lake Titisee**, forget your car and take the train. The half-hour journey, along tracks that were laid in 1887, is an unforgettable experience. The stretch runs from the station at **Himmelsreich** (Realm of Heaven) to **Höllsteig** (Hell's Rise) station, climbing about 625 metres (2,050 feet) as it does so, a record for German railways. The journey up the gorge can be broken at the hill resort of **Hinterzarten** where Queen Marie Antoinette once dined. At weekends the road leading down to the picturesque Lake Titisee is choc-a-bloc with visitors. It is a popular retreat from the

towns and cities, where people like to stroll around the lake (approx. 1½ hours' walk) or opt for the more strenuous ascent of the **Feldberg** (1,493 metres/ 4,900 feet), the highest mountain in the Black Forest. Beyond Lake Titisee the road follows the bank of the more peaceful Schluchsee to **Bonndorf**, with its tempting culinary speciality, the Black Forest Ham. To the north lies the **Wutachsschlucht** nature reserve.

The maritime winds blowing through the Rhine Valley result in the mild climate that has made the western part of the Black Forest an important region for the cultivation of fruit. The vineyards among the foothills of the **Markgräfler-land**, dropping gently down to the plain to the south of Freiburg, are reminiscent of more southern climes. The picturesque little town of **Staufen**, 20 km (12 miles) to the south-west of Freiburg, became famous in 1539 when the alchemist Dr Faustus was murdered in the Gasthaus zum Löwen (Lion Inn) by one of the higher-ranking devils. Faustus was later immortalised by Goethe's famous drama. Today, the "devil" waits in the form of Markgräfler wine.

Situated on a rounded hill, **Baden-weiler** has been a health resort ever since AD 100. Peace and quiet are guaranteed here, as cars are barred from the town. The spa gardens contain the remains of an old Roman Baths.

Around the **Kaiserstuhl** (Emperor's Seat), the climate is perfect for the cultivation of fruit and vines. The rock is of volcanic origin and during periods of intense sun the ground can heat up to temperatures of 70°C (158°F). This creates a unique micro-climate where wild orchids and unusual butterflies abound. Small wine-producing villages such as **Oberbergen** have retained their traditional character. The visitor can sample the full-bodied *Sylvaner* in **Achkarren**, the aromatic *Gewürztraminer* in **Bickensol** and the velvet-red *Spätburgunder* in **Oberrotweil**. The town of **Breisach**, perched on basalt cliffs above the Rhine, is dominated by the **Minster** which was built between the 12th and 14th centuries and contains a huge wooden carved altar by the unknown

"Zum Bären" in Freiburg is the oldest inn in Germany.

master "H.L.", rated as one of the most beautiful examples of German wood carving. The town is a very lively place in summer with art festivals and, in July, one of the best known wine festivals – the Hock Festival. This is the ideal starting-point for a trip over the border into France. **Colmar** is well worth a visit with its **Unterlinden Museum** and Dominican church. The Alsatian cuisine should also not be missed while you are in the area.

Idyllic road to Stuttgart: The whole length of the road from Freiburg to Stuttgart winds along small river valleys through an area of outstandingly beautiful landscape, where the traveller is constantly tempted to stop to admire the scenic views.

By way of contrast, mechanical intricacies can be admired in the **Clock Museum** in **Furtwangen**. Clocks of all shapes and sizes are on display, except for one. The largest cuckoo clock in the world is in **Schonach**. Its cuckoo measures nearly 1 metre (3 feet) from its beak to its tail.

The **Triberg Falls**, with a height of 103 metres (338 feet), is the highest waterfall in Germany. From Triberg or St Georgen, the Black Forest Railway runs to **Hausach**, where the nearby **Vogtsbauernhof Open Air Museum** (on the B33) is well worth a visit. The museum consists of houses and farm buildings from the different regions of the Black Forest.

Turning east from Freudenstadt, the road leads to **Nagold**, a town beautifully situated on the river of the same name where four valleys meet. Alongside old, half-timbered houses, the 1,000-year-old **Church of St Remigius** contains some beautiful frescoes and an unusual statue of the Holy Mary.

"The most beautiful place I know on the Nagold is **Calw**," declared the writer Hermann Hesse (1877–1962), who was born here. After a visit to the **Museum** dedicated to Hesse, a wander through the little town with its delightful half-timbered town houses (17th–18th century) will confirm this opinion. The ruins of the once-powerful **Benedictine**

These Black Forest carvings show the traditional costume of the region.

Abbey (AD 830), in the town's district of Hirsau, are a reminder of the 11th century, when the abbey was one of the mainstays of the reform movement begun in Cluny.

Freiburg's Swabian counterpart is the university town of **Tübingen**, which has attracted poets and philosophers since the 16th century. There was Johannes Kepler (1571–1630), the first man to calculate the elliptical orbit of the planets; and Wilhelm Schickhardt who, in 1623, invented the world's first mechanical calculator. The philosophers Hegel and Schelling also lived here, as did such writers as Hölderlin, Mörike, Uhland and Hauff. All were students at the **Tübingen Foundation**, an evangelical theological seminary established in 1536.

Tübingen is built at the foot of two hills overlooking the Neckar and Ammer rivers. Its medieval attractions all survived World War II intact. Particularly worth seeing are the 15th-century Gothic **Collegiate Church**, and behind it the oldest parts of the **University** founded in 1477, where the reformer Philipp Melancthon lectured from 1514 to 1518. Down on the Neckar among weeping willows is the **Hölderlin Tower** where the poet Hölderlin, who had become insane, lived from 1807 until his death in 1843. From there the Bursagasse leads past the church to the **Town Hall**, a half-timbered building dating from 1435. On the old Market Place, farmers still come, in rural costume, to sell their wares. Above, the **Burgsteige** path climbs to the 16th-century **Hohentübingen Castle** which offers splendid views over the rooftops down to the Neckar.

City of the luxury limousine: Capital of the federal state of Baden Württemberg, **Stuttgart** (pop. 560,000), has the highest per capita income of any city in Germany. This is due in part to it being chosen in 1926 as the location for the manufacture of Germany's luxury Mercedes cars.

Opulence was displayed differently by the rich and powerful in earlier times, as evidenced by the 16th-century **Old Palace** on Schillerplatz. Op-

Half-timbered houses of Tübingen.

posite here is the **New Palace** (1746–1807) which currently houses the Ministries of Culture and Finance. The Schlossplatz, or Castle Square, is popular for shopping. Behind the New Palace the State Parliament building is not far from the **State Theatre**, the domicile of the world-famous **John Cranko Ballet**, which stands opposite the palace gardens. The **State Art Gallery,** containing one of southern Germany's leading art collections, now occupies a post-modern building behind the theatre. Situated near the main station, the **Linden Museum** has an interesting anthropological collection.

In the district of Untertürkheim automobile fans will find the fascinating **Daimler Benz Museum**. On the right bank of the Neckar, in the district of Bad Cannstatt, Gottfried Daimler demonstrated the world's first petrol-driven car in 1886. This is also where the **Cannstatter Volksfest**, Stuttgart's answer to the Munich Oktoberfest, is held every autumn.

An excursion to Ulm: It is said that "the fortune of **Ulm** rules the world". The townspeople of the former free imperial town demonstrated their wealth by building a great **Minster** (1377–1543), which was crowned in 1890 by a 161-metre (530-ft) **tower**, the highest in the world. The **Bread Museum** is dedicated not to spiritual but physical sustenance, as it tells the history of this staple food enjoyed since time immemorial. If this gives you an appetite, you will be welcomed in one of the many cosy inns in the picturesque **Fishing Quarter** by the water.

From Stuttgart to Karlsruhe: All those who admire valuable jewellery should make a point of stopping in **Pforzheim**. The reputation of Pforzheim's goldsmiths can be compared with that of the diamond cutters of Amsterdam, and their history is displayed in the **Jewellery Museum** in the Reuchlinhaus.

North-east of Pforzheim in **Maulbronn**, the 12th-century **Cistercian Monastery** is the best-preserved medieval building of its kind in Germany.

The existence of **Karlsruhe** (Karl's Rest) is entirely due to the palace which Margrave Karl Wilhelm of Baden-Durlach had built around 1715. Around 100 years later, however, the city had become the capital of the Grand Duchy of Baden. Most of its attractions are found around the palace, which today houses the **Baden State Museum**. The State Majolica Manufactory, with a fine display of faience pottery, the State Art Gallery containing one of the best displays of European painting in southern Germany, and the Botanical Gardens, are all nearby.

The town is the seat of the **Federal Constitutional Court**, guardian of the Basic Constitutional Law, and the **Federal High Court**, responsible for protecting the rights of the individual.

European summer capital: Although the spa tradition of **Baden-Baden** goes back to Roman times, it was not revived until 1838 when Jacques Benazet opened his **Casino**, a luxurious fun palace, in the Kurhaus. It suddenly became fashionable to visit Baden-Baden. The **Great Race Week** at Iffezheimer on the outskirts of the town, is the highlight of the German horse-racing calendar.

Medieval Neustadt.

Situated at the heart of Germany, Frankfurt-am-Main is the hub of all national road, rail and air traffic. Having tried extremely hard to be at the forefront of high-rise building, it has been given the nickname "Mainhattan". Although the city is the undisputed banking metropolis of Germany, it is not, as many people assume, the capital city of the federal state of Hessen. The state capital is Wiesbaden which lies opposite Mainz on the Rhine. Every year during carnival one can see how this place really lets its hair down. One wonders whether the all important archbishops enjoyed watching these heathen practices in the past as much as people do today. Be that as it may, the people in authority were then, and are now, the target of the buffoonery.

There are massive contrasts between the various regions within easy reach of Frankfurt, from the romantic castles strung out along Germany's river of destiny, Old Father Rhine, to the country's largest industrial area, the Ruhrgebiet, further downstream, where new clean industries are moving in to replace the old, providing new opportunities for employment as the coal and steel industries have become less profitable.

But before the Rhine even reaches the Ruhrgebiet, there are two neighbouring cities competing against each other. There is Düsseldorf, a city symbolised by art and fashion, and there is the cathedral city and media centre of Cologne. Beer, ice-hockey and football are all important here, and so is the unforgettable carnival season. The Romans also once settled in this region – at least to the left of the Rhine – and the most impressive examples of Roman architecture are to be found on the banks of the Moselle, in Trier. Just adjacent, the beautiful countryside of the Eiffel unfolds. Romanticism, even that of bands of robbers, is guaranteed in Heidelberg and the surrounding forests of the Spessart and Odenwald, where there are also many castles to be explored.

Hardly a German state is left untouched by a trip around Frankfurt, except for the five new states in the east and those in the extreme north. By following the Rhine you pass through Hessen, Rhineland Palatinate and North Rhine Westphalia (the largest of the federal states). The river Neckar flows through Heidelberg in Baden-Württenberg, and the Odenwald even stretches as far as Bavaria. The Fairytale Road of the Brothers Grimm leads through Hessen, Lower Saxony and up to Bremen in the north.

Preceding pages: the densely wooded areas of the Spessart, Rhön and Odenwald can be easily reached from Frankfurt; among Frankfurt's shining facades. **Left**, a panoramic view of the Rhine with Oberwesel Castle in the foreground.

FRANKFURT AM MAIN

Frankfurt has developed into a pulsating metropolis. Thanks to its location at the intersection of important road, rail and air traffic routes, the heart of this vast conurbation has become the conduit for fast bucks and rapid careers.

The new cathedrals of the world of finance – the spires of the skyscrapers which house the international banks and financial corporations – create a dramatic skyline which epitomises the power of this bustling city: the Bundesbank, the German Stock Exchange, plus many of the leading financial institutions of Germany and Europe, are concentrated within a very small area at the heart of the city.

Frankfurt's infrastructure was not really ready for the spectacular growth which has occurred: the old shops and the resident population were forced out into other parts of the city or into the surrounding countryside as the tenants could no longer afford to pay the astronomical rents. Even the oldest profession in the world was forced to vacate its original site in Kaiserstrasse near the main station. The ladies of the night can now be found on a distant, industrial estate. It was the wish of the city fathers that the area around the main station be designated as a showcase – a vision that was emphatically fulfilled by the **Messeturm**, built in 1989 and at that time the highest office building in Europe, rising to 265.5 metres (870 feet).

But Frankfurt may well pay a heavy price for progress and prosperity, as it is in danger of losing its past and everyday charm: the corner kiosk, or *Wasserhäusschen*, the friendly pub with a garden, and the *Lädsche*, that little store that sells practically everything and where people meet for a chat in the old Frankfurt dialect. Nevertheless, if you take a little time, it is still possible to discover the remnants of old Frankfurt. This city on the Main is also an important seat of learning. There are students everywhere and that means lively bars and a cultural paradise.

Paradoxically, in a spiritual sense Frankfurt stands for anything but the might of capitalism. In 1923 the Institute for Social Research was established here under the leadership of the philosopher Max Horkheimer and the sociologist Theodor Adorno. This was the "Frankfurt School", which soon acquired a worldwide reputation. Although the institute that revised the theories of Marx, Freud and other great thinkers had to move to Geneva in 1933–34 and then on to New York, Horkheimer and Adorno returned to Frankfurt in 1950.

One example of the socio-political involvement of Frankfurt's students was the 1980s campaign against the construction of the airport's western runway. Joschka Fischer, now a leading light in the Green Party, was one of the protagonists in the battle, which was instrumental in raising awareness about environmental issues.

A great past: A settlement by the banks of the Main was first mentioned in documents in 794 when an Imperial gathering was held under Charlemagne. Since

Left, the Messeturm in Frankfurt is the tallest office building in Europe. **Right**, street buskers are part of the everyday scene on the Römerburg.

then, Frankfurt has always been at the centre of political events. From 1356 the election of the king took place here and, after 1502, the German emperor was crowned in Frankfurt Cathedral.

The Kaisersaal or Emperor's Room in the **Römer**, Frankfurt's town hall, serves to remind visitors of the great moments in the country's distant past. It was here that the magnificent coronation celebrations took place. The **Römerplatz** with the **Gerechtigkeitsbrunnen** (Fountain of Justice) at its centre is a good place to start and finish a two-hour tour of the city's historic sites. If a little sustenance is required before or after, then **Haus Wertheim**, a 16th-century, half-timbered structure with a richly ornamented facade, can provide a friendly atmosphere.

The next point of interest is the **Historische Ostzeile**, a row of restored, medieval half-timbered houses opposite the Römer. The **Leonhardskirche** has a late Romanesque-Gothic interior. The **Historische Museum** at Saalgasse 19 is an amalgam of modern architecture and ancient buildings from the Hohenstaufen period – the Saalhof chapel dates from around 1170. On display here are exhibitions documenting the history of Frankfurt.

The Protestant **Nikolaikirche** (1290) and the **Kaiserdom**, the emperor's cathedral (13th–14th centuries), are close to one another. Among the many art treasures in the cathedral, the most notable are the sculptures to the side of the chancel and Hans Backofen's *Crucifixion* (1509) in the tower hall. Modern art in touring exhibitions as well as action art shows are the specialities of the **Schirn-Kunsthalle** at Römerberg 6A. The historic significance of the **Paulskirche** (built between 1789 and 1833) derives from the events of 1848–49 when the German National Assembly, the first all-German parliament, met here. After suffering considerable damage in World War II, it was converted into a concert hall in 1948. The Goethe prize and the peace prize offered by the German publishing industry are awarded here every year.

The Ostzeile, Römerplatz.

224

Connoisseurs of German literature will find the **Goethehaus** at Grosser Hirschgraben 23–25 of interest. The house where Johann Wolfgang von Goethe, Germany's most famous playwright, was born and raised has been restored and converted into a museum.

Shopping: The best place to start a shopping expedition is at the **Hauptwache** (1730), formerly the city's police station and now a café. The **Zeil**, Germany's longest shopping street, starts here. Opposite is a pedestrian zone known as the **Fressgass**, literally "Glutton's Lane". It acquired its name from the many delicatessens and restaurants that are located here.

Culture: Situated at the end of the Fressgass is the **Alte Oper** building. The old opera house now has a number of different functions, one of which is as the studio for a popular German TV chat show called *Life aus der Alten Oper.* Around the corner is the Jazz Cellar, an important venue for jazz enthusiasts and one reason why Frankfurt is regarded as Europe's capital of jazz.

As well as the lively theatre scene, the city boasts a number of superb museums and these alone justify a visit to Frankfurt. Perhaps the most interesting one is the **Senckenberg Museum of Natural History** with its world-famous collection of fossils and dinosaur skeletons (Senckenberganlage 25). Eight museums line the south bank of the Main, a district known as the **Museumsufer**. The **Städelsche Kunstinstitut** is one of Germany's most famous art galleries and displays paintings dating from the 14th century up to the present day, whereas the **Liebighaus** exhibits sculptures from antiquity to the baroque period. The **Deutsche Filmmuseum** documents the German film industry, but film performances are also staged here. On or near the Schaumainkai are the **Deutsche Architekturmuseum**, the **Museum für Kunsthandwerk** (Museum of Applied Arts), **Museum für Völkerkunde** (Ethnological Museum), the **Deutsche Postmuseum** (Postal Museum) and the **Ikonmuseum** (Icon Museum) at Brückenstrasse 3-7.

Street cafés in the "Fressgass".

"Ebbelwoi": After such a wide choice of cultural delights, it will be time for some gastronomic pleasures and one of the pubs, beer gardens or jazz bars in the district of **Sachsenhausen** to the southeast of the museum quarter is sure to have something suitable. In the cafés around the Klappergass, the favourite tipple of the locals is a drink called *Ebbelwoi*, which is a kind of apple wine.

Frankfurt's trade fairs: The gigantic, multi-storey tower with its pointed roof is a landmark that no visitor to Frankfurt could possibly miss. The tower marks the venue for the trade fairs that take place in Frankfurt. Every October, thousands of publishers arrive to do deals at the **Internationale Buchmesse**, the biggest book fair in the world. The **Internationale Automobilausstellung**, in which the German car industry displays its new models, is another important annual event.

If now is the time for a little relaxation away from the traffic, then try the **Palmengarten**, one of the most beautiful botanical gardens in Europe.

Excursions from Frankfurt: Frankfurt lies within easy reach of the Taunus mountains and many Frankfurters wishing to escape from the stresses and strains of city life seek refuge here at weekends. **Bad Homburg vor der Höhe** (pop. 51,000), only 17 km (10 miles) from Frankfurt in the foothills of the Taunus range, is a favourite destination. Even in Roman times the healing power of the local waters was well known. In subsequent years, celebrated guests have included emperors, tsars and kings. English visitors were responsible for marking out the first tennis court on continental Europe and later Germany's first golf course.

There are some interesting sights in the large Kurpark, such as a **Siamese temple**, a **Russian Chapel** and also a casino. The baroque **Landgrafenschloss** (1680–85) overlooking the town was built by Friedrich II.

From Bad Homburg it is only a short bus ride to **Saalburg**, a rebuilt Roman fort (AD 83–260) that once guarded the Limes, the border of the Roman Empire. The **Saalburgmuseum** displays a collection of artefacts from this period.

Line S4 of Frankfurt's suburban railway (S-bahn) takes 25 minutes to cover the distance to **Kronberg** (pop. 18,000), whose skyline is dominated by a castle of the same name (1230). Edible chestnuts, once of significant commercial value, can still be collected in the **Hardtwald**. First take a stroll through the delightful medieval town centre and then give the children a break from sightseeing by visiting the **Opelzoo**.

Oberursel is the gateway to the Taunus. The U3 undergound line from Frankfurt town centre will take you there in only 25 minutes. Footpaths up into the hills start at the Hohenmark underground station, but the highest peak in the range, the **Grosse Feldberg** (880 metres/2,886 feet), can be reached by car. On a clear day the view extends across the Upper Rhine plain as far as Alsace. Many different birds of prey are bred at the falconry. Opposite stands the more peaceful **Altkönig** (798 metres/2,617 feet). There is no road to the top – the footpath starts in Falkenstein.

Left, children will enjoy the Opel Zoo. **Right**, at the summit of the Feldberg.

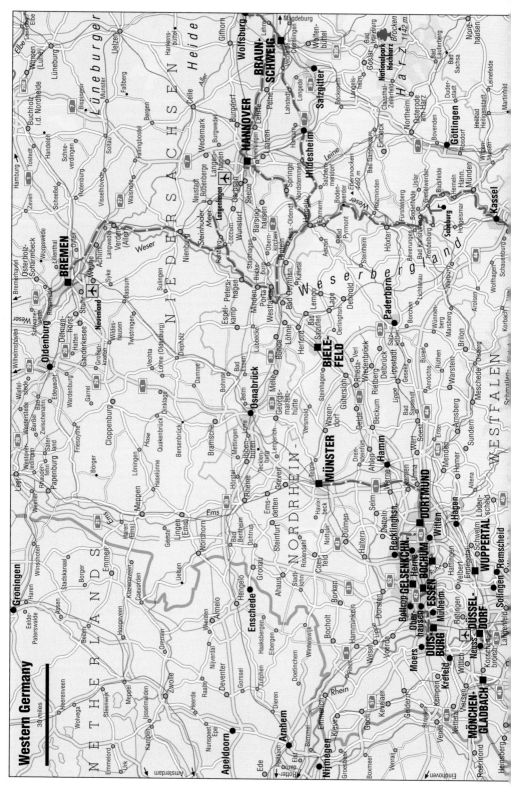

Western Germany

30 miles

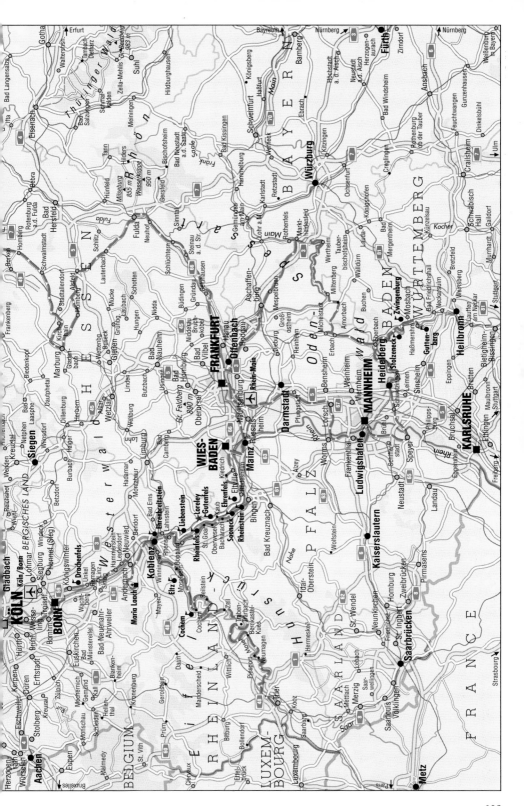

FROM THE RHINE TO THE MOSELLE

The Rhine has been Germany's "river of destiny" since time immemorial. Before AD 55, when Julius Caesar had the first bridge built across the river near Andernach, north of Koblenz, the Rhine formed the last frontier between the Roman Empire and the Germanic tribes. But when the Romans crossed this river the Germans were irrevocably drawn into the process of world history.

Countless vineyards and castles, idyllic towns and sombre legends have for centuries symbolised the conflicting traits which are said to mark the German national character: a zest for living and sentimentality on the one hand, broodiness and haughtiness on the other. The belligerent and the romantic, the bustling and the idyllic exist side by side in the landscape of this river.

With a total length of 1,320 km (820 miles, of which 539 flow in Germany), the Rhine is the third-longest river in Europe, after the Volga and the Danube. It has its source at the base of the Gotthard Massif in the Swiss Alps and flows into the North Sea near Rotterdam. For the last 883 km (552 miles) from Rheinfelden near Basle to its estuary, the Rhine is the busiest waterway in Europe. Nearly 10,000 barges and freighters ply its waters every month with all kinds of cargo, while the water itself also carries seawards much of the waste which was created in the manufacture of those goods and in waste-recycling.

The Rhine is a heavily polluted river, however – and not only during emergencies like the disastrous Sandoz chemicals fire near Basel in 1986 but also on any normal day. Its waters are enriched by a cocktail of some 60,000 different chemicals which are released quite legally from the giant chemical plants strewn along its banks.

Nevertheless, the Rhine appears to have lost none of its romantic appeal, and for the millions of tourists from all over the world who come here every year it remains a symbol of both German history and the German spirit. The symbolism of the Rhine was reinforced by the German, and also the English, Romantic poets.

Gutenberg's city: Not far from the confluence of the River Main and the Rhine lies the ancient city of **Mainz** (pop. 187,000), which was founded as Mongotiacum in the year 38 BC. After several hundred years of decline, the former capital of the Roman province *Germania superior* embarked on a long period of prosperity in AD 747 when St Boniface, the "German Apostle", made it the seat of an archbishop. The city thereby became the centre of Germanic Christendom. The archbishops of Mainz were not only spiritual shepherds, but in simultaneously performing the role of chancellor to the Reich and elector of the emperor, they became one of the strongest secular powers in the Roman Empire of German Nations. In 1254 Mainz joined with Worms in founding the Rhenish League of Cities, which grew to a group of 70 cities before very long. Together they succeeded in releasing the Rhine from the grip of the

Left, quality control on the Moselle. *Right*, Burg Katz, near the famous Lorelei.

robber knights, who during the vacuum of the Great Interregnum (1250–73) had gained a hold on most of Germany.

Mainz's most famous son is undoubtedly Johannes Gensfleisch zum Gutenberg (circa 1397–1468), who is regarded as the inventor of printing. It was while living in Strasbourg, from about 1439 onwards, that he developed the revolutionary system of printing with moveable letters. After returning to his home town in 1448, he won the patronage of the Mainz tradesman Johann Fust, who advanced the necessary capital to print the 42-page Latin Gutenberg bibles, of which 47 copies are known to exist today. One of them can be seen in the **Gutenberg Museum**, which also contains a replica of the master's workshop. In 1477 a university bearing Gutenberg's name was founded in Mainz

The mighty Romanesque **Cathedral** (975) stands opposite the museum and, with its six red sandstone towers, remains the dominant feature of a city that practically had to be rebuilt after the devastation of successive bombing raids during World War II. Mainz is the capital of the federal state of Rhineland-Palatinate, founded in 1949. Near the cathedral stands the 14th-century Church of St Stephen (Stephanskirche), where the artist Marc Chagall worked on painting the window until shortly before his death in 1985. The **Electoral Palace**, a late-Renaissance building, houses the **Roman-Germanic Central Museum** as well as the banqueting halls in which the famous annual carnival performances are held.

A glass of wine in Rüdesheim: From Mainz the Rhine begins to meander its way through the steep valley separating the Taunus and the Hunsrück mountains. In addition to the barges, there are now countless pleasure steamers plying up and down this romantic stretch of the river, which is accompanied by ever-changing vistas of quaint villages with pointed church spires and golden weather cocks, narrow gorges and steeply sloping vineyards.

Following the river downstream towards Koblenz, the traveller soon ar-

The morning mist over the Rheingau slowly lifts.

rives in **Eltville**, the *alta villa* of Roman days, seat of the electors of Mainz for 150 years. The **Wohnturm** (dwelling tower) of the electoral castle recalls the days when the archbishops of Mainz sought refuge here in times of war and rebellion. Many 16th- and 17th-century town houses and former residences of the landed gentry are worth seeing in the town centre, as indeed is the **Parish Church of Saints Peter and Paul** (built from 1350). The historic Rhine promenade which at one time was going to have to make way for a road and railway has been saved by the efforts of a local action group.

In the north of Eltville, a narrow road branches off to the wine village of **Kiedrich** with the ruins of **Scharfenstein Castle** and **Eberbach Monastery**. Here, in 1116, Augustinian monks first started cultivating their Rheingau vines, pressing specially-cellared communion wine from their grapes.

The town of **Rüdesheim**, with its famous **Drosselgasse**, has somehow managed to market itself to millions of visitors as your typical, quaint wine "village". Despite the **Brömserburg** (the oldest castle on the Rhine, built in the 9th century), there is very little to distinguish Rüdesheim from other settlements along this stretch of the river. All have typical half-timbered houses and all have narrow back alleys and *Weinstuben* (wine bars). The visitor would be well advised to steer clear of the crowds on the Drosselgasse itself and head for less busy pubs and eateries, where the atmosphere can still be enjoyed – and at remarkably low prices.

Germania, a Valkyrie: From Rüdesheim a cable lift makes the journey to the 37-metre (121-feet) high **Niederwald Monument**, whose scale and position high above the Rhine are breathtaking. Created as an expression of Wilhelminian aspirations of power after the Franco–German war (1870–71), the statue they call **Germania**, symbolically depicted as a sword-brandishing Valkyrie, gazes defiantly westwards.

There is a ferry from Rüdesheim across to **Bingen** at the confluence of

Mainz, an old imperial city.

the Rhine and River Nahe. Together with the **Mäuseturm**, perched on a rock in the middle of the river, **Castle Klopp** controlled the Rhine at this point for Bishop Hatto of Mainz, who was thus able to derive considerable income from taxation of the commercial traffic both beside and on the river. The Mäuseturm later served as a signal tower to warn the passing traffic of **Bingen Hole** and its treacherous reef. The reef was cleared some years ago.

A string of castles: The next 16 km (10 miles) after Bingen Hole will make any visitor appreciate why the Rhine has played such a central role in so many fairy tales and fables, legends and songs. The majestic Rhine, with its steep valley sides, forested slopes, vineyards and castles, holds not only those of a romantic disposition in its spell. Train passengers have a panoramic view from the comfort of their seats, for the railway line follows the river's course for the entire dramatic stretch between Bingen and Bonn. The castles recall the days when the robber knights, having ren-

dered the land routes impassable, blocked the river with chains in order to demand tolls from the traders.

Just before Bingen the **Ehrenfels** fortress stands sentinel above the right bank of the river. Nearby is the riverside town of **Assmannshausen**, famous for its fine red wine. A ferry takes you to the left bank, where castle after castle – Rheinstein, Reichenstein, Sooneck, Hohneck, Fürstenberg and Stahleck – mark the riverside like milestones all the way to Bacharach (linger in its lovely Old Town).

Napoleon's defeat: A few kilometres beyond Bacharach, the middle of the river is dominated by the picturesque **Pfalzgrafenstein** Island and its castle, a picturesque customs post built here in its watery location in the 14th century. It was at this point that Marshal Blücher crossed the Rhine on New Year's Eve 1813–14 with the help of a pontoon bridge. He was in pursuit of Napoleon's forces who had just suffered a heavy defeat at the Battle of Nations near Leipzig. Opposite stands the small town of

Left, the Niederwald Monument, near Rüdesheim, with the statue of Germania. Below, the Drosselgasse, Rüdesheim.

Kaub and **Gutenfels Fortress** which was built in the 13th century. A little further on, the ruins of **Schönburg** come into view above the left bank of the river near Oberwesel, a medieval town well worth visiting.

Lorelei and other maidens: Immediately beyond Oberwesel the smooth flow of the Rhine is disturbed by seven underwater rocks, the **Seven Maidens**. According to legend seven girls were turned to stone because they were so prudish. At least that's what the local lads would tell their girlfriends if they resisted their advances. By contrast, the **Lorelei** sealed the fate of many hapless boatmen. On the overhanging cliffs above the dangerous currents, the siren Lorelei – so goes the legend – would sing seductively and comb her long blonde hair.

A few minutes' drive further on, three castles appear simultaneously: **Katz Castle** and **Maus Castle** above the right bank and **Rheinfels Castle** on the left bank near **St Goar**. This is the location of an annual September firework display on the river, the "**Rhine in Flames**".

Not far away, castles **Sterrenberg** and **Liebenstein**, known as the two "hostile brothers", are separated from each other by a high wall.

Endless vineyards: Boppard, with its Rhine promenade, more than a mile in length, is the centre of the largest wine-producing region on the Middle Rhine. On the **Bopparder Hang** alone, there are no fewer than 1 million vines. A cable lift climbs to **Gedeons Eck** (302 metres/991 feet), where a magnificent view of the meandering Rhine divides the river into what look like four separate lakes – hence the name of this spot, the **Vier-Seen-Blick** (Four Lakes View).

Rivalling Bacharach for the sheer number of its half-timbered buildings is the little town of **Braubach**. The 13th-century **Marksburg Castle** above the town houses the fascinating **Museum of Castles**. A medieval festival is held here every two years.

Diagonally opposite lies the small town of **Rhens**, in medieval times one of the main centres of power of the German realm. It was here, at the **Kings'**

Burg Pfalzgrafenstein, near Kaub.

Chair, that the seven electors assembled to choose their kings and emperors. Downstream near **Lahnstein**, at the confluence of the Lahn, stands the **Wirtshaus an der Lahn**. A summer theatre festival is held in the Lahneck castle. Across the river stands the **Stolzenfels** castle.

Where the Rhine and Moselle meet: At the confluence of the Rhine and Moselle rivers stands **Koblenz** (pop. 108,000), the largest city on the Rhine after Mainz. The **Landesmuseum** has an interesting selection of cultural and historical exhibitions. From the fortress of **Ehrenbreitstein** above the right bank, there are excellent views of the city with the towers of the **Church of our Dear Lady** (12th–13th centuries) and the **Church of St Castor** (13th century).

The fortress not only houses the largest youth hostel in Germany but also the interesting **Museum of the Rhine**. The Middle Rhine Museum on Florinsmarkt contains works of art from the past five centuries. The origins of the city lie on the other side of the river (reached via the Pfaffendorf Bridge), at the magnificent **Electoral Palace** (1777–86). The last Elector of Trier had it built on the site of the ancient *castrum ad confluence,* the Roman encampment which was established here in 9 BC.

On a promontory at the confluence of the Rhine and Moselle is a hallowed piece of ground known as the **German Corner** (Deutsches Eck). A memorial to Kaiser Wilhelm stood here until 1945, when American troops blew it up. In 1953 the surviving pedestal was renamed the **Monument to German Unity**.

Above the Pfaffendorf Bridge, with the Moselle on the left and the Rhine on the right, is the famous **Wine Village**. It was built in 1925 as a replica of a wine-producing village complete with authentic vineyards and typical half-timbered houses from the most celebrated German wine-growing regions. Here you can take a breather in a Rhineland–Moselle tour and enjoy a glass of refreshingly fruity Moselle wine in preparation for the journey through that lovely valley of vineyards.

Boppard by night.

The wonderful Moselle Valley: The idyllic Moselle Valley is the best-known of all Germany's wine-producing areas, and here enjoyment of good wine is inseparable from the lovely landscape and the region's 2,000-year history. For the Romans knew how to sweeten life so far away from home and they bequeathed the Germanic tribes their Elbling grape.

To the left and right of the Moselle rise the uplands of the Eifel and Hunsrück. The steep, slatey southern slopes produce the best wine, although they are very difficult to work. In earlier times many of the vineyards were cultivated part-time, with as many as 12,000 vintners sharing an equivalent number of hectares (about 30,000 acres). Nowadays there are 8,000, mostly larger concerns, their land worked in a more productive and effective way, a necessary development in view of increased competition from other countries of the European Union. The competition has taken away nothing of the popularity of the Moselle wine, though.

Everything about Moselle Wine: The wine of the Moselle Valley wasn't discovered by visitors to the region, but it certainly figures at the centre of most tourist itineraries; visits to wine cellars, vineyard tours, tastings and seminars all offer the opportunity to get to know everything about the noble grape. Every vineyard has its "open day", when visitors are invited to drop in and enjoy a free glass or two of its vintage.

Holidays on the Moselle: Although wine is at the centre of so much Moselle life, all kinds of leisure activities are also cultivated for the visitor: angling, hiking and biking tours along the winding river and sight-seeing excursions, to name just a few.

Winningen is the first of many typical Moselle villages, with its narrow streets and market squares, hemmed in by half-timbered houses, old wine vaults and new wine cellars that are found only on the Moselle. Take a look into the back courtyards and try some delicious cake in one of the charming cafés. And for more information on the wine and history of the Moselle Valley it's worth calling in at Winningen's **Wein und Heimatmuseum** (Wine and Local History Museum)

Eltz Castle: One of Germany's most beautiful castles, 6 km (4 miles) from the railway station at Moselkern, it is surrounded on three of it sides by the Eltz River. The castle was first mentioned in documents in 1150, and since then has belonged to the family of the Count of Elce. Thousands of visitors have been inspired by its towers, high gables and beautiful ornamentation. The treasures that the counts collected in the course of centuries can be admired in the weapons hall, the painting collection and the expensively-appointed rooms, but only when the present owners are not at home.

The **Reichsburg Cochem** (Imperial Castle) at **Cochem**, 13 km (8 miles) from Eltz Castle, built in 1027, looms above the delightful little town which gave it its name. The Cochem Krampen is the first of many idyllic bends in the river, typical of the Moselle. From its walls, a fine view of the Moselle Valley

Bernkastel-Keus, the heart of the Moselle.

and of Cochem's maze of little streets can be enjoyed. The Kapuziner Monastery (built 1623–35) is also worth a visit. The **Moselle Promenade**, with its numerous wine bars, cafés and restaurants, entices the visitor to take a stroll. Near Cochem's Moselle bridge is the entrance to Germany's longest railway tunnel, the 4,203-metre (4,596-yard) **Kaiser-Wilhelm-Tunnel** (built in 1877), which cuts through the **Cochemer Krampen** and detours the biggest bend of the Moselle.

Right on the bend is romantic **Beilstein**, whose historic houses, town hall and parish church (Pfarrkirche) snuggle up to each other between the river and the bordering slopes, crowned by a monastery and castle ruins.

No less dreamlike is the wine-town **Zell**, famous for its "Schwarze Katze" vineyard. Thirty-seven kilometres (23 miles) from Cochem lies **Traben-Trarbach**, a spa and wine-centre in one. An international motorboat race takes place here once a year. From here you can also take an excursion to **Mont Royal**, one of the largest European fortresses under the French King Louis XI, and to the ruins of **Grevenburg** (14th century), from where there is a wonderful view of the Moselle Valley.

After another 22 km (14 miles), you arrive in **Bernkastel-Kues** (pop. 7,500), in the heart of the central Moselle, one of the region's best-known wine areas. The romantic market place with the ruined castle of Landshut rising over it has become a symbol of the Moselle. No less than 65 million litres of wine, the product of more than 5,000 wine growers, are stored in its central wine cellars. Bernkastel is world-famous for its pretty, half-timbered houses, the filigreed fountain railing in the market square and the artistic weathervanes on the gables of the houses – an incomparable picture that has long decorated calendars.

The **Cusanusstift**, for over 500 years a hospital and hospice, was named after the famous cardinal and philosopher Nikolaus von Kues (in Latin, Cusanus, 1401–64). Kues was an important sup-

The Porta Nigra in Trier is one of Germany's best-preserved Roman structures.

porter of German humanism who spoke out for religious tolerance.

The trip continues along the winding course of the Moselle from Bernkastel-Kues to Trier, past vineyards and through idyllic wine villages such as **Piesport** and **Neumagen**.

Germany's oldest city: Founded in the year 16 BC by the Emperor Augustus, **Trier** (pop. 100,000) is considered Germany's oldest city. It has the most impressive Roman constructions north of the Alps. Trier was the residence of Diocletian, Constantine the Great and other Roman emperors. Evidence of the city's long history can be seen throughout the city.

The **Porta Nigra** (2nd-century), which was once the gate of a Roman fortress and is 36 metres (118 feet) wide and 30 metres (98 feet) high, is considered the best-preserved construction of its kind north of the Alps. The Porta Nigra gets its name from the dark patina that has built up on the limestone blocks.

The **Aula Palatina**, a basilica built in the 4th century as Constantine the Great's coronation chamber, and the **Imperial Baths**, begun but not completed under Constantine, also date back to Roman times, as does the **Roman Bridge**. It is only a short distance from the baths to the ruins of the antique amphitheatre, where 25,000 spectators once attended theatre presentations and bloody gladiatorial battles.

The fortress-like **Cathedral**, one of Germany's oldest churches in the Romanesque style (11th–12th centuries), bears witness to the Christian Middle Ages. The foundations date from the 4th century. Its treasure contains many precious works including the 10th century gold Portable Altar of St Andrew.

From the church it is only a few steps to the **Main Market**, an impressive, picturesque square surrounded by Gothic, Renaissance and rococo buildings, a living art-history textbook. And from here, it is only a few minutes to Brückenstrasse 10, the house where Karl Marx was born in 1818. The house is now a museum and attracts visitors from all over the world.

The Neumagener Weinschiff – a Roman wine-barge.

THE ROUTE TO COLOGNE

In the extensive region between Koblenz's "German Corner" and the western frontier of Germany lies the bleak but beautiful upland range of the Eifel. For those who followed the meanderings of the Moselle river all the way to Trier, there's a direct route back to the Rhine across these Eifel hills. For those who remained at the Rhine the riverside town of Andernach, near Koblenz, is the best starting point for a tour of the Eifel.

The **Eifel** is an area of great natural contrasts, even in climate. Rolling uplands covered with thick fir woods alternate with bare peaks and highland moors, such as the **Hoher Venn**. Rivers and streams flow between steep rock faces. Sandstone and basalt rock formations beckon climbers. Chalk caves like the Kakus caverns near Weyer are another challenge for the adventurous. Typical of the landscape are the so-called Maare, round lakes of volcanic origin, among which the Laacher See and the Dauner Maare are two significant examples.

Andernach itself is a former Roman settlement, *Antunnacum*. A medieval wall still surrounds the town, in the middle of which stands the splendid **Mariendom**.On the shores of a crater lake near Andernach stands the Benedictine monastery and church of **Maria Laach Abbey**, whose abbey church (built 1093–1220) is among the most important Romanesque buildings in Germany. The entire abbey complex, whose monks have long since become experienced tour guides, marks the very apogee of Romanesque architecture.

Back on the right bank of the river, the road leads through Leutesdorf to the small village of **Hammerstein**, watched over by the ruins of the 10th-century **Ley Castle**, where Count Otto von Hammerstein managed to defend himself and his wife Irmgard for three long months against the emperor Henry II.

The Remagen Bridge: The prime attractions of **Linz** are the city gate towers, the late-Gothic town hall and the excellent local wine. From the **Imperial Castle** (Kaiserberg) there are wonderful views across the river to the Eifel massif and the valley of the River Ahr. From Linz it is possible to take a ferry to the bridge at **Remagen**. At the end of the war German forces blew up the bridges across the Rhine in order to slow down the allied advance. Miraculously though, while 43 other bridges were destroyed the one at Remagen remained standing long enough for the Americans to cross it, so shortening the war by several days. The dramatic events are recalled by the **Peace Museum** which is located in the only surviving tower of the former railway bridge.

From the town of **Unkel** it is possible to make a detour to **Arenfels** and **Ockenfels** castles. The road leads through the picturesque **Siebengebirge** (Seven Mountains) hills, said to have been created by seven giants who dug a channel for the Rhine and left seven mounds of earth. Atop the Drachenfels (Dragon Rock) stand the ruins of the

12th-century **Drachenfels Castle**. It was named after Siegfried, hero of the *Nibelungen Saga*, who slew the dragon and bathed in its blood to make himself invulnerable to attack.

Provisional capital: Before 1949, the major claim to fame of the sleepy electoral residence city and university town of **Bonn** (pop. 295,000) was as the birthplace of Ludwig van Beethoven (1770–1827). But it was then chosen as the provisional seat of the new Federal Government and transformed into a modern capital, with thousands of officials moving into the stately old buildings and new high-rise blocks built to house the various ministries and administrative bodies. When the Berlin Wall collapsed, the authorities were in the process of investing billions in still more governmental construction projects, including a new parliamentary chamber.

Under the terms of the reunification treaty of 1990, Bonn returned the function of German capital city to Berlin. Heated debates broke out about the future division of responsibilities between Bonn and Berlin. In June 1991 the German Parliament voted by a narrow majority for a motion ruling that Berlin should assume its full role as seat of parliament and government within 10 to 12 years. More than half of the ministries, the Chancellor's office and other departments are to move to Berlin, with the year 2000 set for the removal of the parliament to Berlin's Reichstag. In spite of these far-reaching plans, so far not much has really changed. Government business continues as usual on the banks of the Rhine; the Bundestag (Lower House) moved into the new parliamentary building in 1992. Bonn is becoming accustomed to its new title of "Federal City" and is turning its attention increasingly to science and culture. Thanks to its "Museum Mile" it already has quite a lot to offer in this respect, including the **Art and Exhibition Hall** with changing exhibitions of art, technology, history and architecture. **The Museum of Art** houses works by August Macke and Joseph Beuys. The **House of History** displays exhibits describing the

Drachenfels and Petersburg castles near Bonn.

history of the Federal Republic of Germany, whilst zoology is the theme of the **Alexander Koenig Museum**.

The history of Bonn goes back to the Ubii, a Germanic tribe who were subsequently driven out by the Romans. Remains of the medieval city walls can still be seen in the **Star Gate** and the **Old Customs House**; the latter also affords a lovely view across the Rhine.

Northeast of the market place, at Bonngasse 20, is the **Beethovenhaus**, where the great composer was born in 1770 and grew up. Since 1889 the 16th-century building has housed the world's most important Beethoven museum, whose exhibits include the piano made specially for Beethoven in Vienna. Nearby, the **Beethovenhalle** on the Rhine promenade is today the setting for concerts and festivals. To the southwest on **Münsterplatz** stands the venerable Romanesque **Minster** with its 12th-century cloister.

In the wealthy suburb of **Bad Godesberg** stands the **Godesberger Redoute**, a fine rococo electoral palace built in 1791–92, where Beethoven once performed concerts.

The cathedral city: The most rewarding and certainly most comfortable way to enter the cathedral city of **Cologne** is by train. Looking out of the window as the train clatters over the **Hohenzollernbrücke** you can enjoy one of the world's most spectacular city panoramas: the Rhine embankment with its colourful facades and pointed gabled-roofs above which tower the mighty spires of **Cologne Cathedral**.

From the railway station a broad flight of steps leads up to the **Domplatte**, a windy open space where buskers and pavement artists perform before the great backdrop of the cathedral. With its awesome dimensions – 142 metres (472 feet) long by 43 metres (143 feet) high – the cathedral is the unmistakable landmark of this city of one million inhabitants. A winding staircase of 509 steps leads to a viewing platform 95 metres (312 feet) up in the south tower, where the view amply rewards the effort of getting there.

In the grounds of Poppelsdorfer Castle, Bonn

On the opposite side of the river, you can pick out on the tower of the famous **4711 Eau de Cologne** factory, established in the city in 1709 by the Italian chemist Giovanni-Maria Farina. Directly adjacent are the exhibition halls of the Cologne trade fair. The mighty steel bridge is called the Hohenzollernbrücke and connects Deutz on the right bank by rail with the main train station. The other side of the tower offers views of the inner city, including the roof of the Wallraf-Richartz Museum, in the shadow of the cathedral, and the Westdeutsche Rundfunk building. The pedestrian-zone shopping streets **Hohe Strasse** and **Schildergasse** cut their way through the area.

Back down at street level, it's useful to know the history of the cathedral. It was built as a new repository for the **Shrine of the Magi** which had been housed in the old cathedral since 1164. When in 1248, the Archbishop Konrad von Hochstaden gave his blessing to the commencement of construction work, Cologne was one of the world's wealthiest cities, Germany's largest city and the third largest in Europe after Paris and Constantinople. After the university was founded in 1388, the city became, both from a religious, intellectual and artistic point of view, the enlightened focal point of the Rhine Valley.

In 1322 the cathedral's choir, the work of masters Gerard, Arnold and Johannes, was completed and eight years later the construction of the towers began. In 1560, however, work ceased and the cathedral remained just a torso with a choir but no transept or nave and uncompleted towers.

The building would never have been completed if the spirit of historicism and wave of enthusiasm for the Middle Ages had not spread across Europe in the 19th century and fuelled the revival of the Gothic style. In 1842 the Prussian King Friedrich Wilhelm IV laid the foundation stone for the resumption of work and by 1880 the cathedral was completed, the most perfect example of "French" high-Gothic architecture. When it was complete the cathedral's

Facades on Colognes Old Market Place.

157-metre (515-foot) south tower was the highest in the world.

Although allied air raids devastated the old town, the cathedral miraculously escaped heavy damage. The wartime damage is still being repaired, as are the ravages of city pollution which have dug deep into the cathedral's sandstone.

Cologne Cathedral leaves a deep impression on the visitor on account of the unmatched harmony of its individual elements and the perfection of its exterior. The interior reaches to the heavens with uplifting Gothic clarity. The centrepiece of the choir is the Shrine of the Three Magi, made in 1225 and the largest gold sarcophagus in the western world. It was to have held the remains of the Magi. The **Treasury**, which contains gold, precious stones and ivory work as well as liturgical robes and documents from many centuries, testifies to the extraordinary wealth of the Catholic Church. The **Cross of Gero** (around 971) is the oldest wood-carved crucifixion work north of the Alps.

Romanesque churches: Apart from its cathedral, Cologne is famous for its wealth of Romanesque churches. Not far to the southwest of the cathedral is the Romanesque **Church of St Martin**, surrounded by the steep-eaved houses of the **Old City**. The triple-naved columned basilica with its beautiful trefoil-formed choir was razed to the ground in the wartime bombing, but since being rebuilt in 1963 it has resumed its role as the outstanding landmark of the old city. A second Romanesque church of note, **St Gereon's**, stands at the other end of the pedestrian zone, near Appellhofplatz. The 11th-century church, built on a decagonal, oval floor plan, is worth visiting for its interior frescoes, the dome of its nave, its baptistery and sacristy.

The heart of Cologne can be explored on foot and the visitor will constantly be reminded of the city's Roman past. Ancient cobbled streets and an intact thermal bath have been excavated and the **Roman-Germanic Museum** contains priceless treasures and offers a fascinating glimpse into life as it was

Below, the modern Olivandhof shopping centre. <u>Right</u>, street performers.

some 2,000 years ago after the Romans had established their camp of *Colonnia* here on the Rhine. The museum was built over the world-famous **Dionysos Mosaic** which was discovered during construction work on an air raid shelter. The 2nd-century masterpiece covers an area of 70 sq. metres (84 sq. yards) and consists of over one million ceramic and glass components. It once covered the dining room floor of a Roman villa.

Next door is the museum complex whose controversial roof construction stands out so clearly when the city is viewed from the cathedral tower. The interior design of the modern complex – which contains the Philharmonie concert hall, the **Wallraf-Richartz Museum** and the **Ludwig Museum** – has been received positively enough by Cologne critics and public, but the roof construction, incorporating design elements of the cathedral, is still cause for debate. The Wallraf-Richartz Museum is considered to be one of Germany's leading art collections, incorporating medieval Cologne painters such as Stefan Lochner, panel-artists of the 14th–16th centuries (Cranach, Dürer and others), Dutch and Flemish works of the 16th–18th centuries (including Rembrandt and Rubens), as well as French painters of the 19th century (Renoir, Monet, Degas, Manet and Cézanne).

The Ludwig Museum is named after the well-known German art collector and chocolate factory owner Peter Ludwig, who bequeathed the city his collection of 20th-century art. Among its treasures are works by Schwitters, Ernst, Dalí and Magritte, the Blauer Reiter group (Marc and Macke), the Brücke (Kirchner, Schmidt-Rottluff, Nolde), the Bauhaus (Klee, Schlemmer), paintings by Picasso and Braque, sculptures by Barlach and Kollwitz. Nouveau Realisme and Pop Art are also represented (Warhol, Rauschenberg, Lichtenstein).

The **Museum of Applied Art** is also well worth a visit. It is among the most important such museums in Germany and displays a wide spectrum of textiles, glass, furniture, ceramics and jewellery, ranging from medieval times to

Pavement decoration outside the Cathedral.

design objects of the 20th century. Finally, the **Schnütgen Museum** should not be forgotten. It is named after the art-loving cathedral capitular Alexander Schnütgen, who built up an extensive collection of religious art, specialising in sculptures (crucifixes and Madonnas above all).

Secret television capital: Cologne isn't just a city of churches and museums, however. Over the years it has developed into Germany's secret television capital. The headquarters of the Westdeutscher Rundfunk (WDR) are within a stone's throw of the broadcasting house on Wallrafplatz. In terms of political programmes, WDR is among the most progressive of the public television and radio stations in Germany. But more popularity is enjoyed among the German public by long-running soap-operas like *Lindenstrasse* and *Verbotene Liebe*, which are produced in the WDR studios at Köln-Bocklemünd. On some weekends in summer Böcklemünd opens its gates Hollywood-style to the general public, and reports of traffic jams on roads leading there are eloquent testimony to the numbers of people who make the journey just to try to catch a glimpse of their favourite stars and see where they work.

Live-and-let-live: Finally, Cologne has rightly earned a reputation as a city whose inhabitants "live and let live". The people of Cologne are proud of their past without living in awe of it, they are truly attached to their roots and that's their first principle of life. The best way to meet them is away from the crowds, in areas like the **Severinsviertel**. In a *Kölschen Weetschaff*, as the pubs are called, and served a glass of *Kölsch* (the local beer) by a *Köbesse*, as the waiters are known, it's very easy to catch the prevalent good mood.

The people of Cologne fully embody the Rhineland good humour, and there's no better proof of that than at carnival time – the famous, riotous Cologne Carnival – with its Rosenmontag (Monday before Ash Wednesday) procession, when virtually the entire population pours out onto the streets. Up goes the

Henry Moore's "Reclining Figure in Two Parts" (1969) in the Hofgarten.

cry *Kölle alaaf* – Long Live Cologne, and live it certainly does.

The Rhineland Paris: Lying 40 km (25 miles) of the north of Cologne, not far from the industrial Ruhr, the city of **Düsseldorf** (pop. 576,000) is the capital of Germany's most populated federal state of North Rhine Westphalia. It sits conveniently at the centre of a network of good communications, served by autobahns and at the junction of important north–south and east–west rail routes. Its airport is number two after Frankfurt am Main in numbers of charter flights. The city even has a harbour, shipping freight up and down the Rhine.

The central city areas lie right of the Rhine – in contrast to all the Rhineland cities of Roman origin – and are connected by five bridges with the other bank and its considerably older neighbour, Neuss. The city rose to importance from being a *Dorf* (village) on the river Dussel (a tributary of the Rhine) because of its elevation to the seat of the local Dukes of Berg back in the 14th century.

Although it was never as important as Cologne, Düsseldorf's royal patronage nevertheless resulted in it becoming a centre that attracted artists, writers and musicians. The Art Academy, founded in 1777, developed into one of the most respected such institutions in the country. The German writer and francophile Heinrich Heine (1797–1856) was born in Düsseldorf. He was an admirer of Napoleon whom he celebrated in his book *Le Grand*. Napoleon referred to Düsseldorf as "mon petit Paris".

Düsseldorf's trademarks, the **Schlossturm** tower and the church of **St Lambert** (the Lambertuskirche), with its characteristic slightly crooked spire, stand directly on the Rhine. The former thoroughfare which ran alongside the river, separating it from the old town, has now been banished underground, giving Düsseldorf an additional riverside open space, the Uferpromenade. It is now possible to walk unhindered by traffic from the river bank to the bustling old town, a square mile packed so solidly with pubs and restaurants that it **Düsseldorf's Rhine Promenade.**

has come to be known as the "longest bar in the world".

Another name that has stuck is "the office desk of the Ruhr", earned by Düsseldorf in the years after 1945 when banks, courts, multinational firms, organisations of all kinds, state government departments, service industries and the state stock exchange all established themselves there. Düsseldorf is also a very important centre of trade and industry (iron, steel and chemicals), and it is significant that Japanese firms are much more strongly represented here than in Frankfurt.

City of art and fashion: The city's importance for trade is reflected in the numerous trade fairs, the best known of which are the **Modemessen** – the fashion fairs. Its prominent place in the world of fashion and the arts has a long tradition. The **Academy of Art** was founded in 1777 and rapidly grew into one of the most respected in the whole country, a reputation reinforced by the artists Peter von Cornelius and Wilhelm von Schadow, among others. But the academy never rested on its laurels, and important modern impulses were released there, thanks to the work of Paul Klee, who was a professor there from 1931–33, and the sculptor and "action" artist Joseph Beuys (1961–72).

The city maintains its reputation as a centre of the arts, and it has many good museums: for instance, the **Kunstmuseum** (Museum of Art) in the Ehrenhof, with a collection of French, Italian and Dutch works from the 15th to the 20th centuries.

The municipal **Kunsthalle**, on Grabbeplatz, stages regular exhibitions of modern art. Opposite, behind a highly-polished marble facade, is the **Kunstsammlung Nordrhein-Westfalen**, the state art collection, with 20th-century works by artists ranging from Picasso to Lichtenstein and a comprehensive collection of works by Paul Klee.

Within the **Heinrich-Heine Institute** on Bilkerstrasse is the country's largest collection of documents illustrating the life and work of the great poet, who was born in Düsseldorf in 1797. The ba-

Eating out on the Königsallee.

roque **Jägerhof Palace** in Jacobistrasse houses a **Goethe Museum**.

Besides its artistic scene, Düsseldorf also has a lively theatre and opera programme. Its opera house and theatre are among Germany's most innovative. Fresh Rhineland has found its forum here in political cabaret, the **Kom(m)ödchen**, which has been performing since the early post-war years and which was given national fame by the late Kay and Lore Lorentz.

The Rhineland metropolis is also the undisputed capital of the art trade. Apart from large exhibitions in the trade fair halls, many small galleries with a good sense of the newest trends have set up business in the city.

Finally, art as a decorative form for the body. The international fashion fairs in March and September have reinforced Düsseldorf's world fame as a fashion centre. You can, though, follow fashion trends just as well from a café on the celebrated Königsallee (the "Kö" for short) as from a seat next to a fashion house catwalk.

The great Rhineland rivals: Cologne and Düsseldorf do not regard themselves as serious rivals in a number of spheres. Düsseldorf has little to offer in the way of Romanesque churches, while Cologne can't compete in the world of fashion. Yet in many areas these two cities are permanently engaged in traditional rivalries of a more or less serious nature.

The most important, first of all: **Kölsch** or **Düssel**, that's the question when it comes to beer. The real Rhinelander knows no neutrality in this pub contest, unless a beer from a completely different area is ordered. Either one loves the light, top-brewed Kölsch from Cologne or one swears by the malt-coloured, more bitter but also top-brewed Düsseldorfer Alt.

Up until only about 20 years ago, every Cologne publican would have shown you the door if you had dared to order an Altbier and a Düsseldorfer would react similarly to an order of Kölsch. But nowadays you can find the two kinds of beer in practically every pub in the rival areas, with the exception of the breweries' own pubs and taverns. The multicultural society that is now Germany has made all this possible.

Rivalries have been taken more seriously for years past on the ice and soccer turf. Local derbies between the ice-hockey clubs **Eissportclub Düsseldorf** and the **Kölner EC** are sell-out fixtures. The Düsseldorf fans are particularly renowned for the unbounded enthusiasm with which they cheer on their team in home matches.

Direct confrontations between the two rival soccer clubs **Fortuna Düsseldorf** and **1 FC Köln** (or **Fortuna Köln**) became a thing of the past in Germany's premier league when the goddess of good fortune, after which Fortuna Düsseldorf and Fortuna Köln are named, failed to prevent the relegation of both. Fortuna Düsseldorf managed to climb back into the premier league for the current season, however, so tense matches in Cologne's Müngersdorfer stadium and Düsseldorf's Rheinstadion are back on the programme in future.

Finally, an area where fun rules instead of money: **carnival**. Both cities treasure equally highly their own ways of celebrating carnival, from the official start of the season at 11am on the eleventh day of the eleventh month until Ash Wednesday. It's impossible to judge, though, where the fun is greater or more intensive.

Bergisches Land: To the east of the Rhine, just a short drive from Cologne and Düsseldorf, lies an upland area which offers all kinds of recreation for city-dwellers: the **Bergisches Land Nature Park**. Rivers of the rainiest areas, such as the Ruhr, Wupper and Sieg, have formed idyllic valleys.

Extensive fir forests beckon hikers and walkers. The region's reservoirs offer secure habitats for endangered species and attractive areas for people in search of rest and recreation. In many areas the rain water of millions of years has carved out labyrinthine caves in the limestone, creating bizarre worlds of stalactites. The **Aggertal** caves, near Ründeroth, have exceptional aragonite crystals, while the stalactite caves (**Tropfsteinhöhle**) of Wiehl have beautiful sinter cascades.

Düsseldorf: major centre of fashion.

THE RUHR

To the northeast of Cologne lies Germany's largest industrial region, the *Ruhrgebiet*, the district of the Ruhr, a tourist destination of a very special kind. Every city here has its own special mix of industry, culture and reclaimed countryside. According to UNESCO, the Ruhr belongs alongside cities like Paris and New York to the greatest of the world's cultural landscapes.

The coal and steel crises of recent years have presented great problems for the Ruhr communities. But many have managed to take at least the first steps out of the deadend street in which they had found themselves. Through the development of new industrial and service sectors they have tried to get to grips with unemployment. Examples of creative solutions are provided by the closed collieries which have been converted to places of cultural activity.

The Social Democratic Party, which ruled practically unchallenged in the Ruhr cities for decades, reaped the reward at the last local and state elections for the deterioration in living standards. The party had to content itself with a red–green coalition in many local city halls and council chambers and in some places even with alliances of conservative CDU representatives and the Greens. Yet a lot has remained unchanged despite the general mood of crisis: the people of the Ruhr, because of their tradition of living alongside people of the most varied backgrounds, are more tolerant than anywhere else in Germany. And, above all, the tough labour struggles have strengthened the traditional feeling of solidarity.

Duisburg: The economic upswing of this industrial city (pop. 530,000), located north of Düsseldorf and on the western edge of the Ruhr, began in 1831 with the construction of the world's largest river port. A tour by boat of the 40 docks of the Duisburg harbour, in which iron ore, coal, slag and oil are principally loaded and shipped on the Rhine, is a unique experience. Its Museum of German River and Lake Shipping (Museum der Deutschen Binnenschiffahrt) should also be visited.

But Duisburg also has its cultural side: apart from the cruise around the harbour, Duisburg today has other attractions. Together with Düsseldorf, it is the home city of the **German Opera on the Rhine** as well as the **Wilhelm Lehmbruck Museum** in which the works of the famous German sculptor (1881–1919) are displayed. Duisburg has few other names of note to boast of, although it is the home of Germany's most famous television policeman, Superintendant Horst Schimanski.

Oberhausen: Duisburg's neighbour (pop. 231,000) is the birthplace of Ruhr industry, for the first iron foundry was built here at the end of the 18th century. It holds an annual film festival, under the motto *Wege zum Nachbarn* (Routes to the Neighbours). A visit to nearby **Bottrop** is worth it because of its **Josef-Albers Museum**, featuring the work of the local-born artist, who also taught at the Bauhaus.

Left, a future in steel. Right, Duisburg has Europe's largest inland harbour.

Essen: Once known as the "armourer of the nation", **Essen** (pop. 600,000) no longer produces any steel. None of the original 22 collieries now operate. But it was in Essen that the industrialisation of the Ruhrgebiet actually began back in 1837, largely thanks to the innovative ability of one man, the pioneer of industry Franz Haniel. He developed a way of getting the miners to the previously inaccessible bituminous coal, which enabled the furnaces to produce pig iron very competitively. The steel boom began in earnest.

When the mines went into decline, Essen won importance as a centre of trade and service industries. Today many an international industrial combine has its headquarters in Essen, such as Ruhrkohle AG, the largest German producer of coal, and RWE, the biggest power company in Europe and the Ruhrgas AG. The city is also an episcopal seat, it has a university and is the shopping eldorado of the Ruhr.

With its extensive **Stadtwald** woodlands, the **Baldeneysee** lake recreation area and the **Grugapark**, Essen exemplifies perfectly the "green Ruhr" image. The city's Gruga Hall stages six-day cycle races, orchestral concerts and rock spectaculars, as well as exhibitions and trade fairs.

The **Zeche Carl**, like so many independent and officially-subsidised complexes in other German cities, is an integral part of the Essen cultural scene. The city's **Folkwangschule** has won international fame in the areas of music, dance, theatre and design, and the exhibitions in the **Folkwang Museum** are renowned far beyond the state borders.

Bochum: The last mine in Bochum (pop. 400,000) closed in 1973, but other branches of industry (steel, clothing, vehicle-production) established themselves. The Ruhr University, founded in 1965, was the first in the region. The city theatre, the Schauspielhaus is among the country's best, and hosted a long-running production of Andrew Lloyd Webber's *Starlight Express*.

The **Museum of Mines** is the most popular technical museum in Germany

The "Kneeling Girl" by Wilhelm Lehmbruck in Duisburg.

and the most important of its kind in the world. With replicas of mining villages, mines and real machinery, the museum guides the visitor through the history of industrialisation in Germany and examines its social consequences. The climax of the visit – great fun for children – is a trip down the demonstration mine.

From the winding tower of the museum it is possible to see the two Bochum Krupp steelworks, out towards **Wattenscheid**. To the north lies **Gelsenkirchen** home to the area's most famous football team, Schalke 04.

To the north-west lies **Wanne-Eickel**, where the largest popular fair in Germany, the *Cranger Kirmes*, takes place over 11 days in August.

Herne (pop. 187,000) forms the northern extremity of Bochum. One of the first mines in the Ruhrgebiet was located here, the **Shamrock** colliery, founded by Irishmen. On the road leading out of town from the mining museum (Dorstener Strasse), a well-maintained mining settlement still stands, the **Zeche Hanover**, which is worth a visit.

Tour of the Mining Museum in Bochum.

Opel Cars, a subsidiary company of General Motors, settled in Bochum when the big decline in mining began. Today, its three factories employ 20,000 people working around the clock.

Recklinghausen (pop. 125,000), on the northern edge of the region, is best known for the *Ruhrfestspiele*, an international festival of theatre since 1946.

Dortmund: The modern city on the eastern edge of the Ruhr is actually very old. It was granted the right to hold a market way back in 880, and, much more important, in 1293 it was given leave to start brewing beer. While its coal and steel industries have declined, Dortmund remains at the top of the German brewing league. Indeed, more brewing goes on in Dortmund than in any other city in Europe, including its rival to the south, Munich. Dortmund's primary position is documented in a **Brewery Museum**.

Dortmund's revival began in the 19th century with the growth of the coal and steel industries. The city was heavily bombed in World War II and was rebuilt

in its present form, with a number of its historic buildings restored. It suffered again with the decline of mining in the region, and in the mid-1980s unemployment rose to 15 percent. Today steel is a thing of the past. The **Westphalian Museum of Industry** is currently in the process of creating a series of exhibitions portraying working and living conditions during the 20th century on the site of the former coal mine Zollern II/IV. The surface equipment and machinery rooms can be visited.

Dortmund's harbour, connected with the Ems river by the Dortmund-Ems Canal and with the Rhine by the Lippe-Seiten Canal, is the largest canal port in the whole of Europe.

Dortmund's **Wesphalia Hall**, with the capacity to hold 16,500 spectators, is the scene of mass popular events like six-day cycle races, various equestrian events, ice-skating revues and rock concerts. In the large **Westphalia soccer stadium** Borussia Dortmund has won the highest honours, while athletics and swimming events are held in the stadi-um's neighbouring competition halls.

Münsterland: The northern fringes of the Ruhrgebiet give way to the Münsterland, the so-called "green belt of Germany". Between large isolated farms and flat fields, surrounded by streams and canals, hundreds of moated castles, many of which are open to the visitor, lie hidden in the clearings in the woods. One of the best ways of discovering them is by bicycle and these are available for hire in the towns and villages. The region is well-equipped with cycling paths and is therefore ideal for a family outing.

Münsterland also faces environmental and economic problems, and although the area is traditionally farming country few can make a living these days from the land.

Münster: The geographic and commercial centre of the Münsterland, **Münster** (pop. 266,000) was granted its city charter in the 12th century and it soon became a member of the Hanseatic League. The Treaty of Westphalia, which marked the end of the Thirty Years' War in 1648, was signed in Münster. The ceremony took place in the Gothic **Town Hall** (14th century) on the large main market square.

The wonderfully restored square is dominated by the **Cathedral** (13th–14th century), the largest church building in Westphalia. From the tower of the **Church of St Lambert** (15th century) hang the three iron cages in which the corpses of the leaders of the reformist Anabaptists, who were executed in 1536, were displayed. Much of the splendid Baroque architecture is by the talented Westphalian architect Johann Conrad Schlaun – the baroque **castle**, now part of the university, and the **Fine Arts Museum** with magnificent altarpieces and Lucas Cranach paintings of Luther and his wife, should be visited.

The quality of life in Münster is considerably heightened by the banishment of motor traffic from the **Promenade**, which runs around the city along the course of the old fortification wall. Other sights which are worth a visit in Münster include the **Planetarium**, **Zoo** and **Natural History Museum**.

Vishering Castle: Münsterland is famous for its moated castles.

RECLAIMING THE RHUR

To the northeast of Cologne lies Germany's largest industrial region, the Ruhrgebiet. Today, much of the heavy industry has gone and, although it has a lot to offer, it still has to live with a reputation of smoke and sweat.

The River Ruhr gave this tract of land its name, for it was here that the first coal mines were excavated, back in 1820. At that time the population was 274,000. Originally, the Irish, Silesians and East Europeans came to work and settle here and, from the 1960s, they were followed by migrant workers from Italy, Turkey, Greece, Portugal and Spain. This cosmopolitan community transformed the area into a unique melting pot of European nationalities. The population of the Ruhrgebiet today numbers more than 5½ million people.

In the course of the region's development, many of the small towns grew and merged into one another until there came a point when the only way of telling where one ended and another began was by the yellow town signs. From the air, the Ruhrgebiet appears to be one massive conurbation, with dozens of sub-centres. At the local level, parish-pump based political structures are in place to ensures that a unitary Ruhrgebiet regional council does not have overwhelming authority and that all the local communities are properly represented.

Right up until the 1980s the perception of the Ruhrgebiet was characterised by toil and sweat. Men in protective clothing standing before the furnaces, silhouetted by the bright glow of molten iron; miners, their faces blackened by the coal dust, appearing at the surface after a day underground. This "romantic" vision of the Ruhr no longer holds, no longer reflects the ever-changing world of the people who live and work here today. Widespread and far-reaching structural changes have occurred, brought about by innovations in the area of research and technology, the growing awareness of the impact of heavy industry on the environment, as well as recent economic conditions.

The employment figures speak for themselves: at the end of the 1960s the coal mines employed around 266,000 people, but by the mid-1990s the figure had dropped dramatically to a mere 84,000. The numbers of people employed in the steel industry have also shrunk from 170,000 to 100,000 in the past 20 years. In the 1960s, a large part of the economy depended predominantly on the steel and coal industries but this dependence has been diminishing every year.

One of the leading roles in structural changes has been played by the sciences. Right up to the 1950s the policy towards culture and education was governed by the maxim "we need workers, not intellectuals". The first university was founded in Bochum in 1965. Now, the universities of the Ruhrgebiet employ around 7,000 lecturers and 154,000 students are presently enrolled. Culturally speaking, there is no other region in Germany with such a rich concentration of museums, theatres and concert halls.

Preconceived ideas about the industrial landscape of the Ruhrgebiet usually contradict the reality of the situation. Admittedly, it is difficult to imagine that more than 60 percent of the 4,432 sq. km (2,754 sq. miles) is actually made up of farmland, forests and meadows. There are the scenic river landscapes of the river Ruhr itself, whose artificial lakes provide excellent recreation possibilities, as do the five major parks in Dortmund, Duisburg, Herne, Gelsenkirchen and Oberhausen. In some of the towns where the land has been forsaken by the mines and industry, it is being reclaimed for agriculture. This is a process that seems set to continue in the future. ■

Essen's Zollverein Schacht XII (Customs Union Pit XII) is an important industrial monument.

HEIDELBERG AND THE CASTLE ROAD

A peaceful contrast to the German financial metropolis – whose modern office blocks and skyscrapers have earned it the punning name "Mainhattan" as another name for the city – is offered by the countryside which borders on Frankfurt and the region to the south. There you will find thousand-year-old cities with glittering histories, medieval castles, the picturesque valleys and meadows of the river Neckar and the thick forests of the Spessart, long ago a hunting ground for bands of robbbers. A high point of the tour is Heidelberg, a city which was the very essence of the Middle Ages for the German Romantics.

Driving south from Frankfurt on, the A5 and then the A67 lead (via the Lorsch exit) to the old imperial city of **Worms** (pop. 75,000), whose history goes back some 5,000 years to the Celts. During the time of the Migration of Peoples, Worms was the capital of the Burgundian realm which was destroyed by the Huns in AD 437, events which provided the basis for the *Nibelungen Saga* with its hero Siegfried and grim villain Hagen.

Numerous imperial diets were held in Worms. In 1521, Martin Luther defended his theses here against Rome and the emperor. The visitor can learn more about the city's past in the extensive **Municipal Museum**.

In the city centre stands the **Cathedral** (12th–13th century). Particularly fine is the Gothic south door, with 700-year-old "pictorial bible" reliefs. The interior contains a number of Romanesque and Gothic statues and the east choir of this double-choir church is dominated by the baroque **High Altar** created by Balthasar Neumann in 1741. The red-sandstone church is regarded as the very model of late-Romanesque ecclesiastical architecture. The heaviness of the walls is reduced by the use of glass, including the magnificent rose window.

To the west of the cathedral (at the junction of Andreasstrasse and Andreasring) is the **Jewish Cemetry**, Germany's oldest (11th century) and, with 2,000 graves, the largest. The partly-rebuilt **Jewish Quarter (Judengasse)**, is on the other side of town. Also of interest are the **Town Hall**, the **Church of the Holy Trinity** (1709–25) and the **Red House**, a fine Renaissance building on Römerstrasse dating from 1624.

Industrial centre on the Rhine: The region around Mannheim, together with its sister-city Ludwigshafen, is one of Germany's leading industrial centres. Nevertheless, **Mannheim** has much to offer the visitor in the way of art and culture. The city is marked by the sharp contrast between the busy river harbour and the stylish and elegant baroque architecture in the centre.

Mannheim was also founded by the counts of the Palatinate, on the foundations of an 8th-century settlement. In 1606 the Elector Friedrich IV ordered the town to be fortified, However, this did not prevent it from being destroyed twice in war, in 1622 and 1689. It was subsequently rebuilt on a grid pattern that still characterises the city centre and in which the streets are named only by letters and numbers.

The city flourished from 1720 onwards after the elector Carl Philipp moved his residence here from Heidelberg, but the glorious days ended when Karl Theodor chose Munich as his electoral seat. In the 19th century the Rhine became a major industrial waterway, and Mannheim developed into an important river port. But in World War II the city was almost completely destroyed and now Mannheim has a modern character, but with many of the contemporary buildings incorporating attractive historical features.

Mannheim's major sight, the **Electors' Palace**, built between 1720 and 1760, is one of the largest baroque palace complexes in all Europe. After suffering severe damage in the war, the main stairway, the palace church and the Knights' Hall were all rebuilt. Today, the palace is part of the university.

Opposite the palace stands the **Jesuit Church**, completely rebuilt after 1945. The splendid interior decoration is true to the original. A few blocks towards

Heidelberg and its castle.

the centre is the **Reiss Museum**, housed in the former arsenal. It provides a comprehensive insight into the history of the city and has a number of collections, including some exquisite porcelain. Here also is the first bicycle made by Baron von Drais in 1817 and a replica of the world's first car, invented by Carl Benz in 1886. Art-lovers make for the **Municipal Art Gallery**, which has a collection of wonderful works from the 19th and 20th centuries.

A boat trip around the huge harbour completes a visit to Mannheim. The boats depart from near the **Museum Ship** (replete with models of ships) at the Kurpfalz bridge from June to September.

The free imperial city of Speyer: After a detour to the Schwetzingen Palace, a royal summer residence surrounded by one of the most beautiful baroque gardens in Germany, a stop on the road to Speyer is recommended on the bridge over the Rhine for a fine panoramic view, dominated by the city's imposing Romanesque cathedral.

Speyer was founded in Roman times around AD 50 and was first mentioned as a bishopric in AD 343. A century and a half later it was taken by the Franks. Between 1294 and 1797, it was one of the seven free Imperial Cities of the Holy Roman Empire of German Nations. More than 50 imperial diets were held within its walls. While Speyer survived the Thirty Years' War unscathed, in 1689, during the Palatine War of Succession, it was practically destroyed, its medieval heritage annihilated. As a result, only a few historical buildings remain to recall the glorious past.

The Romanesque **Cathedral**, with its six spires, rises majestically over the city. The basilica, built during the Salier period between 1030 and 1125, set new standards for scale and design. At a first glance the exterior seems plain and austere; only after very close inspection do the open dwarf galleries and their numerous columns and beautifully carved capitals catch the eye. Nor do the large decorative windows in the transept do very much to alter first impressions. This severity corresponds perfectly with the solemn mood within the building.

The whole structure is supported by relatively slim columns with heavy Corinthian capitals and pilasters carved with geometric designs.

In the impressive nave are the statues of eight German emperors who all found their final resting place here. Their tombs and those of their wives are located in the **Imperial Vault**. The crypt is the largest and, some say, the most beautiful in Germany.

Just south of the cathedral is the **Museum of Palatinate History**, containing a number of interesting collections as well as a section devoted to the history of wine. Other sights include the 12th-century **Jewish Baths**, formerly part of a synagogue, the **Altpörtel**, one of the old city gates from the 13th century from where there is a fine view of the city, and the Protestant **Church of the Holy Trinity** (1701–17) with imposing ceiling frescoes.

Heidelberg is for many people the very embodiment of German Romanticism, and its location alone certainly reinforces that impression. Located on

Speyer Cathedral.

the edge of the Odenwald Forest, where the river Neckar reaches the Rhine Plain, the city nestles against the riverside slopes, overlooked on the northern hillside by the famous castle ruins.

Homo heidelbergiensis: Human settlers must have been attracted to this place 500,000 years ago, for that is the age of the jaw bone of *homo heidelbergiensis* – the oldest human bone ever discovered in Europe – found at nearby **Mauer**. Much later, the Celts came and settled here and the Romans constructed a fort. The city was first officially mentioned in 1196 as "Heidelberch" and from 1214 it came to be ruled by the powerful counts of the Palatinate. For almost 500 years the Electoral College, the body responsible for electing the German kings, was controlled by these counts. And the city bears their unmistakable mark to this day. Its major landmarks are the castle, the university (founded in 1386) and the church of the Holy Ghost.

The city suffered greatly during the Thirty Years' War. It was occupied and plundered by the troops of the Catholic General Tilly. The **Bibliotheca Palatina**, the library built up by the counts, did not escape the pillage. Its priceless books were sent as spoils of war to the Vatican and only the German language volumes were ever returned.

The climb to the castle: The main thoroughfare of the old city centre is the High Street which today, together with the surrounding lanes, is a pedestrian precinct linking Bismarckplatz and **Market Square** in the west with the **Kornmarkt** (Corn Market) in the east. Here begins the 15-minute climb up Burg Weg and the Kurzer Buckel to the **Castle**. Alternatively, take the funicular (from Kornmarkt); it stops at the castle before continuing to the Königstuhl Heights (558 metres/1,860 feet).

It took 400 years before the whole complex, with its fortifications, domestic quarters and palaces, was complete, so the building styles evolved all the way from 14th-century Gothic to baroque. The castle is a testimony in stone not only to the power but also to the artistic taste of its creators. To the left of

The Rhein-brücke at Ludwig-shafen.

the massive gate tower (the Ruprechts-bau), the simple **Gothic House** is the oldest part of the complex. Here lived the Elector Ruprecht III, who was also responsible for the **Church of the Holy Ghost** in the city. The northern side of the courtyard is occupied by the **Friedrichs Building** (1601–7) with its impressive Renaissance facade bearing statues of the German kings.

The most interesting part of the castle is the **Ottheinrichs Building** at the east side of the courtyard, which combines elements of Italian, Dutch and German Renaissance. The portal's composition of statues and ornamentation is very harmonious. As well as Christian saints, Roman gods are also depicted: Jupiter and Mars and the five virtues – strength, faith, love, hope and justice. The richly-decorated doorway resembles a classical triumphal arch and above it stands Count Ottheinrich who had the building constructed between 1556–66. Passing the Friedrichs Building, the visitor arrives at the Castle Terrace, where there is a fine view over the city.

Some buildings are now in ruins. Others have been restored and are used for banquets, concerts and theatrical performances. The Ottheinrichs Building houses the **German Apothecary Museum** which has a collection of furniture, books, medical instruments and medicine bottles of all shapes and sizes.

The Old City: Heidelberg is a typical medieval Gothic town, with magnificent Renaissance palaces added in the 16th century. During the War of Succession (1688–97) which, due to the unacceptable claims of the French King Louis XIV, involved half of Europe, Heidelberg was devastated by French troops, first in 1689 and again in 1693. The castle was in ruins for many years and even when reconstruction did begin fate stepped in with a fire, sparked by lightning, which put paid to the restoration once and for all.

The tour through the old city begins at the **University**. This world-famous institution was founded in 1386 by Ruprecht I and is the oldest university in Germany. During the wars of the 17th

One of the world's largest wine vats.

century it lost much of its importance, regaining it only after reinauguration by Karl Friedrich of Baden in 1805.

Today, the university has more than 28,000 students (about one-fifth of the town's population). In 1930–32, to cope with the increasing numbers of students, a new university complex was built behind Universitätsplatz with the help of donations from America. The establishment later expanded to the other side of the Neckar. Student life today doesn't quite compare with the student days of yore. A reminder of the riotous past is the former **Studentenkarzer** (student lock-up) in Augustinerstrasse which, until 1914, served as a jail for students who were guilty of particularly bad or "indecorous" behaviour

Merianstrasse and Ingrimmstrasse lead back to the Kornmarkt and the market square, where two of the most famous of Heidelberg's student taverns, **Zum Sepp'l** (Sepp's Place) and **Roter Ochsen** (The Red Ox) – are to be found. Traditional pubs such as these remain the haunts of various student fraternities, whose customs are not only perpetuated by hard-drinking contests, but also by the "duels" where the aim is, as in the 19th century, to have a facial scar inflicted by an opponent.

The **Church of the Holy Ghost** stands to the north of the Kornmarkt. The mighty late-Gothic edifice (circa 1450) is the largest church in the Palatinate. Its founder, Ruprecht III of the Palatinate, who later became king of Germany, lies buried here, and the church also once housed the ill-fated Palatinate Library. Opposite (at Hauptstrasse 178) is the **Hotel Ritter** with one of the finest Renaissance facades in Germany. The building survived the depredations of 1693 because it was the French commander's headquarters. Equally worth seeing is the adjacent former **Court Apothecary** (Hauptstrasse 190).

From the church, Steingasse leads down to the river. The **Old Bridge**, which crosses the Neckar at this point, is one of the city's symbols: the other one is the castle. Goethe thought the bridge one of the wonders of the world, an opinion based not on its technical

qualities but on the wonderful view it affords. Upstream looms the **Benedictine Monastery of Neuburg** and downstream the river gradually widens out into the Rhine Plain. Looking back, the city is perfectly framed by the archway of the bridge gate.

Across the river, a steep path winds its way up the Heiligenberg. The tranquillity of the **Philosophenweg** (Philosophers' Path), leaves the hustle and bustle of the city far behind. Barges chug slowly up and down the river below. The path leads to Bergstrasse which runs down to the new **Theodor Heuss Bridge**. Back on the other side of the river the visitor arrives at **Bismarckplatz**, at the western end of the pedestrian precinct.

Modern Heidelberg: Thanks to its students, Heidelberg is a young city, yet life here doesn't only revolve around the university. The city is the headquarters of the German Cancer Research Society and the Academy of Sciences. A Heidelberg printing machine factory is worldwide the largest exporter of the most modern offset-printing equipment.

Typical alley in the city centre.

Germany's largest publisher of scientific literature, annually publishing more than 8,000 scientific publications and 190 specialist magazines is also based here. These statistics show that Heidelberg's development did not end in the 19th century and that the city remains as vital as ever.

Heidelberg's river, the Neckar, has its source in the Black Forest and runs nearly 400 km (250 miles) before joining the Rhine. Its wooded valley is a haven of peace, best explored from the deck of one of the white cruise ships which ply the winding river.

After Heidelberg come the villages of Neckargemünd and Hirschhorn and the resort of Eberbach, with its ruined Emichsburg Castle (11th–13th centuries), once the largest of the Hohenstaufen forts.

The castles around Mosbach: Before leaving the Neckar to strike out north into the Odenwald forest, a detour is recommended along the Castle Road to the ruined **Stolzeneck Castle** and **Zwingenberg**, a resort with a majestic castle (13th–15th centuries). The picturesque little town of **Mosbach**, which began as an 8th-century Benedictine monastery, is known as the "Odenwald town of half-timbered houses".

Hornberg Castle (1148) has an interesting history. Götz von Berlichingen, who lived here until his death in 1562, played a key role in the peasants wars. The Götz von Berlichingen house, dungeon, knight's armoury and wine-growing estates are the attractions here. **Guttenberg Castle**, near Hassmersheim, is not only one of the oldest Neckar castles but among the best preserved.

Through the Odenwald forest: From Eberbach, the B45 road runs through one of the loveliest upland areas of Germany, to **Erbach**. This former residence of the Counts of Erbach-Erbach has a well-preserved old town with quaint, narrow streets. The town also has a rare Ivory Museum.

Further on, the German Holiday Road reaches the resort of **Michelstadt**, with a jewel of a town hall, built in 1484. Behind it is the parish church of St

Treasures of Guttenberg Castle.

Michael (1461–1537) with Glockenspiel and the tombs of the Erbach nobility.

Focal point of the old Franconian, baroque town of **Amorbach** is its abbey. The abbey church, with a Romanesque west tower, was reconstructed in baroque style between 1742 and 1747. Its interior is an example of the purest rococo. Of special beauty is the iron gate to the choir, which once separated monks from the congregation. The huge baroque organ, in keeping with the mighty high altar, has 3,000 pipes and 63 registers, and is the second largest such instrument in Germany.

The German writer Elly Heuss said about **Miltenberg**: "For me, the market square and fountain are the perfect embodiment of medieval Germany." The ensemble of Renaissance fountain and old half-timbered buildings, the 17th-century wine tavern **Zur gülden Cron** and the **Weinhaus am alten Markt** are world-renowned.

Moated castle and robbers' den: A very pretty road along a bend of the Main river brings you to **Wertheim**. Narrow streets and high-eaved buildings give this old Franconian town its character. The half-timbered buildings lining the market square of **Marktheidenfeld** are still in good order. Just to the north stands **Rothenfels Castle**, 224 metres (735 feet) over the Main. Its stout defence walls and keep were built in the 12th and 13th centuries.

The journey to Mespelbrunn brings you to the heart of the **Bavarian Spessart Nature Park**. In the middle of a forest on one side of town stands the moated castle of the Echter von Mespelbrunn family. It was built in 1564 in Renaissance style and still belongs to the Counts of Ingelheim.

The Spessart, which encloses the Main river in almost a square, is one of Europe's finest nature parks, with extensive oak woods and idyllic meadows. The author Wilhelm Hauff (1802–27) was inspired by the region to write his picaresque tale *Das Wirtshaus im Spessart*, which in turn gave filmmakers ideas for locally-shot scenarios featuring robber bands and ghosts.

Below, the moated castle of Mespelbrunn. Right, Michelstadt market square.

GERMANY'S FAIRY TALE ROAD

The German Fairy Tale Road cuts right through the region where the brothers Jacob and Wilhelm Grimm (1785–1863, 1786–1856) collected and wrote up the traditional stories which are known today as the *Grimms' Fairy Tales*. The story-telling talent of Wilhelm Grimm is to be credited for the rapid spread of the stories and their translation into more than 140 languages.

Both Grimm brothers also devoted themselves to language research. In their professions as high school teachers they developed the basics of German grammar and published the first volumes of the German Dictionary. They also involved themselves decisively in campaigns against undemocratic forms of rule and for popular freedoms, which led to their expulsion from school service, along with other professors of the "Göttingen Seven". Jacob Grimm was a member of the Frankfurt National Assembly in 1848.

The journey along the Fairy Tale Road begins in the town where the two brothers were born, in **Hanau am Main** (pop. 93,100). An atmospheric start to the journey is a presentation of Grimm fairy tales on the summer open-air stage of the **Schloss Philippsruhe**. Within the palace, the **Hanau Museum** has local history exhibits as well as a collection of regional and Dutch art. On Hanau's Altstädter Markt stands a fine, half-timbered building, the **Deutsches Goldschmiedhaus** (German Goldsmiths House, 1538–50).

The nearby **Wilhelmsbad** has a lovely park laid out in English country-house style. Wilhelmsbad's **Hessisches Puppenmuseum** (Hessian Dolls Museum) is very popular with families. From the **Grimm Memorial** on Hanau's market square, the Marktplatz, the Fairy Tale Road runs north 595 km (370 miles) to the "free Hanseatic city" of Bremen.

Gelnhausen (pop. 21,000), some 20 km (12 miles) from Hanau, prospered at the junction of important trading routes and was made an imperial free city in 1170. In that same year the emperor Frederick Barbarossa built a castle there, the **Kaiserpfalz** (1170–80), which developed into the centre of the Staufer dynasty. The first imperial assembly, or Reichstag, took place here in 1180.

The journey across the **Kinzigtal Valley** takes the traveller through **Wächtersbach**, which has retained the magic of a small residence town, as well as the health resorts of **Bad Orb** and **Bad Soden**. The old trading route between Frankfurt and Leipzig followed this road.

The Grimm brothers spent their childhood in the **Amtshaus** (now a museum) in the romantic little town of **Steinau an der Strasse** (population 11,700), in the midst of one of Germany's most beautiful stretches of countryside, the **Bergwinkel**. Picturesquely set among the rolling hills is the old monastery town of **Schlüchtern** (pop. 16,000), where the **Bergwinkel Museum** exhibits Grimm memorabilia as well as items recalling Ulrich von Hutten (1488–1523), a knight and poet who fought for a strong, united German emperor.

Left, Göttingen's "little goose girl" has been kissed by countless newly-graduated students. Right, the Grimm Brothers memorial in their birthplace, Hanau.

Side trip to the Rhön: An excursion to **Fulda** (pop. 60,000) is to be recommended. The history of the episcopal city, set between uplands of the Rhön and Vogelsberg, goes back to 744, when Saint Boniface built a **monastery** on the ruins of a Merovingian castle. The monastery rapidly grew into the major centre of religion and science of the Frankish empire. Boniface was martyred in 745 in Friesland. His tomb, then still in the monastery's Church of the Redeemer, became a place of pilgrimage.

Fulda's baroque quarter is unique in its unity. Johann Dientzenhofer, working for the prince-abbots, reconstructed the Renaissance palace between 1706 and 1721, into today's **Stadtschloss**. He was also responsible for the plans for the cathedral, the **Dom St Salvator und Bonifatius** (1704–12), where the **remains of St Boniface** lie in the crypt. A baroque alabaster relief, framed by black marble, depicts his martyrdom.

The **Fulda Vonderau Museum** has been enriched with additional cultural and natural history exhibitions, paintings and sculptures. Children can enjoy the touch-sensitive displays and experiments in the **Kinder-Akademie Fulda**.

Outside Fulda is the **Fasanerie,** a small baroque palace or *Lustschloss*, while the Romanesque **St Lioba's Church** (Grabeskirche St Lioba), on the Petersberg, has some fine frescoes.

Between Fulda and Bad Kissingen lies the barren upland landscape of the **Rhön,** the remains of a volcanic massif. A mixture of high moorland and windy plains, the area is partly a nature preserve. Its highest point is the **Wasserkuppe** (950 metres/3,135 feet), whose name – meaning "water dome" – derives from the many springs to be found there. Today it's a centre of every kind of flying sports. There's a **museum of gliding** (Segelflugmuseum) and round trips are organised by the gliding school.

To the northwest rises the summit of the **Milseburg** (835 metres/2,755 feet), where a pilgrimage chapel and the remains of a Celtic camp are to be found. To the northeast lies **Tann,** where a **Freilichtmuseum** (Open Air Museum) illustrates the way the miners used to live. In the valley of the Franconian Saale lies **Bad Kissingen** (pop. 23,000), one of Bavaria's popular health resorts.

Back on the Fairy Tale Road: At the little town of **Lauterbach** (pop. 15,000) one is back on the Fairy Tale Road. Hundreds of thousands of garden dwarfs are produced annually here and despatched all over the world. The many half-timbered houses around the **Ankerturm** give a foretaste of the next town, for **Alsfeld** (pop. 18,000) is well-known for its historic style of architecture. Its market square, or Marktplatz, has an impressive town hall, or **Rathaus** (1512–16), **Weinhaus** (1538) and **Hochzeithaus** (1564–71).

Other impressive stone and half-timbered houses (mostly from the 14th century) line the streets of the Altstadt, the old town quarter. Many of them were only recently freed of disfiguring facades, revealing massive oak beams, carved cornerposts and transoms with carved inscriptions bearing testimony to the high standard of medieval craftsmanship in Alsfeld.

Closely-clustered houses in Marburg.

Forty kilometres (24 miles) west of Alsfeld is the university city of **Marburg** (pop. 76,000), the cradle of the German Romantic movement. The Grimm brothers began their research work into German fables here. The old town centre, with its narrow streets and beautiful market square, extends from the banks of the Lahn up to the slopes of the Schlossberg. The **Elisabethkirche** (St Elizabeth's Church, 1235–83) an early-Gothic masterpiece, with aisles of equal height and impressive stained glass in the three middle windows of the choir. In the **Landgrafenschloss** castle, with its great Gothic knights hall, Luther and Zwingli held their famous "Marburger Religionsgespräche" in 1529. Apart from the historic rooms, a **Cultural History Museum** (Museum für Kulturgeschichte) can be visited. The **university**, founded in 1527, was the world's first Protestant university, and it has a strong hold on Marburg life.

Little Red Riding Hood Country: The story of Red Riding Hood and the Wolf originates in the Schwälmerland area east of

Marburg. Red Riding Hood's characteristic head-covering is part of the traditional costume still worn on local holidays, in the processions which are part of such festivities as the **Salatkirmes** in **Ziegenhain** and **Hutzelkirmes** in **Treysa**. Examples of the local traditional costume can be seen in the **Schwalm Museum** in **Schwalmstadt** (pop. 19,000).

Back on the Fairy Tale Road, the route leads through the health spas of **Neukirchen** and **Oberaula** on the southern slopes of the **Knüllgebirge** to **Bad Hersfeld** (pop. 30,000). This upland health resort is well known for its annual theatre festival in the **Stiftsruine**, the most extensive Romanesque church ruins north of the Alps. The **Lullus** and **Vitalis** springs are valued for their health-giving waters, while every October the town's founder is commemorated with a festival known as the Lullusfest.

The administrative centre of the region, **Homberg** (pop. 14,500), has many half-timbered buildings to admire, particularly on the market square, the

Marktplatz, where old patrician houses share space with the large Gothic church of St Mary's, the **Marienkirche**. The **Krone** tavern, built in 1480, is the oldest still functioning hostelry in Germany.

In **Fritzlar** (pop. 15,000), Boniface destroyed a sacred shrine of the heathen Germans: he felled the oak tree of the god of thunder and lightning, Donar, and founded a Benedictine monastery in its place in the year 724. An imperial city developed, whose importance can be judged today by the impressive medieval centre with its defence walls and the half-timbered houses around the market square. The **Cathedral** (11th–14th centuries) is the symbol of the city, which belonged to the prince-bishops of Mainz for centuries.

City of the Dokumenta: The once sleepy Residence city of **Kassel** (pop. 200,000) has become the most modern centre of this German region. After its almost complete destruction by allied bombing in 1943, reconstruction changed the original city plan and only a few historical buildings were restored.

The city's symbol is the enormous **Hercules** statue which looks down on Kassel from the heights of the **Wilhelmshöhe Palace Park**, laid out in the 18th and 19th centuries. With its soaring fountain, the **Grosse Fontäne**, numerous waterfalls and artificial ruins, it can claim to be one of Europe's most grandiose parks. The palace itself (1786–1802) has a fine interior and collections of paintings by Dutch and Flemish masters, and of antiques. The **Hessian State Museum** (Hessisches Landesmuseum) contains a small gem of an attraction: the **Tapestry Museum** there has a panorama tapestry from 1814 depicting the Battle of Austerlitz, as well as a lovingly created display of the history of tapestry. The **Brüder-Grimm-Museum** recalls the 30 years the Grimm brothers worked in Kassel.

Since 1955 the city has been a mecca for artists and art-lovers from all over the world: the **Dokumenta**, Kassel's presentation of contemporary art, is held every five years (next one in 1997). For 100 days the world's best is on show in a series of exhibitions, held in such venues as the **Museum Fredericianum**, continental Europe's oldest museum building, and the Orangerie in the Karlsaue baroque park.

Where the Little Goose Girl gets kissed: The Grimm brothers also worked in the university city of **Göttingen**. From 1351 until 1572 the city (pop. 135,000) belonged to the Hanseatic League. Its prosperity came to an end, however, in 1547 with the defeat of the Lutheran Schmalkadian Federation.

The founding of the **university** by Prince Georg August von Hannover in 1734 gave Göttingen new impulse. In 1777 it was Germany's biggest, and more than 30 Nobel Prize-winners have studied or taught here. The city retains a special flair, and many fine buildings testify to its former prosperity, among them the Gothic **Church of St John** and the old town hall, the **Altes Rathaus** (1369–1443). Centrepiece of the market square, the Marktplatz, is the bronze **Gänseliesel,** a statue of the Little Goose Girl, who is traditionally kissed by every graduating student.

The Documenta in Kassel is held every five years.

ALONG THE WESER TO BREMEN

The Werra and the Fulda join together in Münden to form the River Weser. From here the river snakes along, twisting around countless bends on its 440-km (273-mile) journey through picturesque landscape to Bremen. Riverside meadows, spruced up towns and villages, castle ruins and Renaissance palaces lead one to believe that, just as in the fairy tale of Sleeping Beauty, time actually could stand still here.

Green rolling hills, some reaching a height of 500 metres (1,640 feet), stretch along both sides of the river. The Weser-talstrasse runs along the right side. From here the panoramic views of the fishermen and rowing boats, freighters and excursion boats are equally lovely as those from the German Fairy Tale Road along the left bank.

At the end of the 16th century the Weser valley served as one of central Europe's granaries. The wealth of the area's rulers and residents can still be seen in the beautiful palaces, town halls and patrician buildings.

The sleepy Weser Valley: The picturesque town of **Hann. Münden** (pop. 28,000) was founded in the year 1170 by the Thuringian landgraves. Münden has more than 700 well-preserved half-timbered houses built over six centuries. The **Town Hall**, an early Weser-Renaissance structure, is worth a visit, as is the **Welfen Palace**. This dates from the 16th and 17th centuries and is a local history museum. The **Ägidien Church** contains the grave of the notorious Dr Eisenbarth (1663–1727). During the summer, a play about his radical methods of healing is performed over two Sundays from May to August. His house still stands in Langen Strasse. Boat trips along the Weser from Münden to Hameln are operated by the **Oberweser Personenschiffe** company.

Some 10 km (6 miles) to the north, a passenger ferry driven by the river current crosses the river to **Hemeln**. **Bursfelde**, further downstream, is noted for

Preceding pages: grazing near the coast. Below, the Pied Piper of Hamlin.

its 12th-century Benedictine monastery which has some medieval frescoes and a bell dating from the 14th century.

Huguenots and members of the Protestant *Waldenser* sect who had been subjected to persecution in their homeland were granted asylum in **Gottstreu** by the landgrave Karl von Hessen-Kassel (1677–1730). After the devastation of the Thirty Years' War (1618–48), these devout immigrants were instrumental in rebuilding the area.

The hills on the left bank of the Weser are densely wooded. In the heart of the **Reinhardswald** and perched on a high plateau lies the **Sababurg,** where the Sleeping Beauty could well have been aroused from her slumbers. Although half of the castle is in ruins, the other half has been turned into a hotel with modern comforts. Nearby is a zoo which has specialised in the preservation of native species of animals. Towards Beberbeck lie 70 hectares (172 acres) of **primeval forest** where centuries-old beeches and oaks have survived.

A bizarre geological phenomenon can be found between Friedrichsfeld and the **Trendelburg** (a 15th-century hotel). Known as the **Nasser Wolkenbruch** (Wet Cloudburst), it is a 12-metre (40-foot) deep crater lake that was formed when overlying strata collapsed.

Bad Karlshafen, the "white town", was founded in 1699 by Karl von Hessen Kassel. In order to avoid paying customs duties, he drew up plans for a canal from the Diemel to Kassel, but only the harbour and 14 km (9 miles) of waterway were completed.

Huguenots also settled here and the many well-preserved relics in the **German Huguenot Museum** provide an insight into the history and culture which these refugees brought with them. The revenues from the town's era as a health spa, which began in 1730, made possible the construction of a multi-storey white baroque building which gave the town its nickname.

After Meissen, **Fürstenberg** is the oldest porcelain factory in Germany (founded 1747). A **Porcelain Museum** is housed in the **Renaissance Palace**.

Weser
Renaissance
in Vlotho.

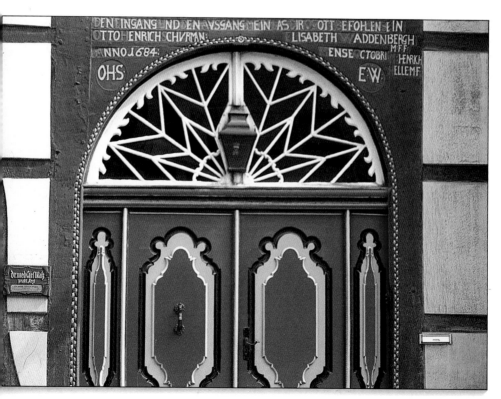

Nearby is **Höxter** (pop. 35,000) with its ancient city walls, half-timbered houses and typical Weser-Renaissance **Town Hall**. To the northeast the former **Imperial Abbey of Corvey** dates from 822. In medieval times this was a cultural centre of European-wide importance and in the 12th century the parliament of the German Empire often met here.

The Lying Baron: Baron von Münchhausen (1702–97), better known as the "Baron of Lies" (*Lügenbaron*), was born in **Bodenwerder**, a town of well-preserved city walls and half-timbered houses. A monument in front of the Town Hall was built in memory of the baron's "ride on half a horse". This building used to be the Münchhausen's family home and now houses the **Münchhausen Museum**.

From the **Ebersnacken** hill (460 metres/1,508 feet) to south of the town, a fine view extends across to the Harz mountains and also over the beautiful **Swiss Rühle** countryside.

The Castle of **Hämelschenburg** near **Emmern** is the best example of a Weser-Renaissance castle. Constructed between 1588–99, the entire building, including the oriels and octagonal towers, is extremely well-preserved.

The city of the Pied Piper: Hameln (pop. 58,000), which grew out of a monastery in the 8th century, proudly and rightfully calls itself "the city of the Weser-Renaissance". Just one among many beautiful buildings, the **Rattenfänger-haus** recalls the famous story of the *Pied Piper of Hamlin.*

In the year 1284 the city was suffering a plague of rats. A fancifully dressed man named Bundtig who happened to be passing through the town promised to end the plague and was hired by the city fathers. He lured the rats out of the city by playing his flute, but the city fathers refused to pay him his due reward. One Sunday, when all the adults were in church, he earned his revenge by once again playing his flute, this time luring away 130 children. Every Sunday from July to October, a play depicting this legend is performed in front of the **Hochzeithaus**.

Hanover's town hall is on a lake.

An excursion to Hanover: Hanover (pop. 514,000), the capital of Lower Saxony, is within easy reach of Hameln. This city, the state's centre of trade and industry, is also well known as the location of the **Hanover Messe**, the world's largest industrial fair which is held annually in April. Founded in 1163, Hanover soon became a member of the Hanseatic League. From 1636–1866 the city was the seat of the dukes of Calenberg and for much of that time (1714–1837) Hanover and Great Britain were governed by the same ruler. In 1866 it came under Prussian control.

Because of the devastation suffered during World War II, this city has only a few remaining noteworthy structures. However, the 14th-century **Ägidien Church**, the old **Town Hall** and the **market place** merit a visit. The grave of the famous philosopher G.W. Leibniz (1646–1716) is in the Neustädter Church which is located near the 17th-century **Leine Castle** (now the State Parliament). The **Kestner Museum** displays ancient Greek, Roman and Egyptian

The Böttcherstrasse is Bremen's attractive main street.

art. However, for many art-lovers, the fine collection of 20th-century art (for example, Kurt Schwitters) in the **Sprengel Museum** is the main highlight. The **Lower Saxony State Museum** has an impressive collection of German impressionist paintings. The geometrically laid out **Grosse Garten**, a beautiful baroque garden, is located in the western part of Hanover along the Herrenhäuser Allee.

Braunschweig, northeast of Hanover, has a population of 260,000, making it Lower Saxony's second largest city. Destroyed in World War II, it was quick to regain its position of economic significance. Henry the Lion, Duke of Bavaria and Saxony, lived here from 1166 onward. The **Dankwarderode Castle** with its Braunschweiger lions, located in the centre of the old city, serves as a reminder of this ruler. His gravestone, a splendid example of Romanesque stone-masonry, lies in the nave of **St Blase Cathedral** (1173–95).

A half hour's drive to the north is **Wolfsburg**, home of Europe's largest automobile manufacturer: Volkswagen. Some 140 models of VWs and Audis are exhibited in the **Automuseum**.

A short detour to **Hildesheim** can be quite rewarding. In this bishop's city (in existence since 815), the Romanesque **Cathedral**, with its beautiful cloisters and superb art treasures, and **St Michael's Church** (1001–33) have been designated as World Cultural Heritage monuments. The Egyptian collection in the **Römer- Pelizäus Museum** also justifies a visit to the city.

Back to the Weser: North of **Rinteln** on the Weser, **Schaumburg Castle** offers a delightful view of the valley. At **Porta Westfalica** the river has carved a 600-metre (1,968-foot) wide gorge on its way from the Weserbergland region into the northern German plains.

North of the gorge is the old city of **Minden** whose 13th-century **Town Hall** is one of Germany's oldest. The nearby **Wasserstrassenkreuz** is where the **Mittelland Canal** crosses the Weser in a cement trough 375 metres (1,230 feet) long and 13 metres (43 feet) wide. This technological masterpiece, a water-con-

ducting canal-bridge with three sluices, serves as a link between the Havel in Brandenburg and the Ems in the west of the country.

The well-preserved Cistercian monastery of **Loccum** (12th–13th centuries) lies to the north. The church is noted for its sumptuous interior. Cloisters, a hospital and other monastic buildings provide a vivid picture of life in a monastery. A side road leads from here to **Steinhuder Meer**, the largest German lake between Lake Constance and the North Sea. With a surface of 32 sq. km (12 sq. miles), it has a maximum depth of only 3 metres (10 feet). The southern and eastern shores are nature reserves. Secure walkways bring visitors closer to the varied flora and fauna.

At the junction of the Aller and the Weser just outside Bremen lies **Verden**, a small town with a **Fairy-tale and Leisure Park**. An equestrian centre and museum will enthrall horse-lovers. The **cathedral** in the centre of the city, built in the year 786, is the oldest brick church in northern Germany.

Bremen: This old Hanseatic town (pop. 555,000) together with the port of **Bremerhaven**, 57 km (35 miles) further to the north, comprises Germany's smallest state. The city was founded in the 8th century and was raised to the status of a bishop's city in 789 by Charlemagne. It was known for a long time as the "Rome of the north" due to the fact that it was the departure point for the missionaries who converted the Scandinavians to Christianity. In the year 1358 Bremen joined the Hanseatic League and in 1646 became a free city of the German Empire.

Today, Bremen is Germany's second largest port after Hamburg, important for the shipment of motor vehicles, cereals, cotton, wool, coffee and tobacco. The **Overseas Museum** has an ethnographic collection as well as replicas of Japanese and Chinese gardens and buildings. The **Bremen State Museum for Art and Cultural History** also documents the region's maritime past.

Most of the attractions in the old part of the city are in or around the market square. The first building of interest is the 15th-century Gothic **Old Town Hall** with its ornate Renaissance facade. Its **Great Hall** is the venue for the annual **Schaffermahlzeit**, the world's oldest fraternal dinner. The **Ratskeller** in the cellar is famous for its Gothic vaults.

Close to the northwest tower is the **Bremen Town Musicians**. These four figures, a dog, a donkey, a cat and a rooster, are from a Grimm Brothers' fairy tale. The 10-metre (33-foot) high statue of **Roland**, is located beside the Town Hall. It was erected in 1404 and serves as a symbol of Bremen's freedom and independence. The **Cathedral** with its 98-metre (321-foot) high steeples embodies 1,200 years of history.

Near the **Schütting**, the old merchants' house, is the entrance to **Böttcherstrasse** whose restored medieval buildings present a kind of open-air museum. From here it is only a few steps to **Schnoor**, which is the oldest part of Bremen and the site of many houses, pubs and shops dating from the 15th century. The North Sea is now only another 57 km (35 miles) away. **Time for a break.**

THE VW BEETLE

The customs officers at New York's LaGuardia airport could not believe their eyes. They had asked a businessman from Germany to open his baggage and were presented with blueprints and plans for a four-wheeled hunchbacked thingumajig. The man insisted that the drawings were of a car, a car that he intended to sell in America. But the officials were not the slightest bit impressed and told him he wouldn't be able to pass his "thing" off as a car anywhere in the world. The documents were declared as "graphic art" on which the German had to pay $30 import duty.

The incident is supposed to have occurred around Easter time in 1949. The businessman was Heinrich Nordhoff, head of Volkswagen, Inc. His deft marketing skills turned this car into an overnight sensation and it became a German best-seller even in the heart of Chevrolet and Cadillac country.

No fewer than 5 million Beetles were eventually sold in the States. By 1972, Volkswagen had surpassed the sales record set by Henry Ford's "Tin Lizzy". Ford's car, the first to be manufactured by mass production, had sold 15 million. In the end, more than 20 million Beetles which were exported to 147 countries were produced, a world record that still stands.

"Volkswagen" literally translates as the "people's car". In 1933, Adolf Hitler, who was a car enthusiast, contracted the gifted designer Rudolf Porsche to develop a car that the ordinary working man could afford. Despite opposition from the German automobile industry, the Nazi state financed the building and testing of the first prototypes.

In 1938, Hitler personally laid the foundation stone of the first Volkswagen factory. A whole town was built upon reclaimed swampland – modern-day Wolfsburg. By the end of the war, the town's German population of 14,000 was outnumbered by more than 18,000 forced labourers from Russia and Poland. Today, 130,000 people live in Wolfsburg.

At the beginning of 1939, the regimented subjects of the totalitarian German state were encouraged to open special savings plans to enable them to buy a VW. But the 270,000 people who did so never saw the "car for the common man", whose arrival had been hailed for years by the Ministry of Propaganda. During the war civilian projects were sacrificed to the requirements of the *Wehrmacht* and the projected VW was trans-

formed into an all-purpose military vehicle which could be adapted to all terrains and climates.

The Beetle's success after the war, its reputation as the world's best-built small car, is largely thanks to the punishing trials that Porsche's military vehicles had to undergo during the war: they had to be as reliable in the blazing sands of the North African desert as they were in sub-zero temperatures on the Russian steppe.

Immediately after the war in 1945, the British occupation authorities began the first limited production of the Beetle. Heinrich Nordhoff took over management in 1948. During his time at the company a car that had initially been criticised as having as many design faults as a dog has fleas, became a hallmark of the German "economic miracle", the symbol of quality German workmanship. During those 20 years, VW engineers developed 36 new prototypes, but Nordhoff clung to the myth of the Beetle and would not let any of them go into production. Seen from the outside, there is hardly any difference between the 1948 and 1958 models, but in fact practically every single part was redesigned. VW went on improving the Beetle right into the 1970s and it was only in the 1980s that production finally ceased. ■

Rudolf Porsche's all-time best-seller.

The beauty of the north and its coast always conquers the hearts of its guests. The spectacular drama of the landscape is matched by the drama played out in the skies, particularly when the winds blow, the heavens turn dark, and the sun suddenly breaks through to drench the land and sea in a magical light.

Emil Nolde, the great northern expressionist painter, never tired of bringing to life in his paintings the different moods and contrasts created by this light. He placed black peasant cottages next to violet blue larkspur in front of blood-red skies. The tempestuous deep blue sea whips up a yellowy brown spray that foams under the poisonous yellow light. Foals stand teetering in the deep green marshland under skies of clouds torn by the winds. Nolde was a master of colour who opened many people's eyes.

Along the Baltic Sea coast on the East Frisian islands, as well as on Amrum, Sylt and Föhr, you can encounter beautiful wide beaches of fine sand which are an open invitation for strollers and a paradise for water-sports fans. The Surf World Cup is competed off the coast of Sylt and Kiel is the home of the summer sailing regatta in what is known as the Kiel Week (*die Kieler Woche*).

Hamburg, the lively metropolis on the river Elbe, is situated between the three federal states of Schleswig-Holstein, Mecklenburg-Vorpommern and Lower Saxony. Hamburg lives off the sea, the North Sea to the left and the Baltic to the right. Apart from trade the seas also bring the storm tides – Hamburg's last major floods were in 1962 and killed 308 people. The city's long tradition of trade is based on its own ethos and pride. Search as one may for magnificent buildings and beautiful examples of architecture, it becomes clear through the cityscape that Hamburg was always a city of the people rather than of the rulers.

East and West are combined in this capital. Millions of West Germans now visit the Mecklenburg-Vorpommern Baltic sea coast. Until reunification, most people only knew the chalk cliffs of Rügen through the paintings of Caspar David Friedrich. Despite the modern influx, the region has managed to maintain its charm.

On the route from the coast through the Brandenburg Marches to Berlin, you will drive along roads flanked by long avenues of trees. Such avenues are quite a rarity in Germany – in the western part of the country they were all cut down to facilitate speedy driving.

Preceding pages: Hamburg's crowded harbour; shielded against the elements. Left, the sound of flutes is a fitting scenario, Hamburg.

HAMBURG

Hamburg claims to be Northern Germany's leading city. It is the second largest city after Berlin, is Germany's biggest port, produces half of all the newspapers and magazines in the country and in addition has a lively cultural scene involving all sectors of the community.

This great city with its trading roots is truly cosmopolitan, and its inhabitants are known for their balanced, liberal world view. Traditionally, the SPD holds the majority in the Senate. The long-serving Federal Chancellor Helmut Schmidt came from Hamburg – he was known for his characteristic Hanseatic yachting cap and his sailor's pipe.

The city is well-known for its colourful bars, providing a lively night-life which knows no closing time, even away from the St Pauli district. Those who prefer a quieter life will enjoy the many green corners and comfortable cafés to be found in the city. Waterways can be found throughout Hamburg. Many an enjoyable day can be spent exploring canals and the port area by boat, discovering Hamburg from the new perspective of the water.

This big, lively city has as its setting a wonderful hinterland, including the regions of Mecklenburg, Schleswig-Holstein and Lower Saxony. However, you are never far away from the open sea – be it the quiet and charming Baltic coast or the forbidding, tidal North Sea. You can even try your hand at freshwater sailing on the Alster – the legendary fresh breeze is never far away from Hamburg.

An early trading centre: Water has always been the lifeblood of the city. Ludwig the Pious, son of Charlemagne, was perhaps the first to realise that the location of the Hammaburg settlement, at the confluence of the Alster, Bille and Elbe rivers, had the potential to be extremely profitable, and promoted it to an Archbishopric in 831. His construction of a fortress here in the 9th century served the dual purpose of intimidating the inhabitants of the surrounding Saxon villages as well as providing a secure harbour from which to carry out commercial trade with the neighbours to the north and to the west. Around 100 years later the settlement was granted market status.

After years of continuous power struggles, with the constant danger of raids from the neighbouring clan of Slavic Obotrites, the settlement at last entered a period of stability under the rule of Adolf von Schauenburg. A new town emerged, centred around the dwellings of sailors and merchants near the site of today's Nikolaifleet. The evolution of Hamburg into a prosperous commercial city began with the granting by Frederick Barbarossa of free trade licences, along with customs exemptions and the right to free traffic, in the year 1189.

From the 13th century, Hamburg served as the North Sea port for the wealthier city of Lübeck. The Hanseatic League developed out of this common trade bond. It became an autonomous free German city in 1510, and, with its

Left, enjoying the highlife near the city. **Right**, Hamburg's town hall, in the heart of the city.

conversion to Protestantism 19 years later, demonstrated its desire for independence from the German emperors. Owing to its well-constructed fortifications, Hamburg was able to withstand the Thirty Years' War (1618–48) quite unscathed.

A boost to development: The transport of goods and people from Europe to the New World, starting in the 17th century, proved to be very profitable for Hamburg's merchants. It was during this growth period that the city made its major contributions to the development of German intellectual life. Among the best known names of the Hamburg cultural scene were the composers Georg Friedrich Händel and Georg Philipp Telemann who lived and worked in the city. Gotthold Ephraim Lessing, from 1767 the chief dramatist at the newly founded German National Theatre, wrote his *Hamburgische Dramaturgie*. Matthias Claudius published the *Wandsbecker Boten* between 1771 and 1776. The city's cultural life in the 19th century was further enriched by Felix Mendelssohn-Bartholdy, Heinrich Heine, Friedrich Hebbel and Johannes Brahms.

The world's third largest port: The decision to join the German Customs League, vehemently opposed by many of the city's residents, actually brought immense trade advantages as well as the development of new industry. By 1913 Hamburg was the world's third largest seaport after New York and London. When Germany was forced to surrender almost its entire merchant fleet to the victors of World War I in 1918, it naturally hit the port very hard.

It did not take too many years, however, for the losses to be recouped. The towns of Harburg and Wandsbeck were incorporated into Hamburg in 1937 bringing the city to its present size of 755 sq. km (290 sq. miles). Due to its strategic economic importance, Hamburg was the target for many bombing raids during World War II and these resulted not only in severe damage to the city but also in great losses to the civilian population, with a total of 45,000

Dress codes in the Hansaviertel.

dead and 1 million refugees. Even this blow was met with typical Hanseatic composure as the rubble was cleared and a new start made. In 1949 the city-state of Hamburg became a federal *Land*.

The loss of its hinterland behind the East German border was a heavy blow, but the city's population of 1.6 million sought successfully to compensate for this by attracting new industries. Only the future can tell how this development will continue after the reunification.

The port: For many visitors to Hamburg the first point of attraction is the **St Pauli Landungsbrücken** near the Old Elbe Tunnel. In former times, before the centre of commercial shipping activities was moved to the outskirts, steamers and sailing ships berthed at these piers. The **Rickmer Rickmers** (1896), a fine example of one of these windjammers, which now houses a restaurant, can be found close by. Today the landing stages serve as the departure point for boat tours of the harbour, an experience to be recommended. A high point of these tours is the world's largest

warehouse complex, to be found in the old **Speicherstadt** with its maze of canals. Coffee, tea, tobacco, spices and other products are still kept here today in the typical neo-Gothic brick buildings, specially constructed to provide the perfect conditions. Goods stored in this **free port**, an enclosed area measuring 10 sq. km (4 sq. miles), are not subject to customs formalities.

Most of the 13,000 ships which arrive annually in Germany's largest port are loaded and unloaded on the island of Steinwerder, reached via the **Old Elbe Tunnel** (1911) with its vehicle elevators and tiled walls. The elegant **Köhlbrand Bridge** (1974) stretches above this swarm of ships and cranes, large and small barges, tugboats and motor launches. The bridge shares the load of the north–south Autobahn traffic with the **New Elbe Tunnel** (1974).

In the 1980s, the **Hafenstrasse**, with its "autonomous" squatters' houses, was the scene of violent confrontations between the government and young people who seemed to have lost their way in

Backstreet restaurants.

what was now an extremely prosperous nation. It is worth venturing into this area to see the brightly painted houses which remain unchanged to this day.

The nearby **Reeperbahn** derives its name from the 17th-century rope-makers (*Reeper* in German) who worked in this area producing the riggings for the sailing ships. Today this street and the immediately adjacent **Grosse Freiheit** and **Herbertstrasse**, form the port's infamous "mile of sin". In **Harry's Harbour Bazaar** in **Bernhard Nochtstrasse** you can rummage to your heart's content and discover a wealth of curiosities. In the same street, the **Erotic Art Museum** makes its own contribution to the character of the area. The multitude of bars, cabarets and cheap entertainments in the red-light district have been known to distract many a Saturday-night visitor until the early hours of Sunday morning, when they head off to sample the unique atmosphere of the **Fish Market.**

The stalls here have already disappeared by the time the clock on the nearby **Church of St Michael** strikes nine. This baroque symbol of Hamburg with its outstanding view over the harbour is affectionately called the "**Michel**". The church itself has been destroyed many times in the past, but always rebuilt. Its owes its present form to the design by Leonhard Prey and the renowned architect Ernst Georg Sonnin (1751–62).

In the vicinity are the **Shopkeepers' Flats**, established by the shopkeepers' guild in 1676 and administered as an early form of widows' pension. This function was finally abandoned in 1969 and the flats now house an interesting **Museum**, as well as galleries and pubs. Among the open spaces of the **Great Embankments**, at Am Holstenwall 24, is the informative **Museum of Hamburg History**, which has a large collection of model ships and the biggest model railway in Europe.

The city centre: The more elegant side of Hamburg can be seen by strolling from the Main Railway Station into the city centre. The **Deutsche Schauspiel-**

There's little you can't find at Harry's Harbour Bazaar.

haus (1900), immediately opposite the station, is the theatre where Gustav Gründgens used to direct, and Peter Zadek courted controversy with some stirring productions.

Around the corner the city's shopping district begins in the **Mönckeberg-strasse**, but be sure not to miss the **Church of St Jacob** (1340) with its Lucas altar (1499) and precious 17th-century organ by the famous organ-maker Arp Schnitger. The ancient settlement of Hammaburg once lay to the south of here. On the far side of the Burchardplatz is the **Chilehaus**, built by a rich city merchant, and of interest for its expressionist architecture.

Back on the Mönckebergstrasse is the **Church of St Peter**, Hamburg's oldest church (1050). It was destroyed by the Great Fire in 1842, when it assumed its present form. Many valuable treasures from the church are now on display in the Art Gallery.

The **Market Square** provides an appropriate setting for the **Town Hall** (1886–87), the seat of Hamburg's Senate, Bürgerschaft (City Parliament) and Council, which reflects the prosperity of the Hamburg citizens of old. Many of the building's 647 rooms can be seen on a guided tour. The facade is decorated in Renaissance style with figures depicting the German emperors. You can relax under the **Alster Arcades** over a cool beer and watch the swans glide by on the water. The atmosphere is a little hotter, however, in the financial world of the adjacent **Stock Market** (1841).

Around the Alster: A few minutes away from the Town Hall is the **Binnen-alster**, the inland lake. The **Jungfern-stieg** with its department stores and shops facing the city and the **Alster Pavilion** facing the water, is the point of departure for guided boat tours of the city.

Top-quality specialist shops, expensive department stores, glass arcades and first-class restaurants and cafés are located all around this lake. In wet weather, covered arcades such as the **Hanseviertel** are inviting places for a stroll. Nearby is the **Hamburg State Opera** (Grosse Theater Strasse 35).

The tranquil suburban villas of Blankenese.

Exquisite museums: Among the many museums in the city, the **Kunsthalle** (Art Gallery) on the Glockengiesserwall has one of the most magnificent collections in Germany. Many great artists from the 14th to 20th centuries are represented here, including Caspar David Friedrich, Philipp Otto Runge and Edvard Munch along with Dix, Kandinsky, Picasso, Beuys and Warhol. Picasso, Miró and Chagall can be seen in the **Museum of Art and Trade** south of the main railway station, which also has an exhibition of commercial art from a wide variety of cultures and a display documenting the history of photography. The **Ernst Barlach House** is in the Jenisch park on the Elbchaussee; this can be combined with a short trip from Altona to the Schulau Ferry House.

Altona: Once an independent small town, **Altona** was incorporated into Hamburg in 1937. Founded in 1520, the village came under the rule of the Danes 100 years later. The **Altona Museum** provides a good insight into the eventful history of this area. The luxurious

Elbchaussee, lined with luxurious villas, follows the bank of the river. The village of **Övelgönne** with its many old houses, some dating back to the 18th century, once the homes of captains and pilots, is also the location of the **Harbour Museum**. The romantic houses in the former fishing village of **Blankenese** are now occupied by some of the city's richest inhabitants. At this point the **Bismarck Stone** affords a wonderful view across the water.

Downstream from here, near the **Schulau Ferry House** with its "ships in bottles" museum, is the **Willkommhöft** from where all ships entering or leaving Hamburg are greeted or bade farewell. The national flag of the ship's home port is hoisted and its national anthem is played over a loudspeaker.

Recreation in Hamburg: There are various opportunities to escape the routine of daily life in Hamburg. These include the grounds of the **Wallanlagen**, the **Old Botanic Gardens** and the **Plant and Flower Park** with its greenhouses, playgrounds, fountains and Japanese Garden. **Hagenbecks Tierpark**, the world's first private zoo, has been in existence since 1907. A short boat trip takes you from the Inland Alster to the Outer Alster or **Aussenalster**, where the Alster Park was laid out for the International Garden Exhibition.

Excursion to Lüneburg: South of Hamburg, near Undeloh, lies the **Lüneburg Heath National Park**. This was named after the old commercial city of Lüneburg whose meteoric rise was based on the mining of salt which has been taking place here since 936. The monopoly on the salt trade, which Lüneburg gained when the neighbouring city of Bardowick was destroyed, brought immense wealth. The large number of Gothic brick homes ("Am Sande") is evidence of this affluence, and the magnificent Town Hall is a notable product of this period (1300–1706).

The old warehouses, mills and harbour facilities can still be found along the Ilmenau River, bearing a lasting testimony to the splendid era during which Lüneburg and Lübeck controlled the salt trade.

Left, seasonal fruit. **Right,** the "Hope of Lübeck (17th century).

THE HANSEATIC LEAGUE

What do the towns of Bruges and Novgorod, Lübeck and Bergen, Braunschweig and Riga have in common? Between the 12th and 16th centuries they and a further 200 cities joined together to form the Hanseatic League. This association enjoyed greater economic and political influence than any German state before 1871. In addition, its military might exceeded that of many a kingdom of its time.

This exercise of power was not one of the League's original aims. It was created as an association of German traders abroad, as a means of providing mutual protection from attack. It also offered a more effective means of representation, and the advantages of shared office and warehouse accommodation. The loosely-knit organisation expanded over the years to include more towns, especially in north Germany. From the middle of the 14th century, under the leadership of Lübeck, it controlled all trading on the North Sea and Baltic coasts. The economic, military and political power of the Hanseatic League lay in the strict code of regulations with which all members had to comply. The penalties for not doing so were severe. Council meetings were held at which decisions were taken on matters of common interest; these were then binding upon all members. Any trader who failed to abide by them was threatened with a total boycott by all members. A town sentenced to such sanctions could no longer sell its goods in any of the member towns nor was it permitted to use the League's offices and warehouses abroad.

Thus the Hanseatic League governed not only the economic development of a town, but also its politico-social climate. No duties were levied on goods imported from member towns, they used a common system of weights and measures and all paid in the same currency. The combined representation lowered costs overseas, made transport cheaper and kept competitors at bay.

Over the years the Hanseatic League became so powerful that in 1370 it even dared to declare war on the King of Denmark in order to claim its rights in that country as well as access to the Baltic. The League was victorious, forcing the kingdom to accept another monarch and insisting that all their demands were met. Thus the association protected its market, which extended from Bruges and London in the west to Novgorod in the east. Its role was to act as a turntable between east and west. In its cavernous

Koggen, high-sided freight ships with a capacity of 120–160 tons, the Hanseatic League brought raw materials such as furs, wax, salt, honey and amber from the Orient and transported metal goods, textiles, wine and beer from the West. It maintained transport routes to almost every sizeable town in northern and central Europe.

The heavily laden *Koggen* were also a popular prey for pirates determined to make a quick fortune. For a long time the Hanseatic League undertook a campaign against such incursions. Pirate raids were particularly bad between 1370 and 1402. One of the boldest pirates, Klaus Störtebeker, plundered every ship unable to escape his clutches, yelling as he did so, "God's friend – man's enemy!" No prisoners were ever taken; any survivors were unceremoniously flung overboard. The other side was equally barbarous; vanquished pirates were summarily executed on shore.

The Hanseatic League had passed its zenith by the end of the 15th century. Increasing numbers of princes gained control over the cities within their jurisdiction, and the rise of nation states such as Sweden, Russia and England placed further restrictions on the League's expansion, thereby breaking its united front. In 1598 it abandoned its last overseas branch office, in London. ∎

Sailing ship from Lübeck, Queen of the Hansa.

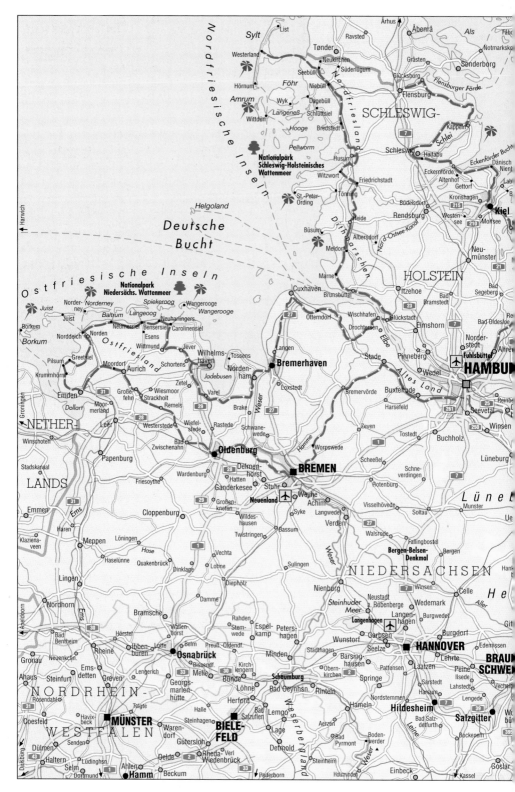

Nordfriesische Inseln

Sylt
List
Westerland
Hörnum
Amrum
Wittdün
Föhr
Wyk
Langeneß
Hooge
Pellworm

Tønder
Neukirchen
Süderlügum
Seebüll
Niebüll
Dagebüll
Schlüttsiel
Bredstedt

Ravsted

Århus
Åbenrå
Als
Notmarksko

Gråsten
Glücksburg
Flensburg
Flensburger Förde

Sønderborg

SCHLESWIG-

Schlei
Schleswig
Haitabu
Kappeln
Eckernförder Bucht
Dänisch
Nient
Lab

Nationalpark
Schleswig-Holsteinisches
Wattenmeer

St-Peter-Ording
Tönning
Witzwort
Husum
Friedrichstadt

Eckernförde
Altenhof
Gettorf

Kiel

Helgoland

Deutsche
Bucht

Heide
Büsum
Meldorf
Albersdorf
Rendsburg
Büdelsdorf

Nord-Ostsee-Kanal

Kronshagen
Westen-
see
Mölfsee

Neu-
münster

← Harwich

Marne

HOLSTEIN

Bad
Segeberg

Ostfriesische Inseln

Nationalpark
Niedersächs. Wattenmeer

Juist
Norder-
ney
Norderney
Spiekeroog
Langeoog
Wangerooge
Wangerooge
Neuharlingers.
Baltrum
Borkum
Neßmersiel
Bensersiel
Carolinensiel
Borkum
Norddeich
Norden
Esens
Wittmund
Jever
Wilhelms-
haven
Greetsiel
Moordorf
Schortens
Nordenham
Pilsum
Aurich
Tossens
Krummhörn
Zetel
Jadebusen

Cuxhaven
Brunsbüttel
Itzehoe
Bad
Bramstedt
Otterndorf
Wischhafen
Glückstadt
Elmshorn
Bad Oldesloe
Langen
Drochtersen
Norder-
stedt
Ahre
Bremerhaven
Stade
Pinneberg
Fuhlsbüttel
Loxstedt
Wedel
HAMBUR

NETHER-
Emden
Große-
fehn
Wiesmoor
Strackholt
Remels
Leer
Moor-
merland
Dollart
Westerstede
Wiefel-
stede
Rastede
Varel
Brake
Schwane-
wede
Weser

Winschoten
Papenburg
Bad
Zwischenahn
Oldenburg
Hatten
Delmen-
horst
Ganderkesee
Stuhr
Neuenland
Wardenburg
Wildes-
hausen

Bremervörde
Harsefeld
Zeven

Worpswede
Hamme
Scheeßel

BREMEN
Weyhe
Achim
Syke
Langwedel
Bassum

Buxtehude
Seevetal
Winsen
Buchholz
Lüneburg
Schne-
verdingen

Soltau

Munster

LÜNE

LANDS

Emmen
Haren
Klaziena-
veen
Meppen
Löningen
Hase
Quakenbrück
Cloppenburg
Friesoythe
Groben-
knaten
Vechta
Lohne
Dinklage
Twistringen
Diepholz
Damme
Sulingen
Nienburg

Rotenburg

Visselhövede
Verden

Walsrode
Fallingbostel
Bergen

Bergen-Belsen-
Denkmal

NIEDERSACHSEN
Han

He

Nordhorn
Bramsche
Rahden
Stemwede
Espel-
kamp
Peters-
hagen
Wunstorf
Steinhuder
Meer
Neustadt
a. Rübenberge
Langen-
hagen
Wedemark
Burgwedel

Burgdorf
Gif

Bad
Bentheim
Hörstel
Ibben-
büren
Wallen-
horst
Belm
Preuß.-Oldendf.
Minden
Stadthagen
Barsing-
hausen
Seelze
Garbsen
Langenhagen
HANNOVER
Lehrte
Edemissen

Gronau
Neuenkch.
Rheine
Lotte
Kirch-
lengern
Obern-
kirchen
Pattensen
Laatzen
Peine
Ilsede
BRAUN
SCHWE

Ahaus
Steinfurt
Ems-
detten
Lengerich
Greven
Osnabrück
Bissendf.
Melle
Bünde
Löhne
Schaumburg
Schaumburg
Springe
Nordstemmen
Sarstedt
Lahstedt
Lengede
Vecher

Rosendahl
Georgs-
marien-
hütte
Herford
Bad Oeynhsn.
Rinteln
Hamburg
Hildesheim
Harsum
Salzgitter
Wo
bü

Coesfeld
Havix-
beck
Telgte
Halle
Steinhagen
BIELE-
FELD
Lemgo
Lage
Bad
Salzuflen
Aerzen
Boden-
werder
Bad
Pyrmont

Bockenem

Goslar

NORDRHEIN-
MÜNSTER
Waren-
dorf
Güntersloh
WESTFALEN
Senden
Lüdinghsn.
Oelde
Rheda-Verl
Wiedenbrück
Paderborn
Detmold
Steinheim
Holzminden

Einbeck

Kassel

Dülmen
Haltern
Selm
Ahlen
Beckum
Hamm
Dortmund

294

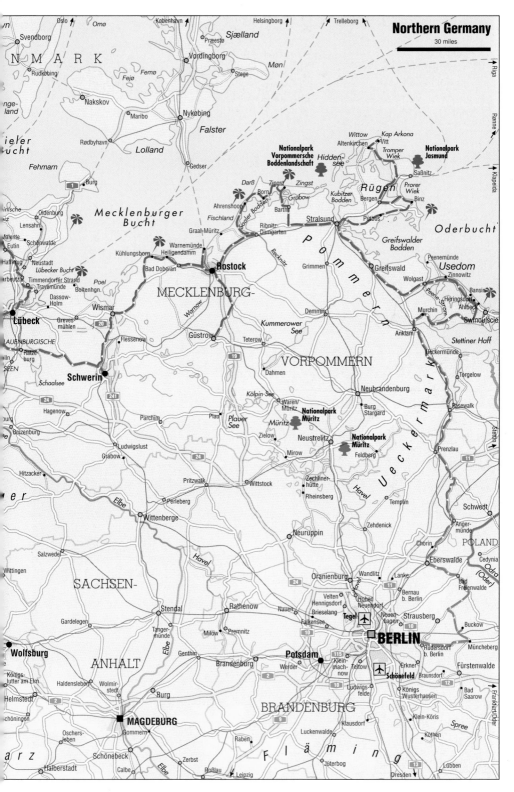

Oslo ↑   Omø   København ↑   Helsingborg ↑   Trelleborg ↑

Svendborg   Sjælland   Riga →

DENMARK   Præstø   Vordingborg   Møn

Rudkøbing   Femø   Stege
Fejø

Nakskov   Maribo   Nykøbing   Falster   Rønne ↑

Langeland   Rødbyhavn   Lolland   Gedser   Klaipeda →

Fehmarn   Wittow   Kap Arkona

Burg   Nationalpark   Altenkirchen   Vitt   Nationalpark
Vorpommersche   Tromper   Jasmund
Boddenlandschaft   Hidden-   Wiek
see   Saßnitz

Oldenburg   Mecklenburger   Darß   Zingst   Zingst   Rügen   Prorer
Bucht   Born   Wiek
Lensahn   Ahrenshoop   Grabow   Kubitzer   Bergen   Binz
Schönwalde   Fischland   Barth   Bodden   Pulitz
Eutin   Kieler   Graal-Müritz   Ribnitz-   Stralsund
Bucht   Damgarten   Oderbucht

Neustadt   Kühlungsborn   Heiligendamm   Recknitz   Greifswalder
Haffkrug   Lübecker Bucht   Warnemünde   Bodden
Timmendorfer Strand   Bad Doberan   Peenemünde
Travemünde   Poel   Rostock   Grimmen   Greifswald   Usedom
Dassow-   Boltenhgn.   Wolgast   Zinnowitz
Holm   Warnow   Demmin   Peene-Strom   Heringsdorf
Wismar   Bansin
Lübeck   Greves-   Ahlbeck
mühlen   MECKLENBURG-   Kummerower   Murchin   Swinoujscie
See   Anklam

LAUENBURGISCHE   Flessenow   Güstrow   Teterow   Stettiner Haff
Ratze-   VORPOMMERN
burg   Schwerin   Dahmen   Ueckermünde
SEEN   Schaalsee   Neubrandenburg   Torgelow

Hagenow   Parchim   Kölpin-See   Burg   Pasewalk
Waren/   Stargard
Müritz   Nationalpark
Plau   Müritz
Müritz   Prenzlau
Brüzenow   Ludwigslust   Plauer   Zielow   Neustrelitz   Nationalpark
Grabow   See   Mirow   Feldberg   Müritz

Hitzacker   Pritzwalk   Zechliner-   Stettin →
Wittstock   hütte   Havel
Perleberg   Rheinsberg   Templin   Schwedt

Elbe   Wittenberge   Zehdenick   Anger-   POLAND
münde   Cedynia

Salzwedel   Neuruppin   Chorin   Eberswalde   Oder (Odra)

Wittingen   Havel   Bad
Freienwalde

SACHSEN-   Oranienburg   Wandlitz   Lanke
Stendal   Rathenow   Nauen   Velten   Bernau   Buckow
Gardelegen   Hennigsdorf   Hohen   b. Berlin
Tanger-   Milow   Premnitz   Brieselang   Neuenhagen   Strausberg
münde   Falkensee   Tegel ✈   10

Wolfsburg   Genthin   BERLIN   Rüdersdorf   Müncheberg
b. Berlin
Königs-   ANHALT   Brandenburg   Werder   Potsdam   Klein-   Erkner   Fürstenwalde
lutter am Elm   mach-   Teltow   Schönefeld ✈   Braunsdorf
Haldensleben   Wolmir-   now   Bad
Helmstedt   stedt   Burg   Ludwigs-   Königs   Saarow
Schöningen   felde   Wusterhausen   Frankfurt/Oder →

Oschers-   MAGDEBURG   BRANDENBURG   Klein-Köris
leben   Gommern   Klausdorf   Köthen
Luckenwalde   Spree   Lübben
Harz   Raben   Jüterbog
Halberstadt   Schönebeck   Zerbst   Elbe   FLÄMING   Lübbenau
Calbe   Roßlau   Leipzig   Dresden ↓

TWO TRIPS ALONG THE COAST

"The murderous sea" is how the Hamburg director Hark Bohm described the North Sea for his film *"Nordsee ist Mordsee"*, grimly reflecting the uneasy relationship between this unruly element and the fisherfolk, shipwrights, traders and pirates of Germany's northwest coast who, down the centuries, made it their livelihood. For all too often this was at the cost of their lives, and all too often they were to see its waters carry away whole islands and sweep inland right up to their homes.

The landscape along the North Sea coast takes three forms – the mudflats of the **Watt**, covered by the Wattenmeer, the fertile **marshland**, and the hilly morainic heathland of the sandy **Geest**.

The Watt extends between mainland and islands for over 565,000 hectares (2,180 sq. miles), a vast expanse of mudflats like nowhere else in the world, and with protected status as the **Wattenmeer National Park**. Here over 250 life forms make up the specialised food chain created by the North Sea's relatively shallow tidal waters.

Both routes around the coast described below are easy to join from Hamburg: either head west to East Friesland, or north to North Friesland and Dietmarschen.

A sea of blossom: Every spring the lovely countryside of **Alte Land**, the marshland south of the Elbe between Hamburg and Stade, becomes a sea of blossom as the apple, cherry and plum orchards in Germany's largest fruit-growing area burst into flower. There have been fruit-growers here since the 14th century. Beautifully embellished half-timbered houses lend added charm to the landscape.

In the heart of Alte Land lies **Buxtehude** (pop. 35,000), with its lovely Old Town, half-timbered houses, old market hall, **Town Hall, St Peter's Church** (1296, Gothic vaulted basilica), and, particularly worth seeing, the 13th-century **canal complex** on the Este. This served as a harbour until 1962. The town's **Regional Museum**, modelled on an old farmhouse, dates from 1913. A **museum train**, with a 1926 carriage, runs to neighbouring **Harsefeld** every other Sunday from May to September.

The county town, **Stade** (pop. 45,000), also has a fine Old Town. High above it looms the baroque tower of **St Cosmas' Church** (13th century), which has an organ by Arp Schnitger. For purposes of musical comparison there is also the Bielfeldt organ in **St Willehad's Church**. The streets are resplendent with half-timbered buildings such as the **Town Hall** (1667), the **Bürgermeister-Hintze House** (1621), the **Höker House** (1650) and the **Hahnentor** (Cock Gate, 1658). The pictures on show at the **Kunsthaus** offer an early introduction to the work of the Worpswede School (*see below*), while the **Local History Museum** (Heimatmuseum), **Schwedenspeicher Museum** and **Open Air Museum** (Freilichtmuseum) record the life and times of this town on the Schwinge. Stade first began to flourish as a trading port when

Left, part of the fishing fleet. **Right**, lazing on a sunny afternoon.

it joined the Hanseatic League in 1267. Its port continues to be important but nowadays modern industry has firmly established itself alongside traditional shipbuilding.

Artists and their landscapes: The route now leads inland to the little village of **Worpswede** (pop. 9,000). This owes its fame to the artists who chose to work here and who drew their inspiration from the primeval landscape of the **Teufelsmoor** (Devil's Moor). Among the first, in 1889, were Fritz Makens, Otto Modersohn and Hans am Ende, later to be followed by the likes of Heinrich Vogeler and Fritz Overbeck. Their work can be seen in the **Haus im Schluh** and the **Grosse Kunstschau** but they also left their mark on the streetscape. Vogeler was responsible for the **Station** and the art nouveau reworking of the **Barkenhoff** (boatyard), while the **Logierhaus** (guest-house), Grosse Kunstschau and **Café Worpswede** – still a popular meeting place for painters and craftspeople – were all the work of Bernhard Hoetger.

The nearby Teufelsmoor, now a nature conservancy area, was at one time the largest unbroken stretch of moorland in Lower Saxony but most of the moors have since been lost to peat digging and drainage. Worpswede's **Torfschiffswerftmuseum** (Peat-Shippers Wharf Museum) affords a glimpse of the life and hard times of those who worked on the moors.

On the River Hamme at Worpswede there are berths for the **passenger ships** which ply the Lesum and the Weser down to Bremen-Vege (May–September, Wednesday and Sunday, buses to Bremen city centre).

Grand-ducal seat: Oldenburg (pop. 145,200), the largest place between Dollart and Jadebusen, became the seat of the Gottorfer Grand Dukes in 1785. Fine 17th-century town houses, neoclassical buildings and lovely art nouveau villas testify to the wealth of the town. The period rooms in the **Schloss**, the grand-ducal palace, are adorned with paintings by Johann Heinrich Wilhelm Tischbein and Ludwig Münstermann. Works by Old Mas-

ters can also be seen in the impressive gallery of the **Landesmuseum**, the regional art and art history museum. The **Augusteum** is the place to see paintings by the Worpswede School, Emil Nolde and Franz Radziwill. This bustling university town is the commercial and cultural capital of the region and has a packed programme of events, among them the annual **Oldenburg Kultursommer** (summer arts festival) held in July and August.

Peat moors and windmills: Heading north-west, past the moorland spa of Bad Zwischenahn, and Westerstede, with its Ammerland wildlife park, you come to **Grossefehn**. Colonisation of the moors began with the first settlement here on the fen in 1633. The rich black peat was cut for fuel, an unhealthy job which was often forced labour for convicts, as can be seen in the **Fen Museum** at **Westgrossefehn**. The peat was transported along the drainage canals to the port at Emden, away from this landscape of, canals, bridges, windmills and locks.

Protecting the coast is a full-time job.

"East Frisian capital": The secret capital of the East Frisians is **Aurich** (pop. 37,000), at one time the seat of the Cirksena and subsequent ruling dynasties. The **Schloss**, palace (1852), and many other neo-classical buildings, including both churches and some town houses, date from this period.

The modern market place is very eyecatching. Its new **Market Hall** in white steel, and Aachen sculptor Albert Sous's **Tower** were initially quite controversial. The **Historical Museum** is in the former **Chancery**, the Stiftsmühle holds the **Mill Museum**, and the Renaissance-style **East Frisian Landschaft** building (1900) houses a collection of furniture from the region. The town landmark is the free-standing 14th-century **Tower** of **St Lambert's Church**, dating from 1825.

By far the most graphic of East Friesland's museums on the life and hard times of the moorland colonists is the **Open Air Museum** (Freilichtmuseum) at Moordorf about 10 km (6 miles) from Aurich.

Hub of commerce: Two famous sons of **Emden** (pop. 51,000), the next stop on the route, are Otto Waalkes, whose comic mementoes can be seen in the **Otto Hus**, and Henri Nannen, whose bequest to the town was his collection of works by artists such as Emil Nolde, Paula Modersohn-Becker and August Macke, together with the **Kunsthalle** in which they are displayed.

Emden is the commercial hub of East Friesland with its North Sea port (one of the world's largest for car shipments) and Volkswagen plant. To get a good impression of Emden's size climb the tower of the **Old Town Hall**, a modern building incorporating parts of its forerunner which was destroyed in 1944. The town hall also houses the **East Frisian Museum** with an exhibition on Emden's development. **Harbour cruises** leave from the Ratsdelft steps opposite. Another insight into the shipping world is to be had in the **Shipping Museum** on the Amrumbank lightship. Parts of the Old Town which still exist in the area of the Friedrich-Ebert-Strasse

Preparing to set sail.

include the **New Church** (1648) and some fine rows of houses.

Seven pearls in the sea: From Emden a car ferry sails to **Borkum**, the first of the seven East Frisian islands. Like the others it grew from the sandbanks formed here in the seas on the edge of the Continental Shelf. Like them too, Borkum is very much at the mercy of the sea and the storm tides which used to flood ever larger expanses of land. People and livestock were drowned and whole villages would be washed right out to sea.

But time and again the islands would be resettled, since there was no gainsaying that the North Sea, with its rich fish stocks, still constituted a plentiful supply of food. In the 18th century the men also used to work as merchant seamen and whalers.

The key to survival here nowadays is the concept of "gentle tourism": nature and countryside conservation are top of the agenda and every island includes guided nature walks among its attractions. Cars are only allowed onto the two largest and busiest islands, Borkum and **Norderney** (ferry from Norddeich). On the others it is a matter of light railway, horse-drawn transport and bikes only. **Baltrum**, at 6.5 sq. kilometres (2½ sq. miles) and with only 492 inhabitants, is the smallest of the islands, and **Spiekeroog** (ferry from Neuharlingersiel) is the greenest and most intact. **Langeoog** (ferry from Bensersiel) is the best for families, **Juist** (ferry from Norddeich) the most natural, and **Wangeooge** (ferry from Carolinensiel), which for a time belonged to Czarist Russia, has the most chequered history.

The coast: The best place on the East Frisian coast for harking back to the past is **Greetsiel**, and the locals certainly know how to cash in on nostalgia. Despite this commercialisation it is a real pleasure to stroll around the beautifully restored and pedestrianised streets in the centre. The hub of village life is the harbour with its crab boats; Greetsiel's chief feature, however, is its great windmills, the two **Galerieholländer**. One is still in working order (open for visits) **The far north.**

and the other has a tea room and an art gallery. In fact this is just one gallery among many in the village – Greetsiel's **Kunstwochen** (art weeks) are famous throughout the country.

Norden (pop. 25,000), with its sandy beaches and green dunes at **Norddeich**, is East Friesland's largest coastal resort. Leisure facilities include the **seawater indoor pool**, a **small zoo** and a **leisure centre**. A particular favourite is the **seal sanctuary** where orphaned seal pups are lovingly hand-reared.

The **harbour** is a hive of activity with the comings and goings of ferries, fishing boats and yachts. At the heart of the town, around the large **Marktplatz** (market place), there is a very fine cluster of buildings formed by the three **Bürgerhäuser** (from around 1600), next to the **Town Hall** (1884) and the **Mennonite Church** (1662–1835). The **St Ludger Church** (13th–15th centuries) is the largest church in the region, and has a fine organ by Arp Schnitger. The **Alten Rathaus** (old town hall, 1542) contains a **Tea Museum** and an interesting **local history museum** (Heimatsmuseum) which vividly recreates scenes from domestic and working life.

Wittmund (pop. 19,000) is like an open university all summer long for anyone who fancies a course in the East Frisian lifestyle. Subjects include pottering about, drinking tea and milking the cows – and you can only qualify if you join in the fun and have a good sense of humour. As he was inclined to do in so many churches in the region, Arp Schnitger also bestowed one of his fine instruments on **St Nicholas Church** (1776).

Jever (pop. 12,800) is another place to polish up your knowledge of East Frisian traditions when it comes to tea, beer and fish. There are guided tours around the local **Brewery**, along with an opportunity to taste its Pilsener bitter. Jever's harbour enabled it to become an important entrepôt in the Middle Ages but the most imposing reminder of its eventful past is the magnificent **Schloss** (palace) in which hangs a portrait of Csarina Catherine II who

Maritime motifs are everywhere.

ruled Jever between 1793 and 1818. The palace also contains a **Regional Museum** which is worth a visit. A lot of green space and plenty of canals and fine buildings, some of them art nouveau, complete the townscape.

All this is in sharp contrast to **Wilhelmshaven** (pop. 91,000) whose brief history only dates back to 1854 when King Wilhelm I of Prussia founded a naval port here in 1853. Life still revolves around the **port** which, thanks to oil, has since expanded to become highly commercial. The **Coast Museum** on the Rathausplatz tells the story of the area and its shipping.

Wilhelmshaven's opposite number, on the far side of the Weser estuary in Bremen, the smallest of Germany's *Länder*, is the town of **Bremerhaven** (pop. 150,000), Europe's largest fishing port and container terminal. It was from its Columbus pier, the "pier of tears", that over 10 million Europeans embarked for the New World. The Old Harbour also holds the **German Shipping Museum** (Deutsches Schiffahrts-museum) and its collection of historic ships including a Hanseatic merchant ship (Hansekogge). A good place to take time out is the nearby **Columbus Center** with its restaurants and shopping mall.

At the tip of the headland between the Elbe and Weser estuaries the port of **Cuxhaven** (pop. 56,000) squares up to the open sea. All the ocean-going giants pass by here on their way to Hamburg, making a wonderful sight to behold from the **Alte Liebe** pier and nearby **lighthouse**. At low tide horse-drawn carriages cross the mudflats to the islands of **Neuwerk**.

Red rock in the sea: From Alte Liebe boats also depart for **Heligoland** (pop. 1,800), the small island of red sandstone rock which rises up out of the sea 70 km (44 miles) off the mouth of the Elbe. Its exposed location explains why the island has changed hands so many times. It served as a pirate stronghold in the 13th century, then came to be owned by the Danes followed by the British who eventually handed it over to the Ger-

Such dunes are common on the East Frisian Islands, as well as Sylt, Amrum and Föhr.

mans in 1890 in exchange for the island of Zanzibar. Heligoland served as a naval base in both world wars but the population eventually fled the bombing of World War II. Thereafter it was used for target practice by the British Air Force. A peaceful sit-in by young Germans led to the island being handed back to its former occupants in 1952.

It has since developed into a popular destination for visitors and can be reached from almost all the North Sea ports. Its best-known landmark is **Big Anna** (Lange Anna), the free-standing rock stack at the north end of the island. The **Aquarium** recreates the underwater world of the North Sea.

Northwards to Dithmarshen: To pick up the second leg of this journey along the North Sea coast, this time in the *Land* of Schleswig–Holstein, cross the River Elber at **Wischhafen**.

When the Danish King Christian IV founded **Glückstadt** (pop. 12,000) in 1617 he was pursuing the ambitious aim of creating a flourishing centre for trade which would rival neighbouring Hamburg. To this end he attracted Jews, Mennonites and Dutch Protestants to live here by promising them freedom of religion and freedom from taxes. The face of Glückstadt reflects those lofty aims, especially in the old buildings around the **Marktplatz** (Market Place) and the **Harbour.** These include the Dutch Renaissance **Town Hall** (1642) and the late-Gothic **Town Church** (1621). The **Detlefsen Museum** in the **Brockdorff-Palais** features some interesting displays on whaling and regional history.

The town of **Brunsbüttel** (pop. 13,500) owes its leading role in the petro-chemical industry and energy distribution to its position at the start of the **North Sea–Baltic Canal**, the world's busiest canal in terms of traffic. In the period between 1959, when its oil terminal came on stream, and 1995 – the centenary of the canal – Brunsbüttel handled 190 million tons of crude oil and mineral and chemical products. You can watch the huge canal locks in action from a viewing platform. For background information, visit the **Locks**

Museum (Schleusenmuseum). The focus is also on navigation in the **Local History Museum** (Heimatsmuseum), which includes an authentic saloon from an around-the-Horn sailing clipper. Something of the atmosphere of the old church parish still lingers on in the **Marktplatz** (Market Place).

The Dithmarschen Peasant Republic: It was a collection of church parishes that formed the framework for the "Dithmarschen Peasant Republic", an association of wealthy peasant families which held sway between 1070 and 1559 in the fertile marshland. Well shielded by the surrounding moors against attack by potential overlords, together they organised the building of the sea dyke which was so vital for protection of their land. The "Council of Forty-eight" arrived at all their important decisions "on the heath (*Heide*)" and sold their abundant harvests to the Hanseatic towns. It was not until 1559 that they were eventually forced to accept the rule of the Danish kings. The **Dithmarschen Cathedral** (9th–13th century) in **Meldorf**

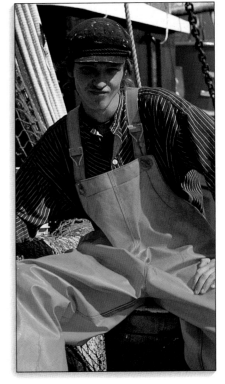

Fishing has an uncertain future.

testifies to the peasants' early conversion to Christianity.

The place where the council met developed into what is now the county town of **Heide** (pop. 20,000), with one of Germany's largest **Marktplätze**. Heide is also the birthplace of Johannes Brahms and the wordsmith and professor Klaus Groth, Heide has a **Museum** dedicated to each of its famous sons. Another interesting museum here is the **Museum of Dithmarschen Pre-History**.

Dutch architecture: Lying on the Eider is the town of **Friedrichstadt** (pop. 2,600). Founded in 1621, it was largely built up by Dutch religious refugees. They modelled their second home entirely on their home towns: hence the little canals (boat tours) and the lovely gabled houses, like the **Alte Münze**, which line the cobbled streets.

The Dutch were also responsible for the construction method of the *haubarge*, the large, handsome farmhouses characteristic of the **Eiderstedt** peninsula where some can still be seen today.

They are built so that the wooden superstructure, anchored deep in the ground, would still be holding up the lofty central section even when a storm tide had ripped all the walls away. The most famous is the **Red Haubarg** at Witzwort (Museum of Landscape Development) which the poet Theodor Storm visited as a child.

It was Storm who christened his native town of **Husum** (pop. 22,000) that "grey town by the sea" and his novellas convey a vivid impression of life here and on the peninsula. Many of the places he described can still be visited. These include the **Schloss** (1582–1752) in the midst of its **Park**, which is carpeted with purple crocuses in the spring; and the 19th-century **Merchants' Houses** by the **Old Harbour**.

On the waterfront, look out for the **Stormhaus** (Storm House) and the **Tobacco Museum**. The museum in the **Nissenhaus** tells of sea dykes and storm tides. Paradoxically, it was a storm tide in 1362 which made the town's fortune since instead of being inland Husum

Dutch settlers built these houses in Friedrichstadt.

found itself on the coast and thus acquired a harbour. From here ferries sail to the Halligen and the North Frisian Islands.

St Tropez of the North: Off the coast of Husum lie the islands of **Nordstrand** (causeway to the mainland), **Pellworm** and the **Halligen**. All this used to be part of the mainland until the 1360s when storm tides flooded over the marshes and only the odd few acres were left behind. On the Halligen the farmsteads are perched on earthbanks (*warften*) for safety, for the flood warning is still sometimes sounded.

The Halligen and the tiny ports of Schlüttsiel and Dagebüll, north of Husum, are the departure points for ferries to the three biggest North Frisian islands.

On **Amrum** the main bathing beach is a 17-km (11-mile) long sandspit (the Kniepsand) which gets pushed 50 metres (55 yards) further north by the wind and the waves every year. **Föhr**, on the other hand, is comparatively well served with vegetation. In Wyk the **Frisian Museum** traces the history of the Frisians, the tribe which settled the region, who came from East Friesland, in the 8th century.

Germany's northernmost point is on **Sylt**, the island which owes its **"St Tropez of the North"** reputation to the jetsetting crowd who love to hang out in places like **Westerland**, and **Kampen**, with its beautiful Red Cliff. But Sylt also has plenty to offer for more ordinary mortals such as families and young people. They prefer **List**, **Rantum** and **Hörnum**. Idyllic **Keitum**, that "loveliest of Frisian villages", also manages to retain its charm far removed from the madding crowd. Evidence of the Neolithic presence on the island is provided by **Denghoog**, the megalithic tomb at **Wenningsted**. To get to Sylt by land take the train from Niebüll, which carries cars over the Hindenburg causeway.

Back on the mainland the **Nolde Museum** makes a fitting conclusion for this trip to the far north. The studio of the unconventional artist, Emil Nolde, is in **Seebüll**.

VIA LÜBECK TO FLENSBURG

Germany's northernmost state is strange but beautiful. The landscape of Schleswig-Holstein, sandwiched between the North Sea and the Baltic, is characterised by windswept trees, lovingly maintained brick houses, thatched cottages, grand farmsteads and hundreds of lakes set amid extensive deciduous forests. It is possible to cruise for miles through the lakes and rivers of the Holstein lowlands, just one of five nature reserves in the eastern part of the state.

In the east, long *Förden* (fjords) cut inland wherever cliffs or sandy beaches have failed to check the Baltic Sea's advance. In most places, though, the scene around this tideless 55-metre (180-foot) deep sea is peaceful.

A lack of minerals has prevented the development of industry, thus earning the region a post-war reputation as a "structurally weak area", a polite term for poverty-stricken, but this has not always been the case. For centuries trade between Scandinavia and the countries of eastern Europe flourished. During medieval times, Schleswig-Holstein's wealth came not only from agriculture but also from its strategic location. The people of this region controlled the land and sea routes which the other Baltic merchants had to use if they were to sell their goods. The most powerful force in this lucrative business was, of course, the Hanseatic League.

The quickest way from Hamburg to Lübeck is via the E22 but a more leisurely route takes in **Schloss Ahrensburg**, the old town of **Bad Oldesloe** and **Reinfeld**.

Queen of the Hanseatic towns: For 250 years, **Lübeck** (pop. 220,000) was the undisputed commercial metropolis of the Holy Roman Empire. Founded in 1143 by Count Adolf II of Schauenburg on an island in the Trave River, Henry the Lion later acquired the settlement and granted it a town charter. It was 1226 before Lübeck received the status of Free Imperial City. It eventually grew into an important port for traders with partners around the Baltic Sea and in the west. Furs, tar, honey and amber from the Baltic were used as barter for wool, copper and tin from England. At that time, salt was a valuable commodity, being used in food preservation. By 1356, Lübeck was the most powerful of all the towns in the Hanseatic League.

Lübeck is famous for its Gothic brick churches. Those arriving from the direction of Hamburg can spot the city's seven towers from a great distance. **The Church of St Mary** was built in the 13th century and served as a model for many of the brick churches around the Baltic. The foundation stone for the **Cathedral** was laid in 1173. This building, planned as a Romanesque basilica, was constructed in its present Gothic form in the 13th and 14th centuries.

The 14th-century churches of **St Ägidien**, **St Catherine** and **St Peter**, as well as the 13th-century **Church of St Jacob** which houses one of Europe's oldest organs (15th century), are all grouped closely together in the old part of the city. There's a fine view from St

Left, the Holsten Gate, symbol of Lübeck. Right, tucking in tio a local delicacy.

Peter's tower and the west front of St Catherine's displays three terracotta sculptures by Ernst Barlach. The **St Annen Museum** is situated nearby. The exhibits in the cloisters of this former monastery are particularly interesting.

The **Holsten Gate** (1466), the most impressive of the few remaining sections of the city wall, formerly guarded the western entrance to the city and the 16th- and 17th-century **salt warehouse**, where Lüneburg salt was stored. Today it houses a **museum** with a large model of the city from the year 1650.

In the centre of the city is the Gothic **Town Hall**. Dating from 1484 it is one of the oldest in Germany and a monument to the Swedish King Gustav Wasa can be found in the lobby. Until well into the 19th century, the unusual openings in the facade and arcades served as a protection against the weather for the numerous market booths. Cafés on the market square sell the world-famous **Lübeck marzipan**.

A few steps further on is the 18th-century **Buddenbrook House**, former home of Thomas and Heinrich Mann. Thomas Mann's novel of the same name turned the house in Mengstrasse into a popular destination for literary pilgrimages. The nearby **Schabbel House** is a good place to dine. The **Shippers' Society House** (Breite Strasse), though less fancy, offers an interesting maritime atmosphere.

The **Holy Ghost Hospital** with 13th-century frescoes in the cross vaults was one of Germany's first old people's homes. Cross Glockengiesserstrasse to the **Füchtingshof**, the finest of Lübeck's 82 **Wohngänge** settlements, which were built in the 16th century in gardens behind large middle-class homes, to house the growing population.

Beaches and bathing areas: Located to the northeast in Lübeck Bay is **Travemünde**, which has been a part of Lübeck since the 14th century. From the beginning of the 19th century, the rich and the powerful, including many Scandinavians, have been enjoying this resort, whose main attraction is the **Casino**. Travemünde is a terminal for many ferry

The *Passat* docks in Travemünde.

services linking Germany and Scandinavia. Stretching further to the north are the beaches and bathing areas of Lübeck Bay. Models in sand of original German castles are the trademarks of **Timmendorf Beach**, **Scharbeutz** and **Haffkrug**, to name the most famous. At Hemmeldorfsee, between Travemünde and Timmendorf, is Germany's lowest point – 44 metres (144 feet) below sea level.

Holstein's Little Switzerland: A mere 10 km (6 miles) further to the north the "mighty" heights of Schleswig-Holstein's "Little Switzerland" appear with their beech and oak forests surrounding approximately 200 lakes. It was below these gentle, terminal moraine hills, formed in the Ice Age, that water from the melting glaciers accumulated. Deciduous forests cover the banks with *Knicks*, or earth mounds, guarded by hedges designed to protect the sandy soil from wind erosion.

The health resort of **Eutin** (pop. 18,000) is known as the "Weimar of the north". Here Johann Heinrich Voss (1751–1826) translated Homer's epics.

Historic pictures painted by the 18th-century artist Tischbein during his stay in Eutin are exhibited in the moated **castle**. Summer concerts in honour of Eutin's most famous native son, Carl Maria von Weber (1786–1826), take place annually in the castle's park.

At the centre of the region, between the **Grosser** and **Kleiner Plöner See** is the town of **Plön** (pop. 10,500). During the 18th century a Renaissance-style moated castle by the lakeside was used by the Danish king as a summer residence. The tower of the **Church of St Peter** in Bosau provides a wonderful view across the entire region. This little church is just one of the venues for the annual **Schleswig-Holstein Music Festival**. North of Plön, the little town of **Preetz** (pop. 16,500) boasts a 13th-century Benedictine **monastery** with a triple-nave brick church. A visit to the **Circus Museum** in pretty Mühlenstrasse will open up a whole new world. The **Seelenter See** north of Preetz provides a sanctuary for rare birds. Several manor houses and small castles are situated nearby, as is the **Bungsberg**. Only 164 metres (538 feet) in height, it is the highest point in the region.

The capital of Schleswig-Hostein: With its port and modern industrial area, **Kiel** (pop. 249,000) is not only the capital, it is also the largest and commercially the most important city in the state of Schleswig-Hostein. However, this has not always been the case. Since its foundation by Adolf IV of Schauenburg in 1233, the local economy has experienced many ups and downs. Kiel's role was not clearly established until 1865 when Prussia annexed Schleswig-Holstein. In 1871, the Imperial naval harbour was founded, and in 1895, the Kaiser-Wilhelm Canal (Kiel Canal) was opened. In 1917 Kiel was named capital of the Prussian province of Schleswig-Holstein and in 1945 capital of the new federal state.

Because of its strategic importance, Kiel fell victim to heavy bombing during World War II. While no longer able to boast about the beauty of its historic buildings, Kiel nevertheless has considerable charm thanks to its location on

The Voss-Eck in Eutin.

the wide bay of the **Kieler Förde**. The railway station is only a few yards from the water's edge, from where passenger boats leave to zig-zag their way across the fjord, passing **Oslo Quay** where larger ferries lie at anchor, the **Hindenburg Quay** with its yachting marina and the **Gorch Fock**. The lock gates of the great **Kiel Canal** can also be seen to the left. At the mouth of the estuary lies the resort of **Laboe**, where you can either squeeze into an old U-Boat or enjoy a wide panoramic view from the **German Naval War Memorial**.

Near the railway station, a modern, covered shopping centre, **Sophienhof**, offers an impressive range of shops. At the far end of the pedestrian precinct is the **Old Market** which, although modern in design, still has a quaint and lively atmosphere. Outside the **St Nicholas Church** (13th–15th century, rebuilt in 1951), stands one of Ernst Barlach's sculptures known as *Der Geistkämpfer.*

The modern **Schloss** is now used as a concert hall, while the **Kunsthalle** exhibits works of art by local artists.

To the south-west of Kiel, the **Schleswig-Holstein Open Air Museum** (Freilichtmuseum) in **Molfsee** is well worth a visit. Not far from here is the **Westensee Naturpark,** a nature reserve that is a popular place for a stroll, particularly at weekends.

Towards the Danish border: Travel north along the cliff-lined coastline past the farmsteads at Knoop, Dänisch Nienhof and **Altenhof** (tel: 04351/41428 to arrange a visit) to reach the seaside resort of **Eckernförde** (pop. 23,000) with its fine **Town Hall Market**. Eckernförde is a traditional fishing port where it is still possible to watch the fishermen landing their catch.

Near to the resort of **Haddeby**, you can still make out the ring-shaped earthworks of **Haithabu**. Up until the 11th century, an important Viking trading centre was situated at this junction of the ancient north–south trade route and the waterway formed by the rivers Schlei, Eider and Treene. The **Viking Museum** at Haddebyer Noor houses finds from the surrounding region.

Shipbuilding in miniature in the Kiel Museum.

On the other side of the Schlei is **Schleswig** (pop. 29,800), the oldest town in the state – it acquired its municipal charter in 1200. Close to the old town, which is well worth a visit, is the Renaissance castle of **Gottorf**, the largest princely residence in Schleswig-Holstein. This castle also houses the two most important museums in Schleswig-Holstein: the **Schleswig-Holstein Museum** (art collections from the Middle Ages to the 20th century) and the **Archaeological Museum**, the largest museum of its kind in Germany. It houses a number of valuable finds such as the Nydam Ship, a 4th-century Viking long boat, and bodies that were discovered preserved in the bog. The Bordesholm Altar by Hans Brüggemann can be seen in **St Peter's Cathedral** (12th–15th century), a Gothic church built from brick. The **Angeln** peninsula to the north-east of Schleswig also has distant historical connections: it was from here that the Angles, an ancient Germanic tribe, emigrated to England in the 5th and 6th centuries.

Schleswig-Holstein is a fertile land.

For the remainder of the trip to Flensburg, take the coastal road from Kappeln which passes through a richly varied landscape. The coast offers not only countless bathing beaches but many fine views of the sea open out along the way. Near **Glücksburg**, stands a beautiful moated castle of the same name (1587). Once the summer residence of Danish kings, the castle gardens are now used as a venue for cultural events.

From its early days as a fishing village (12th century), **Flensburg** (pop. 90,000) emerged as an important trading centre. In the 16th century, the town was Denmark's most important port, as illustrated in the **Maritime Museum**. The narrow streets are lined with fine houses and medieval merchants' courtyards. The **Alt-Flensburger Haus**, which is set out like a merchant's house, is now a top-class restaurant. The **Norertor** or Northern Gate (16th century), with its stepped gables, is the symbol of the home of rum making, a skill that arrived here in the 18th century from the Danish West Indies.

ALONG THE BALTIC SEA TO BERLIN

Bismarck used to quip that he would move north before the end of the world as everything happens 100 years later up there, a saying as popular today as it was then. Travellers through Mecklenburg-Vorpommern may at first be inclined to agree and then be just as likely to find evidence to the contrary. It is true that the fruits of progress are not too apparent in this area, but neither could this sparsely populated federal *Land* be said to be behind the times. The whole area is more or less flat land and everything seems to happen on the shores of one of the 1,800 lakes or along the 340-km (211-mile) stretch of coast between the Bay of Lübeck and the Stettiner Haff.

This lovely coastline is deeply indented with many bays, and a plethora of islands and peninsulas. There are four prosperous Hanseatic towns and numerous bathing resorts, which have done well to preserve their traditional seaside architecture. The steep coast can rise up to 120 metres (390 feet) above sea level, and the never-ending beaches give way to marshy meadows and woodland. The *Bodden* landscape, inland expanses of water leading out into the open sea, often looks like the Baltic equivalent of the North Sea mud flats.

Castles, towns and lakes: On setting out from Hamburg, the first place encountered is **Ahrensburg** (pop. 27,000), where there is a **Renaissance Palace**, constructed in 1595, to visit. Inside there is an exhibition on the noble house of Schleswig-Holstein. The nearby 16th-century **Gottesbuden** (God's Hut) shows how the less well-off used to live. These two small brick houses used to be a refuge for the poor and the sick.

To the east, the town of **Ratzeburg** (pop. 13,000) lies in a beautiful setting on an island. Once an outpost for the conversion to Christianity of West Mecklenburg, it was elevated to the status of bishopric during the reign of Henry the Lion, and the romantic brick-built **Cathedral** was completed in the 12th century. The Cathedral Lodge of Ratzeburg was responsible for the construction of many churches in the area. Pillaging by the Danes in the 17th century accounts for the lack of medieval building, with the exception of the Cathedral and the early Gothic **Church of St George**. For this reason many of the town houses date from the subsequent two centuries; along with the fact that it is enclosed by three lakes, this gives the town a harmonious feel. The sculptor and poet Ernst Barlach (1870–1938) spent his youth here. The **Museum** can be found next to the classicist **Parish Church** (1787–91). In the **Cathedral Chapter** the Andreas Paul Weber Room has an exhibition of fantastical and satirical pencil drawings.

The border between West and East Germany ran not far from here for several decades. For the local population this meant a severe restriction of freedom, but for the flora and fauna it was a time of prolific growth. The **Lauenburg Lakes** west of the former no-man's-land, and the **Schaalsee** directly adjacent to the course of the former border, are a unique wooded water paradise whose rich inheritance includes orchids, sundew, cotton grass, marsh marigolds, cranes and storks. This lake area is now a nature reserve to ensure it remains undisturbed. It is best explored on foot or by bicycle, as the slower pace makes it easier to discover the hidden treasures of the lakes, pools and bogs, and observe the freshwater eco-systems.

The region of Mecklenburg-Vorpommern begins just beyond **Mühlenmoor** on the B 208. Among its population of 2 million, tourism is the watchword, for many see new employment opportunities in this service industry. For the federal *Land* is not only rich in bright yellow rape fields and beautiful scenery, but also, regrettably, in unemployment.

The village pubs round here give the opportunity to look beneath the surface and see the area from a more intimate perspective.

The first to profit from the tourist trade have been the larger towns and cities, rich in culture and history. Typi-

Ahrenshoop on Darss has a history as an artists' colony.

cal of these is the state capital **Schwerin** (pop. 125,000), the former ancestral seat of the Dukes of Mecklenburg. The **Palace**, built between 1843 and 1857 and much rebuilt and extended, is proving a popular destination. Situated between the Burgsee and the Schweriner See, it is said to have 365 towers and turrets. There will always be those who wish to check up on this by counting them. Their job is easier when it comes to counting the nearby lakes – from the lofty heights of the tower of the brick **Cathedral** (1270, tower added 1892) all seven can be seen, an amphibious world populated by swans and boats.

Yet Mecklenburg's oldest town has much more to offer: a variety of half-timbered frontages in the **Schelfstadt**, fine examples of classicism on the Pfaffenteich, and an exquisite collection of the works of the Flemish and Dutch Masters in the **State Museum**.

The coast: The Hanseatic town of **Wismar** (pop. 57,000) is the first port we come to and our first glimpse of the sea. Its favourable location led to its swift expansion in the past. Ships sailed to Bergen and Bruges, and waggons travelled along the coast to Lübeck and the Baltic. It entered a rapid decline after the Thirty Years' War, and its fortunes did not improve again until the industrialisation of the 19th century. Despite heavy losses in World War II, a number of historical buildings were saved from the ruins, including the churches of **St George** (15th century) and **St Nicholas** (14th–15th century) and the classicist **Town Hall** (1817–19), all cheek by jowl with numerous Gothic town houses. Even more variety is provided by baroque buildings and Renaissance facades. The old Hanseatic town will be unrivalled once its programme of restoration is complete.

To the north-east of Wismar are the seaside resorts of **Kühlungsborn** and **Heiligendamm**. The first of these positively glows, with its kilometre-long beach and new bridge, and the second, too, with its epithet "the white town by the sea". This description is justified by the appearance of the resort, founded in

Rostock, historic bridgehead to the north.

1793 and thus the oldest in Germany. White classicist villas line the narrow strip of coast, reflecting the desire of noble and wealthy citizens to savour the beneficial effects of the salt waters in suitably opulent surroundings. A sea view was always guaranteed.

Bad Doberan (pop. 12,300) can be reached via the "green tunnel", the longest avenue of lime trees in Europe, or by leaving the car behind and taking the narrow-gauge railway on board *Molli*, chugging through the countryside at a leisurely 35 kph (20 mph). Doberan is best represented by its imposing 14th-century **Minster**, the Gothic brick-built church with richly furnished interior, which was the centrepiece of a powerful Cistercian convent. From the 18th century it was visited annually by the Mecklenburg court entourage wishing to take the summer air.

Europe's very first horse-racing course was opened in Doberan in 1807. The title "Bad" (spa) was added to its name in 1929 because of its iron-rich mud baths.

Where there are few openings, a gateway must be found. This purpose was served by **Rostock** (pop. 237,000) in the difficult years of the GDR. Walter Ulbricht and his entourage created a "gateway to the world" from the ruins of the war, thereby bringing to the nearly 800-year-old Hanseatic town an international port, docks, and a population explosion, giving it a new prominence. Its sense of civic pride and tradition, which were not diminished in the years following 1945, are amply illustrated by its stepped gables, rooftops, eaves and attics, three large churches, four magnificent city gates and the oldest university in Europe.

A full tour of the town will certainly take a few days. The **Cultural History Museum** contains all manner of information on local history, the **Shipping Museum** tells amusing tales of sea voyages, and the **Church of St Mary** (13th–15th century) has an astronomical clock from 1472, whose calendar goes right up to the year 2017. The 14th-century fishing village of **Warnemünde** is perfect for an outing on a warm summer's day, with its thatched cottages and broad expanse of beach frequented by nudist swimmers.

Anyone who is staying in Rostock should not miss an excursion to **Güstrow** (pop. 37,000). Here there is a lot to see in a small area, including a brick **Cathedral** (1236), the **Parish Church**, the largest **Renaissance Palace** (16th century) in the north, and many traces of Ernst Barlach, who lived in the former provincial seat from 1910 onwards. Examples of his sculpture, can be seen in the Cathedral, the Gertrude Chapel (1430) and in the **Atelierhaus**, the sculptor's former studio.

The "amber coast" is actually in Poland, but some years a few hundred-weight of amber can be found washed ashore on the German Baltic coast. If a stroll along the beach in search of this "northern gold" proves unsuccessful, results are guaranteed in **Ribnitz-Damgarten** (pop. 17,500), to the east of Rostock. The Recknitz, the river which forms the border between Mecklenburg and Vorpommern, flows through the

On the promenade in Warnemünde.

town, and in the Amber Museum the fossilised resin glows in all its glory.

On the **Fischland-Darss-Zingst** peninsula a strong inshore wind always seems to be blowing, and human beings seem insignificant. It is a desolate wilderness of reeds, echoing to the continuous pounding of the waves. Small resorts try to attract holidaymakers to their vast expanses of beach, with camp sites and wicker beach chairs.

Ahrenshoop (pop. 800) has the usual sailors' and fishermen's houses, but also has a history as an artists' colony. One hundred years ago a painter discovered this remote spot, and brought a number of young, mainly female, artists to join him. Sand dunes, windswept cottages and shelters, and strangely twisted and storm-tossed trees, were all committed to paper and canvas. Other popular subjects were the Darsser Forest, and the *Bodden*, the still lagoons sheltered from the wind by islands and peninsulas. Those who are familiar with the song *"Wo de Ostseewellen trecken an den Strand"* ("Where the Baltic waves wash on to the sand"), can pay their respects to the local writer Martha Müller-Grahlert at **Zingst** (population 3,000). She penned this song, and is buried in the little village.

Stralsund (pop. 71,000) is a veritable showcase for brick, the typical building material of northern Germany. Red bricks give this town, Vorpommern's counterpart to Lübeck, its unmistakable appearance, which conservationists and visitors alike hold in high regard. The community, which received its charter in 1234, lived through and survived all the European self-destructive activities of the past, including the Thirty Years' War when the Swedes drove out Wallenstein and stayed themselves until 1815, and World War II, which made way for socialist influences.

Despite all the upheaval, Stralsund resembles a huge museum, honoured by the Federal Government with an award for its town renewal projects. The Gothic **Town Hall** (facade from 1370–80) is an outstanding example of how filigree can be reproduced in brick. There is also

Stralsund, Hanseatic town on the Baltic.

the **Church of St Nicholas** (around 1366), with its *Nowgorodfahrer* pews, the **Church of St Mary** (15th century), with a baroque organ, and **St Catherine's Monastery** (13th–14th centuries), home of both the **Culture and History Museum** and the **Maritime Museum**.

From Stralsund's harbour, and from the fishing village of Schaprode on the island of Rügen, boats set sail for the small Baltic island of **Hiddensee** (pop. 1250). Its name is reminiscent of a fairytale, recalling sun, wind and storms, mussels, amber and the unique northern quality of light, the cries of seagulls and the flight of cranes. People who allows themselves to be carried away by the magic of the name will not be disappointed by a visit to the "Söten Länneken" (sweet little place). There he will find no cars, four villages nestling in the landscape and, to the north of the island, 70-metre (230-foot) high cliffs with a lighthouse. This was the summer refuge of the poet Gerhart Hauptmann (1862–1946), but it did not remain his secret for

long, and in the first half of the 20th century the island became a meeting place for great German minds.

Germany's largest island: If this region has a truly spiritual landscape, this has to be on **Rügen**, Germany's largest island. Caspar David Friedrich (1774–1840) immortalised its tall chalk cliffs in 1818. As we approach the end of this century, the stream of traffic across the Rügendamm and the stream of visitors to the **Stubbenkammer** is never-ending. The island of the romantics has now become a holidaymakers' eldorado, and not without reason. The sea encroaches at various points on the 1,000 sq. km (386 sq. mile) island, producing a unique scenery composed of bays, gulfs and peninsulas, with wide beaches and steep cliffs. Inland it is characterised by avenues of limes and chestnuts, broad-leafed woods, fields and small villages. But Rügen does have other landmarks, including the two lighthouses at **Kap Arkona**, **Putbus** (pop. 5,200), the Baden-Baden of the north, and also the narrow-gauge railway "Rasender

The famous chalk cliffs of Rügen.

Roland" (Racing Roland), the conservation village of **Vitt**, and finally the **Granitz Hunting Seat** near Binz.

Returning to the mainland, the Federal Highway 96 leads to the venerable university town of **Greifswald** (pop. 70,000). At first sight it would appear that the town has not changed since the days when Caspar David Friedrich captured it in his paintings. The skyline punctuated by the towers of the churches of **St Mary** (13th–14th century) and **St Nicholas** (13th–14th century), the imposing town houses on the Market Square, and the ruins of the **Eldena Monastery**, the foundation of this town, which was later to join the Hanseatic League, are all still there. However, a closer inspection will lead to the conclusion that the German *Realsozialisten* are not without reproach, having caused some irrevocable destruction of the town which was given up without a struggle in World War II.

Since the 19th century, people have escaped from the capital to take the summer air at **Usedom**, hence the nickname "The Berliners' Bath". The second largest island in Germany is now reviving these traditions, dusting down its guesthouses and hotels.

Resorts abound on Usedom: in the past, they reflected a social hierarchy; **Heringsdorf** (pop. 3,700) attracted a different kind of visitor from **Bansin** (pop. 2,500) or **Zinnowitz** (pop. 4,200). Some catered for the aristocracy and high financiers, while others accommodated officers and civil servants. Common to all are the picturesque beaches and the typical resort architecture with its promenades and villas seeking to outdo each other, with bay windows and turrets, large conservatories and ornate balconies.

At the narrowest point of the island, at **Lüttenort**, there is an unusual museum, the refuge of the painter Otto Niemeyer-Holstein (1896–1984). This consists of a studio full of Baltic landscapes and portraits, a railway luggage van connecting two houses, and a garden abounding in sculptures. A museum of a completely different kind awaits the curious in **Peenemünde**. In the military research establishment here in the 1940s, Wernher von Braun developed the world's first liquid-fuel rockets. In the form of the V-bomb, these brought death and destruction to the south of England.

Towards Berlin: The road continues through Anklam, Pasewalk and Prenzlau, towns which were 80 percent destroyed in World War II, but still entice the visitor with their interesting histories and one or two small remaining treasures. We are now in the region of the **Uckermark**, the historical borderland between Pommern and Mecklenburg, an area characterised by lakes and peaceful waterways. This excellent walking country also takes you through forests with clearings often as small as a single field.

Near Federal Highway 2 there is one of the finest examples of local Gothic brick architecture, the **Chorin Monastery** (13th century). This was founded by Cistercian monks and after the Reformation was used as a cattle shed and plundered for its building materials. The Romantics recognised its significance and the monument was restored.

When Berliners take a trip out into the countryside, the **Märkische Schweiz** (Little Switzerland of the Brandenburg Marches), is one of their favourite destinations, with its beeches and oaks, lakes and heaths, villages where time seems to stand still and houses which have more the character of lowly cottages than opulent farmsteads.

Buckow (pop. 2,500), is the undiscovered capital of the region, and is not entirely unjustified in claiming the title "Pearl of Little Switzerland". The mellow charm of the little town was well-loved by the playwright Bertolt Brecht (1898–1956), and the actress Helene Weigel (1900–17). In 1952 they moved into the "not ignoble" house by the lake, as Brecht himself described it, which is today a museum.

Here he wrote *The Elegies of Buckow* poem cycle, which contains the lines: *Vom Dach steigt Rauch. / Fehlte er / Wie trostlos dann waren / Haus, Bäume und See* ("Smoke rises from the chimney. / If it were not so / How bleak would be / House, trees and lake").

A tranquil corner of Brandenburg's "Little Switzerland".

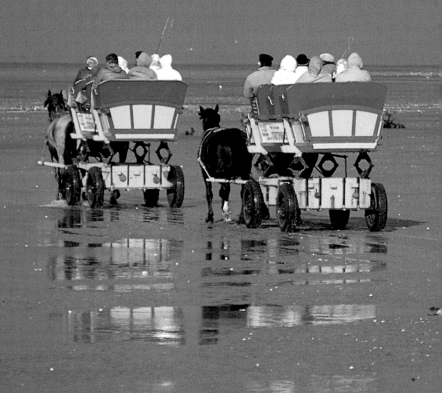

Travel Tips

Your vacation.

Your vacation after losing your hard-earned vacation money.

 Lose your cash and it's lost forever. Lose American Express® Travelers Cheques and get them replaced. They can mean the difference between the vacation of your dreams and your worst nightmare. And, they are accepted like cash worldwide. Available at participating banks, credit unions, AAA offices and American Express Travel locations. *Don't take chances. Take American Express Travelers Cheques.*

do more

Travelers Cheques

Getting Acquainted

The Place

Area: 357,000 sq. km (138,000 sq. miles).
Capital: Berlin.
Population: 81 million.
Language: German plus small minorities speaking Frisian and Sorb.
Religion: 45 percent Protestant; 37 percent Roman Catholic and 18 percent non-religious and other religions.
Time Zone: Central European Time (MEZ), one hour ahead of GMT.
Currency: Deutsche Mark (DM).
Weights and measures: Metric.
Electricity: 220-volts, two-pin plugs.
International Dialling Code: (49).

Climate

Germany lies within the continental climate zone which means it can be very hot in the summer and bitterly cold in the winter. You will, however, experience a slight change in climate when travelling from the northwest to the southeast. In the north around Hamburg and in Schleswig-Holstein and along the Baltic Sea the weather is more oceanic with milder winters and moderately warm summers. Further south the weather becomes more continental with greater variations.

The average winter temperature varies from –1°C (30°F) in Berlin and surroundings to 2°C (37°F) in Cologne; in the mountains it varies between –10°C and –15°C (14°F and 5°F). The hottest month is July when it can be as hot as 35°C to 40°C (95°F to 104°F). If you come in summer you will hardly ever be disappointed by the weather since German summers are mostly hot and dry, even though July is the wettest month with an average rainfall of 750 mm (30 inches) in the north and 620 mm (26 inches) in the Rhine Valley. The average rainfall in Bavaria, for example, is 1,300 mm (52 inches) with Oberstdorf in the lead, with rainfall up to 1,750 mm (70 inches).

The Alps are by far the wettest region, which also has another climatic phenomenon – the Föhn, a warm dry wind which blows down the Alps into South Bavaria and Swabia. The Föhn has two effects: it clears the sky so that one can see the Alps even in Munich, and it also tends to give many people headaches.

The water temperature of the North and Baltic Seas varies significantly between May and September depending on the weather. But even during the summer months the water temperature doesn't rise over 18°C (64°F).

The best time to travel to Germany is from late May to early October. Skiers will find the best conditions between mid-December and March.

Government & Economy

The Federal President is head of state and the government consists of the Chancellor and ministers. Legislation is delivered by the Bundestag (lower house of the German Parliament) which consists of 662 ministers elected every 4 years. New national laws have to be confirmed by the Bundesrat (upper house of the German Parliament) which comprises 68 federal state representatives.

Germany consists of 16 federal states: Baden-Württemberg, Bavaria, Berlin, Brandenburg, Bremen, Hamburg, Hesse, Mecklenburg-Western Pomerania, Lower Saxony, Westphalia, Rhineland-Palatinate, Saarland, Saxony, Saxony-Anhalt, Schleswig-Holstein and Thuringia.

Even though Germany is one of the leading industrial countries of the world it has had to struggle with serious problems since the reunification, including an increase in unemployment. More than half (56 percent) of the population work in the service industries, 40 percent in industrial production and the rest in agriculture. Tourism plays an important role in the service industry.

The People

Over 90 percent of the population are of German origin. The rest are "guest workers" from Turkey, Italy, Greece, Spain, Portugal and other countries.

Geography

The north is flat and characterised by waterways and marshes, while the south embraces the mountainous part of the country. The most impressive mountains are the Harz, the Variscian mountains of the Schwarzwald (Black Forest), the Elbesandstein Mountains straddling the Czech border in Saxony and the magnificent Bavarian Alps with the highest mountain, the Zugspitze (2,963 metres/9,721 ft).

Planning the Trip

What to Wear

Whatever the season, pack both a raincoat and your sunglasses because the weather can be very unpredictable indeed. Even if you come in the hottest summer months (July and August) you are advised to bring one warm sweater or cardigan. And for your trip to the North Sea and the Baltic Sea you should bring a jacket or a raincoat.

In case you forget to bring one, you can "go native" and buy a *Friesennerz* (a yellow rubber raincoat) and a pair of rubber boots quite cheaply. Good walking shoes are necessary for anyone wanting to walk in the Black Forest, the Harz, the Lüneburger Heide, the March of Brandenburg or to go hiking in the Alps. Otherwise, casual clothing is acceptable. Most Germans are very fashion-conscious, especially in big urban areas like Berlin, Hamburg or Munich. Long evening dresses and tuxedos are still worn by some, but many now attend in casual wear.

Entry Regulations

Visas & Passports

A valid passport is the only requirement to enter the Federal Republic. Members of the European Community and Union (EU) only need identity cards. Holders of Australian, Canadian, Japanese, New Zealand, South African and United States passports automatically get three-month permits on crossing the border, but visas are required for longer stays. Visitors from outside the EU are not allowed to enter any form of employment unless they have the necessary work permit.

Customs

Unlimited amounts of foreign and local currency can be brought into the Federal Republic of Germany. Gifts (including food) which are purchased in non-EU countries are duty free up to a limit of DM350. This doesn' t apply to gifts bought in EU countries. Theoretically there is no import limit for alcohol, tobacco, perfume etc. to EU members, however you might have to prove that the imported goods are for your private consumption.

Non EU countries are restricted to the following allowances:
800 cigarettes or 200 cigars;
2 litres of wine and 1 litre of spirit above 22 percent proof;
50 grams of perfume and 250ml of eau de cologne.

The regulations for imports from non-EU countries apply to purchases made in duty-free shops.

VAT

VAT (*Mehrwertsteuer*) in Germany is charged at two rates: 15 percent and 7½ percent. Fourteen percent VAT (MWST) is added to all goods except food, books and newspapers which are taxed at 7½- percent. All services such as the hairdressers add 15 percent VAT. Restaurant menu prices include 15 percent VAT. The tax can be deducted if you buy expensive articles, provided you fill in a sales form when buying the article. Present both the form and article at customs when you return home, have it stamped and send it back to the shop where you bought the article, which will then reimburse you.

Money

The Deutsche Mark (DM) is a decimal currency made up of 100 pfennigs. The coins come in denominations of 1, 2, 5, 10 and 50 pfennigs, and 1, 2, and 5 DM. The notes are in denominations of 5, 10, 20, 50, 100, 200, 500 and 1,000 DM. Money may be changed at any bank and local money changers (*Wechselstuben*) usually found in train stations, airports and in tourist areas. (For opening times, *see Business Hours* below). It is advisable to carry traveller's cheques instead of cash, as the former can be replaced if lost or stolen; remember to keep the cheque numbers separately noted. Although the Germans are not very fond of credit cards you can pay your bills in hotels, restaurants or big department stores with American Express, Diner's Club, Visa or Master Charge cards. You may have problems, however, in smaller towns or villages. Eurocheques can be cashed practically everywhere. The cities are well-equipped with automatic teller machines, many of which take foreign bankcards.

Public Holidays

The majority of public holidays are enjoyed throughout the Federal Republic. But some are restricted to the mainly Catholics states.

New Year's Day: 1 January.
The Magi: 6 January (in Bavaria and Baden-Württemberg).
Good Friday: March or April; refer to German calendar.
Easter Monday: March or April; refer to German calendar.
May Day: 1 May.
Christi Himmelfahrt: (Ascension Day), May or June; refer to German calendar.
Whit Monday: May or June; refer to German calendar.
Fronleichnam: (Corpus Christi) in June; refer to German calendar (only in Catholic states).
Mariä Himmelfahrt: 15 August (in Bavaria and Saarland).
Day of German Unity: 3 October.
All Saints' Day: 1 November in Catholic states.
Buss–und Bettag: (The Day of Prayer and Repentance) in November; refer to German calendar.
Christmas Day: 25 December.
Boxing Day: 26 December.

Getting There

By Air

Most air-routes into the Federal Republic of Germany lead to Frankfurt; Rhine Main Airport, with 50,000 passengers a day, is the second busiest airport in Europe after Heathrow Airport in London, catering for up to 600 international departures and arrivals every day. Germany's other international airports are: Berlin, Bremen, Düsseldorf, Hamburg, Hanover, Cologne, Munich, Nuremberg, Saarbrücken. Münster/ Osnabrück, Dresden and Stuttgart.

Lufthansa, the German national airline, serves most of the world as well as operating a domestic service. If you book in advance, you may take advantage of special APEX fares and thereby save up to 40 percent on domestic and international flights. The main domestic airports are interconnected by regular Aero Lloyd, Deutsche BA and Lufthansa services.

All airports have regular bus and rail connections to the city centres. Official taxis are ivory-coloured Mercedes or BMWs with a black "TAXI" sign on the roof.

By Sea

There are ferry connections from northern Germany (Hamburg and Rotterdam) with Scandinavia and the UK (Scandinavian Seaways sailings on the Harwich – Hamburg route). The East German port of Warnemünde has sailings to Trelleborg in Sweden.

By Train

From northern Europe, the best train connections to the north of Germany are from the Hook of Holland in the Netherlands. Trains leave in the direction of Venlo and Emmerich.

The south of Germany is better reached via Ostend, from where trains go to Aachen and Cologne, connecting with Euro-City and Inter-City trains to the southern federal states. From the UK, ferry links with the Hook of Holland are via Harwich and with Ostend via Dover.

Practical Tips

Business Hours

Most shops are open 9am–6.30pm Monday to Friday and 8 or 9am until 4pm on Saturday. There are late opening hours on Thursday until 8.30pm and on the first Saturday of the month when shops are generally open until 4pm in summer and 6pm in winter. Shops are closed on Sunday. Different opening times apply to smaller shops and those in rural areas. However small shops such as bakeries, fruit and vegetable shops and butcher's shops open as early as 7am, close for 2½ hours at about noon, re-open at around 3pm and remain open until 6.30pm in the evening. Shops located in the railway stations and airports usually have late shopping hours (some are open until midnight). Business hours are usually 8am–5.30pm. Government offices are open to the public in the morning 8am to noon.

Banking hours are Monday to Friday 8.30am–1pm and 2.30pm–4pm. In most towns, banks are open until 5.30pm on Thursday, with slight variations in the different federal states.

Media

Newspapers & Magazines

The press in the Federal Republic is diverse. The range extends the political spectrum from conservative newspapers like the *Frankfurter Allgemeine Zeitung*, socialist newspapers like the *TAZ* (*Tageszeitung*) highbrow papers like the *Süddeutsche Zeitung*, to the popular press, the most infamous being the *Bildzeitung*. For information on cinema, theatre, exhibitions and concerts, consult any local paper. Foreign newspapers and magazines are available in every town. There are also international bookshops located at railway stations, airports and city centres.

Radio & Television

Radio and television broadcasting in Germany is under public control. There are two national TV stations, the ARD and ZDF, with the ARD having local stations in each state. The ARD also maintains eleven radio stations: NDR, RB, SFB, WDR, HR, SWF, MDR, ORD, SDR, SR and BR. Most of the large regional radio stations produce current traffic reports every half hour. For those who speak or understand German the main news programmes on TV are *Heute* at 7pm (ZDF), and Tag*esschau* at 8pm (ARD). In addition to the national stations, there are a host of privately-run cable and satellite channels.

Postal Services

The post offices (*Postamt*) are usually open from 8am–6pm, with smaller ones closing at noon for lunch. You can have your mail sent care of an individual main post office provided it is marked "poste restante". Your mail will be left at the counter identified by the words *Postlagernde Sendungen*.

Local post boxes (*Briefkasten*) are emptied at least twice a day (morning and evening); those designated with a red point are emptied more often. On Saturday, however, there is only one service. For sending telegrams you have either to dial 1131 on a private telephone or go to the post office.

Telephone

The cost of a single local call costs 20 Pfennigs. For long distance calls you can also dial direct from most of the yellow public phone boxes but remember to have enough 1 and 5 Mark pieces or buy a telephone card, available either in DM12 or DM50 denominations. The majority of public telephone boxes have a telephone card facility. Instead of dialling direct you can go to a post office where an operator will make the connection. Dial 01188 for national directory enquiries and 00118 for international directory enquiries.

Most towns in Germany have their own dialling code, which are listed in the telephone book. Phone calls from abroad should use the country code, 49, and omit- the 0 in the domestic regional code.

Tourist Information

Anywhere in Germany where you find tourists, you should find a tourist authority or information office (marked with an "i"). Write to the office of your destination for any details you require.

Regional Offices

BADEN-WÜRTTEMBERG

Landesfremdenverkehrsverband, Baden-Württemberg e.V., Postfach 102951, 70025 Stuttgart, tel: (0711) 238580. **Fremdenverkehrsverband**, Bodensee Oberschwaben e.V., Schützenstr. 8, 78462 Konstanz, tel: (07531) 90940, fax: 909494. **Touristikverband**, Neckarland-Schwaben e.V., Lohtorstr. 21, 74072 Heilbronn, tel: (07131) 629061. **Fremdenverkehrsverband**, Schwarzwald e.V., Postfach 1660, 79016 Freiburg i.Br., tel: (0761) 31317, fax: 36021.

BAVARIA

Landesfremdenverkehrsverband, Bayern e.V., Postfach 220440, 80545 Munich, tel: (089) 2123970. **Tourismusverband**, Allgäu/Bayerisch Schwaben e.V., Postfach 102529, 86015 Augsburg, tel: (08362) 7077/7078, fax: 39181. **Fremdenverkehrsverband**, Franken e.V., Postfach 269, 90247 Nürnberg, tel: (0911) 264202. **Fremdenverkehrsverband**, Munich-Oberbayern e.V., Postfach 600320, 81203 Munich, tel: (089) 597347. **Fremdenverkehrsverband**, Ostbayern e.V., Landshuter Str. 13, 83047 Regensburg, tel: (0941) 560260.

BERLIN

Berlin Tourismus Marketing GmbH, Karlsbad 11, 10785 Berlin, tel: (030) 2647480, fax: 2647489.

BRANDENBURG

Landesfremdenverkehrsverband, Brandenburg e.V., Schlaatzweg 1, 14473 Potsdam, tel: (0331) 275280, fax: 2752810

BREMEN

Verkehrsverein der Freien Hansestadt Bremen, Postfach 100747, 28007 Bremen, tel: (0421) 308000/19433, fax: 3080030.

HAMBURG

Tourismus-Zentrale Hamburg GmbH, Postfach 102249, 20015 Hamburg, tel: (040) 30051-0.

HESSE

Arbeitsgemeinschaft Deutsche Märchenstrasse, Königsplatz 53, 34117 Kassel, tel: (0561) 707707, fax: 7077200.
Hessischer Fremdenverkehrsverband e.V., Abraham-Lincoln-Str. 38–42, 651-89 Wiesbaden, tel: (0611) 77880-0.

MECKLENBURG -WESTERN POMERANIA

Landesfremdenverkehrsverband, Mecklenburg-Vorpommern e. V., Platz der Freundschaft 1, 18059 Rostock, tel: (0381) 448426, fax: 448423.

LOWER SAXONY

Harzer Verkehrsverband e.V., Postfach 1669, 38606 Goslar, tel: (05321) 20031.
Fremdenverkehrsverband, Lüneburger Heide e.V, Postfach 2160, 21311 Lüneburg, tel: (04131) 52063.
Fremdenverkehrsverband, Nordsee-Niedersachsen-Bremen e.V., Postfach 1820, 26140 Oldenburg, tel: (0441) 92171-0.
Fremdenverkehrsverband, Weserbergland-Mittelweser e.V., Postfach 100-339, 31753 Hameln, tel: (05151) 24566.

WESTPHALIA

Landesfremdenverkehrsverband, Rheinland e.V., Postfach 200861, 53138 Bonn, tel: (0228) 362922, fax: 363929,.
Landesverkehrsverband, Westfalen e.V., Friedensplatz 3, 44135 Dortmund, tel: (0231) 524508.

RHINELAND-PALATINATE

Fremdenverkehrs-und Heilbäderverband, Rheinland-Pfalz e.V., Postfach 1420, 56014 Koblenz, tel: (0261) 915200.
Mosellandtouristik GmbH, Postfach 1310, 54463 Bernkastel-Kues, tel: (06531) 209192, fax: 2093, home address: Gestade 12-14, 54470 Bernkastel-Kues.

SAARLAND

Fremdenverkehrsverband, Saarland e.V, Stuttgarter Str. 53, 66111 Saarbrücken, tel: (0681) 35376, fax: 35841.

SAXONY

Landesfremdenverkehrsverband, Sachsen e.V., Friedrichstr. 24, 01067 Dresden, tel: (0351) 4969703.

SAXONY-ANHALT

Tourismusverband, Sachsen-Anhalt e.V., Grosse Diesdorfer Str. 12, 39108 Magdeburg, tel: (0391) 7384300, fax: 7384302

SCHLESWIG-HOLSTEIN

Fremdenverkehrsverband, Schleswig-Holstein e.V., Niemannsweg 31, 241-05 Kiel, tel: (0431) 560025.

THURINGIA

Landesfremdenverkehrsverband, Thüringen e.V., Postfach 219, 99005 Erfurt, tel: (0361) 5402212.

Local Offices

BADEN-BADEN

Tourist-Information, Augustaplatz 8, 76530 Baden-Baden, tel: (07221) 275200.

BERLIN

Berlin Tourismus Marketing GmbH, Karlsbad 11, 19785 Berlin, tel: (030) 2647480, fax: 2647 4899.

BONN

Tourist-Information, Rathausgasse 5–7, 53111 Bonn, tel: (0228) 773920/19433.

BRANDENBURG

Brandenburg-Information, Hauptstr. 51, 14776 Brandenburg, tel: (03381) 223743.

BREMEN

Verkehrsverein, Hillmannplatz 6, 28195 Bremen, tel: (0421) 308000.

CHEMNITZ

Chemnitz-Information, Stadthalle Chemnitz, Rathausstr. 1, 09009 Chemnitz, tel: (0371) 4508750, fax: 4508 7725.

COBURG

Tourist-Information, Herrngasse 4/Markt, 96450 Coburg, tel: (09561) 74180, fax: 741829.

DESSAU

Dessau-Information, Postfach 14 25, 06813 Dessau, tel: (0340) 214804, fax: 213540, internet: http://www.dessau.de/

DRESDEN

Dresden-Werbung and Tourismus GmbH, Goetheallee 18, 01309 Dresden, tel: (0351) 4919 2123, fax: 35247; Neustädter Markt, 01097 Dresden, tel: 53539.

DÜSSELDORF

Verkehrsverein, Konrad-Adenauer-Platz, 40210 Düsseldorf, tel: (0211) 172020, fax: 161071; Heinrich-Heine-Allee 24, 40213 Düsseldorf, tel: (0211) 8992346.

ERLANGEN

Verkehrsverein, Rathausplatz 1, 91052 Erlangen, tel: 0 91 31/ 2 50 74.

ESSEN

Fremdenverkehrsamt, Rathaus, Porscheplatz, 45121 Essen, tel: 02 01/88-1 53 17, fax: 88-1 50 05.

FRANKFURT AM MAIN

Verkehrsamt, Hauptbahnhof, 60329 Frankfurt/M., tel: 0 69/21 23 88 49-51; Römerberg 27, 60311 Frankfurt/M., tel: 0 69/21 23 87 08/09

FRANKFURT AN DER ODER

Tourist-Information, Karl-Marx-Str. 8a, 15230, Frankfurt/O., tel: 03 35/32 52 1, fax: 2 25 65.

FREIBERG

Freiberg-Information, Burgstr. 1, 09599 Freiberg, tel: 0 37 31/2 36 02.

FREIBURG/BREISGAU

Freiburg-Information, Rotteckring 14, 79098 Freiburg im Breisgau, tel: 07 61/3 68 90 90.

HAMBURG

Tourismuszentrale, Burchardstraße 14, 20095 Hamburg, tel: 0 40/30 05 10.
Tourist-Information, Hauptbahnhof, Hauptausgang Kirchenallee, 20099 Hamburg, tel: 0 40/30 05 12 30.
Hanseviertel, Eingang Poststr., 20354 Hamburg, tel: 30 05 12 20; Hafen, St.-Pauli-Landungsbrücken, 20359 Hamburg, tel: 30 05 12 00; Flughafen, Terminal 4, Fuhlsbüttel, tel: 30 05 12 40.

HAMELN

Tourist-Information, Deisterallee 3, 31785 Hameln, tel: 0 51 51/ 20 26 17.

HANOVER

Hanover-Information, Ernst-August-Platz 2, 30159 Hanover, tel: 05 11/ 30 14 22.

HEIDELBERG

Verkehrsverein, Hauptbahnhof, 69115 Heidelberg, tel: 0 61 21/ 2 13 41.

JENA

Fremdenverkehrsamt, Jena-Information, Löbderstr. 9, 07743 Jena, tel: 0 36 41/58 63-0, fax: 58 63 22; Internet: http://www.uni-jena.de/jena/ jenaallg.html.

KOBLENZ

Touristik- und Congressamt, Verkehrspavillon, 56020 Koblenz, tel: 02 61/ 3 13 04.

COLOGNE

Verkehrsamt, Unter Fettenhennen 19, 50667 Köln, tel: 02 21/72 21 33 45.

LEIPZIG

Leipzig Tourist Service e. V., Sachsenplatz 1, 04109 Leipzig, tel: 03 41/71 04-2 60/-2 65, fax: 71 04-2 71/-2 76; Flughafen Leipzig-Halle, tel: 03 41/ 2 24 18 47.

MUNICH

Fremdenverkehrsamt, Hauptbahnhof, 80335 München, tel: 0 89/2 33 03 00; Stadtinfo, Stachus-Ladengeschoss, 80335 München, tel: 2 33 82 42.

NUREMBERG

Tourist-Information, Frauentorgraben 3, 90443 Nürnberg, tel: 09 11/23 36-0, fax: 23 36-1 66.

POTSDAM

Potsdam-Information, Friedrich-Ebert-Str. 5, 14467 Potsdam, tel: 03 31/27 55 80, fax: 29 30 12.

ROSTOCK

Rostock-Information, Schnickmannstr. 13/14, 18055 Rostock, tel: 03 81/4 92 52 60 or 4 59 08 60.

SCHLESWIG

Tourist-Information, Plessenstr. 7, 24837 Schleswig, tel: 0 46 21/8 14-2 26.

STUTTGART

Touristik-Zentrum, Königstr. 1a, Hauptbahnhof, 70173 Stuttgart, tel: 07 11/22 28-2 40 or 2 41.
Stuttgart Marketing GmbH, Lautenschlagerstr. 3, 70173 Stuttgart, tel: 07 11/22 28-2 40 or 2 41.

WEIMAR

Weimar Information, Markt 10, 99421 Weimar, tel: 0 36 43/2 40 00, fax: 6 12 40.

Embassies & Consulates

Australia: Godesberger Allee 105–107, 53175 Bonn, tel: (0228) 81030, fax: 376268.
Canada: Friedrich-Wilhelm-Strasse 18, 53113 Bonn, tel: (0228) 9680, fax: 230857.
Ireland: Godesberger Allee 119, 53175 Bonn, tel: (0228) 376937-9, fax: 373500.
New Zealand: Bundeskanzlerplatz 2-10, 53113 Bonn, tel: (0228) 228070, fax: 221687.
Netherlands: Strässchensweg 10, 53113 Bonn, tel: (0228) 53050, fax: 238621.
South Africa: Auf der Hostert 3, 53173 Bonn, tel: (0228) 82010, fax: 8201148.
United Kingdom: Friedrich-Ebert-Allee 77, 53113 Bonn, tel: (0228) 9167-0, fax: 9167200.
United States of America: Deichmanns Aue 29, 53179 Bonn, tel: (0228) 3391, fax: 3392663.

Emergencies

Medical Services

The Federal Republic has a national health system whereby doctors and hospital fees are covered by insurance and only a token fee has to be paid for medication. Treatment and medication is also free of charge for EU members and certain other nationalities. All other foreign nationals should ensure that they have adequate health insurance before they leave their home country as medical fees are expensive in Germany.

People using special medication

should either bring a sufficient supply or a prescription from their own doctor. If you have to consult a doctor, contact your consulate for a list of English-speaking doctors.

In the event of an accident, dial **110** for the police, **112** for the fire brigade or **115** for an ambulance or call the Rotes Kreuz (Red Cross). All accidents resulting in personal injury must be reported to the police.

Pharmacies (Apotheken) are normally open 8am–6.30pm. Every pharmacy carries a list of neighbouring pharmacies which are open during the night and on the weekend.

Getting Around

Orientation

When driving in Germany observe the following rules: traffic travels on the right with oncoming traffic on your left. Main road traffic has the right of way. At the junctions of two main roads or two minor roads, traffic coming from the right has priority unless otherwise indicated. Traffic signs follow international standards. The general speed limit (*Geschwindigkeitsbeschränkung*) in towns and villages is 50 kph (31 mph) and on open roads it is 100 kph (62 mph). The recommended speed limit on motorways (*autobahnen*) is 130 kph (80 mph). This is changing, however. Recently the government has been promoting a general speed limit of 100 kph (62 mph) on motorways and 80 kph (50 mph) on open roads due to the rapid increase in the number of dying trees and forests. Vehicles towing trailers are limited to 80 kph (50 mph) on all roads outside towns and villages. Vehicles with trailers and vehicles where rear visibility is impaired due to bulky loads etc must fit additional outside mirrors to both sides of the car.

Rear and front seat safety belts must be worn while travelling. Violation of this results in a hefty fine. Children under 12 years of age are not allowed to sit in the front if the car is fitted with rear seats, unless special safety devices for children are fitted.

Spiked tyres are prohibited. Driving with dipped headlights is obligatory in darkness, fog, heavy rain and falling snow. Driving on parking lights alone is prohibited. Dipped headlights are obligatory for motor-cycles at all times. Crash helmets are compulsory for the drivers and pillion-riders of motorcycles capable of a maximum speed of more than 25 kph (15 mph).

Before setting out make sure you have a first-aid kit and a warning triangle in your car. Should you have an accident, switch on your hazard lights and put up the warning triangle at a safe distance from the scene of the accident. Depending on the severity of the damage, you should summon the police. Always ring the police when an accident results in personal injury. Ask the other party for the name of their insurance company and insurance policy number, and take note of possible witnesses. Do not forget to contact your own insurance company immediately.

The maximum permitted blood alcohol level is 80 mg/100 ml. Stopping is prohibited within 100 metres (328 ft) before or after stop lines (other than at the lines themselves), pedestrian crossings, crossroads and junctions. Parking is prohibited on trunk roads.

By Car

Germany is renowned for its motorways, the *autobahnen*. Altogether there are approximately 13,600 km (8,500 miles) of motorways throughout the Republic, making it one of the densest in the world. The *autobahnen* are marked with an "A" on blue signs while the regional roads are marked with a "B" on yellow signs. There are rest stops (*Raststätten*) every 30–50 km (20–30 miles) along the *autobahnen*. Here you may take refreshments and make use of the toilet facilities. Often you will also find hotels at these rest stops. In addition, there are small rest stops every 4–5 km (2½–3 miles) offering the opportunity to stretch your legs.

Despite many excellent roads, traffic congestion is the order of the day during the holiday season (from the end of June to the middle of September). It is therefore advisable to check traffic conditions on the local radio stations (*Traffic Broadcast/Verkehrsfunk*). The respective wavelengths (VHR) are indicated on the blue square road signs along the motorways and roads. Should you get held up by traffic or some other obstacle, use the diversions indicated by blue signs with the letter "U" (*Umleitung*) and a number referring to the diverting road.

If your car breaks down on the motorway you can call the breakdown services. Use the orange telephones located at the roadside. Black triangles on the posts along the side of the motorway indicate the direction of the next telephone.

The ADAC (Allgemeiner Deutscher Automobil Club) provides road assistance free of charge provided the damage can be repaired within half an hour. Should it take longer, you will have to pay for the repair as well as the cost of all spare parts needed. Road assistance is also free of charge and all recovery costs will be refunded if you have an *Auslandsschutzbrief* (insurance certificate). In fact, you should take out the insurance with your national automobile association before you leave home. The other automobile clubs charge for spare parts, fuel and towing.

Cars can be rented (*Autovermietung*) practically everywhere. International companies with offices throughout Germany are Hertz, InterRent, Avis, Europcar, etc. For local car rentals inquire at your hotel's tourist information desk. If you use the services of an international company such as InterRent and you come from an English speaking country, probably all that is needed is your national driver's licence and cash, credit card or cheque deposit. Smaller companies may insist on an international driver's licence.

Nationwide breakdown services of the Autoclubs:
ACE: (01802) 343 536
ADAC: (01802) 222222
AvD: (0130) 9909.

Further important telephone numbers:
Police/emergency: 110
Fire brigade: 112
Accident recovery: 115.

Nationwide car reservations can be made under the following telephone numbers:
Avis: (0180) 555 77
Hertz: (0180) 533 3535
Interrent: (0130) 22 11.

Cycling

Many book and bicycle shops including the German bicycle club (Allgemeiner Deutscher Fahrrad-Club, Postfach 107747, 28077 Bremen, tel: (0421) 346290, fax: 346250) offer a variety of books and maps for cycling holidays. The Bund Deutscher Radfahrer (Association of German Cyclists), Otto-Fleck-Schneise 4, 60528 Frankfurt, tel: (069) 9678000, fax: 96780080, has cycling guides for special regions on offer, whereas RV Verlag publishes cycling and walking maps entitled *Regio Concept*.

The alternative to taking your own bicycle is the railway service *Fahrrad am Bahnhof* (bicycle at the station) which offers bicycle hire at railway stations. It costs between DM6 and DM25 per day to hire a bicycle, including insurance, with a reduction for rail ticket holders. Brochures available locally provide suggested tours to and from certain stations.

Note: this service is not available on all types of train.

A sophisticated system of well-kept and signposted regional and long distance walking routes such as the Rennsteig in the forest of Thuringia make walking one of the main pastimes in Germany. Many round trips (*Rundwanderwege*) lead through nature resorts.

Some long distance walks are organised by clubs and associations (Youth Hostel Association), tourist offices or tour operators (Ameropa). Further information can be obtained from:
Deutsches Jugendherbergswerk, Bismarckstr. 8, 32756 Detmold 1, tel: (05231) 74010, fax: 740149.
Touristenverein, "Die Naturfreunde", Bundesgruppe Deutschland e.V., Grossglocknerstr. 28, 70327 Stuttgart, tel: (0711) 481076, fax: 3369144.
Deutscher Alpenverein, Praterinsel 5, 80538 Munich, tel: (089) 294940, fax: 226054.

A widespread network of public transport systems is available in every large city. Those cities with a population of 100,000 and more offer an efficient bus system that runs freqently and usually very punctually. You can buy the bus tickets from the driver or at automats available in the bus or at the bus stop. In large cities like Berlin, Hamburg, Cologne, Munich, Frankfurt and Stuttgart, the bus lines are integrated with the underground (U-Bahn) the tram, and the over-ground (S-Bahn) into one large public transport system. The same ticket may be used for all four means of transport.

Trams (Strassenbahn) run on rails throughout the cities. The speed at which they travel allows for some gentle sightseeing. Look out for yellow signs with a green "H" at bus and tram stops; they list the time schedules. Underground (U-Bahn) stations are usually identified by a sign showing a white "U" on a blue background. Every station has detailed route maps displayed on the wall. The S-Bahn will transport you at about the same speed as the U-Bahn. The S-Bahns are suburban trains that travel to the suburbs of the larger cities, and within the city they travel mostly underground. For people living in the suburbs it is a fast way of getting into the city. S-Bahn stations are identified by a white "S" on a green background. The price of tickets varies from town to town. For more detailed information contact the respective information office in each town or city.

Taxis are the most expensive form of transport available. You pay a basic flat rate plus a charge per kilometre. A surcharge might be added for luggage. There are special taxi stands in every large town, but you can aso call for them. (Usually the telephone numbers are listed on the first page of the telephone directory.) In some towns there are also minicabs and call cars which are cheaper and which also have ample space for luggage.

By Train

The Deutsche Bahn AG (DB) provides the most comprehensive transport system in Germany. Their network is expanding steadily. Below is list of services available:

Long distance services: The **Inter-City trains** (IC) which run an hourly service, offer a fast and comfortable connection between two major cities. The ultra-modern **InterCityExpress** trains (ICE) also offer a high-speed service between major cities. The routes listed below run hourly. It is advisable to make seat reservations, and at least 24-hours in advance on the IC services, especially at the weekend, school, and bank holidays. A reservation made without purchase of a ticket costs DM9 but both arranged in a single transaction reduces the supplement to DM3.

ROUTES

- Berlin-Magdeburg-Kassel-Frankfurt-Stuttgart-Munich
- Hamburg-Hannover-Kassel-Würtzburg-Munich
- Hamburg-Hannover-Kassel-Frankfurt-Karlsruhe-Zürich
- Hamburg-Hannover-Kassel-Frankfurt-Darmstadt-Stuttgart
- Bremen-Hannover-Frankfurt

Approximate duration: Munich-Frankfurt 3 hrs, Frankfurt-Hannover 3 hrs, Munich-Hamburg 5 hrs.

Euro-City (EC) trains offer a high-standard connection between major European towns and cities.

There are a number of trains which accommodate overnight travel: The **D-Zug** is a high-speed night train which connects with European cities, as does the **EuroNight** (EN) train, which also offers a high standard of international travel requiring a supplementary charge for sleepers. The **InterCityNight** (ICN) services are 'hotel' trains and are considered good value for money particularly on the Munich–Berlin, Bonn–Berlin and Munich–Hamburg lines. Another good value service is offered on the Dortmund–Vienna, Hamburg–Zurich and Berlin–Zurich lines on the modern **CityNightLine** (CNL) trains.

Local Services: The **Regional-Express** (RE) is a fast train serving the city centres, the **RegionalBahn** (RB) offers a comprehensive local shuttle service and the **StadtExpress** (SE) provides a suburban link, as does the **S-Bahn** (*see page 327*).

The German railways are not only efficient, they also have lots of attractive fare structures, though these are subject to regular revision. The **Bahn Card** permits half-price travel for a whole year for those over 27 years old. Similar passes are available for young people travelling alone and students, though conditions for travel are imposed. The cheapest but slowest and probably most crowded way to get around is by buying a **Wochenendticket** (weekend ticket) for DM35. This allows unrestricted travel on certain trains within Germany on the weekend. Check at any local railway station for further details about fare structures, supplements, reservations and time tables.

A **RailRoad** and **RailAir** link in the form of a car hire service is available to transport you to your destination rail station or airport. A **motorail** service is the best but more expensive method of travel, which provides a comfortable and stress-free way of making your connections, particularly over longer distances. For further information about these services, including hire services, despatch and parking options, call: (0180) 3319419.

German Rail offices abroad

Great Britain: German Rail, Deutsche Bahn AG, Suite 4, 23 Oakhill Grove, Surbiton, Surrey KT6 6DU, tel: (01891) 887755.

United States: German Rail/DER Tours, 11933 Wilshire Boulevard, Los Angeles, CA 90025, tel: (310) 4794140, fax: 4792239.

Canada: German Rail/DER Tours, 904 The East Mall, Etortcoke ONT. M93 6K2, tel: (416) 6951209, fax: 6951210.

Republic of South Africa: World Travel Agency (PTY) Ltd, 13, floor African Life Centre, 111 Commissioner Str, PO Box 4568, Johannesburg 2000, tel: (011) 29-7234.

Australia: Thomas Cook Ltd, Ground Floor, 257 Collins Street, Melbourne VIC 3000, tel: (03) 6502442, fax: 6507050.

By Bus

The so-called *Europabusse* are a cheap way of travelling between cities, many departing from main railway stations, and the *Bahnbusse* (buses owned by the German railway) operate services connecting the smaller villages in the countryside. In remote areas this is usually the only form of public transport.

Germany's rail network

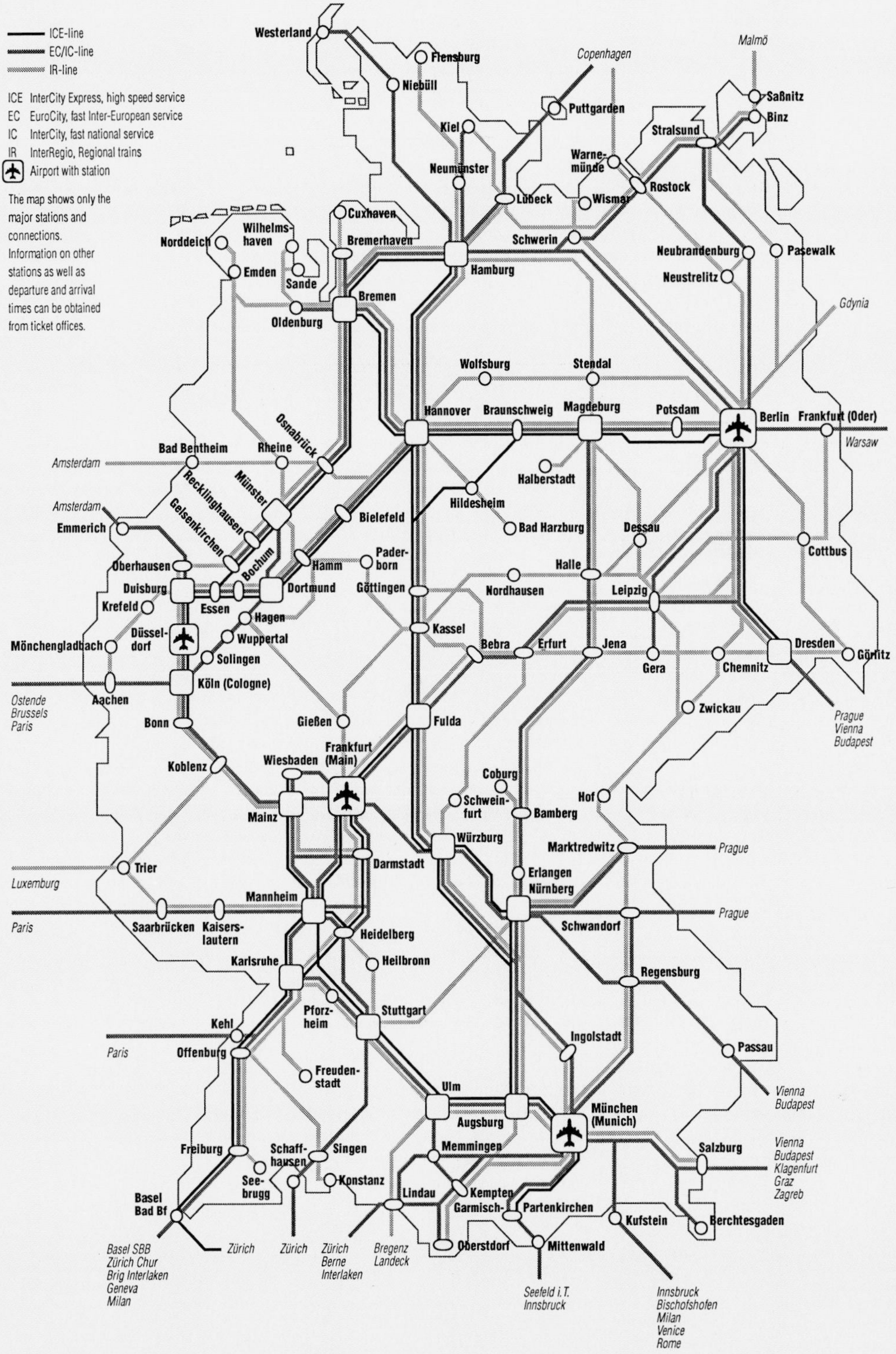

ICE-line
EC/IC-line
IR-line

ICE   InterCity Express, high speed service
EC   EuroCity, fast Inter-European service
IC   InterCity, fast national service
IR   InterRegio, Regional trains
✈   Airport with station

The map shows only the
major stations and
connections.
Information on other
stations as well as
departure and arrival
times can be obtained
from ticket offices.

Westerland
Flensburg
Niebüll
Kiel
Puttgarden
Copenhagen
Malmö
Saßnitz
Binz
Stralsund
Neumünster
Warne-münde
Lübeck
Wismar
Rostock
Cuxhaven
Bremerhaven
Schwerin
Neubrandenburg
Pasewalk
Neustrelitz
Wilhelms-haven
Norddeich
Emden
Sande
Hamburg
Gdynia
Bremen
Oldenburg
Wolfsburg
Stendal
Hannover
Braunschweig
Magdeburg
Potsdam
Berlin
Frankfurt (Oder)
Warsaw
Osnabrück
Bad Bentheim
Rheine
Amsterdam
Halberstadt
Münster
Recklinghausen
Bielefeld
Hildesheim
Bad Harzburg
Dessau
Cottbus
Amsterdam
Emmerich
Gelsenkirchen
Pader-born
Halle
Göttingen
Nordhausen
Leipzig
Oberhausen
Bochum
Hamm
Dortmund
Duisburg
Krefeld
Essen
Hagen
Kassel
Mönchengladbach
Düssel-dorf
Wuppertal
Bebra
Erfurt
Jena
Dresden
Görlitz
Köln (Cologne)
Solingen
Gera
Chemnitz
Aachen
Bonn
Gießen
Fulda
Zwickau
Ostende
Brussels
Paris
Prague
Vienna
Budapest
Koblenz
Wiesbaden
Frankfurt (Main)
Coburg
Hof
Mainz
Schwein-furt
Bamberg
Trier
Würzburg
Marktredwitz
Prague
Luxemburg
Darmstadt
Erlangen
Nürnberg
Paris
Mannheim
Prague
Saarbrücken
Kaisers-lautern
Heidelberg
Schwandorf
Karlsruhe
Heilbronn
Regensburg
Pforzheim
Stuttgart
Kehl
Ingolstadt
Passau
Paris
Offenburg
Freuden-stadt
Ulm
Vienna
Budapest
Augsburg
München (Munich)
Vienna
Budapest
Klagenfurt
Graz
Zagreb
Salzburg
Freiburg
Schaff-hausen
Singen
Memmingen
Basel
Bad Bf
See-brugg
Konstanz
Lindau
Kempten
Garmisch-
Partenkirchen
Kufstein
Berchtesgaden
Basel SBB
Zürich Chur
Brig Interlaken
Geneva
Milan
Zürich
Zürich
Zürich
Berne
Interlaken
Bregenz
Landeck
Oberstdorf
Mittenwald
Seefeld i. T.
Innsbruck
Innsbruck
Bischofshofen
Milan
Venice
Rome

329

Where to Stay

Travellers should have no trouble finding suitable accommodation anywhere. It may not be as luxurious or inexpensive as you would wish, but even in the smallest village there is always some room available. In the peak season (June–August) it is advisable to book in advance if you are visiting a popular place. You may do so through the **Allgemeine Deutsche Zimmerreservierung**, Corneliusst 34, 60325 Frankfurt, tel: (069) 740767, fax: 751056.

Hotels

In the following list you will find different types of accommodation arranged according to region and price:

LL stands for Deluxe (over DM250).
L stands for Luxury (from DM180).
M stands for Moderate (between DM100 and DM179).
E stands for economy (less than DM100).

All prices quoted are for one double room for one night, including breakfast, unless otherwise stated.

The accommodation list is arranged so that it follows the order of the chapters found in the *Places* section of the book.

Berlin

Alsterhof Ringhotel, Augsburger Strasse 5, tel: (030) 212420, fax: 2183949. The large and central hotel close to the "Ku-Damm" features a German restaurant, swimming pool, sauna, solarium, massage and an underground car park. (L–LL)
Hotel Hamburg Ringhotel, Landgrafenstrasse 4, tel: (030) 264770, fax: 2629394. 240 rooms. This modern building is situated close to a shopping centre and only a few minutes' walk from the "Tiergarten" park and the "Gedächtniskirche". It offers a bar and an international restaurant. Dogs welcome. (L–LL)

Meineke, Meinekestrasse 10, tel: (030) 882811, fax: 8825716. Small hotel with 60 rooms in a quiet side street near the "Ku-Damm". 3-bed rooms available. (M–L)
Maritim Grand Hotel, Friedrichstrasse 158, tel: (030) 23270, fax: 2327-3362. This establishment puts the "grand" back into grand hotels. Over 350 elegant and extremely comfortable rooms close to erstwhile Checkpoint Charlie. With fitness club, hairdressing services, pool, sauna and solarium. Don't miss the monumental staircase, the "Peacock Bar", or any of the six exceptional restaurants in the hotel. Multi-storey car park. (LL)
Hotel Unter den Linden, Unter den Linden 14, tel: (030) 238110, fax: 2381100. Modern hotel with over 400 bedrooms on this famous street close to many interesting museums. It features a bar, a café and a restaurant with local cuisine. (M–L)

Berlin to the Harz Mountains

BRANDENBURG
Sorat Hotel, Aldstädter Markt 1, tel: (03381) 5970, fax: 597444. Hotel with 88 rooms in the centre of town. (M–L)

MAGDEBURG
Maritim Hotel, Otto-von-Guericke-Strasse, tel: (0391) 59490, fax: 4949900. Over 500 rooms surrounded by a green landscape in the centre of town. Restaurants, nightclub, sauna. (LL)

Halle, Merseburg & Leipzig

HALLE
Hotel Schweizer Hof, Waisenhausaing 15, tel: (0345) 2026392, fax: 503-068. Centrally located hotel with restaurants and conference facilities. (M)

LEIPZIG
Leipziger Hof, Hedwigstrasse 3, tel: (0341) 69740, fax: 6974150. Hotel with 44 rooms. Located in the town centre, with a restaurant, fitness room, sauna and whirlpool for guests. (L-LL)

WITTENBERG
Goldener Adler, Markt 7, tel: (0451) 2053. This small hotel has rooms with basic facilities. (E)

ROSTOCK
Warnow, Lange Strasse 40, tel: (0381) 45970, fax: 4597800. Tower block with 338 rooms and balconies, surrounded by lawn. The six restaurants offer a regional menu. Other facilities include the Café Riga, a sun terrace, bar, nightclub and souvenir shop. (M–LL)

STRALSUND
Hotel Baltic, Leninplatz 2-3, tel: (0821) 5381. 70-year-old hotel with 40 rooms, next to the station. 3-bed rooms available. The restaurant has a good fish menu. Sea museum located close by. (M)

GREIFSWALD
Boddenhus, Karl-Liebknecht-Ring 1, tel: (03834) 898107, fax: 3105. New building with 80 rooms and bathrooms en suite on the outskirts of town. Tennis Courts, solarium and sauna. (M)

Dresden
Mercure Newa, St Petersburge Strasse 34, tel: (0351) 48140, fax: 4955137. Large hotel with 307 rooms in the middle of a green lawn opposite the station. Several popular restaurants serve national and international cuisine. Sauna and flower shop. From the upper floors you have a superb view over the city. (M–L)
Hotel Ibis, Prager Strasse, tel: (051) 48560. A large hotel with 303 rooms, located near the station. Restaurant with roof garden, sauna. (M–L)
Dresdner Hilton, An der Frauenkirche, tel: (0351) 86420, fax: 8642725. Architecturally interesting five-star hotel in the baroque quarter of Dresden. 327 elegant rooms, 15 restaurants and cafés. The partial glass roof offers a view over the Elbe. Fitness centre, sauna, swimming pool, solarium, underground car park. (LL)

GERA
Stadthotel "Schillerhöhe", Schillerstrasse 9, tel: (0365) 839880, fax: 8398880. 30 rooms, television suite, studios with balcony, garages, disabled access, lift. (L-LL)

BAUTZEN
Pension Lausitz, Bahnhofstrasse 16, tel: (03591) 37810, fax: 47186. Centrally located accommodation, dogs welcome. (M)

Spree Hotel, An den Steinbrüchen 4, tel: (03591) 21300, fax: 213010. Offers group and weekend discounts. 15 additional apartments are also owned by the hotel. Access for the physically disabled. (L)

PIRNA

Hotel Elbparadies, Inh. Familie Richter, Oberposta 2, tel/fax: (03501) 527403. Beer garden situated on the river Elbe. (E-M)

FRANKFURT/ODER

Holiday Inn, tel: (0335) 55650, fax: 5565100. Sauna, solarium, fitness, restaurant. (L-LL)

Congress Hotel "Frankfurter Hof", Logenstr. 2, tel: (0335) 55360, fax: 5536100. Situated in the town centre on the edge of the Oder. Restaurant, bar, beauty/fitness centre with sauna, solarium and hairdressing salon.

Jena

Schwarzer Bär, Lutherplatz 2, tel: (03641) 4060, fax: 23691. 500-year-old building with 65 rooms in the centre of town. Restaurant. Close to lido. (E-M)

Erfurt & Weimar

ERFURT

Radisson SAS Hotel, Juri-Gagarin-Ring 127, tel: (0361) 5510, fax: 551210. Modern hotel with 320 rooms. Centrally located. Restaurants, car rental available. (L)

WEIMAR

Hotel Elephant, Am Markt, tel: (03643) 8020, fax: 65310. 17th-century building with elegant facade and beautiful terracotta roof where Tolstoy and Bach stayed. 106 rooms close to the historic marketplace. Excellent restaurants, Elephantkeller and Belvedere, famous for their salads. (M-L)

Eisenach & Gotha

EISENACH

Hotel Füstenrof, Luisenstrasse 11-13, tel: (03691) 7780, fax: 203682. Hotel with 55 rooms, situated downtown. Stylish restaurant. (E)

Parkhotel, Wartburgallee 2, tel: (0623) 5291. A small hotel, often full of tourist groups, with a gift shop and a restaurant. (E)

GOTHA

Hotel St Gambrim, Schwabhäuserstrasse 47, tel: (03621) 30900, fax: 309040. Central. 24 rooms. (E-M)

Munich

Bayerisher Hof, Promenadeplatz 2-6, tel: (089) 21200. The ultimate in luxury and service. (LL)

Hilton, Am Tucherpark 7, tel: (089) 38450. Super luxurious hotel by the "Englischer Garten" in the city centre. Swimming pool, sauna, car hire.(LL)

Königshof, Karlsplatz, tel: (089) 551360. Luxury hotel right in the city centre

Blauer Bock, Blumenstrasse 16, tel: (089) 2608043. Former monastery (16th-century) directly next to the "Viktualienmarkt". 75 rooms. Vegetarian restaurant. (E-L)

Am Markt, Heiliggeiststr. 6, tel: (089) 226844. Bavarian hospitality in a quiet location at the Viktualienmarkt. (E-M).

STARNBERG

Seehof, Bahnhofsplatz 4, tel: (08151) 6001. Small hotel at the Starnberger See. Directly opposite the lake promenade. (M)

Eastern Bavaria

LANDSHUT

Romantik-Hotel Fürstenhof, Stethaimer Strasse 3, tel: (0871) 92550. Art Deco building with 4 floors in a quiet side street. (M) New: "Non Smoking" floor (L) with individual apartments. Sauna and solarium.

REGENSBURG

Parkhotel Maximilian, Maximilianstrasse 28, tel: (0941) 51042. Listed rococo building, 52 rooms, opposite station. Park close by. (L)

Bischofshof, Krauterer Markt 3, tel: (0941) 59086. The foundation stone of this former bishop's residence was laid in 1648. Beer garden. Danube and huge park only a few minutes away. (M-LL)

WEIDEN

Stadtkrug, Wolframstrasse 5, tel: (0961) 32025. New hotel situated close to the town centre, with country-style decorations. Has a traditional restaurant. (M)

BODENMAIS

Andrea, Am Hölzlweg 10, tel: (09924) 7710. Small hotel close to river Riesbach. Half and full board available. Swimming pool. (M)

ZWIESEL

Kurhotel Sonnenburg, Augustinerstrasse 9, tel: (09922) 2031. New hotel with 40 beds and own swimming pool. (E)

PASSAU

Wilder Mann, Rathausplatz, tel: (0851) 35071. Four 14th-century patrician houses were inter-connected to form this comfortable hotel. Close to the historical town centre and town hall. Pool. Gourmet restaurant. Also houses the glass museum. (M-L)

The German Alpine Road

OBERAMMERGAU

Alte Post, Dorfstrasse 19, tel: (08822) 1091. First registered 550 years ago as an inn on the Roman road. Situated in the town centre, surrounded by green areas. Family rooms available, 60 beds. (E-M)

GARMISCH-PARTENKIRCHEN

Grand-Hotel Sonnenbichl, Burgstrasse 97, tel: (08821) 7020. Large hotel on the outskirts of Garmisch. Swimming pool and sauna. Dogs welcome for a small extra fee. 93 rooms. (LL)

Rheinischer Hof, Zugspitzstrasse 76, tel: (08821) 72024. Family-run hotel on the outskirts of Garmisch. Outside swimming pool and garden. Family apartments available. Restaurant with traditional food and salad bar. (M)

ROTTACH EGERN

Gästehaus Haltmair am See, Seestrasse 47, tel: (08022) 2750. Cosy hotel, situated directly at the Tegernsee. (M)

TEGERNSEE

Seehotel zur Post, Neureuthstrasse 23, tel: (08022) 3951. A medium-sized hotel with direct access to the Tegernsee (sailing, etc), tennis courts and gardens. (E-M)

REITH IM WINKL

Zum Löwen, Tirolerstrasse 1, tel: (08640) 8901. Small hotel in the town centre. (E)

Altenburger Hof, Frühlingstrasse 3, tel: (08640) 8994. Small, family-run hotel at the town entrance, opposite municipal swimming pool and lido. Park nearby. (E)

BAD REICHENHALL

Kurhotel Alpina, Adolf-Schmid-Strasse 5, tel: (08651) 2038. Cosy hotel in country-style. Half and full board available. (E–M)
Kurfürst, Kurfürstenstrasse 11, tel: (08651) 2710. Small hotel with separate family house (incl. terrace). Bicycle hire. (M)

BERCHTESGADEN

Alpenhotel Kronprinz, Am Brandholz, tel: (08652) 6070. Medium-sized, 130 bed mountain hotel. Prices depend on the view. Sauna and solarium. (M)

The Romantic Road

TAUBERBISCHOFSHEIM

Henschker, Bahnhofstrasse 18, tel: (09341) 203040. Near the station. Sandstone turn-of-the-century building. 24 beds. (E–M)

BAD MERGENTHEIM

Bundschu, Cronbergstrasse 15, tel: (07931) 3043. Situated in a residential area near the city centre, close to a large park. (M)

ROTHENBURG O.D. TAUBER

Eisenhut, Herrengasse 3, tel: (09861) 7050. Close to the marketplace, 80 rooms. (L–LL)
Merian, Ansbacher Strasse 42, tel: (09861) 3096. Modern building shortly before the city walls, 60 beds. (M–L)

NÖRDLINGEN

Mondschein, Bauhofgasse 5, tel: (09081) 86074. Hotel in the centre of town with "pick-up" service from the station. Restaurant "Zum Mondschein" with traditional food. (E)

DONAUWÖRTH

Traube, Kapellstrasse 14, tel: (0906) 6096. New building with restaurant. (M)

AUGSBURG

Steigenberger Drei-Mohren-Hotel, Maximilianstrasse 40, tel: (0821) 50360. (LL)
Alpenhof, Donauwörther Strasse 233, tel: (0821) 42040. Grand hotel with 200 beds in the direction of Norden-Oberhausen. Small garden. (M–L)

Franconia

ERBACH

Odenwälder Bauern-und Wappenstuben, Schlossgraben 30, tel: (06062) 2236. Small and cosy little half-timbered house near the castle. 12 rooms. (L)

WÜRZBURG

Maritim, Peichertorstrasse 5, tel: (0931) 30530. 292 rooms in a new building, only 10 minutes from the station. Swimming pool, sauna and solarium. (LL)
Grüner Baum, Zeller Strasse 35, tel: (0931) 450680. Near the bridge across the Main. Two minutes to the river. 38 rooms. (M–L.) Interesting restaurant "Melchior-Keller" in the vaults (16th-century).

BAMBERG

Bamberger Hof Bellevue, Schönleinsplatz 4, tel: (0951) 22216. 100-year-old building opposite the park. (M–L)

COBERG

Romantic Hotel, Goldene Traube, Am Viktoriabrunnen 2, tel: (09561) 8760, fax: 876222. Near the market. (E–M)

LICHTENFELS

Preussischer Hof, Hambergerstrasse 30, tel: (09571) 5015. In the city centre. Sauna inclusive. 75 beds. (E)

KRONACH

Hotel Bauer, Kulmbacherstr. 7, tel: (09261) 94058. Situated in a very quiet area in the centre. (M)

KULMBACH

Hansa-Hotel Hönsch, Weltrichstrasse 2a, tel: (09221) 7995. Ten minutes from the station. 56 beds. Book early for July (10-day beer festival). (M)
Weisses Ross (The White Horse), Marktplatz 12, tel: (09221) 95650. Situated in quiet pedestrianised area of the town centre. 25 beds. (M)

BAYREUTH

Bayerischer Hof, Bahnhofstrasse 14, tel: (0921) 22081. Cosy family hotel with sauna and swimming pool. 50 rooms. (M–L)

NÜRNBERG

Carlton-Hotel, Eilgutstrasse 13, tel: (0911) 20030. Close to the station, sauna and solarium included. (L–LL)
Burghotel, Schildgasse 14–16, tel: (0911) 203040. Situated below the castle. New building with 35 beds. Swimming pool. (M)

Lake Constance

LINDAU

Bayerischer Hof, Seepromenade, tel: (08382) 9150. Traditional hotel close to the station and harbour. Swimming pool. Small children stay for free. (L–LL)
Toscana, Aeschacher Ufer 12, tel: (08382) 3131. The nearby park leads directly to the lake. (E–M)

KONSTANZ

Steigenberger Inselhotel, Auf der Insel, tel: (07531) 1250. Old monastery on Lake Constance with own lakeside lawn and access to the water. With wine cellar and restaurant. (LL)
Seeblick, Neuhauser Strasse 14, tel: (07521) 54018. New, large building with swimming pool. Municipal park close by. (M)

ÜBERLINGEN

Parkhotel St Leonhard, Obere St-Leonhard-Strasse 83, tel: (07551) 808100. Traditional house dating from 1896, own swimming pool, playground and game park. Outside of town on a hill. (M–L)

FRIEDRICHSHAFEN

Zeppelin, Eugenstrasse 41, tel: (07541) 25071. Comfortable hotel with 20 rooms. Double rooms and apartments available. (M)

The Black Forest

FREIBURG

Colombia-Hotel, Rotteckring 16, tel: (0761) 31415. Hotel in city centre, close to the university. Car park. (LL)
Zum Roten Bären, Oberlinden 12, tel: (0761) 387870. Oldest restaurant in Germany (first mentioned 1120 AD). Small patio. Restaurant with regional dishes. (L)

HINTERZARTEN

Park-Hotel Adler, Adlerplatz, tel: (07652) 1270. City hotel close to the station. Swimming pool and playground. Restaurant dates back from 1446, regional cuisine. (LL)

TITISEE

Bären, Neustädter Strasse 35, tel: (07651) 8060. Old hotel close to a forest. Facilities include a swimming pool and fitness centre. Restaurant: local and international cuisine. Close to town centre. (M)

BADENWEILER

Römerbad, Schlossplatz 1, tel: (07632) 700. (LL)

BREISACH

Am Münster, Münsterbergstrasse 23, tel: (07667) 8380. Medium-sized hotel on a hill. Swimming pool. (M–L)

TÜBINGEN

Krone, Uhlandstrasse 1, tel: (07071) 31036. Built during the Romantic period, close to river Neckar (boat hire) and park. Approximately 5 minutes from the station. (M–LL)

STUTTGART

Steigenberger Hotel Graf Zeppelin, Arnulf-Klett-Platz 7, tel: (0711) 299-881. Large city hotel (280 rooms) opposite the station. Swimming pool and sauna. (LL)

PFORZHEIM

Goldene Pforte, Hohenstaufenstrasse 6, tel: (07231) 37920. 115-room hotel with swimming pool and sauna. Summer terrace. Close to jewellery exhibitions and museums. (LL)

KARLSRUHE

Kaiserhof, Karl-Friedrich-Strasse 11, tel: (0721) 26615. 200-year-old, newly renovated hotel with 40 beds in the town centre (marketplace). Three-person bedrooms available. (M–L)
Hasen, Gerwigstrasse 47, tel: (0721) 615076. Small hotel, built in 1912. Gourmet restaurant. (M)

BADEN BADEN

Brenners Parkhotel, Schillerstrasse, tel: (07221) 9000. Very expensive, traditional house with two restaurants, swimming pool, sauna, hairdresser, park, etc. (LL)

Allee-Hotel Bären, Lichtentaler Allee, tel: (07221) 7020. Relaxed hotel surrounded by park, 80 rooms. 7 km (4 miles) from station. Restaurant serving French and traditional cuisine. (L)

Along The Rhine

MAINZ

Hilton, Rheinstrasse 68, tel: (06131) 2450. Super-luxurious hotel near the Rhine. Breakfast buffet or continental breakfast not included. (LL)
Central-Hotel Eden, Bahnhofsplatz 8, tel: (06131) 2760. Near station. (M)
Am Römerwall, Römerwall 51–55, tel: (06131) 232135. Near the station. (M)

WIESBADEN

Aukamm-Hotel, Aukamm Allee 31, tel: (0611) 5760. Luxurious hotel in Wiesbaden-Bierstadt. (LL)
Luisenhof, Bahnhofstrasse 7, tel: (0611) 39431. Only 500 metres from the city centre and the station. (M)
Hotel de France, Taunusstrasse 49, tel: (0611) 520061. (M)

ELTVILLE AM RHEIN

Sonnenberg, Friedrichstrasse 65, tel: (06123) 3081. Outside town. (E)

RÜDESHEIM

Central-Hotel, Kirchstrasse 6, tel: (06722) 2391. (M–L)

BOPPARD

Bellevue-Rheinhotel, Rheinallee 41, tel: (06742) 1020. Luxurious hotel near the ferry across the Rhine. (L–LL)
Rheinlust, Rheinallee 27, tel: (06742) 3001. With view over the Rhine. (M)

BINGEN

Köppel, Kapuzinerstrasse 12, tel: (06721) 14770. In a quiet side street in the pedestrian zone. (E)
Rheingau, Rheinkai 8, tel: (06721) 17496. Close to the river. (E)

Along The Moselle

TRABEN-TRARBACH

Bernkastel Kaiser, Markt 29, tel: (06531) 3038. (E–M)

NEUMAGEN-DHRON

Zur Post, Römerstrasse 79, tel: (06507) 2114. Small central hotel. (E)

TRIER

Ramada Hotel, Kaiserstrasse 29, tel: (0651) 94950. Luxury hotel with play facilities for children. (L)
Deutscher Hof, Südallee 25, tel: (0651) 97780. Situated in the city centre, opposite the station. (M)

Cologne

Haus Lyskirchen, Filzengraben 26–32, tel: (0221) 20970. Right in the city centre, with indoor swimming pool, sauna, solarium. Dogs allowed. (L–LL)

DÜSSELDORF

Hotel an der Kö, Talstrasse 9, tel: (0211) 371048, fax: 370835. (LL)
Hotel an der Oper, Heinrich-Heine-Alee, tel: (0211) 3230621. Located in the town centre. (L–LL)
Günnewig Hotel Uebachs, Leopoldstrasse 3–5, tel: (0211) 360566. Near station and shopping centre, very good hotel restaurant. (M)
Minerva, Cantadorstrasse 13a, tel: (0211) 350961. New building, only 700 metres from the station. (M)

Heidelberg

Prinzhotel, Neuenheimer Landstrasse 5, tel: (06221) 40320. Breakfast not included. Newly renovated building with view over the Neckar, steam sauna, solarium, jacuzzi. (L–LL)
Schönberger Hof, Untere Neckarstrasse 54, tel: (06221) 14060. Established in historical building (since 1772), in the city centre near the Neckar. (L–LL)
Romantik Hotel Zum Ritter St Georg, Hauptstrasse 178, tel: (06221) 1350. In the pedestrian zone, near to marketplace. Over 400 years old. (L)

WORMS

Domhotel, Obermarkt 10, tel: (06241) 6913. Right in the middle of town, near the station. New building. (M)

MANNHEIM

Steigenberger Hotel Mannheimer Hof, Augusta-Anlage 4, tel: (0621) 40050. Situated in the city centre, near the water tower. (LL)
Holländer Hof, U1, 11-12, tel: (0621) 16095. Six-floor building in the pedestrian zone of Mannheim. (M)

Germany's Fairy Tale Road

FRANKFURT/MAIN

Arabella Grand Hotel Frankfurt, Konrad-Ardenauerstr. 7, tel: (069) 29810. Located in the town centre. (L)
Hessischer Hof, Friedrich-Ebert-Anlage 40, tel: (069) 75400. Special offers during the summer. Close to natural history museum Senkenberg. (LL)
Hotel an der Messe, Westendstr. 104, tel: (069) 747979. Close to the fair pavillion. (M)

AIRPORT FRANKFURT/MAIN

Sheraton Hotel, Hugo-Eckener-Ring 15, tel: (069) 69770. Large hotel close to the airport. Cheaper weekend prices, more expensive during the fair. Swimming pool. Close to aeroplane-exhibition at the airport. S-Bahn to the city centre. (LL)

BAD HOMBURG

Maritim Kurhaus-Hotel, Ludwig-strasse, tel: (06172) 28051. Recently built hotel with own pool, sauna and solarium. Cheaper summer rates. Very close to the Taunustherme (water fitness-centre). Bicycle hire. (L–LL)

KÖNIGSTEIN IM TAUNUS

Zum Hirsch, Burgweg 2, tel: (06174) 5034. 30 rooms in new and old building with summer terrace. Close to park, castle ruins and countryside (walking). (M)

FULDA

Maritim Am Schlossgarten, Paulus-promenade 2, tel: (0661) 2820. Former orangery and newly built area with 113 rooms. Swimming pool, skittles, mini golf. Close to castle gardens and cathedral. (LL)
Zum Kurfürsten, Schloss-Strasse 2, tel: (0661) 70001. 18th-century building with 113 beds in the baroque quarter of town. Close to cathedral and castle. Restaurant also serves children's menus. (M–L)

MARBURG

Waldecker Hof, Bahnhofstrasse 23, tel: (06421) 60090. Old hotel (1864) with 70 beds. Swimming pool and sauna. Close to station and old town centre. (M–L)

BAD HERSFELD

Parkhotel Rose, Am Kurpark 19, tel: (06621) 14454. Cosy, family-run hotel built at the turn of the century. A total of 20 rooms. Restaurant with national and international menu. Opposite spa gardens. (L)

KASSEL

Waldhotel Schäferberg, An der B7, tel: (05673) 7951. Traditional hotel in beautiful forest surroundings, 10 km (6 miles) outside Kassel. 95 rooms and "Bauernstube" restaurant with traditional cuisine. Sauna/solarium, fitness centre and skittles. Own car park. Dogs welcome. (M)

GÖTTINGEN

Eden, Reinhäuser Landstrasse 22a, tel: (0551) 76007. Newly decorated hotel with 200 rooms, swimming pool and sauna. Restaurant serving traditional German food. (M–L)

Along The Weser

HANOVER

Maritim, Hildesheimer Strasse 34, tel: (0511) 16531. Newly built hotel with 293 rooms, own swimming pool and sauna. International restaurant. Close to "Herrenhäuser Garten", town hall and city centre. (LL)
City-Hotel, Limburgstrasse, tel: (0511) 326681. Established hotel, newly decorated, 70 beds. Opposite town hall in city centre. (M)

BRAUNSCHWEIG

Deutsches Haus, Ruhfäutchenplatz, tel: (0531) 444422. The former guesthouse to the castle with a view over the cathedral offers 123 beds and an in-house beauty farm. (M)
Mövenpick Hotel, Welfenhof, tel: (0531) 48170. Newly built hotel in the pedestrian zone, adjacent to shopping arcade. Breakfast is not included. "Saunaland" with "snow shower", fitness-centre, swimming pool. (LL)

WOLFSBURG

Holiday Inn, Rathausstrasse 1, tel: (05361) 2070. Large hotel on 9 floors, approximately 2 km (1 mile) from the town centre. Swimming pool and sauna. Opposite planetarium. Has restaurant. (M)

BREMEN

Marriott-Hotel (former Plaza), Hillmannplatz 20, tel: (0421) 17670. Now American-owned, 228 rooms, close to "Bürgerpark". Mini golf, horse riding. Cheap weekend offers (E) if booked 14 days in advance (deposit). Fitness centre and shopping area under glass dome. Three restaurants: gourmet; bistro; piano bar. (E–LL)
Heldt, Friedhofstrasse 41, tel: (0421) 213051. Family-run hotel with 60 rooms on the outskirts of Bremen. Restaurant open Monday–Thursday. (M)

BREMERHAVEN

Nordseehotel Naber, Theodor-Heuss-Platz, tel: (0471) 48770. Medium-sized hotel in the town centre with restaurant, banquet and club rooms, bar and summer garden. (L)

The North Sea Coast

NORDERNEY

Kurhotel Reinke, Bismarckstrasse, tel: (04932) 3051. 70-bed hotel in the centre (zone 1) of the island, close to the beach. (E)

JEVER

Hotel-Pension Stöber, Hohnholzstrasse 10, tel: (04461) 5580. Tiny, family-run hotel with garden, only a short walk from the castle. (E)

WILHELMSHAVEN

Hotel Seestem, Südstrand 116, tel: (04421) 914100, fax: 45263. Small hotel with 11 rooms. Close to the seaside. Restaurant.

OLDENBURG

City-Club Hotel (CCH), Europaplatz 20, tel: (0441) 8080. Modern, purpose-built hotel outside the town centre, close to the "Weser-Ems-Halle" (festival hall). Sauna, solarium, Jacuzzi. (L)

CUXHAVEN

Donners Hotel, Am Seedeich 2, tel: (04721) 5090. New building with 86 rooms. Restaurant with sea view serves North German cuisine. Swimming pool and sauna. (M–L)

FÖHR-WYK

Duus, Hafenstrasse 40, tel: (04681) 708. Small hotel in old building with new annexe on the "outskirts" of Wyk.

Very close to the beach and jetty. Pedestrian zone nearby. (M)

SYLT-WESTERLAND

Stadt Hamburg, Strandstrasse 2, tel: (04651) 8580. Medium-sized central hotel with Frisian decor and close to the beach. Bicycle hire can be arranged. Restaurant serves German and French-style cuisine. (L–LL)

Hamburg

HAMBURG

Vier Jahreszeiten, Neuer Jungfernstieg 9, tel: (040) 34941. 100-room hotel in the city centre. Two restaurants: the upmarket "Herlin" and a barbecue-bar. (LL)

Europäischer Hof, Kirchenallee 45, tel: (040) 248171. Large turn-of-the-century hotel opposite the station with leisure centre, swimming pool and water slide, sauna. (L–LL)

St Raphael, Adenaueralle 41, tel: (040) 248200. Recently redecorated, relaxing hotel with a beautiful view over the port. Fitness centre with sauna, jacuzzi, etc. (M–L)

LÜNEBURG

Hotel Residenz, Münstermannskamp 10, tel: (04131) 45047. Cosy hotel with 35 rooms, own garden and restaurant "Die Schnecke". Close to spa gardens. Bicycle hire and underground car park. Dogs welcome. (M)

From Lübeck To Flensburg

LÜBECK

Lysia-Mövenpick, Auf der Wallhalbinsel, tel: (0451) 15040. Newly renovated, large hotel in the historical quarter of the city. Breakfast not included. Children under 16 stay free of charge. Playroom. Restaurant and conference rooms. (L)

MALENTE

Intermar, Hindenburgallee 2, tel: (04523) 4040. With 10 floors, the largest hotel in town, special weekend rates (M–L). Apartments for groups. Sauna, solarium, bar, restaurant "Friesenstube". Twenty km (12 miles) from "Hansaland" theme park. (LL)

KIEL

"Kieler Kaufmann", Niemannsweg 102, tel: (0431) 85011. Small hotel in a quiet location. Swimming pool, sauna, bicycle hire. Exquisite restaurant with beautiful decor. (M–LL)

FLENSBURG

Historischer Krug, Oeversee, An der B 76, tel: (04630) 300. The oldest inn in the area (since 1519) has been in the same family for many generations. It has a gourmet restaurant with regional specialities, swimming pool, sauna, solarium, massage, fitness centre, beauty farm as well as canoe, kayak and bicycle hire. (M)

Private Accommodation

Please enquire in the local tourist offices for *Pensionen* and *Privatquartiere*. Prices may vary and are not always a clear indication for the facilities offered.

Families with children or large groups may find *Ferienappartements* (holiday apartments) or *Ferienhäuser* (holiday homes) more attractive. You should book your individual apartment or house in your travel office where you can choose from the brochures of the main holiday home companies.

For travellers who would like to arrange their own holiday in the countryside or on a farm, the brochure *Raus aufs Land 97/98* (DM 19.50) will be useful. Contact: Landschriften-Verlag, Heerstr. 73, 53111 Bonn, tel: (0228) 631284, fax: 7669199.

Another reasonable option is the *Gasthof* (Inn), where you can normally expect to be offered good local food. It is here that you will find the best opportunity to talk to the locals and experience local life.

Camping

Camping sites are widespread in Germany. The *Campingführer* (camping guide) published by the automobile clubs provides information on relatively comfortable places. Local tourist authorities and information offices (*see Tourist Information*) will also have lists of local sites. For more global information, write to: **Deutscher Camping-Club**, Mandelstrasse 28, 80802 Munich 40, tel: (089) 3801420.

Youth Hostels

German youth hostels are no longer as old and stuffy as they used to be. Many have been turned into leisure centres which offer windsurfing as well as computer courses.

For people interested in the environment, there are "Umweltjugendherbergen" (environmental youth hostels). About 14 such sites in Germany offer an environment in which to study ecological issues. The hostel managers themselves are known for their ecological management and expect certain criteria to be met by those wishing to take part.

For more information and a map of all German youth hostels contact: the **Deutsche Jugendherbergswerk**, Bismarckstrasse 8, 32756 Detmold, tel: (05231) 74010, fax: 740149.

Eating Out

Where To Eat

Choices of places to eat in Germany range from top quality restaurants to street snack stands. In the wine-growing areas of Germany – Baden, Franken, Rheineland, along the Moselle and Dresden – the wine festivals can be a useful introduction and are always worth checking out.

German cooking differs from region to region. For example, the Northern Germany *Labskaus* will not be found in Southern Germany.

Listed below region by region, are the most typical specialities encountered while travelling from south to north.

What To Eat

Bavaria

Schweinehax'n: pork knuckle usually served with *Blaukraut* (red cabbage) and *Knödel* (dumpling). Very popular beer-garden fare.
Saure Lüngerl: lung in vinegar sauce usually served with *Semmelknödel* (bread dumpling).
Krautwickerl: Minced meat rolled into white cabbage, usually eaten with potatoes.
Weisswürste: Spiced veal and pork sausages which are mainly eaten with sweet mustard (*Weisswurstsenf*). They usually accompany a late-morning beer.
Leberkäs: Meat loaf, taken hot or cold.
Semmelknödel: Bread dumplings often served with *Schweinebraten* (roast pork).
Reiberdatschi: Thinly grated raw potatoes baked in deep fat. Served with apple sauce. In other regions of Germany they are called *Kartoffelpuffer*.
Gugelhupf: Cake made out of yeast with raisins, nuts, almonds etc.
Dampfnudeln: Huge yeast dumplings with plums and served hot with vanilla sauce.

Württemberg/Baden

Flädlesuppe: Clear soup with pancake.
Spätzle: A kind of pasta made of flour, egg, salt and water, grated and boiled, *Spätzle* are served as a side-dish with meat and vegetables.
Maultaschen: Another form of pasta filled with minced meat and spinach. *Maultaschen* are either served as soup or as a separate dish with salad.

Hesse

Handkäs mit Musik: Curd cheese served with onions.
Kasseler Rippchen: Smoked pickled loin of pork, named after a Berlin butcher named Kassel.
Zwiebelkuchen: Yeast cake (almost similar to pizza) filled with onions and bacon and usually served with a glass of young wine (*Federweisser*).
Äppelwoi: Hard cider, another very popular drink.

Rhineland

Sauerbraten: Braised pickled beef lard with bacon, usually served with potatoes and vegetables.
Hunsrücker Festessen: Sauerkraut and peas, *Hunsrücker* pudding with potatoes, horseradish and ham.
Halver Hahn: Rye bread or roll with cheese and mustard.
Kölsch: Light-coloured, surface-fermented beer.
Spekulatius, Muzenmandeln: Almond biscuits.

Westphalia

Westfälischer Schinken: Delicious ham, best when eaten with Pumpernickel bread.
Mettwurst mit Linsen: Pork or beef sausage with lentils.
Westfälischer Reibekuchen: Cakes made of grated raw potatoes and buckwheat flour.

Lower Saxony

Braunkohl mit Brägenwurst: Kale with brain sausage.
Heidschnuckenbraten: Roast lamb served with potatoes.
Braunschweiger Mumme: Very strong dark beer with a high malt content, usually mixed with ordinary beer.

North Germany-Hamburg-Bremen

Kohl mit Pinkel: Cabbage with coarse sausage and potatoes.
Labskaus: Salted meat, herring and mashed potatoes served with fried egg and beetroot.
Lübecker Schwalbennester: Veal olive filled with mashed hard boiled eggs.
Lübecker Marzipan: Favourite sweet, containing lots of almonds ground into a paste.
Rote Grütze: Pudding made from red berries – mainly raspberries – and served with fresh cream.

Berlin

Berliner Schlachtplatte: Fresh blood and liver sausage, pig's kidney and fresh-boiled pork.
Berliner Weisse mit Schuss: Wheaten beer with a shot of raspberry juice or woodruff extract.

Saxony

Sächsischer Mandelstollen: Almond cake.
Leipziger Allerlei: Mixed vegetables.
Gallertschüssel: Boiled pig's or calf's foot in aspic.
Dresdner Christstollen: Christmas cake.
Grüne Klösse: Dumplings made from ground raw potatoes.
Kirschpfanne: Pastry made of white bread, eggs, milk and butter.
Pfefferkuchen: gingerbread.
Eierschecke: Cake with golden-yellow egg-cover, filled with sweet curd.

Brandenburg

Eberswalder Spritzkuchen: Deep-fried ring doughnuts.

Thuringia

Thüringer Klösse: Potato dumplings.
Thüringer Rostbratwurst: Grilled sausage with herbs.
Platz: Thuringian yeast cake.

Saxony-Anhalt

Halberstädter Wurst: sausage.
Salzwedeler Baumkuchen: Cake and chocolate in thin layers.

Mecklenburg-Vorpommern

Salzhering in Sahnesosse: pickled herring in sour cream.
Himmel and Erde: boiled potatoes and apples with bacon.

Culture

Museums & Galleries

Museums and art galleries are usually open daily. However, most establishments close all day Monday.

Ahrensburg
Museum holsteinischer Adelskultur im Schloss, Lübecker Str. 1, tel: 0 41 02/4 25 10. Tuesday–Sunday 10am–12.30pm; April–September 1.30–5pm; October, February, March 1.30–4pm; November, December, January 1.30–3pm.

Altenburg
Lindenau-Museum, Gabelentzstr. 5, tel: 0 34 47/25 10, fax: 25 19. Tuesday–Sunday 10am–6pm.
Schloss- und Spielkartenmuseum, Schloss 2–4, tel: 0 34 47/31 51 93, fax: 50 28 39. Tuesday–Sunday 9am–5pm.

Arnstadt
Museum für Dampflokomotiven, Bahnbetriebswerk im Rehestädter Weg, tel: 0 36 28/60 23 95. groups must book; the factory works are generally always manned.
Puppenstadt "Mon plaisir" im Schloss, Schlossplatz 1, tel: 0 36 28/60 29 32. April–October Tuesday–Sunday 8.30am–noon and 1–4pm; October–March 9.30am–4pm.
Stadtgeschichtliches Museum and Bach-Gedenkstätte, Haus zum Palmbaum, Markt 3, tel: 0 36 28/60 29 78. Monday–Friday 8.30am–12.30pm, 1–5pm; Sat-Sun 9.30am–5pm.

Augsburg
Bert-Brecht-Haus, closed until 1998.
Fuggereimuseum, Fuggerei, Mittlere Gasse 13, tel: 08 21/3 08 68. March–October daily 9am–6pm; November-December Saturday-Sunday 9am–6pm.
Handwerkermuseum, Spitalgasse/ former Brunnenmeisterhaus, tel: 08

21/3 25 92 24. Monday–Friday 2–6pm; Monday-Tuesday 9am–noon; Sunday, public holidays 10am–6pm.
MAN-Museum, Heinrich-von-Buz-Str tel: 3 22 37 91. Monday–Friday 8am–4pm.
Maximilianmuseum, Philippine-Welser-Str. 24, tel: 08 21/34 21 74. Wednesday-Sunday 10am–4pm.
Mozarthaus, Frauentorstr. 30, tel: 08 21/3 24 21 96. Wednesday-Sunday 10am–4pm.
Römisches Museum, Dominikanergasse 15, tel: 08 21/3 24 21 80. Wednesday-Sunday 10am–4pm.
Schaezlerpalais, Maximilianstrasse 46, tel: 3 24 21 75. Wednesday-Sunday 10am–4pm.

Aurich
Freilichtmuseum, see Moordorf.
Historisches Museum, Burgstr. 25, tel: 0 49 41/1 23 16. Tuesday–Saturday 10am–noon and 3-5pm; Sunday 3-6pm.
Mühlenmuseum, Oldersumer Str. 281, tel: 0 49 41/1 88 89. Tuesday–Saturday 10am–noon and 3-5pm; Sunday 3-6pm and on arrangement.
Ostfriesische Landschaft, Georgswall 3–9, tel: 0 49 41/1 79 90. A collection of old Friesian furniture, portraits of famous founders. Tours only during Lower Saxony public holidays Tuesday–Thursday at 11am.

Bad Frankenhausen
Monumentaler Rundbau, Am Schlachtberg 9, tel: 03 46 71/7 17 16. April–September Tuesday–Sunday 10am–6pm; July-August 1–6pm; October–March 10am–5pm.
Barbarossa-Höhle, see Rottleben.

Bad Homburg
Saalbergmuseum, Saalburg, 61350 Bad Homburg, tel: 0 61 75/31 48. Daily 8am–5pm.

Bad Karlshafen
Deutsches Hugenottenmuseum, Hasenstr. 9a, tel: 0 56 72/14 10. 1 April–15 November Tuesday–Saturday 2-6pm; Sunday 11am–6pm; January–15 February closed otherwise Wednesday, Saturday 2-4pm; Sunday 11am–4pm.

Bad Mergentheim
Deutschordens- and Heimatmuseum, Innerer Schlosshof, tel: 0 79 31/96 50. Tuesday–Sunday 10am–5pm.

Bad Muskau
Stadtmuseum im Alten Schloss, Schlossstrasse, tel: 03 57 71/6 03 52. May–September Tuesday–Friday 10am–noon and 1-4pm; Saturday, Sunday, public holidays 10am–noon and 1-5pm; October–April Tuesday–Friday 10am–noon and 1-4pm; Sunday, public holidays, 1-4pm.

Bamberg
Historisches Museum, Domplatz 7, tel: 09 51/87 11 42. May-October Tuesday–Sunday 9am–5pm. Open during winter only for exhibitions.
Sammlung Ludwig im Alten Rathaus, Obere Brücke, tel: 09 51/87 18 71. daily Tuesday–Sunday 9.30am–4.30pm.

Bayreuth
Bayreuther Festspiele. For Information, tel: 09 21/78 78-0. Annually 25 July–28 August. Tours of the Festival Hall daily at 10.15am, 11am, 14.15pm, 3pm; closed November; open mornings only during festival season.
Eremitage. Tel: 09 21/9 25 61. The *Old Castle*: April–September Tuesday–Sunday 9–11.30amd and 1–4.30pm; October–March 10–11.30am and 1–2.30pm. Tours last 30 minutes; must book to visit November-February. *Wasserspiele:* May-mid-October daily at 10am, 11am, 1pm, and hourly until 5pm.
Markgräfliches Opernhaus, Opernstrasse, tel: 09 21/75 96 90. April–September 9–11.30am and 1.30–2.30pm; October–March 10–11.30am and 1.30–3pm. Ticket includes entrance to the *Neues Schloss.*
Neues Schloss, Ludwigstrasse, tel: 09 21/75 96 90. April–September 10–11.20am and 1.30–16.10 pm; October–March 10–11.20 and 1.30–14.50 pm. Tours last 40 minutes; ticket includes entrance to the *Markgräflichem Opernhaus* (Earl's Opera House).

Bautzen
Sorbisches Museum, Ortenburg 3, tel: 0 35 91/4 24 25. April–October daily 10am–12.30pm and 1–5pm; November–March daily 10am–4pm.

Berchtesgaden
Salzbergwerk, 83471 Berchtesgaden, tel: 0 86 52/60 02-0, fax: 60 02-60.

May–15 October and Easter daily 8.30am–5pm; closed Whitsun; 16 October–30 April Monday–Friday 12.30–3.30pm.

Berlin

Ägyptisches Museum: *Berlin-Charlottenburg,* Schlossstrasse 70, tel: 0 30/32 09 11. Book for tours, tel: 8 30 14 65/66. Tuesday–Friday 9am–5pm; Saturday-Sunday 10am–5pm. The Amarna collection: original busts of Egyptian kings; art and cultural history about Egyptian Pharaohs; Papyrus collection.

Museumsinsel, Berlin-Mitte, im Bodemuseum: Eingang Monjibou-brücke, tel: 0 30/20 35 50. Book for tours, tel: 20 35 54 44. Tuesday–Sunday 9am–5pm. Grave and temple reliefs; Mummies; Papyrus collection.

Altes Museum, *Museumsinsel, Berlin-Mitte,* Bodestr. 1–3, Eingang Am Lustgarten, tel: 0 30/20 35 50, Exhibitions office: 20 35 55 00. Rotunde with sculptures of Gods and Caffarelli Sarcophagus. Tuesday–Sunday 9am–5pm.

Antikensammlung, *Museumsinsel, Berlin-Mitte, im Pergamonmuseum:* Am Kupfergraben, tel: 0 30/20 35 50. Book for tours, tel: 20 35 54 44. Tuesday–Sunday 9am–5pm. World-famous examples of antique architectural works of art from the 12th centur; famous Pergamon altar; view of the Market Gate.

Bodemuseum, run by the Egyptian Museum; art gallery; money cabinet; Byzantine art; sculpture collection.

Brücke-Museum, *Berlin-Zehlendorf (Dahlem),* Bussardsteig 9, tel: 0 30/8 31 20 29. Wednesday–Monday 11am–5pm. Book for tours.

Deutsches Historisches Museum, *Berlin-Mitte,* Unter den Linden 2, tel: 0 30/21 50 20. Book for tours, tel: 21 50 23 78. Thursday–Tuesday 10am–6pm. Post-1695 German history collection in the former Armoury.

Friedrichswerdersche Kirche (Schinkelmuseum), *Berlin-Mitte,* Werderstrasse, tel: 0 30/2 08 13 23. Book for tours, tel: 8 30 14 65/66. Tuesday–Sunday 9sm–5pm. Classical sculptures; architectural history of the church.

Gemäldegalerie, *Museumsinsel, Berlin-Mitte, im Bodemuseum:* Eingang Monjiboubrücke, tel: 0 30/20 35 50. Book for tours, tel: 20 35 54 44. Tuesday–Sunday 9am–5pm. Works from 13th-18th centuries.

Berlin-Zehlendorf (Dahlem): Arnimallee 23–27, tel: 0 30/8 30 11. Book for tours, tel: 8 30 14 65/66. Tuesday–Friday 9am–5pm; Saturday, Sunday 10am–5pm. Over 600 European works of art.

Georg-Kolbe-Museum, *Berlin-Charlottenburg,* Sensburger Allee 25, tel: 0 30/3 04 21 44. Tuesday–Sunday 10am–5pm. Early 20th-century figurines and sculptures housed in the former studio of Georg Kolbes.

Hamburger Bahnhof – Museum für Gegenwart Berlin, *Berlin-Tiergarten,* Invalidenstr. 50/51, tel: 0 30/3 97 83 40. Book for tours, tel: 8 30 14 65/66. Tuesday–Friday 9am–5pm; Saturday, Sunday 10am–5pm. Museum with collection of Marxist and contemporary art opened in 1996.

Kunstbibliothek, *Berlin-Tiergarten,* Matthäikirchplatz 6, tel: 0 30/2 66 20 46. Book for tours, tel: 8 30 14 65/66. Monday 2–8pm; Tuesday–Friday 9am–4pm. Costume and art library with graphical art collection.

Kunstgewerbemuseum: *Berlin-Köpenik:* Schloss Köpenik (auf der Schlossinsel), tel: 0 30/6 57 26 51. Book for tours, tel: 8 30 14 65/66. Tuesday–Sunday 9am–5pm. Hand-made art from the 10th century including porcelain, glass.

Berlin-Tiergarten: Matthäikirchstr. 10, tel: 0 30/2 66 29 11. Book for tours, tel: 8 30 14 65/66. Tuesday–Friday 9am–5pm; Saturday, Sunday 10am–5pm. Hand-made art from the Middle Ages to present.

Kupferstichkabinett, *Berlin-Tiergarten,* Matthäikirchplatz 6, tel: 0 30/2 66 20 02. Book for tours, tel: 8 30 14 65/66. Tuesday–Friday 9am–5pm; Saturday, Sunday 10am–5pm. European printed art from the Middle Ages to present day and some North-American drawings.

Münzkabinett, *Museumsinsel, Berlin-Mitte, im Bodemuseum,* Eingang Monbijoubrücke, tel: 0 30/20 35 50. Only study rooms open; book to visit, tel: 20 35 55 10.

Museum für Indische Kunst, *Berlin-Zehlendorf (Dahlem),* Lansstr. 8, tel: 0 30/8 30 11. Book for tours, tel: 8 30 14 65/66. Tuesday–Friday 9am–5pm; Saturday, Sunday 10am–5pm. Stone sculptures; Asian frescos, paintings, arts and crafts.

Museum für Islamische Kunst, *Museumsinsel, Berlin-Mitte, im Perga-*

monmuseum: Am Kupfergraben, tel: 0 30/20 35 50. Book for tours, tel: 20 35 54 44. Tuesday–Sunday 9am–5pm. Architekturdenkmäler, Carpets, wood-carvings, ceramics; remains of the desert castle of Mschatta (8th century.).

Berlin-Zehlendorf (Dahlem): Lansstr. 8, tel: 0 30/8 30 11. Book for tours, tel: 8 30 14 65/66. Tuesday–Friday 9am–5pm; Saturday, Sunday 10am–5pm. History of Islamic art from the 8th-19th centuries; architectural pieces, carpets, jewellery, ceramics, arts and crafts.

Museum für Ostasiatische Kunst, *Berlin-Zehlendorf (Dahlem),* Lansstr. 8, tel: 0 30/8 30 11. Book for tours, tel: 8 30 14 65/66. Tuesday–Friday 9am–5pm; Saturday, Sunday 10am–5pm. Oriental paintings and calligraphy; also East-Asian archaelogical pieces, ceramics, paintings, wood-carvings, sculptures; 400-year-old porcelain.

Berlin-Zehlendorf (Dahlem): Arnimallee 23–27, tel: 0 30/8 30 11. Book for tours, tel: 8 30 14 65/66. Tuesday–Friday 9am–5pm; Saturday, Sunday 10am–5pm. Early Christian and Byzantine ivory carvings; icons and pieces of art from the 4th century.

Museum für Völkerkunde, *Berlin-Zehlendorf (Dahlem),* Lansstr. 8, tel: 0 30/8 30 11. Book for tours, tel: 8 30 14 65/66. Tuesday–Friday 9am–5pm; Saturday, Sunday 10am–5pm. Cultural history of Old America, Africa, Asia; stone sculptures, ceramics of Malasia, Aztecs, Incas; model figures; Chinese theater; West African sculptures, masks;.museum for children and the blind.

Museum für Volkskunde, *Berlin-Zehlendorf (Dahlem),* Im Winkel 6/8, tel: 0 30/8 39 01-01. Book for tours, tel: 8 30 14 65/66. Tuesday–Friday 9am–5pm; Saturday, Sunday 10am–5pm. Furniture, ceramics, textiles, household objects.

Museum für Vor- and Frühgeschichte, *Berlin-Charlottenburg,* im Westflügel des Schlosses, Spandauer Damm 22, tel: 0 30/32 09 11. Book for tours, tel: 32 09 12 82. Tuesday–Friday 9am–5pm; Saturday, Sunday 10am–5pm. Stone Age history, antiquities.

Musikinstrumenten-Museum des Staatlichen Instituts für Musikforschung (Preussischer Kulturbesitz), *Berlin-Tiergarten,* Tiergartenstr. 1, tel: 0 30/25 48 10. Tuesday–Friday 9am–

5pm; Saturday, Sunday 10am–5pm. Tours Saturday 11am; Wurlitzer organ demonstration Saturday noon. Musical instruments from the 16th-20th centuries; computing studio; instrument repair workshops.

Neue Nationalgalerie, *Berlin-Tiergarten,* Potsdamer Strasse 50, tel: 0 30/2 66 26 62. Book for tours, tel: 8 30 14 65/66. Tuesday–Friday 9am–5pm; Saturday, Sunday 10am–5pm. 20th-century art.

Sammlung Berggruen, *Berlin-Charlottenburg,* Schlossstr. 1, tel: 0 30/20 35 54 44. Book for tours, tel: 8 30 14 65/66. Tuesday–Friday 9am–5pm; Saturday, Sunday 10am–5pm. Private collection of modern art since 1996 in the castle, including Picasso.

Schloss Charlottenburg, Luisenplatz, tel: 0 30/32 09 11. Tuesday–Friday 9am–5pm; Saturday, Sunday 10am–5pm. Also the living quarters of Friedrich I. and Friedrich the Great.

Skulpturensammlung (sculpture collection): *Museumsinsel, Berlin-Mitte, im Bodemuseum:* Eingang Monbijoubrücke, entrance over the art gallery, tel: 0 30/20 35 50. Book for tours, tel: 20 35 54 44. Mobile exhibitions in the study rooms Tuesday–Sunday 9am–5pm.
Berlin-Zehlendorf (Dahlem): Arnimallee 23–27, tel: 0 30/8 30 11. Book for tours, tel: 8 30 14 65/66. Tuesday–Friday 9am–5pm; Saturday, Sunday 10am–5pm. Ivory carvings; sculptures by Multscher, Riemenschneider, Leinberger, Donatello and Bernini.

Vorderasiatisches Museum, *Museumsinsel, Berlin-Mitte, im Pergamonmuseum,* Am Kupfergraben, tel: 0 30/20 35 50. Book for tours, tel: 20 35 54 44. Tuesday–Sunday 9am–5pm. History of Near Eastern art and culture; processional street of Babylon and Ischtar Gate.

Bernkastel-Kues

Cusanus-Geburtshaus, Nikolausufer 49. 16 April–31 October Tuesday–Saturday 10am–noon and 2.30–5pm; Sunday 10am–noon; 1 November–15 April Tuesday–Saturday 2.30pm–5pm; Sunday 10am–noon.

Binz

Jagdschloß Granitz, tel: 03 83 93/22 63. May–September daily 9am–5.30pm; October–April Tuesday–Sunday 9am–4pm.

Rasender Roland, Schmalspurbahn between Putbus and Göhren beyond Binz, Jagdschloss Granitz, Sellin, Baabe, tel: 03 83 93/27 64.

Bochum

Deutsches Bergbau-Museum, Am Bergbaumuseum 28, Haupteingang: Wielandstrasse, tel: 02 34/58 77-0, fax: 58 77-1 11. Tuesday–Friday 8.30am–5.30pm, Saturday, Sunday, public holidays 10am–4pm.

Zeche Hannover in Bochum-Hordel, Günnigfelder Strasse. Undergoing construction. Group tours by arrangement, contact: *Westfälisches Industriemuseum,* Zentrale, Grubenweg 5, 44388 Dortmund, tel: 02 31/69 61-0, fax: 69 61 14.

Bodenwerder

Münchhausen Erinnerungszimmer, Münchhausenplatz 1, tel: 0 55 33/4 05 47. April–October daily 10am–noon and 2–5pm or by arrangement.

Bonn

August-Macke-Haus, Bornheimer Str. 96, tel: 02 28/65 55 31. Tuesday–Friday 2.30–6pm; Saturday11am–1pm; Sunday 11am–5pm.

Beethovenhaus, Bonngasse 20, tel: 02 28/63 51 88. April–30 September Monday–Saturday10am–5pm; October–March Monday–Saturday 10am–4pm; Sunday and holidays 11am–4pm.

Haus der Geschichte der Bundesrepublik Deutschland, Adenauerallee 250, tel: 02 28/9 16 50. Tuesday–Sunday 9am–7pm; information centre Tuesday–Friday 9am–5pm.

Kunst- und Ausstellungshalle der Bundesrepublik Deutschland, Friedrich-Ebert-Allee 4, tel: 02 28/91 71-2 00. Tuesday, Wednesday 10am–9pm; Thursday–Sunday 10am–7pm.

Kunstmuseum Bonn, Friedrich-Ebert-Allee 2, tel: 02 28/77 62 60. Tuesday–Sunday 10am–6pm.

Zoologisches Forschungsinstitut und Museum Alexander Koenig, Adenauerallee 160, tel: 02 28/9 12 20. Tuesday–Friday 9am–5pm; Saturday 9am–12.30pm Sunday 9.30am–5pm.

Bottrop

Josef-Albers-Museum, Im Stadtgarten 20, 46236 Bottrop. Tuesday–Sunday 10am–6pm.

Brandenburg

Altstädtisches Rathaus, Altstädtischer Markt 10. Daily 10am–6pm.

Dommuseum, Burghof 11, tel: 0 33 81/20 03 25 or 22 43 90. May–September Monday–Saturday 10am–6pm; Sunday noon–6pm; October–April 10am–4pm; tours daily10.30am and 2.30pm on arrangement.

Braubach

Burgmuseum Marksburg, oberhalb von 56338 Braubach, tel: 0 26 27/2 06. Easter–October daily 10am–5pm; November–Easter daily 11am–4pm; tours hourly.

Bregenz (Austria)

Bregenzer Festspiele, Kartenbüro, tel: 00 43/55 74/40 76 outside Germany. Open July and August.

Bremen

Bremer Landesmuseum (Focke-Museum), Schwachhauser Heerstrasse 240, tel: 04 21/3 61-35 75, fax: 3 61-39 03. Tuesday–Sunday 10am–6pm.

Dommuseum. Monday–Friday 10am–5pm November–April 1–4.30pm; Saturday 10am–noon; Sunday, public holidays 2–5pm. Lead cellar: April–October Monday–Friday 10am–5pm; Saturday 10am–2pm; Sunday, public holidays 2–5pm.

Hafen: Hafenrundfahrt. Abfahrt Martini-Anleger (end of Böttcherstrasse), tel: 04 21/3 08 0-0 and the shipping company Schreiber, tel: 04 21/32 12 29, fax: 32 61 36. March–October daily 11.45am, 1.30pm, 3.15pm; April-September 10am, 4.45pm; tour lasts 1 hours.

Kunstsammlungen Böttcherstraße Bremen, *Paula-Modersohn-Becker-Haus* and *Roselius-Haus,* tel: 04 21/ 3 36 50 77. Tuesday–Sunday 11am–5pm.

Rathaus, Obere Halle/Marktplatz. tours May–October Monday–Friday 10am, 11am, noon; Saturday, Sunday 11am, noon; November–April Saturday, Sunday 11am, noon.

Übersee-Museum, Bahnhofsplatz 13, tel: 04 21/3 61-91 76. Tuesday–Sunday 10am–6pm.

Bremerhaven

Deutsches Schiffahrtsmuseum (plus Museum Harbour), Hans-Scharoun-Platz 1, tel: 04 71/48 20 70. Tuesday–Sunday 10am–6pm. Museum harbour exhibit closed October–March.

Brunsbüttel

Heimatmuseum, Markt 4, tel: 0 48 52/72 12. Tuesday–Sunday 2–5pm; Wednesday 10am–noon and by arrangement.

Schleusenmuseum (canal and shipping exhibition), Gustav-Meyer-Platz, tel: 0 48 52/88 52 13. Daily 10.30am–5pm; tours by arrangment.

Buckow

Brecht-Weigel-Haus, Bertolt-Brecht-Strasse 29, tel: 03 34 33/4 67. April–October Wednesday-Friday 1–5pm; Saturday, Sunday 1–6pm; November–March Wednesday-Friday 10am–noon and 1–4pm; Sunday 11am–4pm.

Buxtehude

Regionalmuseum, Stavenort 2, tel: 0 41 61/40 21. Tuesday–Friday 1.30–5.30pm; Saturday, Sunday 10.30am–5.30pm.
Museumsbahn. Tel: 0 41 64/42 81. May–September open alternate Sundays.

Burg Eltz (Münstermaifeld)

Burg Eltz, 6km from Moselkern, Earl's fortress at Eltz, 56294 Burg Eltz, Münstermaifeld, tel: 0 26 72/13 00, fax: 23 91. April–November daily 9.30am–5.30pm.

Burg Guttenberg (Neckarmühlbach)

Burg Guttenberg, bei 74855 Neckarmühlbach, tel: 0 62 66/2 28. Mid-March–October daily 9.30am–5.30pm; tours by arrangement until December.
Deutsche Greifenwarte, Burg Guttenberg, tel: 0 62 66/3 88. Grounds open April–October 9am–6pm; flight tours March and November 3pm (weather permitting); April–October 11am, 3pm.

Burg Hornburg (Neckarzimmern)

Weingut Burg Hornburg, bei 74865 Neckarzimmern, tel: 0 62 61/41 71, fax: 23 48. Flexible times; tours by arrangement.

Calw

Hermann-Hesse-Museum, Marktplatz 30, tel: 0 70 51/75 22. Tuesday–Saturday 2–5pm; Sunday 11am–5pm.

Chemnitz

König-Albert-Museumsbau, Theaterplatz 1. *Town art collection*: tel: 03 71/4 88 44 24, Tuesday–Sunday 11am–5pm; tours Sunday 11am. *Natural History Museum,* tel: 03 71/4 88 45 51, Tuesday–Friday 9am–noon and 2–5pm; Saturday, Sunday 11am–5pm.
Schlossbergmuseum, Schlossberg 12, tel: 03 71/4 88 45 01, book for group tours 4 88 45 20. Tuesday–Sunday 10am–5pm.

Chorin

Kloster Chorin, tel: 0 33 34/65 73 10. Daily April–October 9am–6pm; November–March 9am–4pm. Use above number to book tickets for the *Musiksommer Chorin,* the music festival in July/August.

Coburg

Coburger Puppenmuseum, Rückertstr. 2/3, tel: 0 95 61/7 40 47, fax: 2 71 16. April–October daily 9am–5pm; November–March Tuesday–Sunday 10am–5pm.
Schloss Ehrenburg, tel: 0 95 61/8 08 80, fax: 80 88 40. April–September tours Tuesday–Sunday 10am, 11am, 1.30pm, hourly until 4.30pm; October–March 10am, 11am, 1.30pm, hourly until 3.30pm.
Veste Coburg, tel: 0 95 61/8 79-0, fax: 8 79-66. *Art collection:* Tuesday–Thursday 2–5pm; Wednesday 10am–noon; art, crafts from the Middle Ages; German paintings *Carl-Eduard-Bau:* Tuesday–Thursday 2–5pm; Wednesday 10am–noon; glass, crafts, copperplate engraving *Herzoginbau:* April–October Tuesday–Sunday 9.30am–1pm and 2–5pm; November–March Tuesday–Sunday 2–5pm; armoury, modern ceramics. *Fürstenbau:* tel: 0 95 61/9 20 88, April–October daily 10am–noon and 2–4pm; tours on the half hour; November–March tours Tuesday–Sunday 2pm, 3pm; Ducal living quarters; Lucas Cranach room.

Colmar (France)

Unterlinden-Museum, 4, rue Unterlinden, tel: 00 33/3/89/41 89 23 outside Germany. April–October daily 9am–6pm; November–March daily except Tuesday 9am–noon and 2–5pm.

Cottbus

Brandenburgische Kunstsammlungen, Spremberger Str. 1, tel: 03 55/79 40 51. Tuesday–Sunday 10am–6pm.
Niederlausitzer Apothekenmuseum, Altmarkt 24, tel: 03 55/2 39 97. Tours Tuesday–Friday 11am, 2 pm; Saturday, Sunday 2pm, 3pm or by arrangement.
Stiftung Fürst Pückler Museum in Schloss Branitz, Zum Kavalierhaus 11, tel: 03 55/75 15 21. Tuesday–Sunday 10am–noon and 12.30–6pm. Exhibitions of the life, work of the writer/garden landscaper Fürst Pückler in the castle; royal stables.
Wendisches Museum, Mühlenstr. 12, tel: 03 55/79 49 30. Tuesday–Friday 8.30am–5pm; Saturday, Sunday 2–6pm.

Creglingen

Fingerhutmuseum, Kohlers Mühle, tel: 0 79 33/6 31. April–October 9am–6pm; November–March 1–4pm; groups by arrangement after hours.

Dessau

Anhaltinische Gemäldegalerie/Schloss Georgium, Puschkinallee 100, Tel/Fax.: 03 40/61 38 74 or 61 19 49. Tuesday–Sunday 10am–5pm.
Bauhaus-Bauten: *Meisterhäuser* (Ebertallee), *Törten settlement:* (Damaschkestrasse, Klein-, Mittel- and Grossring), *Steel house* (Südstrasse), *Fieger house* (Südstrasse), *Consumer goods buildings* (Am Dreieck 1), *labour exchange centre* (August-Bebel-Platz), *Granary* (Elballee), *Laubenganghäuser* (Peterholzstrasse).
Bauhaus Dessau (Museum), Gropiusallee 38, Tel/Fax.: 03 40/65 08-2 50 or 65 08-2 26 . Tuesday–Sunday 10–5pm.
Kurt-Weill-Zentrum im Feininger-Haus, Ebertallee, tel: 03 40/61 95 95. Tuesday 2–4pm; Thursday 10am–noon; Saturday 2–5pm.
Kurt-Weill-Fest, Information/ticket booking, tel: 03 40/61 95 95. Yearly for 2 March (Weill's Birthday).
Museum Schloss Mosigkau, Knobelsdorff-Allee 3, Tel/Fax.: 03 40/ 52 11

39. Tours November–March Tuesday–Friday 10am–4pm; Saturday, Sunday, some public holidays 11am–4pm; April and October Tuesday–Sunday 10am–5pm; May–September Tuesday–Sunday 10am–6pm.

Donauwörth

Käthe-Kruse-Puppenmuseum, Pflegstr. 21a, tel: 09 06/78 91 45, fax: 7 89-2 22. April–October Tuesday–Sunday 2–5pm; November–March Wednesday, Saturday, Sunday, some public holidays 2–5pm.

Dortmund

Altes Hafenamt, Sunderweg 130, tel: 02 31/98 39-6 84. Saturday 2–5pm; Sunday 10am–1pm.

Brauereimuseum, Märkische Strasse 85, tel: 02 31/54 13-2 89. Tuesday–Sunday 10am–5pm.

Westfälisches Industriemuseum, Grubenweg 5, Bövinghausen, tel: 02 31/69 61 10, Fax: 69 61 14. Tour of the plant daily 9am–6pm; machine rooms Saturday, Sunday 10am–6pm; groups by arrangement.

Dresden

Carl-Maria-von-Weber-Museum, in der Dresdner Strasse 44, Dresden-Hosterwitz, tel: 03 51/3 92 34, Fax: 03 51/3 92 34. Wednesday–Sunday 1–6pm.

Gemäldegalerie Alte Meister, Zwinger Semperbau, tel: 03 51/4 84 06 20, Fax: 4 84 06 94. Tuesday–Sunday 10am–6pm.

Gemäldegalerie Neue Meister/Grünes Gewölbe (royal treasury, sculptures, coin collection), Albertinum, Brühlsche Terrasse,Tel: 03 51/4 95 30 56, fax: 4 95 60 19. Monday–Wednesday, Friday–Sunday 10am–6pm.

Kunstgewerbemuseum Schloss Pillnitz, 01326 Dresden, tel: 03 51/2 61 32 01. *Bergpalais:* May–October Tuesday–Sunday 9.30am–5.30pm; *Wasserpalais:* May–October Monday, Wednesday–Sunday 9.30am–5.30pm.

Porzellansammlung, Zwinger, Sophiestr. 2, tel: 03 51/4 84 06 27, fax: 4 84 06 29. Monday–Wednesday, Friday–Sunday 10am–6pm.

Rüstkammer (Historisches Museum), Zwinger Semperbau, tel: 03 51/ 4 84 06 26, fax: 4 84 06 29. Tuesday–Sunday 10am–6pm.

Semperoper, Tour reservations, tel: 03 51/4 91 14 96, fax: 4 91 14 58.

Staatlicher Mathematisch-Physikalischer Salon, Zwinger, tel: 03 51/ 4 95 13 64, fax: 4 84 06 29. Monday–Wednesday, Friday 9.30am–5pm; Saturday, Sunday 9.30am–12.30pm and 1–5pm.

Verkehrsmuseum, Johanneum, Auguststr. 1, tel: 03 51/4 95 30 02, fax: 4 95 50 36. Tuesday–Sunday 10am–5pm.

Düsseldorf

Goethe-Museum, Anton and Katharina Kippenberg Foundation, Schloss Jägerhof, Jacobistrasse 2, tel: 02 11/ 8 99 62 62. Tuesday–Friday, Sunday 11am–5pm; Saturday 1–5pm.

Heinrich-Heine-Institut, Bilkerstr. 12-14, tel: 02 11/8 99 55 71. Tuesday–Friday, Sunday 11am–5pm; Saturday 1–5pm.

Kunsthalle Düsseldorf, Grabbeplatz 4, tel: 02 11/8 99 62 40. Tuesday–Sunday 11am–6pm.

Kunstsammlung Nordrhein-Westfalen, Grabbeplatz 5, tel: 02 11/8 38 10. Tuesday–Sunday 10am–6pm.

Löbbecke-Museum and Aquazoo Scheidt-Keim-Stiftung, Kaiserswerther Str. 380 (in the North Park), tel: 02 11/8 99 61 50. Daily 10am–6pm.

Duisburg

Museum der deutschen Binnenschifffahrt, Dammstr. 11, tel: 02 03/2 83 43 02. Tuesday–Sunday 10am–5pm.

Wilhelm Lehmbruck Museum, Friedrich-Wilhelm-Str. 40, tel: 02 03/2 83 26 30. Tuesday–Saturday 11am–5pm; Sunday 10am–6pm.

Eisenach

Bachhaus, Frauenplan 21, tel: 0 36 91/20 37 14. April–September Monday noon–5.45pm; Tuesday–Sunday 9am–17.45pm; October–March Monday 1–4.45pm; Tuesday–Sunday 9am–4.45pm.

Lutherhaus, Lutherplatz 8, tel: 0 36 91/2 98 30. May–September daily 9am–5pm; October–April Monday–Saturday 9am–5pm; Sunday 2–5pm.

Wartburg. Tel: 0 36 91/2 50-0. April–October 8.30–5pm; November–March 9am–3.30pm.

Eisleben

Heimatmuseum, Lutherstrasse 15/16, tel: 0 34 75/60 29 03. April–October daily 10am–5pm; November–March 10am–4pm.

Luthermuseum Sterbehaus, Andreaskirchplatz 7, tel: 0 34 75/60 22 85. April–October daily 9am–5pm; November–March Tuesday–Friday 10am–4pm; Saturday, Sunday noon–4pm.

Emden

Hafenrundfahrt, Tours depart opposite the Old Town Hall, tel: 0 48 21/89 07 22. Tours hourly (except noon) Monday–Saturday 10am–4pm; Sunday 11am–4pm.

Dat Otto Hus, Große Str. 1, tel: 0 49 21/9 74 00. Monday–Friday 9.30am–6pm; Saturday 9.30am–4pm; April–October Sunday 10am–4pm.

Kunsthalle, Hinter dem Rahmen 13, tel: 0 49 21/9 74 00. Tuesday 10am–8pm; Wednesday–Friday 10am–5pm; Saturday, Sunday 11am–5pm.

Ostfriesisches Landesmuseum im Alten Rathaus, Neutorstrasse, tel: 0 49 21/2 28 55 o. 8 74 78. April.–September Monday–Friday 11am–1pm and 2–5pm; Saturday 1–5pm; Sunday 11am–5pm; October–March Tuesday–Friday 11am–1pm and 2–4pm; Saturday 1pm–4pm; Sunday 11am–4pm.

Museumsfeuerschiff Amrumbank, Im Ratsdelft, tel: 0 49 21/2 32 85. April–October Monday–Friday 10am-1pm and 3–5pm; Saturday, Sunday 11am–1pm.

Erbach

Deutsches Elfenbeinmuseum, Otto-Glenz-Strasse 1, 64711 Erbach (Odenwald), tel: 0 60 62/64 64 o. 64 39, fax: 64 63. Daily 10am–5pm. Closed Monday November-February.

Erfurt

Angermuseum, Anger 18, tel: 03 61/ 5 62 33 11. Tuesday–Thursday, Sunday 10am–5pm; Friday 10am–1pm; Saturday 1–5pm.

Brückenmuseum, Krämerbrücke 20/21, tel: 03 61/5 62 67 71. Tuesday–Sunday 10am–6pm.

Gartenbauausstellung mit Gartenbaumuseum, Gothaer Strasse, tel: 03 61/ 22 32 20. April–October daily 11am–5pm. Gardens; flower exhibitions; tropical houses; leisure centre; observatory; museum.

Kaisersaal, Tel. 03 61/5 68 81 23. Imperial rooms still used for administration; tours by arrangement.

Zitadelle Petersberg, Petersberg, Tourist information, tel: 03 61/5 62 34 36. Tours by arrangement.

Essen

Museum Folkwang, Goethestrasse 41, 45128 Essen (Rüttenscheid), tel: 02 01/88-4 53 00. Tuesday–Sunday 10am–6pm; Thursday until 9pm.

Eutin

Eutiner Sommerspiele GmbH, Kartenzentrale, Jungfernstieg, Postfach 112, 23691 Eutin, tel: 0 45 21/61 40 or 61 69.

Schloss with landscaped gardens and **Remise** in the castle courtyard with Goethean exhibition. Tuesday–Sunday 10am–1pm and 2–5pm; Thursday until 7pm.

Feuchtwangen

Heimatmuseum, Museumsstrasse 19, tel: 0 98 52/25 75. April–October Tuesday–Sunday 10am–noon and 2–6pm; March, November, December Tuesday–Sunday 10am–noon and 2–5pm.

Kreuzgangspiele, programme of events from tourist information, tel: 0 98 52/9 04 44. June-August.

Flensburg

Schiffahrtsmuseum, Schiffbrücke 39, tel: 04 61/85 29 70. Tuesday–Sunday 10am–5pm; Sunday 10am–13pm.

Städtisches Museum, Lutherplatz. Tuesday–Saturday10am–5pm; Sunday 10am–1pm.

Frankfurt am Main

Deutsches Architektur-Museum, Schaumainkai 43, tel: 0 69/21 23 88 44. Tuesday–Sunday 10am–5pm; Wednesday 10am–8pm.

Deutsches Filmmuseum, Schaumainkai 41, tel: 0 69/21 23 33 69. Tuesday–Friday 10am–5pm; Wednesday 10am–8pm; Saturday 2–8pm.

Goethehaus/Goethe-Museum, Grosser Hirschgraben 23–25, tel: 0 69/29 18 84. October-March Monday–Saturday 9am–4pm; Sunday 10am–1pm; April-June Monday–Saturday 9am–6pm; Sunday 10am–1pm.

Historisches Museum, Saalgasse 19, tel: 0 69/21 23 55 99. Tuesday–Sunday 10am–5pm; Wed 10am–8pm.

Ikonenmuseum, Brückenstrasse 3–7, tel: 0 69/ 21 23 62 62. Tuesday–Sunday 10am–5pm; Wed 10am–8pm.

Liebieghaus/Museum alter Plastik, Schaumainkai 71, tel: 0 69/21 23 86 17. Tuesday–Sunday 10am–5pm; Wednesday 10am–8pm.

Museum für Kunsthandwerk/Ikonen-Museum, Schaumainkai 17/Brückenstr. 3–7, tel: 0 69/21 23 40 37. Tuesday–Sunday 10am–5pm; Wednesday 10am–8pm.

Museum für Post and Kommunikation, Schaumainkai 53, tel: 0 69/ 6 06 00, Tuesday–Sunday 10am–5pm; Wednesday 10am–8pm.

Museum für Völkerkunde, Schaumainkai 29, tel: 0 69/21 23 53 91. Tuesday–Sunday 10am–5pm; Wednesday 10am–8pm.

Naturmuseum Senckenberg, Senckenberganlage 25, tel: 0 69/754 2357. Wednesday–Friday 9am–5pm; Wednesday 9am–8pm; Saturday, Sunday, public holidays 9am–6pm.

Schirn-Kunsthalle, Am Römerberg 6a, tel: 0 69/2 99 88 20. Tuesday–Sunday 10am–7pm; Wednesday, Thursday also 7–10pm.

Städelsches Kunstinstitut and Städtische Galerie, Schaumainkai 63/Holbeinstr. 1, tel: 0 69/60 50 98-0. Tuesday–Sunday 10am–5pm; Wednesday 10am–8pm.

Zoologischer Garten, Alfred-Brehm-Platz 16, 60316 Frankfurt/Main, tel: 0 69/21 23 37 35. Summer daily 8am–7pm; winter daily 8am–5pm.

Frankfurt (Oder)

Carl-Philipp-Emanuel-Bach-Konzerthalle (Ausstellung), Collegienstr. 8, tel: 03 35/ 6 80 27 04. Daily 9–7pm.

Kleistmuseum, Faberstr. 7, tel: 03 35/53 11 55. Tuesday–Sunday 11am–5pm.

Freiburg

Freiburger Fasnetmuseum inm Zunfthaus der Narren, Turmstr. 14, tel: 07 61/2 26 11. Saturday 10am–2pm and by arrangement.

Orgelkonzerte im Münster, Mid-June-September every Tuesday evening.

Freising

Diözesanmuseum, Domberg 21, tel: 0 81 61/4 87 90, fax: 48 79 25. Tuesday–Sunday 10am–5pm; closed some public holidays.

Friedrichroda

Marienglashöhle, On the B 88 between Friedrichroda and Tabarz, tel: 0 36 23/30 49 53. 15. April–September 9am–5pm; October-mid-April 9am–4pm.

Friedrichshafen

Zeppelinmuseum, Seestrasse 22, tel: 0 75 41/38 01-0, fax: 38 01-80. Tuesday–Sunday 10am–5pm; Thursday until 8pm.

Füssen

Hohes Schloss. Tel: 0 83 62/90 31 46. April–October 11am–4pm; November–March 2–4pm. The castle houses the state gallery with late-gothic paintings and sculptures.

Schloss Hohenschwangau. Tel: 0 83 62/8 11 27. April–September 9am–5pm; October–March 10am–4pm.

Schloss Neuschwanstein. Tel: 0 83 62/8 10 35 or 8 18 01. April–September 9am–15pm; October–March 10–4pm; closed some public holidays.

Fürstenberg

Porzellanmanufaktur Fürstenberg, Meinbrexener Str. 2, tel: 0 52 71/40 10. 10. April–October Tuesday–Saturday 9am–5pm; Sunday, public holidays noon–6pm.

Fulda

Deutsches Segelflugmuseum: *see* Wasserkuppe.

Kinder-Akademie Fulda, Werkraum Museum, Mehlaustr. 4, tel: 06 61/7 22 76. Monday–Friday 10am–noon and 3–6pm; Sunday 3–6pm; groups by appointment.

Museum Schloss Fasanerie, Fasaneriestrasse, in Eichenau, tel: 06 61/9 48 60. By tour only; groups by appointment. April–October Tuesday–Sunday 10am–5pm. Tours on the half hour until 4pm except 12.30pm. Tour of porcelain and antique collection Tuesday–Friday 11.30am and 3pm.

Stadtschloss, Schlossstr. 1. Tourist information tel: 06 61/10 21 50. Monday-Thursday 10am–6pm; Friday 2–6pm. Tours April–October Monday-Thursday 10.30am and 2.30pm; Friday 2.30pm; November–March Monday–Friday 2.30pm; Saturday, Sunday, public holidays 10.30am and 2.30pm.

Vonderau Museum, Jesuitenplatz, tel: 06 61/92 83 50. Tuesday–Sunday 10am–6pm. Tours April–October Friday-Sunday 3.30pm; November–March Sunday 3.30pm.

Furtwangen

Deutsches pmenmuseum, Gerwigstrasse 11, tel: 0 77 23/9 20-1 17. April–November daily 9am–5pm; November–March daily 10am–5pm. Tours for groups by arrangement.

Gera

Geraer Höhler (caves), Geithes Passage, tel: 03 65/8 38 14 70. Tours by appointment Monday–Friday 11am and 3pm; Saturday 11am, 2pm and 3pm; Sunday 10am, 11am, 2pm and 3pm.

Kunstsammlung Gera, Küchengartenallee 4, Ortsteil Untermhaus, tel: 03 65/8 32 21 47. Tuesday 1–8pm; Wednesday–Friday 10am–5pm; Saturday, Sunday 10am–6pm.

Museum für Angewandte Kunst, Ferbersches Haus, Greizer Str. 37–39, tel: 03 65/2 87 50. Tuesday–Sunday 10am–5pm.

Museum im Höhler Nr. 188, entrance via Geithes Passage or Natural History Museum. Tel: 03 65/5 20 03. Daily 10am–5pm.

Otto-Dix-Haus, Mohrenplatz 4, tel: 03 65/8 32 49 27. Tuesday–Friday 10am–5pm; Saturday, Sunday 10am–6pm.

Gersthofen

Ballonmuseum, housed in former water tower. Tel: 08 21/2 49 11 35. Wednesday 2–6pm; Saturday, Sunday, public holidays 10am–6pm.

Glücksburg

Schloss. May–September Tuesday–Sunday 10am–5pm; October 10am–4.30pm; November–January; March, April Tuesday–Sunday 10am–noon and 2–4pm.

Glückstadt

Detlefsen-Museum im Brockdorff-Palais, Am Fleth 43, tel: 0 41 24/64 48. 2. April–August Tuesday–Sunday 11am–4pm; September–March Saturday, Sunday 11am–4pm.

Görlitz

Städtische Kunstsammlungen im Kaisertrutz, Demianiplatz, tel: 0 35 81/67 13 51. May-October only, Tuesday–Sunday 10am–5pm.

Gotha

Museum der Natur, Parkallee, tel: 0 36 21/5 31 67. Daily 9–5pm.

Museum für Regionalgeschichte, Ekhof Theater and Cartography Museum; Friedenstein castle, tel: 0 36 21/5 40 16. Daily 9am–5pm.

Schlossmuseum, Schloss Friedenstein, tel: 0 36 21/5 30 36. Daily 9am–5pm.

Graupa

Richard-Wagner-Museum, Richard-Wagner-Strasse 6, tel: 0 35 01/54 82 29. Tuesday–Sunday 9am–4pm.

Greetsiel

Galeriehölländer, tel: 0 49 26/8 90. Tours of the mill easter-autumn Saturday and Wednesday 2pm; autumn-easter Saturday only.

Greetsieler Kunstwoche, open July or August; for tourist information, tel: 0 49 26/9 18 80.

Güstrow

Ernst Barlach Stiftung Güstrow, Atelierhaus am Heidberg, Heidberg 15, tel: 0 38 43/8 22 99. May–October 10am–5pm; November–April 11am–4pm.

Gertrudenkapelle, Gertrudenplatz, tel: 0 38 43/68 30 01. May–October 10am–5pm; November–April 11am–4pm.

Museum im Renaissanceschloss, Franz-Parr-Platz 1, tel: 0 38 43/75 20. May–October Tuesday–Sunday 10am–6pm, November–April Tuesday–Sunday 9am–5pm.

Gutach

Schwarzwälder Freilichtmuseum, Vogtsbauernhof, 77793 Gutach, tel: 0 78 31/2 30. April–October daily 8.30am–6pm.

Haddeby

Wikingermuseum Haithabu, see Schleswig.

Halberstadt

Dom St. Stephanus mit Domschatz, Domplatz 16a, tel: 0 39 41/2 42 37. Monday–Friday 9–11.30am and noon–4pm; Saturday 11–11.30am and noon–4.30pm; Sunday noon–4.30pm.

Vogelkundemuseum (Heineanum), Domplatz 37, tel: 0 39 41/55 14 60. Tuesday–Friday 9am–5pm; Saturday, Sunday 10am–5pm.

Halle

Geiseltalmuseum in der Neuen Residenz, Domstrasse 5, tel: 03 45/ 3 77 81 or 83 24 41. Monday–Friday 9am–noon and 2.30pm–5pm.

Händelfestspiele, Information/ticket sales, tel: 03 45/50 09 02 23. Book June to March at the latest to avoid disappointment.

Händelhaus, Grosse Nicolaistr. 5–6, tel: 03 45/50 09 00. April–September Tuesday–Sunday 10am–5pm; October–March Tuesday–Sunday 10am–4pm.

Staatliche Galerie Moritzburg Halle, Friedemann-Bach-Platz 5, tel: 03 45/3 70 31 or 2 02 82 59. Tuesday 11am–8.30pm; Wednesday–Friday 10am–5.30pm; Saturday, Sunday 10am–6pm.

Hamburg

You can purchase the "Hamburg CARD" (valid for one or more days) from tourist information offices or many hotels and which allows unlimited travel on public transport plus free or reduced entrance fees for many Museums. The "Hamburg CARD light" offers similar reductions, but without the travel benefits.

Altonaer Museum, Museumsstr. 23, tel: 0 40/3 80 75 14. Tuesday–Sunday 10am–6pm.

Ernst-Barlach-Haus, Jenischpark, Baron-Voght-Str. 50a, tel: 0 40/82 60 85. Tuesday–Sunday 11am–5pm; tours every last Sunday of the month at 11am.

Erotic Art Museum, Bernhard-Nocht-Straße 69, tel: 0 40/31 34 29. Tuesday–Sunday 10am–midnight. Mobile exhibitions.

Grosse Hafenrundfahrt mit Barkassen oder eleganten Fahrgastschiffen. Launches from St.-Pauli-Landungsbrücken, at bridge 1, 3, 4, and 7, Deichstrasse/Binnenhafen; passenger boats from St.-Pauli-Landungsbrücken, bridges 5–9, tel: 0 40/31 46 44, 4 12 50 05 or 31 31 30. March–October 9am–5pm every half hour; November–February 10am–4pm every hour. Tours last 1 hour.

Grosse Hafenrundfahrt mit HADAG-Schiffen, from St.-Pauli-Landungsbrücken, departures from bridge 2. Tel: 0 40/31 10 07-0. April–October daily 9am–6pm every half hour; November–March daily 10.30–3.30pm every hour. Tours last 1 hour. Additional trips available.

Hamburger Kunsthalle, Glockengiesserwall (near the main station), tel: 0 40/24 86 26 12. Tuesday–Sunday 10am–6pm; Thursday until 9pm.

Krameramtsstuben, Krayenkamp 10, tel: 0 40/31 10 26 24, Tuesday–Sunday 10am–5pm.

Museum für Hamburgische Geschichte, Holstenwall 24, tel: 0 40/35 04-23 60. Tuesday–Sunday 10am–6pm.

Museum für Kunst and Gewerbe, Steintorplatz 1, tel: 0 40/24 86-27 32/28 28, tel: 24 86-26 30. Tuesday–Sunday 10am–6pm; Thursday until 9pm.

Museumshafen Övelgönne, Anleger Neumühlen, tel: 0 40/3 90 00 79. Always open; tours by arrangement; opportunity to board the ships.

Museumsschiff Rickmer Rickmers, St.-Pauli-Landungsbrücken, bridge 1, tel: 0 40/3 19 59 59. Daily 10am–5.30pm.

RathausTours. Tel: 0 40/36 81 24 70, Monday–Thursday 10am–3pm; Friday–Sunday 10am–1pm every half hour; tours in English/French Monday-Thursday 10.15am–3.15pm, Friday–Sunday 10.15am–1.30pm every hour.

St. Michaelis Kirche und Turm, April–September Monday–Saturday 9am–6pm; Sunday 11.30am–5.30pm; October–March Monday–Saturday 10am–4.30pm; Sunday 11.30am–4.30pm.

Tierpark Hagenbeck, Hagenbeckallee 31, tel: 0 40/54 00 01-0, 5 40 01-47/-48. Open daily from 9am-7pm (summer); 9am-4pm (winter). "Jungle nights" held over four Saturdays end-May-June; artists, shows and music.

Hanau

Hessisches Puppenmuseum, Parkpromenade 4, tel: 0 61 81/8 62 12. Tuesday–Sunday 10am–noon and 2–5pm.

Schloss Philippsruhe, Museum Hanau, Philippsruher Allee 45, tel: 0 61 81/29 55 16 or 29 55 10. Tuesday–Sunday 10am–5pm.

Hann. Münden

Städtisches Museum im Welfenschloss, Schlossplatz, 34346 Hann. Münden, tel: 0 55 41 7 52 02. Wednesday–Friday 10am–noon and 2.30–5pm; Saturday 10am–noon and 2.30–4pm; Sunday 10am–12.30pm.

Hannover

Kestner-Museum, Trammplatz 3, tel: 05 11/1 68 27 30. Tuesday, Thursday Friday 10am–4pm; Wednesday 10am–8pm;Saturday, Sunday 10am–6pm.

Niedersächsisches Landesmuseum, Willy-Brandt-Allee 5, tel: 05 11/98 07-5. Tuesday–Sunday 10am–5pm; Thursday 10am–7pm.

Sprengel Museum, Kurt-Schwitters-Platz 1, tel: 05 11/1 68 38 75. Tuesday 10am–10pm, Wednesday–Sunday 10am–6pm.

Wilhelm-Busch-Museum, Georgengarten 1, tel: 05 11/71 40 76. Tuesday–Sunday 10am–5pm.

Historisches Museum, Pferdestrasse 6/Eingang Burgstrasse, tel: 05 11/1 68 30 52. Tuesday 10am–8pm; Wednesday–Friday 10am–4pm; Saturday, Sunday, some public holidays 10am–6pm.

Harburg

Schloss Harburg, Burgstr. 1, tel: 0 90 03/14 46 oder 12 11. *Castle rooms:* Mid-March–September Tuesday–Sunday 9am–5pm; October 9.30am–4.30pm. *Art collection:* Mid-March–October 10am–noon and 2–5pm.

Heide

Brahmshaus, Lüttenheid, tel: 04 81/6 31 86. April–September Monday 3–5pm; Sunday 10.30am–12.30pm, public holidays also 3–5pm; October–March Sunday 10am–noon and 2–5pm.

Klaus-Groth-Museum, Lüttenheid 48, tel: 04 81/6 37 42. April–September daily 9.30am–noon, Monday, Thursday, Friday 2–4.30pm; October–March daily 10am–noon; Monday, Thursday 2–4pm.

Museum für Dithmarscher Vorgeschichte, Brahmsstrasse 8, tel: 04 81/21 83. April–September Tuesday–Friday 9am–noon and 2–5pm; Sunday 10am–5pm; October–March Tuesday–Friday 2–5pm; Sunday 10am–noon and 2–5pm; groups by arrangement mornings also.

Heidelberg

Deutsches Apothekenmuseum, in the Ottheinrich buiding of the castle, tel: 0 61 21/16 57 80, fax: 18 17 62. Late-March to October daily 10am–5pm; November to early March Saturday, Sunday, public holidays 11am–5pm.

Heidelberger Schloss. Tel: 0 61 21/53 84 14, fax: 16 77 02. Tours daily 8am–5pm.

Studentenkarzer, Alte Universität, Augustinergasse, tel: 0 61 21/54 23 34. April–October Tuesday–Saturday 10am–noon and 2–5pm; Saturday 10am–1pm; November–March Tuesday–Friday 10am–noon and 2–5pm.

Herrnhut

Völkerkundemuseum, Goethestrasse 1, tel: 03 58 73/24 03. Tuesday–Friday 9am–5pm; Saturday, Sunday, public holidays 9am–noon and 1.30–5pm.

Husum

Nordfriesisches Museum Nissenhaus, Herzog-Adolf-Strasse 25, tel: 0 48 41/25 45. April–October daily 10am–5pm; November–March Sunday-Friday 10am–4pm.

Schloss. Tel: 0 48 41/89 73-0. April-October Tuesday–Sunday 11am–5pm. Exhibitions; cultural events.

Stormhaus, Wasserreihe 31, tel: 0 48 41/66 62 70. April–October Tuesday-Friday 10am–noon and 2–5pm; Monday, Saturday, Sunday 2–5pm; November–March Tuesday, Thursday, Saturday 2–5pm.

Tabakmuseum, Wasserreihe 52, tel: 0 48 41/6 12 76. Daily 10am–6pm.

Ilmenau

Am Goethewanderweg: *Goethe's memorial:* Am Markt 1, Ilmenau, tel: 0 36 77/20 26 67 or 6 31 12, May–October daily 9am–noon and 1–4.30pm; November–April daily 10am–noon and 1–4pm. Living quarters; local history. *Gabelbach hunting lodge:* Museum of Goethe's scientific studies, tel: 0 36 77/20 26 26, May–September Tuesday–Sunday 9am–noon and 1–5pm; October–April Wednesday–Sunday 9am–noon and 1–4pm. *Goethehaus Stützerbach (Gundelachsches Haus).* Tel: 03 67 84/5 02 77. Opening times as the hunting lodge.

Jena

Botanischer Garten, Fürstengraben 26, tel: 0 36 41/63 26 26. From mid-May daily 9am–6pm.

Optisches Museum, Ernst-Abbe-Stiftung Jena, Carl-Zeiss-Platz 12, tel: 0 36 41/5 51 06 or 44 31 64. Tuesday–Friday 10am–5pm; Saturday 1–4.30pm; Sunday 9.30am–1pm. Additional tours for groups by arrangement.

Romantikerhaus, Städtische Museen, unterm Markt 12a, tel: 0 36 41/2 35 21. Tuesday–Saturday 10am–1pm and 2–5pm; Wednesday until 6pm.
Schiller-Gedenkstätte, Schillergässchen, tel: 0 36 41/63 03 94. Tuesday–Friday 10am–noon and 1–4pm; Saturday 11am–4pm.
Zeiss-Planetarium, Am Planetarium 5, tel: 0 36 41/44 97 01.Tours for children Tuesday, Thursday 10am; Saturday, Sunday 2.30pm; tours for adults Tuesday–Sunday 11am; Tuesday, Thursday noon and 3pm; Saturday, Sunday 3.30pm. Laser show Wednesday 8pm. Additional tours available.

Jever

Friesisches Brauhaus zu Jever, Elisabethufer 18, tel: 0 44 61/1 37 11. Book for tours.
Kulturhistorisches Museum des Jeverlandes (Museum of Local History) Schlossstr., tel: 0 44 61/21 06. March to mid-January Tuesday–Sunday 10am–6pm.

Karlsruhe

Badisches Landesmuseum, Schloss, tel: 07 21/9 26 65 14. Tuesday–Sunday 10am–5pm; Wednesday 10am–8pm.
Botanischer Garten, Hans-Thoma-Str. 6, tel: 07 21/9 26 30 08. November–March Tuesday–Friday 9am–4pm; Saturday, Sunday, public holidays 9am–noon and 1–4pm; April–October Tuesday–Friday 9am–5pm; Saturday, Sunday, public holidays 9am–noon and 1–5pm.
Museum in der Majolikamanufaktur, Ahaweg 6, tel: 07 21/9 26 65 83. Tuesday–Sunday 10am–1pm and 2–5pm.
Staatliche Kunsthalle and Orangerie, Hans-Thoma-Str. 2–6, tel: 07 21/9 26 67 88. Tuesday–Friday 10am–5pm; Saturday, Sunday, public holidays 10am–6pm.

Kassel

Antikensammlung, Schloss Wilhelmshöhe, tel: 0561/9 37 77, fax: 31 58 73. Summer only Tuesday–Sunday 10am–5pm.
Ballhaus am Schloss Wilhelmshöhe. Tel: 0561/9 37 77, fax: 31 58 73. Summer only Tuesday–Sunday 10am–5pm.
Hessisches Landesmuseum (Hessian Regional Museum), Brüder-Grimm-Platz 5, tel: 05 61/7 84 60, fax: 1 45 51. Tuesday–Sunday 10–5pm. Works by Italian/German artists. Carpet Museum, Pre/Early History Museum, Arts, Crafts and Plastics Museum.

Neue Galerie, state and local art collection, Schöne Aussicht 1, tel: 05 61/70 96 30. Tuesday–Sunday 10–5pm. Works by Dutch/Flemish artists.

Kelheim

Befreiungshalle, auf dem Michelsberg, tel: 0 94 41/15 84. April–October daily 9am–5pm; November–March daily 9am–noon and 3–4pm; closed some public holidays.
Museum für Archäologie, Lederergasse 11, tel: 0 94 41/1 04-92 or 1 04-09. April–October Tuesday–Sunday 10am–4pm.

Kiel

Schleswig-Holsteinisches Freilichtmuseum e. V., Hamburger Landstr. 97, tel: 04 31/6 55 55. April–October Tuesday–Sunday 9am–6pm; August also Monday 9am–6pm; November–March Sunday, public holidays weather permitting 11–4pm.
Kunsthalle, Düsternbrooker Weg 1–7. Tuesday–Saturday 10am–6pm; Thursday until 8pm; Sunday until 5pm.
Rathaus, Am Kleinen Kiel. Tours Saturday 3.40pm.
Schleusen des Nord-Ostsee-Kanals in Kiel-Holtenau. Tours from 3 people, times by arrangement, tel: 04 31/3 60 34 07.
Stiftung Pommern im Schloss, Burgstrasse. Tuesday–Friday 10am–5pm; Saturday, Sunday 2–6pm. Paintings and graphical art from the 17th-20th centuries.

Koblenz

Landesmuseum Koblenz, Festung Ehrenbreitstein, Hohe Ostfront, 56077 Koblenz, tel: 02 61/9 70 30. Mid-March to mid-November daily 9am–12.30pm and 1–5pm.
Mittelrhein-Museum, Am Floriansmarkt 15–17, 56068 Koblenz, tel: 02 61/1 29 25 20. Tuesday–Saturday 11am–5pm; Wednesday 11am–8pm; Sunday 11am–6pm.

Kochel am See

Franz-Marc-Museum, Herzogstandweg 43, tel: 0 88 51/71 14. April–October, 25 December to mid-January Tuesday–Sunday 2-6pm.
Walchensee-Kraftwerk, Altjoch, tel: 0 88 51/7 70. Daily 9am–5pm; tours by arrangement.

Köln

Funkhaus des Westdeutschen Rundfunks (WDR), Wallrafplatz, tel: 02 21/2 20 67 44. Tours around the radio and television studios 9am, 11am, 1pm and 3pm by prior arrangement only; single persons preferred Saturday, Sunday.
Wallraf-Richartz-Museum, Bischofsgartenstr. 1, tel: 02 21/2 21 23 72. Tuesday–Friday 10am–6pm; Saturday, Sunday 11am–6pm.
Museum Ludwig, Bischofsgartenstr. 1, tel: 02 21/2 21 23 79. Tuesday–Friday 10am–6pm; Saturday, Sunday 11am–6pm.
Römisch-Germanisches Museum, Roncallipl. 4, tel: 02 21/2 21 23 04. Tuesday, Thursday, Friday 10am–4pm; Wednesday 10am–6pm; Saturday, Sunday 11am–4pm.
Museum für angewandte Kunst, An der Rechtsschule, tel: 0 2 21/2 21 67 14. Tuesday–Friday 11am–5pm; Saturday, Sunday noon–5pm.
Schnütgen-Museum, Cäcilienstr. 29, Tel. 0 2 21/2 21 36 20. Tuesday–Friday 10am–4pm; Saturday, Sunday 11am–4pm.

Konstanz

Haus zum Kunkel, Münsterplatz 5. Private home. Contact the Mack Family to arrange visits, tel: 0 75 31/2 38 70.
Hus-Museum, Hussenstr. 64, tel: 0 75 31/2 90 42. Tuesday–Saturday 10am–noon and 2–4pm; Sunday 10am–noon.

Kronach

Fränkische Galerie in der Festung Rosenberg. Tel: 0 992 61/6 04 10, fax: 9 72 36. April to early-January Tuesday–Sunday 10am–5pm.

Kronberg

Opelzoo, Königsteiner Str. 35, tel: 0 61 73/7 86 70. October–March daily 8.30am–6pm; April–September daily 9am–5pm.

Laboe

Marine-Ehrenmal, daily 9am–6pm; winter 9am–4pm.

Landshut

Burg Trausnitz. Tel: 08 71/2 26 38. Visit by tours only, offered hourly April–September 9am–noon and 1–5pm; October–March 10am–noon and 1–4pm.

Landshuter Fürstenhochzeit, every 4 years. Next event 2001. Tourist information, tel: 08 71/92 20 50.
Stadtresidenz, Altstadt 79, tel: 08 71/ 2 26 38. April–September 9am–noon and 1–5pm; October–March 10am–noon and 1–4pm.

Lauda

Wein- and Heimatmuseum, Rathausstr. 25, tel: 0 93 43/45 17 or 50 11 28. April–October Sunday, public holidays 3–5pm or by arrangement.

Leipzig

Antikenmuseum, Nikolaikirchhof 2, tel: 03 41/9 60 39 35. Tuesday–Sunday 10am–5pm.
Bach-Museum, Thomaskirchhof 16, tel: 03 41/96 44 10. Daily 10am–5pm; Tours 11am and 3pm.
Museum in der "Runden Ecke", Dittrichring 23, tel: 03 41/9 61 24 43. Wednesday–Sunday 2–6pm.
Stadtgeschichtliches Museum im Alten Rathaus, Markt 1, tel: 03 41/9 65 13-0. Tuesday–Friday 10am–6pm; Saturday, Sunday 10am–4pm; collections Wednesday 9am–4pm.
Thomanerchor, entrance via the church. Friday 6pm, Saturday 3pm except school holidays.
Völkerschlachtdenkmal, Prager Str., tel: 03 41/8 78 04 71. May–October daily 10am–5pm; November–April daily 9am–4pm.

Lichtenfels

Korbmacherausstellung im Stadtturm, in the marketplace. May–October Monday–Friday 10am–6pm; Saturday 9am–1pm.
The **Korbmacherwerkstätten** (basket-making workshops) are close by, open during office hours Monday–Friday. A Museum of basketware is situated 4km (2 miles) from Lichtenfels.

Lindau

Stadtmuseum im Haus zum Cavazzen, Marktplatz, tel: 0 83 82/2 75-4 05. Tuesday–Sunday 10am–noon and 2–5pm; tours by arrangement. Paintings, plastics, graphics, arts/crafts, musical instruments.

Linderhof

Schloss Linderhof. Tel: 0 88 22/35 12. April–September daily 9am–12.15pm and 12.45–5.30pm; October–March daily 10am–12.15pm and 12.45–4pm.

Lübeck

Buddenbrookhaus, Museum and Dokumentationszentrum, Mengstr. 4, tel: 04 51/7 77 88. Daily 10am–5pm; Thursday until 7pm.
Heilig-Geist-Hospital, Koberg. Tuesday–Sunday 10am–5pm.
Katharinenkirche mit Museum für lübische Plastik, Königstrasse. Tuesday–Sunday 10am–1pm and 2-5pm.
Rathaus, Breite Strasse. Tours Monday–Friday 11am, noon and 3pm.
St.-Annen-Museum, St.-Annen-Strasse. Tuesday–Sunday 10am-5pm.
St. Petri, (Tower). April–September daily 9am–6pm.
Stadtgeschichtliches Museum im Holstentor. Tuesday–Sunday 10am–5pm; March–October 10am–4pm.

Lüttenort

Otto-Niemeyer-Holstein-Gedenkstätte. Tel: 03 83 75/2 02 13. Visits by tour only, May–September daily 10am, 11am, 2pm and 3pm; Wednesday, Thursday Friday also 1pm and 4pm. October–April Wednesday–Sunday 11am, 1pm, 2pm and 3pm.

Ludwigslust

Staatliches Museum Schwerin, Schloss Ludwigslust, 19288 Ludwigslust, tel: 0 38 74/2 81 14. Summer Tuesday–Sunday 10am–6pm; winter Tuesday–Sunday 10am–5pm.

Magdeburg

Kulturhistorisches Museum, Otto-von-Guericke-Str. 68–73, tel: 03 91/5 36 50 20. Tuesday–Sunday 10am–6pm.
Telemannfesttage. Tel: 03 91/5 43 02 90. Held every year around June.

Mainau (Insel)

The **Bodenseeschiffahrtsbetriebe** offer boat trips from Konstanz, Überlingen, Meersburg, Friedrichshafen, Bregenz. For information, tel: 0 75 31/28 13 89.
Schloss Mainau, Tel. 0 75 31/3 03-0. Daily 10am–5pm. Mobile art and craft exhibitions; "multivision" show on the nature and culture of the Bodensee area.
Schmetterlingshaus. Tel: 0 75 31/3 03-0. Mid-March to October 10am–8pm; November to early-March 10am–5pm.

Mainz

Gutenbergmuseum, Liebfrauenplatz 5, tel: 0 61 31/12 26 44. Tuesday–Saturday 10am–6pm; Sunday 10am–1pm; closed Monday, public holidays.
Landesmuseum Mainz, Grosse Bleiche 49–51, tel: 0 61 31/2 85 70. Tuesday 10am–8pm, Wed-Sun 10am–5pm.
Römisch-Germanisches-Zentral-Museum, Ernst-Ludwig-Platz 2, tel: 0 61 31/23 22 31. Tuesday–Sunday 10am–6pm.

Mannheim

Kurfürstliches Schloss and Schlosskirche. Tel: 06 21/2 92-28 90. Tours: April–October Tuesday–Sunday 10am–1pm and 2–5pm; November–March Saturday, Sunday only 10am–1pm and 2–5pm.
Museumsschiff, Am Museumsufer, tel: 06 21/42 98-8 39. Tuesday–Sunday 10am–5pm; tours on request.
Städtische Kunsthalle Mannheim, Friedrichsplatz, tel: 06 21/2 93 64 13/14/30/52. Tuesday–Wednesday, Friday–Sunday 10am–5pm; Thursday noon-5pm.
Städtisches Reiss-Museum, Zeughaus: C5, Neubau: D5, tel: 06 21/2 93-31 50/51. Tuesday–Wednesday, Friday–Sunday 10am–5pm; Thursday noon–5pm.

Marbach

Schiller-Nationalmuseum/Deutsches Literaturarchiv Marbach (Museumsabteilung), (National Schiller Museum/ German Literature Archives, Museum Department), Schillerhöhe 8–10, Tel. 0 71 44/60 61. Daily 9–5pm.

Marburg

Universitätsmuseum für Kulturgeschichte (University Museum of Regional History), Castle, tel: 0 64 21/ 28 23 55. 1 April–31 October Tuesday–Sunday 10–6pm, 1 November–31 March Tuesday–Sunday 11–5pm.

Meissen

Albrechtsburg (Albrechtsburg Castle), Domplatz 1, tel: 0 35 21/47 07 10, fax: 47 07 11. March–November daily 10–6pm, December and February daily 10–5pm, January closed.
Frauenkirche (Church of Our Lady), An der Frauenkirche 11, tel: 0 35 21/45 38 32. Tower ascent: May–October daily 10–12.30 and 1–3.30 pm.
Staatliche Porzellanmanufaktur Meissen (Meissen Porcelain Factory),

Talstrasse 9, tel: 0 35 21/46 82 08, fax: 46 88 04. Demonstration workshop daily 9–12 and 1–4.45 pm; Exhibition Hall 9–5pm.

Meersburg

Altes Schloss (Old Castle). Tel: 0 75 32/64 41. March–October daily 9–6pm; November–February daily 10–5pm. Knights' Hall, Weapons Hall, Apartments of the poetess Annette von Droste-Hülshoff.

Droste-Museum (Annette von Droste-Hülshoff Museum) **(Fürstenhäusle)**, Stettener Strasse 9, tel: 0 75 32/60 88. Easter–mid-October daily 10–12.30 and 2–6pm, Sunday and public holidays 2–6pm.

Neues Schloss (New Castle). Tel: 0 75 32/4 40-2 65. April–October daily 10–1 and 2–6pm; November–Easter closed. Residence of the prince-bishops, municipal art collection. Also within the castle: Dorniermuseum (Dornier Museum) with an exhibition of German aviation history.

Merseburg

Kulturhistorisches Museum Merseburg im Schloss (Museum of Regional History in Merseburg Castle), Domplatz 9, tel: 0 34 61/40 13 19. Tuesday–Sunday 9–5pm. The museum displays exhibits relating to the prehistory and early history of the region, as well as sitting room, kitchen and bedroom of the Biedermeier period, beadwork and other craft items as well as changing art exhibitions.

Mespelbrunn

Schloss (Castle). Tel: 0 60 92/2 69, fax: 99 59 79. Tours 1 April–mid-November Monday–Friday 9–noon and 1–5pm, Saturday, Sunday and public holidays 9–5pm.

Michelau in Oberfranken

Deutsches Korbmuseum (German Museum of Basketry), Bismarckstrasse 4, tel: 0 95 71/8 35 48. April–October Tuesday–Sunday 9–noon and 1–4.30 pm; November–March Monday-Thursday 9am–noon and 1–4.30 pm, Friday 9am–noon; May–September Basketry Demonstrations (Saturday afternoon).

Mittenwald

Geigenbau- and Heimatmuseum (Museum of Violin-Making and Local History), Ballenhausgasse 3, tel: 0 88 23/25 11. Monday–Friday10–11.45 and 2–4.45 pm, Saturday and Sunday 10–11.45; 1 November– approx. 20. December closed.

Moordorf

Moormuseum Moordorf (Moordorf Marshland Museum), open-air museum, Victorburer Moor 7a in Moordorf, tel: 0 49 42/27 34. May–October Tuesday–Sunday 10am–5.30 pm.

Moritzburg

Käthe-Kollwitz-Museum, Meissener Strasse 7, tel: 03 52 07/8 28 18. April–October Tuesday–Friday 11–5pm, Saturday and Sunday 10–5pm, in winter shorter opening hours.

Museum Schloss Moritzburg. Tel: 03 52 07/8 14 39, fax: 8 14 58. May–October daily 10–5.30 pm; March and November Tuesday–Sunday 10–4.30 pm; December Tuesday–Sunday 10–3.30 pm; April Tuesday–Sunday 10–5.30 pm.

Munich

Alte Pinakothek (Old Pinakothek), Barer Strasse 27. This museum is expected to remain closed for renovation until 1998. Some 300 principal works are on view on the New Pinakothek.

Bayerisches Nationalmuseum (National Museum of Bavaria), Prinzregentenstrasse. 3, tel: 0 89/21 12 41. Tues–Sunday 9.30–5pm.

Cuvilliéstheater (Cuvilliés Theatre), Entrance Residenzstrasse 1, tel: 0 89/29 68 36. Open for viewing: Monday–Saturday 2–5pm, Sunday and public holidays 10–5pm, unless rehearsals are taking place.

Deutsches Museum, Museumsinsel, tel: 0 89/2 17 91. Daily 9–5pm. With planetarium. *IMAX Cinema* in the Forum der Technik (Forum of Technology): Museumsinsel 1, tel: 0 89/2 11 25-1 80.

Fernsehturm (Olympiaturm) (Television Tower), Olympiapark, tel: 0 89/30 67 20 07. Daily 9–midnight, last ascent at 11.30 pm.

Glyptothek, Königsplatz 3, tel: 0 89/ 28 61 00. Tuesday–Sunday 10–5pm, Thursday until 8pm.

Kunsthalle der Hypo-Kulturstiftung (Art Gallery of the Hypo Cultural Foundation), Theatinerstrasse 5, tel: 0 89/ 22 44 12. Daily 10–6pm, Thursday until 9pm.

Münchner Stadtmuseum (Museum of the City of Munich), Sankt-Jakobs-Platz 1, tel: 0 89/23 32 23 70, Tuesday and Thursday–Sunday 10–5pm, Wednesday 10–8.30 pm. (permanent exhibitions etc. in the Museum of Photography and Film and in the Puppet Museum).

Neue Pinakothek (New Pinakothek), Barer Strasse 29, tel: 0 89/2 38 05-1 95. Daily except Monday 10–5 pm, Tuesday and Thursday all day 10–8 pm.

Residenzmuseum (Palace Museum), Max-Joseph-Platz 3, tel: 0 89/29 06 71. Open daily 10–4.30; the morning and afternoon tours cover different areas of the museum. In the morning (10-12.30 pm) the tour covers the Antiquarium etc.; during the afternoon it includes the Kaisersaal etc.

Schack-Galerie (Schack Gallery), Prinzregentenstrasse 9, tel: 0 89/ 2 38 05-2 24. Daily except Tuesday 10–5 pm.

Schatzkammer in der Residenz (Palace Treasury), Max-Joseph-Platz 3, tel: 0 89/29 06 71. Daily 10–4.30 pm.

Schloss Nymphenburg (Nymphenburg Castle). Tel: 0 89/17 90 80, fax: 17 90 86 27. Schönheitengalerie (Gallery of Beauties): April–15 October 9–12.30 and 1.30–5pm, 16 October–March 10–12.30 and 1.30–4pm. Schlosskapelle (Castle Chapel): April–15 October 9–12.30 and 1.30–5 pm, closed in winter.

Marstallmuseum (Carriage Museum): April–15 October 9–12 and 1–5 pm, 16 October–March 10–noon and 1–4pm. Badenburg, Pagodenburg and Magdalenenklause: April–September 10–12.30 and 1.30–5pm.

Spielzeugmuseum im Alten Rathausturm (Toy Museum in the Old Town Hall), Marienplatz, tel: 0 89/ 29 40 01. Daily 10–5.30 pm.

Staatliche Antikensammlung (Collection of Antiquities), Königsplatz 1, tel: 0 89/59 83 59. Tuesday–Sunday 10–5pm, Wednesday until 8pm.

Staatliche Sammlung Ägyptischer Kunst (Collection of Egyptian Art), Residenz, Entrance Hofgartenstrasse 1, tel: 0 89/29 85 46. Tuesday–Friday 9–4pm, Tuesday also 7–9pm, Saturday and Sunday 10–5pm.

Staatliches Museum für Völkerkunde (Museum of Ethnology), Maximilianstrasse 42, tel: 0 89/2 28 55 06. Reconstruction of the museum was completed by the end of 1996. The side wing has already reopened for special exhibitions (Tuesday–Sunday 9.30–4.30pm); the rest of the building will be completed by 1998.

Staatsgalerie moderner Kunst (Gallery of Modern Art), Haus der Kunst, Prinzregentenstrasse 1, tel: 0 89/ 21 12 71 37. Daily except Monday 10–5pm, Thursday 10–8pm.

Städtische Galerie im Lenbachhaus (Villa Lenbach Collections), Luisenstrasse 33, tel: 0 89/2 33 03 20 and 23 23 20 00. Daily except Monday 10–6pm.

Turm des Alten Peter (Tower of St Peter's Church), am Rindermarkt, tel: 0 89/2 60 48 28. In winter Monday–Saturday 9–6pm, Sunday 10–6pm, in summer longer if required.

"Valentin-Musäum", Museum of folk song and folk song pub, in the Isartor tower, tel: 0 89/22 32 66. Monday, Tuesday, Friday Saturday11.01–5.29 pm, Sunday 10.01–5.29 pm.

Münster

Allwetterzoo (Indoor Zoo), Sentruper Strasse 315, tel: 02 51/89 04-0. Daily from 9 pm. Ticket office closes April–September 6pm, March/October 5pm, otherwise 4pm.

Freilichtmuseum Mühlenhof (Mill Open-Air Museum), Sentruper Strasse 223, tel: 02 51/98 12 00. April–October daily 10–6pm, November–March daily 11–16.30 pm.

Rathaus mit Friedenssaal (Town Hall and Peace Hall), Prinzipalmarkt, tel: 02 51/4 92-27 24. Monday–Friday 9–5pm, Saturday 9–4pm, Sunday and public holidays 10–1 pm. Tours of the Town Hall Sunday 11.30 am (except when official functions are taking place).

Westfälisches Museum für Naturkunde mit Planetarium (Science Museum and Planetarium), Sentruper Strasse 285, tel: 02 51/5 91 05. Tuesday–Sunday 9–6pm.

Murnau

Gabriele-Münter-Haus (Russenhaus), Kottmüllerallee 6, tel: 0 88 41/93 05. Closed until approx. autumn 1997 for renovations.

Schlossmuseum (Castle Museum), Schlosshof 4–5, tel: 0 88 41/47 62 07. Tuesday–Sunday 10–5pm; July–September open until 6pm at weekends.

Neuruppin

Heimatmuseum (Museum of Local History), August-Bebel-Strasse 14–15, tel: 0 33 91/33 08. Tuesday–Friday10–5pm, Saturday and Sunday 10–6pm.

Nördlingen

Daniel, Tower of St George's Church. Tel: 0 90 81/8 41 24. April–October daily 9–8pm, November–March daily 9–5.30 pm.

Stadtmuseum (Municipal Museum), Vordere Gerbergasse 1, tel: 0 90 81/ 8 41 20. Visits only as part of the hourly guided tours: Easter–1 November Tuesday–Sunday 10–noon and 1.30–4.30 pm.

Norden

Heimatmuseum mit Teemuseum (Museum of Local History and Tea Museum), Am Markt, tel: 0 49 31/1 21 00. Tuesday–Sunday 10–4pm.

Seehundaufzuchtstation (Seal breeding station), im Wellenpark, tel: 0 49 31/89 19. Daily 10–5pm.

Tiergehege (Miniature Zoo), im Wellenpark. Tel. via Tourist Information Office: 0 49 31/9 86 02. Daily 10–5pm.

Nürnberg (Nuremberg)

Albrecht-Dürer-Haus (Albrecht Dürer House), Albrecht-Dürer-Strasse 39, tel: 09 11/2 31-25 68. March–October Tuesday–Sunday 10–5pm; November–February Tuesday–Friday 1–5pm, Saturday and Sunday 10–5pm.

Germanisches Nationalmuseum (German National Museum), Kartäusergasse 1, tel: 09 11/13 31-0. Tuesday–Sunday 10–5pm, Wednesday until 9pm.

Handwerkerhof (Craftsmen's Yard), am Königstor. Monday–Friday 10–6.30, Saturday 10–4pm. Tuesday Restaurants and taverns are open until 10pm. In December also Sunday 10–6.30 pm, 24. December–19. March closed.

Kaiserburg (Castle). Tel: 09 11/22 57 26. April–September 9–noon and 12.45–5pm; October–March 9.30–noon and 12.45–4pm. Tours every half hour.

Lochgefängnisse, Folterkammer (Dungeons and Torture Chamber), Beneath the Old Town Hall, tel: 09 11/2 31-26 90. Tuesday–Sunday 10–5pm. Mid-October–early April closed.

Stadtmuseum Fembohaus (Fembo

Municipal Museum), Burgstrasse 15, tel: 09 11/2 31-25 95. The museum is expected to be closed during summer 1997 for reconstruction.

Verkehrsmuseum (Traffic Museum), Lessingstrasse 6, tel: 09 11/2 19-24 28. Daily 9.30–5pm.

Oldenburg

Augusteum, Elisabethstrasse 1, tel: 04 41/2 20 26 00. Tuesday–Friday 9–5pm, Saturday, Sunday and public holidays 10–5pm.

Landesmuseum für Kunst und Kulturgeschichte im Schloss (Regional Art and History Museum), Schlossplatz 26, tel: 04 41/2 20 26 00. Tuesday–Friday 9–5pm, Saturday, Sunday and public holidays 10–5pm.

Oldenburger Kultursommer (Oldenburg Summer Festival), Information from the Tourist Information Office, tel: 04 41/1 57 44. Music, dance, drama, street musicians, do-it-yourself circus for children etc.

Peenemünde

Historisch-technisches Informationszentrum Peenemünde (Historical and Technical Information Centre), Bahnhofstrasse 28, tel: 03 83 71/2 05 73. April–October Tuesday–Sunday 9–6pm, November–March 9–4pm.

Pforzheim

Schmuckmuseum (Jewellery Museum), Jahnstrasse 42, tel: 0 72 31/ 39 21 26. Tuesday–Sunday 10–5pm.

Pirna

Barockgarten Grosssedlitz in Heidenau (Grosssedlitz Baroque Garden, Heidenau), Parkstrasse 85, 01809 Heidenau, tel: 0 35 29/51 92 12. April–September daily 7–8pm, October–March daily 8–6pm. A visit is only recommended in summer, as the sculptures are clad in protective cases in winter. Tours by arrangement.

Stadtkirche St. Marien (St Mary's Church): Ascent of the church tower upon application to the parochial office: tel: 0 35 01/52 79 73.

Plau

Burgturm, Am Burgplatz. Contact Tourist Information Office, tel: 03 87 35/ 23 45. Opening times vary.

Wandschneider-Museum, Kirchplatz 2, tel: 03 87 35/22 09. Opening times vary.

Potsdam

Note: The Potsdam "WelcomeCard", permits unlimited use of all public transport run by the Berlin-Brandenburg Transport Authorities (VBB) for a period of 48 hours as well as three days' free entry or reductions on entrance charges to museums, leisure and adventure parks and sightseeing tours in Potsdam and Berlin. Cards are available from the Tourist Information Office, VBB sales offices and hotels.

Babelsberger Studiotour (Tour of Babelsberg Film Studios), August-Bebel-Strasse 26–53, Entrance Grossbeerenstrasse, tel: 03 31/7 21 27 55 (Information), 03 31/7 21 27 50 (Visitors' Service Centre). April–October daily 10–6pm (Last entry 4.30 pm), in winter upon request. Duration of tour: 3-4 hours.

Filmmuseum Potsdam (Potsdam Film Museum), Marstall, tel: 03 31/27 18 10. Tuesday–Friday10–5pm, Saturday, Sunday and public holidays 10–6pm.

Stiftung Preussische Schlösser und Gärten Berlin-Brandenburg (Castles and Parks Foundation Berlin-Brandenburg), tel: 03 31/ 96 94-2 02, -2 03 and -2 04. Cecilienhof Castle and Sanssouci Palace, Mid-May–Mid-October daily 9–5pm, November, December, January 9–3pm, otherwise 9–4pm. Closed on some Mondays, open on public holidays, closed 24 and 31 December.

Pottenstein

Teufelshöhle (Devil's Cave), on the B 470 between Pottenstein and Pegnitz, tel: 0 92 43/2 08. Easter-October daily 9–4.30 pm; November-Easter Tuesday and Saturday 10–noon. Tours take place every 10–15 minutes and last approximately 45 minutes.

Preetz

Zirkusmuseum (Circus Museum), Mühlenstrasse 14. Wednesday 5–8pm, Saturday 3–6pm, Sunday 10–noon and 3–6pm.

Quedlinburg

Domschatz (Cathedral Treasury). Tel: 0 39 46/70 99 00. Tuesday–Saturday 10–6pm, Sunday 11.30–5pm; in winter closes one hour earlier depending on number of visitors. Tours by arrangement.

Ständerbau (Fachwerkmuseum) ((Museum of Timbered Houses), Wordgasse 3, tel: 0 39 46/38 28. April-October daily except Thursday 10–5pm.

Schlossmuseum (Castle Museum), Schlossberg 1, tel: 0 39 46/27 30. Tuesday–Saturday 10–5pm.

Radebeul

Karl-May-Museum (Villa Shatterhand), Karl-May-Strasse 5, tel: 03 51/8 30 27 23, fax: 8 30 99 18. March–October Tuesday–Sunday 9–6pm, November–February Tuesday–Sunday 9–4pm, 24., Closed on December 25 and 31 and January 1.

Staatliche Kunstsammlungen Dresden, Puppentheatersammlung (Dresden Museum of Art and Puppet Theatre Collections), Hohenhaus, Barkengasse 6, Tel. and fax: 03 51/7 43 73. Tuesday–Friday 9–4pm; last Sunday in the month 10–5pm.

Weinbaumuseum Haus Hoflössnitz (Wine Museum), Knohllweg 37, tel: 03 51/8 30 13 22, fax: 8 30 83 56. Tuesday–Friday 2–5pm, Saturday and Sunday 10–5pm.

Rathen

Festung Königstein, (Königstein Castle), Staatlicher Schlossbetrieb, 01824 Königstein, tel: 03 50 231/64-6 07. April–September 9–8pm, October 9–6pm, November–March 9–5pm.

Ratzeburg

A.-Paul-Weber-Haus, Domhof 5, tel: 0 45 41/1 23 26. Tuesday– Sunday 10–1 and 2–5pm.

Barlach-Museum, Barlachplatz 3, tel: 0 45 41/37 89. Tuesday–Sunday 10–noon and 3–6pm; Closed 1 December–1 March.

Regensburg

Reichstagsmuseum (Reichstag Museum), Altes Rathaus am Rathausplatz, tel: 09 41/5 07 44 11. Viewing by guided tour only: Monday–Saturday 9.30, 10.30, 11.30am and 2, 3, 4pm; Sunday and public holidays 10, 11, noon; April–October also at 10 and 11am, noon, 2.30, 3.50pm and Sunday and public holidays 10.30, 11.30am and 2–4pm every half-hour. Closed on January 1. Open by request on: February 11, March 28 and 31, May 1, 19, November 1, December 25 and 31.

Remagen

Friedensmuseum (Peace Museum), an der Remagener Rheinfront, tel: via Tourist Information Office: 0 26 42/2 25 72. March–November daily 10–5pm.

Rheinsberg

Schlossmuseum Rheinsberg (Castle Museum). Tel: 03 39 31/21 05. April-October 9.30–12.30 and 1–5pm, November–January 9.30–12.30 and 1–3pm, February and March 9.30–12.30 and 1–4.30 pm.

Ribnitz-Damgarten

Bernsteinmuseum (Amber Museum), Kloster 1–2, tel: 0 38 21/29 31. May-September daily 9.30–5pm, October, March, April Tuesday–Saturday 9.30–4.30 pm, Sunday 1–4.30 pm, November–February Wednesday–Saturday 10–4pm, Sunday 1–4pm.

Rorschach (Switzerland)

Museum im Kornhaus (Granary Museum), Hafenplatz 2, tel: 00 41/71/8 41 40 62 (from abroad). End April–mid-November Tues–Saturday 9.30–11.30am and 2–5pm, Sunday 10–noon and 2–5pm. At other times by appointment.

Rostock

Kulturhistorische Museen (Historico-Cultural Museums): Kloster zum Kreuz, (Monastery of the Cross) Klosterhof, tel: 03 81/45 59 13. Local medieval art, 20th-century sculptures Kröpeliner Tor, (Kröpelin Gate) Kröpeliner Strasse, tel: 03 81/45 41 77. Municipal History. Opening times for both museums: October–March Tuesday–Sunday 9–5pm, April–September Tuesday–Sunday 10–6pm.

Schiffahrtsmuseum (Navigation History Museum), August-Bebel-Strasse 1, tel: 03 81/4 92 26 97. History of Navigation. October–March Tuesday–Sunday 9–5pm, April–September Tuesday–Sunday 10–6pm.

Schiffbaumuseum (Museum of Shipbuilding), Traditional ship, Liegeplatz Schmal, tel: 03 81/1 21 97 26. October–March Tuesday–Sunday 9–5pm, April–September Tuesday–Sunday 10–6pm.

Rothenburg ob der Tauber

Kriminalmuseum (Museum of Crime), Burggasse 3, tel: 0 98 61/53 59. Daily 9.30–6pm.
Hans-Sachs-Spiele (Hans Sachs Drama Festival), Programme information from the Tourist Information Office, tel: 0 98 61/4 04-92. Annually, mid-September.
Rathausturm (Town Hall Tower). April–October daily 9.30–12.30 and 1.30–5pm, December daily noon–3pm, January–March Saturday and Sunday noon–3pm.

Rottleben

Barbarossa-Höhle (Barbarossa's Cave), 06568 Rottleben, tel: 03 46 71/24 81. October–April daily 9–5pm.

Schleswig

Wikingermuseum Haithabu (Haithabu Viking Museum), on the B 76 in South Schleswig, tel: 0 46 21/81 33 00. April–October daily 9–5pm, November–March Tuesday and Sunday 10–4pm.
Landesmuseen Schloss Gottorf (Gottorf Castle Local Museum), tel: 0 46 21/81 32 22. March–October daily 9–5pm (one section closed on Monday); November–February Tuesday–Sunday 9.30am–4pm, closed on Buss- and Bettag (holiday in mid-November) as well as December 24, 25, 31 and January 1.

Schlüchtern

Bergwinkelmuseum, Schlossstrasse 15, tel: 0 66 61/8 50. 1 April–10 September Tuesday–Saturday 2–4pm, Sunday 10am–noon; 1 October–31 March Wednesday 2–4pm, Sunday 10am –noon.

Schmalkalden

Schloss Wilhelmsburg (Wilhelmsburg Castle), Schlossberg 9, tel: 0 36 83/40 31 86. February–October Tuesday–Sunday 9am–5pm, November–January Tuesday–Sunday 10am–4pm.
Schaubergwerk Finstertal (Finstertal Demonstration Coal Mine), Asbach, tel: 0 36 83/48 80 37. April–October Wednesday–Sunday 10am–5pm.
Technisches Denkmal Neue Hütte (Neue Hütte Technical Monument), Weidebrunn, Gothaer Strasse, tel: 0 36 83/40 30 18. April–October Wednesday–Sunday 10am–5pm.

Schwalmstadt

Museum der Schwalm (Schwalm Museum), Paradeplatz/Ziegenhain, tel: 0 66 91/38 93. 1. April–30 September Tuesday–Friday 10am–noon and 3–5pm, Saturday and Sunday 11am–5pm; October 1–March 31 Tuesday–Friday 10am–noon and 3–5pm, Saturday 10am–noon and 3–5pm, Sunday 11am–noon and 3–5pm.

Schwerin

Schlossmuseum (Castle Museum), Lenné-Strasse 1, tel: 03 85/5 25 29 27. 15. October–14 April Tuesday–Sunday 10–5pm, 15 April–14 October Tuesday–Sunday 10–6pm.
Staatliches Museum (National Museum), Alter Garten 3, October 15–April 14 Wednesday–Sunday 10am–5pm, Tuesday 10am–8pm, April 15–October 14 Wed–Sun 10am–6pm, Tuesday 10am–8pm.

Seebüll

Stiftung Seebüll Ada and Emil Nolde (Seebüll Ada and Emil Nolde Foundation), near Neukirchen, tel: 0 46 64/3 64. March 1–October 31, 10am–6pm, November 10am–5pm.

Speyer

Historisches Museum der Pfalz (Palatinate Museum of History), Domplatz, tel: 0 62 32/1 32 50. Special exhibitions Tuesday–Sunday 10–8pm, otherwise Tuesday–Sunday 10–6pm and Wednesday until 8pm.
Judenbad (Jewish Baths), Judenbadgasse, tel: 0 62 32/7 72 88. 1.4.–31.10. Monday–Friday 10am–noon and 2–5pm, Saturday, Sunday 10–5pm. Closed in winter.

Stade

Freilichtmuseum Auf der Insel, (Open-air Museum). Tel: 0 41 41/32 22. 1 May–10 September Tuesday–Sunday 10am–1pm, 2–5pm.
Heimatmuseum (Folklore Museum), Inselstrasse 12, tel: 0 41 41/40 15 41. Tuesday–Friday 10–1 and 2–4pm.
Kunsthaus (House of Art), Wasser West 7, tel: 0 41 41/32 22. Tuesday–Friday 10–5pm, Sat/Sun 10am–6pm.
Schwedenspeicher-Museum, Am Fischmarkt, tel: 0 41 41/32 22. Tuesday–Friday 10–5pm, Saturday and Sunday 10–6pm.

Steinau an der Strasse

Amtshaus (Wohnhaus der Familie Grimm) (Tribunal), Brüder-Grimm-Strasse 80, Tel. via Tourist Information Office: 0 66 63/9 73 55/-56. April–October daily 2–5pm. Tours by arrangement at any time of year.

Stolberg

Heimatmuseum mit Thomas-Münzer-Zimmer (Folklore Museum and Thomas Münzer Room), Niedergasse 19, tel: 03 46 54/4 54. Tuesday–Saturday 9–12.30 and 1–5pm, Sunday and public holidays 10–noon and 1–5pm.

Stralsund

Kulturhistorisches Museum (Historico-Cultural Museum), Mönchstrasse 25, tel: 0 38 31/2 46 90. Tuesday–Sunday 10–5pm.
Deutsches Museum für Meereskunde and Fischerei (German Museum of Oceanography and Fishing), Katharinenberg 14–20, Entrance Mönchstrasse, tel: 0 38 31/29 51 35. 1 November–30 April Tuesday–Sunday 10–5pm, during local school holidays also open on Monday; May, June, September, October daily 10–5pm, July/August Monday–Thursday 9–6pm, Friday–Sunday 9–5pm.

Straubing

Gäubodenfest (Folklore Festival), early-mid-August, over a period of 10 days. Information from Tourist Information Office, tel: 0 94 21/94 43 07.

Stuttgart

Lindenmuseum Stuttgart, Staatliches Museum für Völkerkunde (National Museum of Ethnology), Hegelplatz 1, tel: 07 11/1 23 12 42/43. Tuesday–Sunday 10am–5pm, Wednesday 10am –8pm.
Mercedes-Benz-Museum (Stuttgart-Untertürkheim), Mercedesstrasse 136, tel: 07 11/1 72 32 56. Tuesday–Sunday 9–5pm, closed public holidays.
Staatsgalerie Stuttgart (Stuttgart National Gallery of Art), Konrad-Adenauer-Strasse 30–32, tel: 07 11/2 12 40 50. Tuesday–Sunday 10–5pm, Tuesday and Thursday also 5–8pm.
Württembergisches Landesmuseum Stuttgart (Württemberg State Museum), in the Old Castle (Altes Schloss), Schillerplatz 6, tel: 07 11/2 79 34 00. Tuesday 10–1 pm, Wednesday–Sunday 10am–5pm.

Tann

Rhöner Museumsdorf und Rhöner Naturmuseum (Museum Village and Nature Museum), Schlossstrasse 3, 36142 Tann (Rhön), tel: 0 66 82/16 55, fax: 89 22. 1 April–31 October 10–noon and 2–5pm, 1 November–31 March open for groups upon request.

Tauberbischofsheim

Kurmainzisches Schloss (Castle), Am Schlossplatz, tel: 0 93 41/8 03 73 (Museum), 37 60 (Museum Guides). Palm Sunday–October Tuesday–Saturday 2.30–4.30pm, Sunday and public holidays also 10am–noon.

Tübingen

Hölderlin-Turm (Hölderlin Tower), Bursagasse 6, tel: 0 70 71/2 20 40, fax: 2 29 48. Tuesday–Friday 10–noon and 3–5pm, Saturday, Sunday and public holidays 2–5pm. Tours Saturday, Sunday and public holidays at 5pm.

Trier

Karl-Marx-Haus, Brückenstrasse 10, tel: 06 51/4 30 11. Tuesday–Sunday 10–6pm, Monday 1–6pm.

Uhldingen-Mühlhofen

Freilichtmuseum Deutscher Vorzeit (Open-air Museum of German Prehistory). Tel: 0 75 56/85 43. April–September daily 8am–6pm; October 9am–5pm; March and November Saturday only, Sunday and public holidays 9am–5pm. Group tours by prior arrangement.

Ulm

Deutsches Brotmuseum (German Bread Museum), Salzstadlgasse 10, tel: 07 31/6 99 55. Tuesday–Sunday 10am–5pm, Wednesday until 8.30pm.

Verden

Deutsches Pferdemuseum (German Horse Museum), Andreasstrasse 17, tel: 0 42 31/39 01. Tuesday–Sunday til 4pm.
Märchen- and Freizeitpark (Fairy-tale and Leisure Park), Osterkrug 5–7, tel: 0 42 31/6 40 83. Beginning of Easter holidays–End of autumn half-term holidays) daily 9–6pm, closed in winter.

Waren

Müritz-Museum and Süsswasseraquarium (Müritz Museum and Freshwater Aquarium), Friedenstrasse 5, tel: 0 39 91/66 76 00. October–April

Tuesday–Friday 10–4pm, Saturday, Sunday and public holidays 10–noon and 2–4pm; May–September Tuesday–Sunday 9–6pm, during school holidays sometimes also open on Monday.

Wasserkuppe

Deutsches Segelflugmuseum (German Gliding Museum), auf der Wasserkuppe, 36129 Gersfeld-Rhön, tel: 0 66 54/77 37. 1 April–1 November 9–noon and 1–6pm; 2 November–31 March 10–noon and 1–5pm; Closed December 24 and 25.

Weikersheim

Schloss Weikersheim (Weikersheim Castle), Marktplatz, tel: 0 79 34/83 64. April–October 9–6pm, November–March 10–noon and 1.30–4.30 pm.

Weimar

Bauhaus-Museum der Kunstsammlungen zu Weimar (Bauhaus Museum of Art, Weimar), Burgplatz 4, tel: 0 36 43/54 61 61, fax: 54 61 01/02. Tuesday–Sunday 10–6pm.
Gedenkstätte Buchenwald (Buchenwald Memorial Site). Tel: 0 36 43/43 02 00. May–September daily 9.45–6pm, October–April daily except Monday 8.45–5pm.
Herzogin Anna Amalia Bibliothek (Duchess Anna Amalia Library), Platz der Demokratie, Rococo Hall, April–October daily except Sunday 11–12.30 pm, closed November–March.
Museen der Stiftung Weimarer Klassik (Museums of the Weimar Classic Foundation). Tel: 0 36 43/54 51 02.
Goethes Gartenhaus im Park an der Ilm, (Goethe's Summer-House). Daily except Tuesday 9–noon and 1–5pm, November–February until 4pm.
Goethes Wohnhaus am Frauenplan, (Goethe's House) Tuesday–Sunday 9–5pm, November–February. 9–4pm.
Schillerhaus, (Schiller's House) Schillerstrasse, daily except Tuesday 9–5pm, November–February to 4pm.
Wittumspalais, Theaterplatz, Tuesday–Sunday 9–noon and 1–5pm, November–February to 4pm.

Westgrossefehn

Fehnmuseum, Leerer Landstrasse, tel: 0 49 45/13 33. April–September Tuesday–Saturday 10–5pm, Sunday 10–7pm, Groups by arrangement, also outside the normal opening times.

Wilhelmshaven

Küstenmuseum (Coastal Museum), Rathausplatz 10, tel: 0 44 21/16 14 60. Tuesday–Friday and Sunday (July and Aug. also Monday) 10–1 and 2–5pm, Saturday 10–1pm.

Winningen

Wein- und Heimatmuseum (Wine and Folklore Museum), Schulstrasse 7, 56333 Winningen, tel: 0 26 06/21 26. Wednesday and Saturday 3–4.30 pm.

Wittenberg

Lutherhaus (Luther House), Collegienstrasse 54, tel: 0 34 91/40 26 71. April–September Tuesday–Sunday 9–6pm; October–March Tuesday–Sunday 10–5pm.
Melanchthonhaus (Melanchthon House), Collegienstrasse 60, tel: 0 34 91/32 79. April–October Saturday–Thursday 10–6pm; November–March Saturday–Thursday 9–5pm.
Museum für Natur- and Völkerkunde "Julyus Riemer" (Julius Riemer Museum of Nature and Ethnology), Schlossplatz, tel: 0 34 91/40 26 96. Tuesday–Friday 9–5pm, Saturday and Sunday 10–12.30 and 2–5pm.

Witzwort

Museum zur Entwicklung der Landwirtschaft (Museum of Agricultural Development) im Roten Hauarg, Adolfskoog, 25889 Witzwort, tel: 0 48 64/8 45. Tuesday–Sunday 10–10pm.

Wolfsburg

Automuseum (Automobile Museum), Dieselstrasse 35, tel: 0 53 61/5 20 71. Daily 10–5pm, Closed December 23–January 1.

Worms

Städtisches Museum im Andreasstift (Municipal Museum), Andreasstrasse, tel: 0 62 41/94 63 90. Tuesday–Sunday 10–noon and 2–5pm.

Worpswede

Barkenhoff, Ostendorfer Str. 10, tel: 0 47 92/39 68. Daily 10–6pm.
Grosse Kunstschau (Art Exhibition), Lindenallee 3, tel: 0 47 92/13 02. Daily 10–6pm.
Haus im Schluh, Im Schluh 35–37, tel: 0 47 92/95 00 61. Daily 2–6pm, closed on Monday in winter. The museum contains the Vogeler Collection

as well as the widow's old boarding house and weaving atelier, run today by two granddaughters of the artist.
Personenschiffahrten auf der Hamme (Cruises on the River Hamme), the Haferkamp family in Elsfleth, tel: 0 44 04/35 14. Cruises from May until September, to Bremen-Vege (departures mornings only!) or round trips on the Hamme.
Torfkahnfahrten (Tours on peat-cutters barges), Information from the Tourist Information Office: tel: 0 47 92/95 01 21.
Torfschiffswerftmuseum Heimatverein Schlussdorf (Museum of peat-cutters' boats), Schlussdorfer Strasse 20, tel: 0 47 92/6 43. Opening times vary as the association is run by volunteers. Phone in advance.

Würzburg

Mainfränkisches Museum (Franconian Museum of the Main), Marienberg Fortress, tel: 09 31/4 30 16. April–October Tuesday–Sunday 10–5pm; November–March Tuesday–Sunday 10–4pm.
Residenz, Rennweg. Paradezimmer (Parade Room). Tel: 09 31/3 55 17 12, April–October Tuesday–Sunday 9–5pm, November–March Tuesday–Sunday 10–4pm. Hofkirche (Court Church): April–October Tuesday–Sunday 9–noon and 1–5pm, November–March Tuesday–Sunday 9–noon and 1–4pm. Hofgarten (Gardens): open daily until dusk.

Zwickau

Automobilmuseum "August Horch" Zwickau (August Horch Motor Museum), Walther-Rathenau-Strasse 51, tel: 03 75/3 32 38 54, Ticket Office 3 32 22 32. Tuesday and Thursday 9–noon and 2–5pm, Saturday and Sunday 10–5pm.
Robert-Schumann-Haus, Hauptmarkt 5, tel/fax: 03 75/21 52 69. Tuesday–Saturday 10–5pm.
Zwickauer Trabbi-Treffen (Zwickau Trabant Reunion), held in June each year. Includes tests of driving skill and election of the "Super Trabant". Old Trabant films are shown during the evenings (production and advertising films); a Trabant Memorial in Zwickau. Information from the editorial office of *Super-Trabbi*, Dr.-Fridrichs-Ring 12, 08056 Zwickau or from Mr Haschke, tel: 01 72/3 70 46 34.

Theatre & Concerts

German cities offer a wide range of cultural activities. These include municipal and state opera companies and theatres, as well as commercial and independent theatres. All municipal and state theatres close for approximately six weeks in the summer, during the local school holidays.

Augsburg

Augsburger Puppenkiste (Augsburg Puppet Theatre), Spitalgasse 15, tel: 08 21/43 44 40. Advance ticket sales Tuesday–Sunday 10–noon.

Bad Hersfeld

Bad Hersfelder Festspiele (Bad Hersfeld Festival), 36251 Bad Hersfeld. June–August, the first part drama and musicals; the last three weeks are devoted to opera. Information from the Festival Administration (Tel: 0 66 21/20 12 72) or via the Tourist Information Office (Am Markt 1, 36251 Bad Hersfeld, tel: 0 66 21/1 94 33). Central ticket office, tel: 7 20 66.

Berlin

Information about current events can be found in the two city magazines *Tip* and *Zitty*. Central advance booking for evening performances: Theaterkasse Centrum, Meinekestrasse 25, Charlottenburg, tel: 0 30/8 82 76 11; Theaterkasse Europa-Center, Tauentzienstrasse 9, Charlottenburg, tel: 0 30/2 61 70 51. Ticket sales by telephone via Ticket Hotline, tel: 0 30/8 02 24 24 (Credit cards).

Berliner Ensemble, Bertolt-Brecht-Platz 1, tel: 0 30/2 82 31 60. Monday–Saturday 11–6pm, Sunday and public holidays 3–6pm. Ticket sales for same-day performances one hour before the start of the performance. The original Brecht theatre.
Berliner Philharmonie, Matthäikirchstrasse 1, tel: 0 30/2 61 43 83. Monday–Friday 3.30–6pm, Saturday, Sunday and public holidays 11am–2pm. Ticket office for same-day performances one hour before the start of the performance.
Deutsche Oper Berlin (Berlin German Opera), Bismarckstrasse 35, tel: 0 30/3 43 84 01. Advance ticket sales: Monday–Saturday 11am–7pm or one hour before the start of the perform-

ance, Sunday 10am–2pm. International star singers; excellent touring ballet ensembles.
Deutsches Theater und Kammerspiele, Schumannstrasse 13a, tel: 0 30/28 44 12 25. Ticket office, Deutsches Theater, tel: 28 44 12 26 (Kammerspiele). Monday–Saturday noon–6pm, Sunday 3–6pm. Ticket sales for same-day performances one hour before the start of the performance.
Distel, Friedrichstrasse 101, Mitte, tel: 0 30/2 00 47 04. The East Berlin cabaret.
Friedrichstadtpalast, Friedrichstrasse 117, Mitte, tel: 0 30/23 26 24 74. The East Berlin revue. Excellent ballet ensemble.
Komische Oper, Behrenstrasse 55–57, Mitte, tel: 0 30/2 83 25 55. Harry Kupfer's productions are well worth seeing.
Komödie, Kurfürstendamm 206, Wilmersdorf, tel: 0 30/8 82 78 93. Favourites from television in an amusing boulevard theatre.
Maxim-Gorki-Theater, Am Festungsgraben 2, Mitte, tel: 0 30/2 29 25 55. Small theatre offering intellectually demanding performances.
Mehringhof Theater, Gneisenaustrasse 2a, Kreuzberg, tel: 0 30/6 91 50 99. Cabaret: political, critical, literary and pointed.
Metropol-Theater, next to the station, Friedrichstrasse 101, Mitte, tel: 0 30/20 36 41 17. Classical musical stage, also performing operetta; small stage in the foyer.
Schaubühne am Lehniner Platz, Kurfürstendamm 153, tel: 0 30/89 00 23, Monday–Saturday 11am–6.30 pm, Sunday and public holidays 3–6.30pm. Ticket on sale before the evening performance. The realm of Peter Stein.
Schauspielhaus Berlin, Gendarmenmarkt, tel: 0 30/2 03 09 21 or 00/2 03 09 01 (Ticket office). Theatre ticket office: 2 03 09 94/2 03 09 05. Monday–Saturday noon–6pm, Sunday and public holidays 2–6pm, Recorded announcements regarding performances: 2 04 47 62, Ticket sales for same-day performances one hour before the start of the performance.
Schiller-Theater, Bismarckstrasse 110, Charlottenburg, tel: 0 30/25 48 92 41. Since subsidized performances were driven away from the thea-

tre, only commercially-produced New York Musicals.

Staatsoper Unter den Linden (State Opera), Unter den Linden 7, tel: 0 30/2 00 47 60 (Ticekt office). Advance ticket sales: Monday–Saturday noon–6pm; Ticket sales for same-day performances one hour before the start of the performance, Sunday and public holidays 2–6pm. Artistic direction: Daniel Barenboim.

Theater am Halleschen Ufer, Hallesches Ufer 32, Kreuzberg, tel: 0 30/2 51 09 41. Musical theatre and avant-garde dance performances; many visiting ensembles.

Theater des Westens, Kantstrasse 12, Charlottenburg, tel: 0 30/8 82 28 88. Well-produced entertainment in a theatre dating back to 1900.

Wintergarten, Potsdamer Strasse 96, Tiergarten, tel: 0 30/2 62 70 70 oder 2 61 60 60. Europe's Leading Variety Theatre, directed by André Heller and Bernhard Paul. Performances daily at 8pm, Saturday also at 11.45pm and Sunday also at 3.30 pm.

Die Wühlmäuse, Nürnberger Strasse 33, Wilmersdorf, tel: 0 30/2 13 70 47. Cabaret by (and sometimes with) Didi Hallervorden.

Bochum

Schauspielhaus Bochum (Bochum Municipal Theatre), Königsallee 15. Advance ticket sales, tel: 02 34/3 33 31 11, Monday–Friday 10am–7pm, Saturday 6–7pm, Sunday 5–6pm.

Starlight Express Theatre, Stadionring 24. Advance ticket sales through Stella Musical Company, tel: 0 18 05/44 44, Monday–Friday 8am–8pm, Saturday and Sunday 9–7pm. Advance ticket sales at the ticket office: Monday 11.30am–5pm, Tuesday–Friday 11.30am–7pm, Saturday, Sunday 11.30am–2pm, 3–4pm and 4.30–7pm and ticket sales for same-day performances one hour before the start of the performance.

Dortmund

Westfalenhalle Dortmund GmbH, Rheinlanddamm 200, tel: 02 31/12 04-0, fax: 12 04-5 60. Ticket Service: 12 04-6 66.

Dresden

Dresdens Kabarett-Theater Die Herkuleskeule, Sternplatz 1, tel: 03 51/4 92 55 55.

Dresdner Philharmonie, Kulturpalast am Altmarkt, tel: 03 51/4 86 63 06.

Dresdner Zentrum für zeitgenössische Musik (Dresden Centre for Contemporary Music), Schevenstrasse 17, tel: 03 51/37 82 81.

Jazz Club "Tonne", Waldschlösschenstrasse., tel: 03 51/4 95 13 54.

Kulturpalast, Schlossstrasse 2, tel: 03 51/4 86 60.

projekttheater dresden, Louisenstrasse 47, tel: 03 51/5 30 41.

Sächsische Staatsoper/Sächsische Staatskapelle Dresden (State Opera of Saxony, State Orchestra of Saxony), Schinkelwache/Theaterplatz, tel: 03 51/4 91 17 05.

Staatsoperette, Pirnaer Landstrasse 131, tel: 03 51/2 07 99 29.

Staatsschauspiel Dresden (Dresden State Theatre): Schauspielhaus, Theaterstrasse 2, tel: 03 51/4 91 35 55.

Kleines Haus, Glacisstrasse 28, tel: 4 91 35 65.

Theater in der Fabrik, Tharandter Strasse 33, tel: 4 21 45 05.

Theater Junge Generation, Meissner Landstrasse 4, tel: 03 51/4 21 45 67.

Theaterkahn Dresdner Brettl, Terrassenufer/Augustusbrücke, tel: 03 51/4 96 94 50.

Duisburg

Deutsche Oper am Rhein, Theater der Stadt Duisburg, Neckarstrasse 1, tel: 02 03/30 09-1 00. Ticket Office: Monday–Friday 10am–6.30pm, Saturday 10am–1pm, Sunday and public holidays 11am–1pm.

Düsseldorf

Deutsche Oper am Rhein, Heinrich-Heine-Allee 16a. Advance ticket sales, tel: 02 11/8 90 82 11, Monday–Friday 9am–5pm, Saturday 11am–1pm. Ticket sales for same-day performances 11am–6.30pm.

Düsseldorfer Schauspielhaus, Gustaf-Gründgens-Platz 1, tel: 02 11/36 99 11 and 3 68 73 41, Monday–Friday 11am–6.30pm, Saturday 11am–1pm and ticket sales for same-day performances one hour before the start of the performance.

Kom(m)ödchen, in der Kunsthalle, Eingang Hunsrücker Str, tel: 02 11/32 54 28. Ticket office: Monday–Saturday 1–8pm.

Essen

Folkwang-Hochschule Essen, Abtei Werden, Clemensborn 39. Ticket sales, tel: 02 01/49 03-231, Monday–Friday 10am–6pm.

Initiative Zeche Carl, Wilhelm-Nieswandt-Allee 100, tel: 02 01/8 34 44 10.

Theater and Philharmonie, Aaltotheater (opera and ballet) and Grillo-Theater (drama). Advance ticket sales, tel: 02 01/81 22 00, Monday–Friday 9am–4pm.

Zeche Zollverein, Schacht XII, Gelsenkirchener Strasse 181, tel: 02 01/30 30 18 0. 30 30 19.

Frankfurt am Main

Schauspielhaus, Neue Mainzer Strasse 15. Advance ticket sales, tel: 0 69/21 23 79 99, daily except Saturday 10am–6pm.

Oper, Am Willy-Brandt-Platz. Advance ticket sales, tel: 0 69/21 23 79 99, Monday–Friday 10am–6pm, Saturday 2–6pm.

Alte Oper, Opernplatz 8. Advance ticket sales, tel: 0 69/1 34 04 00, Monday–Friday 10–8pm.

Jazzkeller, Kleine Bockenheimer Strasse 76, tel: 0 69/28 85 37 or Wednesday–Saturday 28 49 27. Famous jazz club.

Hamburg

Deutsches Schauspielhaus, Kirchenallee 39, tel: 0 40/24 87 13. The theatre was twice nominated Theatre of the Year (1994 and 1996).

Hamburger Staatsoper, Grosse Theaterstrasse 34/Dammtorstrasse 28, tel: 0 40/3 56 80. Classical and modern opera performances, ballet; new forms of music theatre on the studio stage Opera Stabile.

Hansa-Theater, Steindamm 17, tel: 0 40/24 14 14. Closed July/August. Magicians, jugglers and acrobats.

Imperial-Theater, Reeperbahn 5, tel: 0 40/31 31 14. Broadway hits.

Kampnagelfabrik, Jarrestrasse 20–26, tel: 0 40/2 79 10 66. Free dance and theatre; international performers.

Musikhalle, Karl-Muck-Platz, tel: 0 40/34 69 20. Concert hall used by Hamburg's three great orchestras: the State Philharmonic Orchestra, the North German Radio Symphony Orchestra and the Hamburg Symphony Orchestra. There are also guest performances here.

Neue Flora, Stresemannstrasse 159, tel: 0 40/27 07 52 70. The *Phantom of the Opera*.

Ohnsorg-Theater, Grosse Bleichen 23, tel: 0 40/35 08 03-21. Theatrical perfomances in local dialect (Plattdeutsch).

Operettenhaus, Spielbudenplatz 1, tel: 0 40/27 07 52 70. "Cats".

St.Pauli Theater, Spielbudenplatz 29, tel: 0 40/31 43 44. Boulevard theatre.

Thalia-Theater, Alstertor, tel: 0 40/32 26 66. Classical and modern drama.

Das Schiff, Holzbrücke 2, tel: 0 40/36 47 65. Literary cabaret in an old ship.

Schmidt Theater und Schmidts Tivoli, Spielbudenplatz 27, tel: 0 40/31 12 31. Variety, Shows and the television personality Ms Plaschke.

Köln

Oper der Stadt Köln, Offenbachplatz. Advance ticket sales, tel: 02 21/2 21 82 48.

Deutschlandfunk, Raderberggürtel 40, tel: 02 21/34 51. Concerts in the recording studio of the radio station.

Halle Kalk, Neuerburgstrasse. Advance ticket sales, tel: 02 21/87 57 41. Operettas, musicals, cabaret, experimental theatre.

Hänneschen-Theater. Advance ticket sales, tel: 02 21/2 58 12 01. Cologne's puppet theatre; performances are often sold out.

Kammerspiele, Ubierring 45. Advance ticket sales, tel: 02 21/32 79 90. Smaller performances by the Municipal Ensemble.

Philharmonie, Bischofsgartenstrasse 1, tel: 02 21/20 40 80. Not just classical music, but also jazz, pop, rock.

Schauspielhaus, Offenbachplatz. Advance sales, tel: 02 21/2 21 82 52.

Schlosserei im Schauspielhaus, Krebsgasse. Advance ticket sales, tel: 02 21/2 21 83 21. Modern drama.

Staatliche Hochschule für Musik (State Conservatory), Dagobertstrasse 38, tel: 02 21/12 40 33. Concerts by young performers.

Theater am Dom, Glockengasse 11. Advance ticket sales, tel: 02 21/2 58 01 53. Boulevard theatre with well-known local actors.

Volkstheater Millowitsch, Aachener Strasse 5. Advance tickets, tel: 02 21/25 17 47. Folk theatre (in local dialect).

WDR-Funkhaus, Wallrafplatz 5, tel: 02 21/22 01. Concerts in the recording studios of the radio station.

Munich

Altes Residenztheater (Cuvilliés Theatre), Entrance Residenzstrasse, tel: 0 89/29 68 36. Open for viewing: Monday–Saturday 2–5pm, Sunday and public holidays 10–5pm. Advance ticket sales: 21 85 19 40.

Black-Box im Gasteig, Rosenheimer Strasse 5, tel: 0 89/4 80 98-0. Small-stage performances, usually of an experimental nature.

Deutsches Theater, Schwanthalerstrasse 13, tel: 0 89/55 23 44 44. Touring musical ensembles and original Broadway productions.

Drehleier, Balanstrasse 23, tel: 0 89/48 43 37. Satire and cabaret, including the well-known Lower Bavarian cabaret artist Sigi Zimmerschied.

Heppel & Ettlich, Kaiserstrasse 67, tel: 0 89/34 93 59. Every Monday, improvisational theatre in a minute stage in a room next door to the pub. At other times cabaret performances.

Herkulessaal der Residenz. Tel: 0 89/29 06 72 63. Ticket sales for same-day performances one hour before the start of the performance. Classical concerts.

Hinterhoftheater, Sudetendeutsche Strasse 40, tel: 0 89/3 11 60 39. Cabaret, grotesque sketches and satire, accompanied by Weissbier and white sausages.

Komödie am Max-II-Denkmal, Maximilianstrasse 47, tel: 0 89/22 18 59. Professional light entertainment.

Lach- und Schiessgesellschaft, Ursulastrasse 9, tel: 0 89/39 19 97. The home stage in Schwabing of national stars of cabaret, including Dieter Hildebrandt and Hanns Dieter Hüsch.

Münchner Kammerspiele (Schauspielhaus), Maximilianstrasse 26, Ticket sales, tel: 0 89/23 72 13 28. Monday–Friday 10–6pm, Saturday 10–1pm. Ticket sales for same-day performances one hour before the start of the performance.

Münchner Lustspielhaus, Occamstrasse 8, tel: 0 89/3449 74. Concerts and cabaret in an attractive hall, with waiter service.

Philharmonie im Gasteig, Rosenheimer Strasse 5, tel: 0 89/4 80 98-0. Classical music; ocassional jazz performances.

Nationaltheater (Bayerische Staatsoper), Bavarian State Opera, Max-Joseph-Platz, tel: 0 89/21 85 19 20.

Advance ticket sales at the ticket office of the Bavarian State Theatre, Maximilianstrasse 11–13: Monday–Friday 10-6pm, Saturday 10–1pm. Ticket sales for same-day performances one hour before the start of the performance. Opera and ballet.

NT. – Neues Theater München, Entenbachstrasse 37, tel: 0 89/65 00 00. Private experimental theatre with high artistic standards.

Pathos-Transport, Dachauer Strasse 110d, tel: 18 42 43. In search of contemporary dramatic themes in an old factory.

proT-ZEIT, Steinseestrasse 2, tel: 7 25 42 81 and 40 74 61. Experimental and visual (Music) theatre by Alexeij Sagerer, whose artistic fame has spread well beyond the boundaries of Munich.

Residenztheater (Bayerisches Staatsschauspiel), Bavarian State Theatre, Max-Joseph-Platz 1. Ticket office, tel 0 89/21 85 19 40. Monday–Friday 10–6pm, Saturday 10–1pm. Ticket sales for same-day performances one hour before the start.

Staatstheater am Gärtnerplatz, Gärtnerplatz 3, tel: 0 89/2 01 67 67. Advance ticket sales at the theatre: Monday–Friday 10-6pm, Saturday 10–1pm or via the ticket office of the Bavarian State Theatre, Maximilianstrasse 11–13.

Theater links der Isar, Auenstrasse 19, tel: 0 89/2 02 28 95. One of Munich's oldest private theatres. Critical, political-satirical, occasionally serious.

Nürnberg

Städtische Bühnen, Richard-Wagner-Platz 2–10. Ticket sales, tel: 09 11/2 31-38 08. Information and advance ticket sales for groups from out of town: Fränkischer Besucherring Nürnberg, tel: 2 29 90. Advance ticket sales from the theatre ticket office: Monday–Friday 9.30–6pm, Saturday 9–1pm. Sunday and public holidays no advance ticket sales.

Stuttgart

Staatstheater Stuttgart, Oberer Schlossgarten 6. Advance ticket sales, tel: 07 11/20 20 90. Monday–Friday 10–2pm.

Altes Schauspielhaus, Kleine Königstrasse 9. Advance ticket sales, tel: 07 11/2 26 55 05. Monday–Saturday 10–2pm and 5–7pm.

Recklinghausen

Ruhrfestspiele Recklinghausen (Ruhr Festival, Recklinghausen). International theatre festival every year in May/June at various venues in Recklinghausen. Information and tickets, tel: 0 23 61/91 84 40, fax: 91 84 20.

PUBS AND TAVERNS

Aschinger, Kurfürstendamm 26, tel: 0 30/8 82 55 58. Daily 11am–midnight. Stews and grilled meats to accompany the beer from the pub's own brewery.

Café Westphal, Kollwitzstrasse 64. Daily 9–3am. The rendezvous in Prenzlauer Berg.

Dicke Wirtin, Carmerstrasse 9, tel: 0 30/3 12 49 52. Daily noon–4am. Beer and more beer, served with nostalgic bric-a-brac and spiced with pert waitresses.

E & M Leydicke, Mansteinstrasse 4, tel: 0 30/2 16 29 73. Monday, Tuesday, Thursday Friday 4pm–midnight; Wednesday, Saturday, Sunday 11–1am. Seedy and amusing; just the way you'd imagine a Berlin tavern.

Goldener Hahn, Pücklerstrasse 20, tel: 0 30/6 18 80 98. Monday, Tuesday from 9pm; Wednesday–Sunday from 7pm. For 70s fans.

Heidereiter, Hasenheide 58, tel: 0 30/6 91 30 82. Daily from 10am. Low prices, loud music; tavern atmosphere with garden.

Luisenbräu, Luisenplatz 1, tel: 0 30/3 41 93 88. Daily 11–2 am. The place to exchange opinions about Berlin with other tourists.

Mauerblümchen, Wisbyer Strasse 4, tel: 0 30/4 44 79 04. Daily 11–4am. GDR nostalgia.

Mommsen-Eck, Mommsenstrasse 45, tel: 0 30/3 24 25 80. Daily from 10 am. If you want to try all 100 different types of beer, you will need to come early.

Pasternak, Knaakstrasse 22–24, tel: 0 30/4 41 33 99. Thursday–Sunday noon–2am, Friday and Saturday until 3am. The ideal place for those who want to taste Russian food in a casual atmosphere.

Sophienhof, Sophienstrasse 11, tel: 0 30/2 83 21 36. Monday–Friday noon–1am, Saturday and Sunday 7–1am.

Small tavern with a garden; very pleasant atmosphere.

Wirtschaftswunder, Yorckstrasse 81, tel: 0 30/7 86 99 99. Daily from 4pm. Expensive with a 1950s flair.

BARS

Berlin Bar, Uhlandstrasse 145, tel: 0 30/8 83 79 36. Daily 10–7am. small, elegant, excellent cocktails.

Chamäleon Variete, Rosenthaler Strasse 40–41, tel: 0 30/2 82 71 18. Open daily from 7pm. Variety show from 9pm.

Cut, Knesebeckstrasse 16, tel: 3 13 35 11. Daily 10–6 am. Exclusive and elegant.

Harry's New York Bar in the Hotel Esplanade, Lützowufer 15, tel: 0 30/2 54 78-8 21. Daily from noon. Bar with atmosphere, for prosperous guests.

Hudson, Elssholzstrasse 10, tel: 0 30/2 16 16 02. Monday–Friday from 9pm. One of Berlin's nicest bars.

Le Bar, Grolmanstrasse 52, tel: 0 30/ 3 12 87 02. Daily from 7pm. The right choice for those who like things exclusive and expensive.

Mey's Cocktailbar, Pfalzburger Strasse 83, tel: 0 30/8 82 42 62. Monday–Thursday 7–3am, Friday and Saturday until 5am. Crowded and stylish.

DANCING

Abraxas, Kantstrasse 134, tel: 0 30/ 3 12 94 93. Tuesday–Thursday and Sunday 10–5am, Friday and Saturday 10–6am. Soul, jazz, funk and Latin music on a small dance floor.

Bunker, Albrechtstrasse 24, tel: 0 30/ 2 82 81 90. Friday and Saturday from 11pm. Pure techno.

Café Keese, Bismarckstrasse 108, tel: 0 30/3 12 91 11. Monday–Saturday from 8pm, Sunday from 4pm. Dance café for the 40-somethings; velvet and plush interior; ladies' choice.

Café Moskau, Karl-Marx-Allee 34, tel: 0 30/2 79 16 70. Thursday–Sunday from 11pm. Live music in former GDR tavern.

Club Bodrum, Kurfüstendamm 143, tel: 0 30/8 91 97 01. Wednesday and Thursday 9pm–4am, Friday–Sunday 9–5 am. Turkish do-it-yourself disco for the Teens and Twenty-somethings. Turkish pop music, sometimes mixed with folk music.

Delicious Doughnuts Research, Rosenthaler Strasse 9, tel: 0 30/2 83

30 21. Café open daily from noon, Club 8pm–5am. Soul, funk and jazz in a relaxed atmosphere.

E-Werk, Wilhelmstrasse. 43, tel: 0 30/2 52 20 12. Thursday–Saturday from 11pm. Techno and jungle music in a huge warehouse.

El Barrio, Potsdamer Strasse 84, tel: 0 30/2 62 18 53. Friday–Sunday from 9pm. Salsa for pros and would-be pros. A delight to watch.

Junction Bar, Gneisenaustrasse 18, tel: 0 30/6 94 66 02. Daily from 8.30pm. Live music, Thursday–Saturday recorded music thereafter.

Kapkara, Bismarckstrasse 90, tel: 0 30/3 13 90 41. Wednesday–Sunday 10–5am. Turkish Disco with Turkish pop music as well as soul and funk.

Quasimodo, Kantstrasse 12a, tel: 0 30/3 12 80 86. Wednesday–Sunday from 9pm. Long-established rendezvous on the jazz scene.

Salsa, Wielandstrasse 13, tel: 0 30/3 24 16 42. Daily 5–4am. Casual Latin Club with a pleasant atmosphere. With live music.

Cologne

KÖLSCH BEER TAVERNS

Brauereiausschank Alt Köln, Trankgasse 7–9. Typical Rhineland beer tavern near the cathedral.

Brauhaus Sion, Unter Taschenmacher 5–7. Large beer tavern in the city centre.

Em Golde Kappes, Neusser Strasse 295. Typical local meeting place (Veedeltreff), north of the city centre.

Früh am Dom, Am Hof 12–14. Famous beer tavern, near the cathedral.

Früh em Veedel, Chlodwigplatz 28. Local meeting place (Veedeltreff) south of the city centre.

Päffgen, Friesenstrasse 44–66. The most fanmous beer tavern in Cologne; an institution.

Päffgen in der Altstadt, Heumarkt 62. Branch of the original Päffgen in the city centre.

Peters-Brauhaus, Mühlengasse 1. Traditional beer tavern.

Weiss Bräu, Am Weidenbach 24. For homesick Bavarians in Cologne.

BEER GARDENS

Biergarten an der Rennbahn, Scheibenstrasse 40. A good place to relax after the excitement of the racetrack.

Küppers-Brauhaus, Alteburger Strasse 157. Beer garden beside the brewery.
Stadtgarten, Venloer Strasse 40. Popular meeting place in the park.
Volksgarten, Volksgartenstrasse 27. Another popular meeting place in the park.

PUBS AND TAVERNS

Biermuseum, Buttermarkt 39. As the name indicates, some 50 types of beer are on offer here.
Keule, Heumarkt 56. Rustic In-place.
Klein Köln, Friesenstrasse 53. Officially a "night tavern"; typical.
Roxy, Aachener Strasse 2. The place to see and be seen. Musical accompaniment.
Spielplatz, Ubierring 58. "Blasphemous" Tavern with good food.

LIVE MUSIC

Luxor, Luxemburger Strasse 40. Rock, blues, soul.
Stadtgarten, Venloer Strasse 40. Headquarters of the "Cologne Jazz House Initiative", mostly modern jazz.
Subway, Aachener Strasse 82. Mostly mainstream jazz, with a disco.
Tanzbrunnen, Rheinparkweg 1. Open-air setting by the trades fair centre; concerts, art, festivals.

BARS AND NIGHTCLUBS

Chin's, Im Ferkulum 18–24. Popular with artists.
Hotel Timp, Heumarkt 25. Drag show at night from 1am.
Tingel Tangel, Maastrichter Strasse 6–8. Pleasant nightclub with a touch of elegance.

Frankfurt am Main

WINE BARS

VINUM, Rheingauer Weinkeller, Kleine Hochstrasse 9, tel: 0 69/29 38 61. Monday–Friday 4–1am, Saturday 7–1am.
Weinkeller Blaubart, Kaiserhofstrasse 18, tel: 0 69/28 22 29. Sun–Thurs 5–1am, Friday and Saturday 5–2am.
Weinkeller Fabrik, Mittlerer Hasenpfad 1–5, tel: 0 69/62 44 06. Tuesday–Thursday 6–1am, Friday and Saturday 6–2am.
Weinstube im Römer, Römerberg 19, tel: 0 69/29 13 31. Monday–Saturday 4–11pm, Sunday 11.30–8pm.

APPLE WINE TAVERNS

Affentorschänke, Neuer Wall 9, tel: 0 69/62 75 75. In summer: Monday–Saturday 4pm–midnight, Sunday noon–midnight. Closed in winter.
Apfelwein Klaus, Meisengasse 10, tel: 0 69/28 28 64. Monday–Sunday 11–11pm.
Dauth Schneider, Neuer Wall 7, 0 69/61 35 33. Monday–Friday 4pm–midnight, Saturday–Sunday noon–midnight.
Dauth's Hinnerkopp, Grosse Rittergasse 53–59, tel: 0 69/61 50 25.
Eichkatzerl, Dreieichstrasse 29, 0 69/61 74 80. Tuesday–Saturday noon–midnight.
Klaane Sachsehäuser, Neuer Wall 11, tel: 0 69/61 59 83. Monday–Saturday 4pm–midnight.
Lorsbacher Tal, Grosse Rittergasse 49, tel: 0 69/61 64 59. Monday–Saturday 4–11.30pm, Sunday 10.30–2pm and 7–11pm.
Steinernes Haus, Braubachstrasse 35, tel: 0 69/28 34 91. Monday–Sunday 11–1am.
Struwwelpeter, Neuer Wall 3, tel: 0 69/61 12 97. Monday–Sunday 4–1am.
Wagner, Adolf, Schweizer Strasse 71, tel: 0 69/61 25 65. Monday–Sunday 11–1am.
Zum Böckchen, Grosse Ritterggasse 52, tel: 0 69/62 67 81. Monday–Sunday 6pm–midnight.
Zum Fichtekränzi, Wallstrasse 5, tel: 0 69/61 27 78. 4pm–midnight.
Zum Gemalten Haus, Schweizer Strasse 67, tel: 0 69/61 45 59. Wednesday–Sunday 10–midnight.
Zum Grauen Bock, Grosse Rittergasse, tel: 0 69/61 80 26. Monday–Saturday 5–1am.

Hamburg

PUBS AND CAFÉS

Bel Café, Belcalliancestrasse 17, tel: 0 40/43 89 22. Excellent breakfast.
Café Fees, Holstenwall 24, tel: 0 40/3 17 47 66. In the Museum of Hamburg History. Culture fans meet during the day or at night under the glass dome.
Café Oriental, Marktstrasse 21a, tel: 0 40/4 39 21 37. Delightfully kitschy café with red-brown walls and brightly-coloured ornaments. A comfortable place to relax.
Café Monsun, Friedensallee 20, tel: 0 40/3 90 31 48. Theatre café in a pretty green inner courtyard on the

Friedensallee, the focal point of the local culture scene.
Eisenstein, Friedensallee 9, tel: 0 40/3 90 46 06. First-class pizza from the wood-burning oven. Favourite meeting-place for young, dynamic creative talents from the advertising scene.
Filmhauskneipe, Friedensallee 7, tel: 0 40/39 34 67. Popular meeting point for film fans in a converted propeller factory now housing three cinemas.
Geyer, Hein-Köllisch-Platz, tel: 0 40/31 03 18. Fine for an espresso before or after a stroll through the Kiez.
Machwitz, Schanzenstrasse 121, tel: 0 40/43 81 77. Trendy-alternative scene.
R & B, Weidenallee 20, tel: 0 40/41 10 44. "Soul food" café for creative souls.
439, Vereinsstrasse 39, tel: 0 40/4 39 15 50. The counter is a trendy meeting place.

DANCING, LIVE MUSIC AND BARS

After Shave, Spielbudenplatz 7, tel: 0 40/3 19 32 15. Dance until you drop in a large disco.
Birdland, Gärtnerstrasse 122, tel: 0 40/40 52 77. Jazz concerts, also with international artists.
Cotton Club, Alter Steinweg, tel: 0 40/34 38 78. Famous jazz cellar.
Docks/Prinzenbar, Spielbudenplatz 19, tel: 0 40/3 19 43 78. One of the largest discos in town, following all the latest trends and playing anything you can dance to. Live music.
EDK, Gerhardstrasse 3, no Tel. For fans of house music.
Fabrik, Barner Strasse 36, tel: 0 40/39 10 70. Cultural centre; as well as good flea markets; the programme includes concerts from rock and jazz to experimental music.
Grosse Freiheit 36, Grosse Freiheit 36, tel: 0 40/3 19 36 49. Large concert hall for rock fans.
Kir, Max-Brauer-Allee 241, tel: 0 40/43 85 18. Club for independent music.
Lounge, Gerhardstrasse/Ecke Herbertstrasse, tel: 0 40/31 25 47. Orange dance bar, comfortable in spite of the modern design. Open from 10pm. Music varies according to the day of the week (reggae, soul, jazz, jungle).
Markthalle, Klosterwall 49, tel: 0 40/33 94 91. Concerts; rock music as well as the latest trends; including the hard stuff.

Mojo-Club, Reeperbahn 1, tel: 0 40/3 19 19 99. Acid jazz and dancefloor soul, also concerts; small café for meeting friends.

Sam Brasil, Silbersackstr. 27, tel: 0 40/31 33 98. Temperamental, sensuous salsa.

Unit, Nobistor/Holstenstrasse, no telephone. First-class DJs have made this a cult centre for local techno fans.

Munich

BAVARIAN RESTAURANTS

Augustiner-Gaststätten, Neuhauser Strasse 27, tel: 0 89/5 51 99-2 57. Traditional restaurant; tables and chairs in the courtyard in summer.

Hundskugel, Hotterstrasse 18, tel: 0 89/26 42 72. The oldest tavern in town (1440).

Münchner Hofbräuhaus, Platzl 9, tel: 0 89/22 16 76. The most famous Bavarian beer restaurant in Munich.

Spöckmeier, Rosenstrasse 9, tel: 0 89/ 26 80 88. Traditional tavern serving typical Munich specialities.

Straubinger Hof, Blumenstrasse 5, tel: 0 89/2 60 84 44. Down-to-earth Bavarian dishes at down-to-earth prices.

Weisses Bräuhaus, Tal 10, tel: 0 89/ 29 98 75. Pure Bavaria; noisy downstairs, quieter upstairs; the staff is sometimes a bit offhand.

BEER GARDENS

Augustinerkeller, Arnulfstrasse 52. Next door to the headquarters of Bavarian Radio. Augustiner beer is served - considered by many locals to be the best beer in town.

Chinesischer Turm, in the Englischer Garten near the Monopteros. Munich's most famous beer garden, where you will find not only tourists.

Hirschgarten, Hirschgartenallee 1. Large, attractive beer garden with a deer enclosure; some distance from the city centre.

Viktualienmarkt. Not large, but in the very heart of Munich, tucked away between the market stalls. Packed to bursting point on fine Saturdays. The numerous snack bars in the vicinity offer everything from local white sausages to fish from the North Sea.

Waldwirtschaft, Georg-Kalb-Strasse 3, Grosshesselohe. Outside Munich; A good destination for a Sunday

Atzinger, Schellingstrasse 9, tel: 0 89/28 28 80. Classic student pub with Bavarian cuisine.

Café im Stadtmuseum, St.-Jakobs-Platz 2, tel: 0 89/26 69 49. Trendy meeting place for the arts scene; near the Film Museum.

Café Iwan, Sonnenstrasse 19, tel: 0 89/55 49 33. Exclusive atmosphere on two levels.

Wunderbar, Hochbrückenstrasse 3, tel: 0 89/29 51 18. A must for cocktail fans; chic and attractive with a cave-like atmosphere.

DANCING, MUSIC, PUBS AND TAVERNS WITH LIVE MUSIC

Alabamahalle, Domagkstrasse 33, tel: 0 89/ 3 24 42 53. Concerts from rock to jazz.

La Cumbia, Taubenstrasse 2, tel: 0 89/65 85 01. Latin-American bar with good food; live music on Friday; on other days Latin-American disco with salsa, tango, merengue, cumbia.

Far out, Am Kosttor 2, tel: 0 89/22 66 61. Classic disco; light and civilized.

Feierwerk, Hansastrasse 39, tel: 0 89/7 69 36 00. Independent hall with concerts, pub and theatre.

Kaffee Giesing, Bergstrasse 5, tel: 0 89/6 92 05 79. The right place for a civilized Sunday brunch with live music and views across the Isar valley and the city.

Liberty, Rosenheimer Strasse 30, tel: 0 89/48 48 40. Disco people who don't like house and techno can let their hair down.

Loft, Friedenstrasse 22, tel: 0 89/40 88 28. Live performances and recorded music. Often African or Latin-American, sometimes with a touch of jazz.

Mandarine-Lounge, Herzogspitalstrasse. Fridays for gays; on Saturday the house disco club in Munich.

Max-Emanuel-Brauerei, Adalbertstrasse 33, tel: 0 89/2 71 51 58. Every Wednesday salsa dancing in the room next door to the main beer hall; beer garden in summer.

Metropolis, Entrance Zweigstrasse, tel: 0 89/59 85 41/42. Salsa dancing on Saturday; often free salsa lessons from 9-10pm; then things really get going.

Mister B.'s, Herzog-Heinrich-Strasse 38, tel: 0 89/53 49 01. Secret pub for initiated music fans. Live perform-

ances – sometimes good, sometimes not so good – on the tiny stage.

Muffathalle, Zellstrasse 4, tel: 0 89/45 87 50 00. The hottest rendezvous of the artsy crowd in the city centre, directly by the Isar. Bar-café. A large hall for drama, recorded and live music. On Friday, dancing in the **Muffat Café** to acid jazz; changing DJs.

Nachtwerk, Landsberger Strasse 185, tel: 0 89/5 78 38 00. Hall for letting your hair down to live music or disco. Includes the **Nachtwerkclub** (with special nights: Friday – Afro Cosmic, Sunday – House, Monday – Hit Parade) and the **Tanzlokal**.

P 1, Prinzregentenstrasse 1, tel: 0 89/29 42 52. In Disco for cool beauties.

Parkcafé, Sophienstrasse. 7, tel: 0 89/59 83 13. Meeting place of the "Crème de la crème". Rock/funk, rap/soul/acid jazz, soul/hip hop in rotation.

Soulcity, Maximiliansplatz 5, tel: 0 89/55 33 01. Thursday: Easy Listening Night with German pop singers, disco sound as long as supplies last. Saturday: House and techno.

Ultraschall, Grafinger Strasse im Kulturpark Ost, tel: 0 89/49 00 21 50. The techno pioneer of the Munich scene.

Unterfahrt, Kirchenstrasse. 96, tel: 0 89/4 48 27 94. Small jazz bar of high quality.

Further Attractions

There is much to see and do in Germany – castles, palaces, country houses, museums, nature parks, etc. The selection listed below is restricted to castles, nature parks and adventure/amusement parks, arranged according to the principal chapters in this book.

Berlin and surroundings

CASTLES

Schloss Charlottenburg lies at the heart of Berlin, in the district of the same name. Surrounded by a lovely park, it houses several important collections.

Schloss Sanssouci, near Potsdam, is a rococo-style palace built by Frederick II during the 18th century. It is surrounded by a large park (717 acres/ 290 hectares) in which there are a number of pavilions. The mortal remains of "Old Fritz", the original owner of the palace, were removed from the Soviet-occupied zone in 1945 but have since been reinstated with great ceremony in the mausoleum at Sanssouci.

Schloss Cecilienhof lies in the second most important park in Potsdam, the Neuer Garten, a landscaped park on the western shores of the Heiliger See. Built between 1913-17 in the style of an English country house, it was the setting for the Potsdam Conference in 1945.

The Humboldt-Schlösschen in Berlin-Reinickendorf was built in 1824 by Wilhelm von Humboldt.

The Lakes of Mecklenburg

CASTLES

Schloss Oranienburg. The baroque-style castle was built during the 17th century as the country house of the Princess of Anhalt-Dessau. It is surrounded by a formal baroque park.

One of the castle wings houses a printing exhibition.

Schloss Rheinsberg, near Neu-Ruppin, is a small moated castle (16th century).

Schloss Neustadt-Glewe, near Ludwigslust Castle, combines Renaissance and baroque architectural elements.

Schloss Ludwigslust (18th century), S of Schwerin, is surrounded by an extensive park.

NATURE PARKS

There are three nature parks within the Mecklenburg Lake Plateau: **Nationalpark Müritzsee**, **Naturpark Nossentiner-Schwinzer Heide** and the **Naturpark Feldberg-Lychener Seenlandschaft**. The region is characterized by countless lakes, ponds and pools and offers the visitor a variety of opportunities for sailing or surfing.

Through the Harz to Leipzig

CASTLES

Burg Falkenstein (12th century), stands high above the Selke valley in the Harz mountains. The "Sachsenspiegel", the most famous law book of the German Middle Ages, was written here during the 13th century.

Schloss Spiegelsberge, south of Halberstadt, is a baroque hunting lodge which now contains a restaurant. The vaults house a 16th-century wine barrel which will hold 132,760 litres (29,207 gallons).

Schloss Wernigerode in the Harz mountains was built in 1862 on the site of the 12th-century Grafenburg. Today it serves as a musuem. The narrow-gauge "Harzquerbahn" railway stops in Wernigerode; the section from here to Nordhausen dates from 1899.

Schloss Ballenstedt (18th century), on the southern edge of the Harz mountains, was built in the baroque style on the site of a ruined monastery.

To the northwest of Halle stands the **Moritzburg** (15th century). It houses the **National Moritzburg Collection**, one of the most important art museums in the new Bundesländer. It contains outstanding works by 19th and 20th-century artists.

The Rudelsburg and Burg Saaleck were built in the 12th century to maintain control over the Salle valley. Leave

your car in Bad Kösen and walk up the limestone mountains by foot. The view over the Saale valley is ample reward for the effort.

Burg Anhalt (11th century), 6 km/ 4 miles south of Ballenstedt, was formerly the residence of the Dukes of Ballenstedt (later the Dukes of Anhalt).

Schloss Bernburg, on the lower reaches of the Saale, dominates the surrounding area from a sandstone rock high above the river. It is a Renaissance building which incorporates older sections dating from the 16th century.

Schloss Dessau (Schloss Mosigkau), in the Mosigkau district of Dessau, was designed by the architect of Sanssouci, Georg Wenzeslaus von Knobelsdorff. The castle museum exhibits workd by 17th and 18th-century Flemish masters (Rubens, van Dyck etc.) as well as craft items, porcelain and pottery.

North of Oranienbaum lies the neoclassical **Schloss Wörlitz**, surrounded by a notable landscaped park in the English manner dating from the 18th century. The castle's art collection includes items of furniture, ancient sculptures and a collection of paintings.

Schloss Pretzsch lies 6 km/ 4 miles from Bad Schmiedeberg on the border with Saxony. The baroque-style park, the main castle building and the church were all designed by Daniel Pöppelmann.

NATURE PARKS

The Harz mountains lie right in the heart of Germany and extend from Lower Saxony to Saxony-Anhalt. They include three nature parks: **Nationalpark Hochharz**, **Naturpark Harz** and **Naturpark Elm-Lappwald**. The Brocken forms the focal point of this mountainous region, sections of which are densely forested and stretch from Leine in the West to Salle in the East, and from the Lüneburger Heide in the North to the Thüringer Becken in the South. With an altitude of 1,142 m/ 3,747 ft it is the highest mountain in North Germany.

Although there will probably be no strange happenings on the legendary Blocksberg, the Harz can still offer remarkable natural sights.

From Berlin to Dresden

CASTLES

Schloss Branitz, near Cottbus, is surrounded by the lovely castle park designed by Prince Pückler-Muskau.
Schloss Bad Muskau (16th century), on the border with Poland, was burned down in 1945 but was quickly restored to its former glory. The Municipal Museum explains the development of the park.
Schloss Krumlau (19th century) lies west of Bad Muskau. **Jagdschloss Weisswasser** also lies nearby.
Burg Stolpen, 20 km (13 miles) east of Dresden, includes the famous basalt Cosel Tower.
Dresdner Zwinger, Dresden, baroque masterpiece (1711–28).
Schloss Pillnitz (18th-19th century), 12 km (7 miles) upstream from Dresden, surrounded by a beautiful park, consists of the Wasserpalais, the Bergpalais and the Neuer Palais.
Schloss Moritzburg, north of Dresden; the original 16th-century hunting castle was enlarged in the 18th century and resulted in a glorious baroque castle in magnificent surroundings. Some rooms in the castle contain memorabilia of the famous artist Käthe Kollwitz and a baroque musuem containing porcelain, furniture, paintings etc.
Augustusburg, southeast of Chemnitz, a hunting castle (16th century) now houses a youth hostel, a museum and a restaurant.

NATURE PARKS

Sächsische Schweiz, rocks of sandstone mountains south of Dresden with more than 1,000 km (600 miles) of well-marked footpaths criss-crossing the area through canyon-style valleys and gorges, to caves and platforms. Almost 1,000 individual peaks for keen mountaineers.

From Weimar to the Wartburg

CASTLES

Weimarer Schloss (18th-19th century), destroyed and rebuilt several times, now houses a remarkable art collection.
Grünes Schloss (16th-century) contains the Central Library of the German Classical Period.

Schloss Tiefurt, built in the baroque style, it lies 3 km (2 miles) northeast of Weimar.
Schloss Belvedere (17th-18th century) is another baroque castle complex 4 km (2 miles) south of Weimar.
Schloss Friedensstein (17th century), was the first German baroque castle in Gotha. Today, it houses several interesting museums.
Wartburg (from 11th century), in Eisenach is one of the most famous castles in Germany. It was here that Martin Luther translated the Bible in to German.

NATURE PARKS

Thüringer Wald is an area that is excellent for rambling and winter sports, which consists of a continuation of the landscape found in the Rhön and the Bavarian Frankenwald. The Saale and Unstrut river valleys are fruit and wine-growing areas.

Munich and Surrounds

CASTLES AND MONASTERIES

Schloss Nymphenburg, a late-baroque castle (18th century) in the northwest of Munich. Famous park containing the Amalienburg, Pagodenburg and Badenburg pavilions.
Residenz (16th-17th century), the seat of the Wittelsbachs, lies on Max-Joseph-Platz in the heart of Munich.
Schloss Oberschleissheim (18th century), lies 15 km (9 miles) north of Munich.
Schloss Herrenchiemsee was built by King Ludwig II on the Herreninsel, one of the three islands in the Chiemsee.
Benediktinerkloster St. Maria on the Fraueninsel in the Chiemsee, was founded in 766. The convent is worth a visit primarily for its Romanesque wall paintings dating from the 12th century.

AMUSEMENT PARKS

Märchenwald im Isartal, fairyland park near Wolfratshausen 28 km (17 miles) southeast of Munich.

The German Alpine Road

CASTLES AND MONASTERIES

Kloster Ettal. The Gothic monastery church was transformed in the baroque style during the 18th century. A rococo-style tower was added later.

Schloss Linderhof, in the Graswang valley, is a neo-rococo palace dating from the 19th century. It is surrounded by a baroque park. Built by King Ludwig II, it lies approx. 10 km (6 miles) from Oberammergau.
Schloss Hohenschwangau (19th century) was built by King Maximilian II as a hunting lodge.
Schloss Neuschwanstein (1th century) is the "fairy-tale" castle of King Ludwig II of Bavaria. Like Schloss Hohenschwangau, it lies near the town of Füssen.
Kloster Steingaden, with its 12th-century monastery church, lies a few miles from the Wieskirche (18th century). The famous pilgrimage church represents the zenith of Bavarian rococo.

NATURE PARK

Nationalpark Berchtesgaden extends across the area surrounding the Königssee.

AMUSEMENT PARKS

Märchenwald Ruhpolding, fairyland leisure park near Ruhpolding.

The Romantic Road

CASTLES AND MONASTERIES

Schloss Leitheim, rococo castle near Donauwörth.
Schloss Harburg, (12th and 18th century) overlooking the Wörnitz valley near Harburg.
Schloss von Weikersheim, one of the most important castles in Baden-Württemberg. It is known for its beautiful baroque interior.
Schloss Bad Mergentheim, dominates the town of Bad Mergentheim.
Kurmainzisches Schloss, in Tauberbischofsheim (14th-16th century) houses a folklore museum

NATURE PARK

Augsburg-Westliche Wälder, lies near the Ulm-Munich autobahn, take the Augsburg, Adelsried, Zusmarshaussen or Burgau exits.

From Würzburg to Munich

CASTLES AND MONASTERIES

Würzburger Residenz, a baroque palace designed by Balthasar Neumann (18th century) lies at the heart of the residential city of the prince-bishops.
Marienberg Fortress (13th century),

former residence of the prince-bishops of Würzburg. Houses the Franconian Museum of the Main, including works by the sculptor Tilman Riemenschneider.

Kloster Banz (Monastery), near Lichtenfels, is a former Benedictine monastery (built form the 11th century). Today it is the training centre of the Hanns Seidel Foundation.

Schloss Weissenstein is a baroque palace in Kulmbach.

Altes Schloss (Old Castle). Built in the 18th century this was the residence of the Margraves.

Neues Schloss (New Castle) is an 18th century rococo palace in Bayreuth (Ludwigstrasse).

Schloss Eremitage is the old castle on the eastern edge of Bayreuth.

A castle complex (11th-15th century), consisting of the **Kaiserburg**, the **Hohenzollern-Burggrafenburg** (Burgrave's Castle) and the **Kaiserstallung der freien Reichsstadt**, (Imperial Stables of the Free Imperial City) dominate the countenance of Nuremberg.

Burg Trausnitz (13th-16th century) stands sentinel over the town of Landshut.

Stadtresidenz, Renaissance building (16th century) in the heart of the city.

NATURE PARKS

Naturpark Hassberge, northwest of Bamberg.

Naturpark Fränkische Schweiz lies between Bamberg and Bayreuth; to the south lies the **Naturpark Veldensteiner Forst**.

Naturpark Frankenhöhe, can be reached by the autobahn Nuremberg-Ansbach, exits: Aich-Ansbach, Ansbach-West.

Naturpark Bayerischer Wald lies on the road from Passau to Regensburg.

ADVENTURE PARKS

Erlebnispark Schloss Thurn, adventure park and zoo, near Forchheim.

Lake Constance (Der Bodensee)

CASTLES

Schloss Mainau lies on the "Flower Island" of Mainau in the middle of Lake Constance.

The **Altes Schloss** (16th-17th century) and the **Neues Schloss** (18th century) dominate the picturesque town of Meersburg.

From the Black Forest to Stuttgart

CASTLES

Schloss Hohentübingen (16th century) overlooks Tübingen.

Neues Schloss (18th-19th century) dominates the the Schlossplatz at the centre of Stuttgart.

Altes Schloss is a Renaissance-style buliding (16th century) which also lies at the heart of the city of Stuttgart.

Grossherzogliches Schloss (18th century) is the focal point of Karlsruhe.

Neues Schloss (16th century) is a Renaissance castle overlooking Baden-Baden.

NATURE PARKS

Naturpark Schönbuch can be reached via the Stuttgart-Ulm autobahn (exit: Stuttgart-Degerloch) or via the Stuttgart-Singen autobahn (exits: Böblingen, Herrenberg, Tübingen).

ADVENTURE PARK

Altweibermühle Tripsdrill, this huge adventure park lies 23 km (14 miles) east of Heilbronn.

Frankfurt

CASTLE

Saalburg. The reconstructed Roman fort lies 7 km (4 miles) northwest of Bad Homburg. The castle museum contains finds dating back to Roman times.

The Rhine to the Mosel

CASTLES

Schloss Biebrich, 5 km (3 miles) southeast of Wiesbaden, built in the 18th century.

Schloss Gutenfels, in Kaub (12th century).

Burg Pfalzgrafenstein, also in Kaub (14th century).

Burg Katz, close to St Goarshausen.

Burg Thunberg (known as "Mouse"), near St Goarshausen.

Burg Rheinfels, the ruins from the 13th century rise above St Goar.

Burg Lahneck, 8 km (5 miles) southeast of Koblenz.

Feste Ehrenbreitstein, above Koblenz.

Schloss Stolzenfels, 12 km (miles) south of Koblenz.

Burg Stahleck, ruined castle dating from the 12th century in Bacharach.

Burg Sooneck, near Niederheimbach. **Burg Reichenstein**, near Trechtlinghausen.

NATURE PARKS

Nassau, via the Cologne-Frankfurt autobahn exits: Höhr-Grenzhausen, Montabaur, Diez, Limburg.

Rhein-Taunus, via the Cologne-Frankfurt autobahn or via the B260 Wiesbaden-Bad Ems, B54 Limburg-Wiesbaden.

Along The Moselle

CASTLES

Burg Eltz, overlooking Moselkern (1157).

Reichsburg Cochem, 13 km (8 miles) from Burg Eltz upstream of Cochem.

Burg Landshut, ruins in Bernkastel-Kues.

On the way to Cologne

CASTLES

Burg Drachenfels, ruins lie on a hill overlooking Königswinter near Bonn.

Schloss Augustusburg, castle and hunting lodge (1689), in Brühl.

NATURE PARKS

Rhein-Westerwald, **Siebengebirge**, **Kottenforst-Ville**: these three nature reserves can be reached via the Cologne-Frankfurt autobahn (any exit from Bonn-Siegburg and Montabaur) as well as from the Cologne-Koblenz autobahn (any exit from Bonn-Lengsdorf to Koblenz).

Naturpark Bergisches Land can be reached via the A3 or the B506.

Naturpark Nordeifel and **Naturpark Südeifel**.

AMUSEMENT PARKS

Phantasialand Brühl, just outside Brühl there is a huge amusement park.

From Heidelberg to the Castle Road

CASTLES

Kurfürstliches Schloss in Mannheim, the Electoral Palace is one of the largest baroque residences in Europe.

Heidelberger Schloss, Renaissance castle overlooking the river Neckar in Heidelberg.

Schloss Schwetzingen, former water castle in a lovely park in Schwetzingen (near Heidelberg).

Burg Eberbach (11-12th century), the ruins of the former Stouffer fortress lie a few miles from Eberbach.
Burg Stolteneck (13th century), the ruins lie outside Zwingenberg.
Burg Guttenberg, a few miles south of Hassmersheim.
Schloss Erbach, baroque castle in Erbach.
Miltenburg (13th century), in the heart of Miltenburg.
Wasserschloss Mespelbrunn castle (16th century) outside Mespelbrunn.
Burg Löwenstein, ruins above the town of Wertheim.
Burg Rothenfels, castle ruins (13-14th century) dominate the Main valley near Marktheidenfeld.

NATURE PARKS

Bergstrasse- Odenwald, northeast of Heidelberg; can be reached by car from the Mannheim-Frankfurt road or the Heidelberg-Darmstadt road.
Naturpark Bayerischer Spessart, can be reached via the autobahn Frankfurt-Nuremberg by taking any exit between Aschaffenburg and Marktheidenfeld.

The German Fairytale Road

CASTLES

Schloss Philippsruhe (18th century), in Kesselstadt, a surburb of Hanau. The historic museum displays exhibitis relating to the history of the town and its economic development as well as objets d'art from the Netherlands and the vicinity.
Kaiserpfalz, the ruins of Barbarossa's castle are in Gelnhausen.
Burg Brandenstein, a castle just outside Schlüchtern.
Stadtschloss (18th century), lies in the baroque centre of Fulda.
Die Fasanerie, a baroque summer palace, lies just outside Fulda.
Landgräfliches Schloss (13th-16th century) dominates the town of Marburg.
Schloss Wilhelmshöhe (17th-18th century) is a neo-classical building set in the baroque castle park in Kassel, not far from the famous Hercules Memorial. In addition to the magnificent interior furnishings, the castle contains paintings by Dutch and Flemish artists as well as other exhibits.

NATURE PARKS

Hessischer Spessart, via the Frankfurt-Nuremberg autobahn, any exit between Aschaffenburg and Marktheidenfeld.
Hessische Röhn, the nature park stretches east of Fulda and can be reached via the Frankfurt-Kassel autobahn (exits: Bad Kissingen, Bad Brückenau, Fulda, Hühnfeld).
Hoher Vogelsberg park begins 20 km (12½ miles) southeast of Lauterbach and can be reached via the Giessen-Kassel and Würzburg-Kassel autobahnen.

Along The Weser

CASTLES

Welfenschloss (16th-17th century), castle on the shore of the Werra in Münden (Hannoversch-Münden). Houses the Municipal Museum.
Sababurg, castle about 20 km (12½ miles) north of Münden.
Trendelburg, a castle close to the Sababurg, southwest of Karlshafen on the B83.
Hämelschenburg (16th-17th century), Renaissance-style castle close to Emmern.
Leineschloss (17th century), castle above the old town of Hanover.
Schaumburg, a castle on the Weser north of Rinteln.
Schloss Bückeburg (12th century), surrounded by a moat, lies in Bückeburg.

NATURE PARKS

Naturpark Münden stretches east of Münden. Take the exit Münden-Lutterberg on the autobahn Kassel-Göttingen.
Naturpark Solling/Vogler park can be reached via autobahn exits Göttingen-Nord, Nörten-Hardenberg and Northeim-West on the autobahn Kassel-Göttingen-Hanover.
Weserbergland Schaumburg-Hameln: The Bielefeld-Hanover autobahn skirts the northern edge of the park. Take the exits Eilsen, Rehren, Bad Nenndorf, Lauenau.

ADVENTURE PARKS

Rasti-Land, amusement park 32 km (20 miles) east of Hameln.
Potts Park Minden, 10 km (6 miles) south of Minden.

Hamburg and Surrounds

NATURE PARKS

Naturpark Harburger Berge. Take the Hamburg-Bremen autobahn and use exits Emsen, Nenndorf, Hittfeld.
Naturschutzpark Lüneburger Heide, west of Lüneburg; can be reached via the Hanover-Hamburg autobahn (exits Behringen/Evendorf, Egestorf, Garlstorf).

Excursions to the North Sea

CASTLE

Schloss Oldenburg (17th century), in the centre of Oldenburg

NATURE PARKS

The two nature parks **Schleswig-Holsteinisches Wattenmeer** and **Niedersächsiches Wattenmeer** extend along the entire German North Sea coast, providing a unique refuge for flora and fauna.

ADVENTURE PARKS

Babyzoo Wingst, 20 km (12 miles) southeast of Otterndorf.

From Lübeck To Flensburg

CASTLES

Schloss Eutin (17th–18th century) lies on the shores of the Eutiner See.
Schloss Gottorf, a Renaissance castle, lies on an island in the Schlei-Bay, Schleswig.
Schloss Glücksburg, white water castle dating back to the 16th century near Ringsby.

NATURE PARKS

Naturpark Holsteinische Schweiz, on the autobahn A7, exit Neumünster or autobahn A1, exit Eutin.
Naturpark Aukrug, on the Hamburg-Kiel autobahn A7, Neumünster exit.
Naturpark Westensee, on the same autobahn further north, exit: Blumenthal-Bad Bramstedt. If you take the Hamburg-Flensburg autobahn, use the Warder exit.
Hüttener Berge: the northernmost park in Germany can be reached on the Hamburg-Flensburg autobahn, exits Rendsburg-Büdelsdorf, Owschlag, or Schleswig-Gottorf.

Hansaland, 10 km (6 miles) from Timmendorfer Strand.

Along the Baltic to Berlin

CASTLES

Schloss Ahrensburg, the white Renaissance castle of Ahrensburg lies 32 km (20 miles) northeast of Hamburg.
Schloss Schwerin was rebuilt in the 19th century in the style of a Loire château.
Schloss Gadebusch (16th century), northwest of Schwerin. The well-proportioned facade is richly decorated with terracotta ornaments.
Schloss Güstrow (16th century), south of Rostock on the F4, is the most important Renaissance castle in Germany. Built as the residence of the Dukes of Mecklenburg-Güstrow, both the castle and the surrounding park have been fully restored.

NATURE PARKS

Naturpark Lauenburgische Seen/ Schaalsee, surrounding Ratzeburg. From Hamburg the park can be reached via the A24.
The Boddenlandschaft on the Baltic coast near Fischland-Darss-Zingst has been declared a national park.
The **Naturpark Märkische Schweiz,** which lies to the east of Berlin (Mark Brandenburg), can be reached via the B1 and the B5.

Festivals

Annual Events

Germany is a country where festivals are serious business. Often, they are celebrations of religious or historical events, regional and nationwide customs or the end of harvests. There are just too many to list in this book but the following is a rule of thumb to find some of the bigger or national events. Local tourist offices can give you details since precise dates change all the time.

February/March: Carnival, the season of the fools. Also called Fasching, Fasnet or Fasnacht in the South. This event is celebrated by millions at costume parties, balls and colourful street parades. The carnival capitals of Germany are Düsseldorf, Cologne and Mainz, but these sensational events are also widespread all over Southern Germany.

Summer to September: the season of open air events. Every larger city has some sort of festival - music, theatre, folk, pageant plays, dances etc. The wine growing areas of Germany hold Weinfeste where stalls belonging to members of the different wine-growers' organisations sell their products to an accompaniment of music and dance.

Late September/beginning of October: Oktoberfest in Munich. Also known as Wies'n among the local people. A traditional beer-drinking festival with ceremonial participation by innkeepers, the mayor and other local VIPS.

Late November/Advent: the season of Christmas markets (Weihnachts-Christkindlmärkte). These are held in every larger German city with beautifully decorated stalls selling handicrafts and gifts as well as selling food and the famous Glühwein.

Shopping

What to Buy

Germany, being a popular tourist destination, offers lots of souvenirs. The shop to look out for is the Andenkenladen which has anything from valuable souvenirs to all sorts of knick-knacks. Beer mugs (Bierkrüge) are typical gifts. You find them made out of glass, ceramics and pewter, either colourfully painted or plain. Especially fancy, and therefore more expensive, are mugs with pewter lids. For those who do not like beer, there are typical wine glasses. White wine, for example is served in Römer, which are bulbous glasses.

Traditional articles of clothing in the north of Germany are the Schiffermütze, Seemannspullover and the Friesennerz. The Schiffermütze is a blue sailor's cap similar to what ex-Chancellor Helmut Schmidt wore. The Seemannspullover is a big blue sweater sailors wear at sea. It is very comfortable for rough winds over the North Sea coast. The Friesennerz is a raincoat made out of yellow rubber.

Towards the East you will find stylised figures of nutcrackers or wooden figures holding scented candles; in Meissen, watch the porcelain modellers at work.

In practically every town you will find a Fussgängerzone pedestrian zone with all kinds of shops, big department stores, and small specialised shops. Cigarettes, cigars and tobacco may be bought in newspaper shops which also stock postcards, writing supplies, magazines and newspapers.

Sports

Participant and Spectator

Germans enjoy both participant and spectator sports. There is a sports club in every town and many athletic clubs in the cities specialising in disciplines such as wrestling, weightlifting, or boxing. The most popular sport is soccer. During the national soccer league season, millions of Germans follow the results of the games that are usually played on Saturday afternoons and shown in television excerpts at 6pm. Some of the main soccer clubs are Bayern Munich, Hamburger SV, Borussia Dortmund, Werder Bremen, Bornssia Mönchengladbach, Bayer Leverkusen, I.F.C. Cologne.

Your hotel receptionist or the local tourist office should have information on sports activities. Since Steffi Graf, Boris Becker and Michael Stich became successful, tennis has become very popular. Other popular sports are handball, volleyball, squash, basketball, athletics, cycling, motor sports and swimming. There are parks for the dedicated jogger.

Language

Words and Phrases

General

Good morning/*Guten Morgen*
Good Afternoon/*Guten Tag*
Good evening/*Guten Abend*
Good night/*Gute Nacht*
Goodbye/*Auf Wiedersehen*
I don't understand/*Ich verstehe Sie nicht*
Do you speak English?/*Sprechen Sie Englisch?*
Could you please speak slower?/*Könnten Sie bitte etwas langsamer sprechen?*
What's that in English?/*Was heisst das auf Englisch?*
Yes, No/*Ja, Nein*
Please, Thank you/*Bitte, Danke*
Never mind/*Bitte; keine Ursache*
Turn to the right! (left)/*Biegen Sie nach rechts ab! (links)*
Go straight on!/*Gehen Sie geradeaus weiter!*
Above, below/*oben, unten*

At The Hotel

Where is the next hotel?/*Wo ist das nächste Hotel?*
Do you have a single room?/*Haben Sie ein Einzelzimmer?*
Do you have a double room?/*Haben Sie ein Doppelzimmer?*
Do you have a room with a private bath?/*Haben Sie ein Zimmer mit Bad?*
How much is it?/*Wieviel kostet das?*
How much is a room with full board?/*Wieviel kostet ein Zimmer mit Vollpension?*
Please show me another room!/*Bitte zeigen Sie mir ein anderes Zimmer!*
We'll (I'll) be staying for one night./*Wir bleiben (Ich bleibe) eine Nacht!*
When is breakfast?/*Wann gibt es Frühstück?*
Where is the toilet?/*Wo ist die Toilette?*
Where is the bathroom?/*Wo ist das Badezimmer?*

Travelling

Is there a bus to the centre?/*Gibt es einen Bus ins Stadtzentrum?*
Is there a guided sightseeing tour?/*Werden kommentierte Besichtigungstouren durchgeführt?*
church/*Kirche*
memorial/*Denkmal*
castle/*Schloss*
old part of town/*Altstadtviertel*
Where can I buy souvenirs?/*Wo kann ich Souvenirs kaufen?*
Do you know a nightclub/disco?/*Kennen Sie einen Nachtklub/eine Disko?*
Where is the nearest cinema?/*Wo ist das nächste Kino?*
What film does it show?/*Was für ein Film läuft dort?*
Where is the post office?/*Wo ist das Postamt?*
Where is the nearest bank?/*Wo ist die nächste Bank?*
Where can I change money?/*Wo kann ich Geld wechseln?*
Where is the pharmacy?/*Wo ist die Apotheke?*
What time do they close?/*Wann schliessen sie?*
open, closed/*geöffnet, geschlossen*
close, far/*nah, weit*
cheap, expensive/*billig, teuer*
free (of charge)/*kostenlos*
price/*Preis*
change/*Wechselgeld*
Have you got any change?/*Können Sie wechseln?*
telephone booth/*Telefonzelle*
Is this the way to the station?/*Ist das der Weg zum Bahnhof?*
Where is platform one?/*Wo ist Gleis eins?*
Where is the airport?/*Wo ist der Flughafen?*
Can you call me a taxi?/*Können Sie mir ein Taxi rufen?*
Can you take me to the airport?/*Können Sie mich zum Flughafen fahren?*
Where do I get a ticket?/*Wo kann ich eine Fahrkarte kaufen?*
departure, arrival/*Abfahrt, Ankunft*
When is the next flight/train to?/*Wann geht der nächste Flug/Zug nach?*
to change (flights/trains)/*umsteigen*
exit/*Ausgang, Ausfahrt*
entrance/*Eingang, Einfahrt*
travel agency/*Reisebüro*
picnic area/*Rastplatz*
gas (petrol) station/*Tankstelle*
bridge/*Brücke*

crossroads/*Kreuzung*
no parking/*Parken verboten*
no stopping/*Halten verboten*
one-way street/*Einbahnstrasse*
hospital/*Krankenhaus*
ferry/*Fähre*
fee/*Gebühr*
height/*Höhe*
width/*Breite*
length/*Länge*
Have you anything to declare?/*Haben
Sie etwas zu ver zollen?*
customs/*Zoll*

Eating Out

Do you know a good restaurant?/
Kennen Sie ein gutes Restaurant?
Could we order a/*Können wir
meal, please?/bitte bestellen?*
menu/*Speisekarte*
lunch/*Mittagessen*
evening meal/*Abendessen*
knife, fork, spoon/*Messer, Gabel, Löffel*
beer, wine/*Bier, Wein*
bread, cheese/*Brot, Käse*
meat/*Fleisch*
sausage/*Würstchen*
honey/*Honig*
noodles/*Nudeln*
potatoes/*Kartoffeln*
rice/*Reis*
jam/*Marmelade*
egg/*Ei*
milk/*Milch*
coffee/*Kaffee*
tea/*Tee*
sugar/*Zucker*
butter/*Butter*
Can we have the bill, please?/*Können
wir bitte bezahlen?*
to pay/*bezahlen*
tip/*Trinkgeld*
to complain/*sich beschweren*

Days of the Week

Monday/*Montag*
Tuesday/*Dienstag*
Wednesday/*Mittwoch*
Thursday/*Donnerstag*
Friday/*Freitag*
Saturday/*Samstag, Sonnabend*
Sunday/*Sonntag*

Months

January/*Januar*
February/*Februar*
March/*March*
April/*April*
May/*May*
June/*June*
July/*July*

August/*August*
September/*September*
October/*Oktober*
November/*November*
December/*Dezember*

Numbers

0/*Null*
1/*eins*
2/*zwei*
3/*drei*
4/*vier*
5/*fünf*
6/*sechs*
7/*sieben*
8/*acht*
9/*neun*
10/*zehn*
11/*elf*
12/*zwölf*
13/*dreizehn*
14/*vierzehn*
15/*fünfzehn*
16/*sechzehn*
17/*siebzehn*
18/*achtzehn*
19/*neunzehn*
20/*zwanzig*
30/*dreissig*
40/*vierzig*
50/*fünfzig*
60/*sechzig*
70/*siebzig*
80/*achtzig*
90/*neunzig*
100/*hundert*
200/*zweihundert*
1,000/*tausend*
2,000/*zweitausend*
1,000,000/*eine Million*

1st/*erste*(r)
2nd/*zweite*(r)
3rd/*dritte*(r)
4th/*vierte*(r)
5th/*fünfte*(r)
6th/*sechste*(r)
7th/*siebte*(r)
8th/*achte*(r)
9th/*neunte*(r)
10th/*zehnte*(r)
11th/*elfte*(r)
12th/*zwölfte*(r)
13th/*dreizehnte*(r)
20th/*zwanzigste*(r)
21st/*einundzwanzigste*(r)
100th/*hundertste*(r)
1000th/*tausendste*(r)

Further Reading

General

History and Society

George Bailey, *Germans*. (1972)
John Bradley, *The Illustrated History of
the Third Reich*. (1978)
David Calleo, *The German Problem
Reconsidered: 1860–1978*. (1980)
Gordon Craig, *The Germans*. (1982)
William H. Dawson, *German Life in
Town and Country*. (1977)
Hajo Holborn, *A History of Modern
Germany: 1840–1945*. (1969)
Brangwyn G. Jones, *Germany: An Intro-
duction to the German Nation*. (1970)
Henry Kirsch, *German Democratic Re-
public: A Profile*. (1985)
Robert H. Lowie, *Toward Understand-
ing Germany*. (1979)
Ian MacDonald, *Get to Know Germany*.
(1975)
David Marsh, *New Germany at the
Crossroads*. (1990)

People and Culture

To understand the German mentality,
read any of the classical works by
Goethe and Schiller, Heinrich Heine
and Friedrich Hölderlin, to name a few.
Below is a selection of German and
English/American authors:
Günter Grass, *Headbirths*; *The Ger-
mans Are Dying Out*; and *The Flounder*.
Thomas Mann, *Buddenbrooks*.
Catherine Mansfield, *In A German Pen-
sion*.
Madame de Stael, *Germany*.
Mark Twain, *A Tramp Abroad*.

Other Insight Guides

Europe is comprehensively covered by
the 350 books in Apa Publications'
three series of guidebooks which em-
brace the world: *Insight Guides*, which
provide a full cultural background and
top-quality photography; *Insight Compact Guides*, which combine portability
with encyclopedia-like attention to detail and are ideal for on-the-spot reference; and *Insight Pocket Guides*,
which highlight recommendations from
a local host and include a full-size fold-
out map. German cities explored include Berlin, Frankfurt and Munich.

Photography by
Fotografie Archiv für Kunst und
Geschichte 25, 26, 28, 29, 30,
34, 35, 37, 38, 42/43, 44, 46,
47, 48, 49, 50, 51, 54, 57, 58,
72, 73, 184L, 293
Archiv Preußischer
Kulturbesitz 117
Ato 315
David Baltzer 77
V. Barl 251
Michael Bienert 136/137
Bildverlag Traut 264
Siegfried Bucher 31, 260, 263,
265L, 265R
Deutsche Fotothek 55
Deutsche Märchenstraße AG 266
Deutsche Presse Agentur 56, 59
Fritz Dressler 218/219
Filmmuseum München 70
Fotostudio Furtner 179
Fotostudio Schmidt-Luchs 53
M. Frank, Stadtwerbung
Münster 256
Fremdenverkehrsamt Landsberg a.
Lech 184R
Fremdenverkehrsamt Nürnberg
191, 193
Wolfgang Fritz 9, 62/63,
92/93, 125, 126R, 149, 153,
155R, 156, 169, 197, 199, 200,
201, 212, 223, 234L, 234R, 236,
244, 245L, 247, 249, 275
Thomas Gebhardt/Echo 122
Frances Gransden/Apa 18, 103,
105R, 109, 111, 113
Harald Hauswald 96/97, 124,
126L, 140
D. & J. Heaton/Apa Photo
Agency 258
Barbara Hinz 121, 123, 316
Hans Höfer 41
May Hoff 178, 181, 183, 185
Andreas Kämper 65, 68
Ursula Kaufmann 74, 75
Jochen Keute 14/15,
216/217, 224, 225
Rainer Kiedrowski 104, 155L,
159, 252, 257, 261, 267, 268,
269, 270, 274, 277, 278
Nils Koshofer 142
Kurverwaltung Mittenwald 180
Landesbildstelle Berlin 52
Landesbildstelle
Südbaden 24, 27
Britta Lauer 254
Robin Laurence/Apa 20, 21, 23,
84/85, 280/281, 282/283, 284,
286, 287, 288, 290, 291, 292,
297, 301, 302, 303, 304, 305
F. Medau 16/17

Michael Meyborg, signum-fotografie
86, 88, 89
Kai Ulrich Müller 102, 116, 120,
143, 144, 215, 289
Ben Nahayama/Apa Photo
Agency 262
Opel Eisenach GmbH 66
Ulrich Otte, Werbeamt
Düsseldorf 248
Erhard Pansegrau 1, 12/13, 60, 61,
98, 118, 127, 128, 129, 130,
131R, 134, 135, 152, 154, 161,
195, 196, 204/205, 206, 207,
208, 209, 220, 222, 226, 227,
230, 231, 232, 233, 235, 237,
238, 239, 240, 241, 242, 243,
246, 253, 271, 276, 296, 298,
299, 300, 306, 307, 308, 309,
310, 311, 314, 317L, 317R, 319
Gerd Pfeiffer 10/11, 164/165, 171
Photo Jürgens 133
Presseamt Bochum 255
Mark Read/Apa 2, 64, 67, 80, 87,
106, 107, 108, 110, 112, 131L,
132, 138, 141, 145,
146, 147
G. P. Reichelt 22
Dirk Renckhoff/Apa 148, 150,
157, 158
Stefan Maria Rother 119
Carolin Schmitt 312
Günter Schneider 78/79, 90/91
Maja Specht 186, 189
Staatliche Landesbildstelle
Hessen 39
Rolf Steinberg 45
Stiftung Automuseum
Volkswagen 279
Dieter Stroh 82
Süddeutscher Verlag 69
TI Fränkisches Weinland, A.
Gineiger 194
Tourismusverband Franken e.V. 198
Transit Film 70
Klemens Unger 203
Günther/Margarethe Ventur 245R
Verkehrsbüro Oberammergau 182
Verkehrsverein Augsburg 188
Phil Wood/Apa 83, 166, 168, 170,
172, 173, 174
Christoph Zange 162/163,
213L, 213R, 214

Maps Berndtson & Berndtson

Visual Consultant V. Barl

Index

A
B
C
D
E
F
G
H
I
J
a
b
c
d
e
f
g
h
i
j
k
l

The Insight Approach

The book you are holding is part of the world's largest range of guidebooks. Its purpose is to help you have the most valuable travel experience possible, and we try to achieve this by providing not only information about countries, regions and cities but also genuine insight into their history, culture, institutions and people.

Since the first Insight Guide – to Bali – was published in 1970, the series has been dedicated to the proposition that, with insight into a country's people and culture, visitors can both enhance their own experience and be accepted more easily by their hosts. Now, in a world where ethnic hostilities and nationalist conflicts are all too common, such attempts to increase understanding between peoples are more important than ever.

Insight Guides:
Essentials for understanding

Because a nation's past holds the key to its present, each Insight Guide kicks off with lively history chapters. These are followed by magazine-style essays on culture and daily life. This essential background information gives readers the necessary context for using the main Places section, with its comprehensive run-down on things worth seeing and doing. Finally, a listings section contains all the information you'll need on travel, hotels, restaurants and opening times.

As far as possible, we rely on local writers and specialists to ensure that the information is authoritative. The pictures, for which Insight Guides have become so celebrated, are just as important. Our photojournalistic approach aims not only to illustrate a destination but also to communicate visually and directly to readers life as it is lived by the locals.

Compact Guides
The "great little guides"

As invaluable as such background information is, it isn't always fun to carry an Insight Guide through a crowded souk or up a church tower. Could we, readers asked, distil the key reference material into a slim volume for on-the-spot use?

Our response was to design Compact Guides as an entirely new series, with original text carefully cross-referenced to detailed maps and more than 200 photographs. In essence, they're miniature encyclopedias, concise and comprehensive, displaying reliable and up-to-date information in an accessible way.

Pocket Guides:
A local host in book form

However wide-ranging the information in a book, human beings still value the personal touch. Our editors are often asked the same questions. Where do *you* go to eat? What do *you* think is the best beach? What would you recommend if I have only three days? We invited our local correspondents to act as "substitute hosts" by revealing their preferred walks and trips, listing the restaurants they go to and structuring a visit into a series of timed itineraries.

The result is our Pocket Guides, complete with full-size fold-out maps. These 100-plus titles help readers plan a trip precisely, particularly if their time is short.

Exploring with Insight:
A valuable travel experience

In conjunction with co-publishers all over the world, we print in up to 10 languages, from German to Chinese, from Danish to Russian. But our aim remains simple: to enhance your travel experience by combining our expertise in guidebook publishing with the on-the-spot knowledge of our correspondents.